"We Must Be Up and Doing"

"We Must Be Up and Doing"

A Reader in Early African American Feminisms

EDITED BY TERESA C. ZACKODNIK

broadview press

Library and Archives Canada Cataloguing in Publication

   We must be up and doing : a reader in early African American feminisms / edited by Teresa C. Zackodnik.

Includes bibliographical references and index.
ISBN 978-1-55111-917-5

   1. Feminism—United States—History—Sources.
2. African American feminists—History—Sources.
I. Zackodnik, Teresa Christine, 1967-

HQ1419.W4 2010   305.48'896073   C2009-906718-8

Broadview Press is an independent, international publishing house, incorporated in 1985. Broadview believes in shared ownership, both with its employees and with the general public; since the year 2000 Broadview shares have traded publicly on the Toronto Venture Exchange under the symbol BDP.

We welcome comments and suggestions regarding any aspect of our publications—please feel free to contact us at the addresses below or at broadview@broadviewpress.com.

North America
PO Box 1243, Peterborough, Ontario, Canada K9J 7H5
2215 Kenmore Ave., Buffalo, New York, USA 14207
Tel: (705) 743-8990; Fax: (705) 743-8353
email: customerservice@broadviewpress.com

UK, Europe, Central Asia, Middle East, Africa, India, and Southeast Asia
Eurospan Group, 3 Henrietta St., London
WC2E 8LU, United Kingdom
Tel: 44 (0) 1767 604972; Fax: 44 (0) 1767 601640
email: eurospan@turpin-distribution.com

Australia and New Zealand
NewSouth Books
c/o TL Distribution
15-23 Helles Avenue, Moorebank, NSW, Australia 2170
Tel: (02) 8778 9999; Fax: (02) 8778 9944
email: orders@tldistribution.com.au

www.broadviewpress.com

Broadview Press acknowledges the financial support of the Government of Canada through the Book Publishing Industry Development Program (BPIDP) for our publishing activities.

Edited by Betsy Struthers

Designed by Chris Rowat Design, Daiva Villa

This book is printed on paper containing 100% post-consumer fibre.

PRINTED IN CANADA

For Ailsa Brazeau

Contents

CHAPTER I

Roots of Reform and
Early African American Feminism

1

CHAPTER 2

Feminist Black Nationalism

83

CHAPTER 3

Lynching

181

CHAPTER 4

Defending Black Womanhood and the Black Women's Club Movement

231

CHAPTER 5

Woman's Rights, Suffrage, Temperance

279

Acknowledgements

My debts are many as are my thanks. This anthology developed from research originally funded by the Social Sciences and Humanities Research Council of Canada. The University of Alberta's Interlibrary Loan office was patient and diligent in tracking down many of these documents. The assistance of the following libraries, museums and societies was essential: The Ontario Black History Society, the University of Chicago's Department of Special Collections, the Peabody Essex Museum, the British Library's Newspaper Library at Colindale, the Boston Public Library's Rare Books Department, and the Schomburg Center's Rare Book and Manuscript Division and Newspaper Collection. I also wish to thank the University of Alberta's Department of English and Film Studies for funding the research assistance of Younghoon Kim, Heather Kitteringham, Ross Langager, and Dana Wight. The Social Sciences and Humanities Research Council of Canada funded the invaluable research assistance of Jackie Baker, Michael Borshuk, Mridula Chakraborty, Karen Engle, Christie Schultz, and Vivian Zenari. Finally, the University of Alberta's Faculty of Arts Undergraduate Research Scholarship enabled me to work with Sara Ghebremusse on African American women journalists; her research assistance on *The Liberator* was particularly helpful. Finally, I must thank Susan Hamilton for first suggesting I undertake this work and Susan Smith for her keen eye and knowledge of African American women's history.

List of Photographs

Introduction

African American women have been up and doing for their communities for as long as they have been in the United States.[1] Their ability to resist the institution of slavery and its violent attempts at dehumanization was central to the survival of all their people. Alongside and in many ways enabled by those crucial forms of resistance, black women also developed forms of feminist activism and a political culture that advanced claims for freedom and rights in a number of arenas. Yet African American feminists have often been ignored or their importance diminished within histories and studies of "first wave" American feminism. All too often what individual black feminists argued and what their feminism might stand for as a collective politics have been misperceived because of an historical discomfort with the difference "race" makes to feminism.

This is nowhere more evident than in the case of Sojourner Truth who is, for many, *the* African American feminist. Two biographies—Nell Irvin Painter's *Sojourner Truth: A Life, A Symbol* (1996) and Carleton Mabee's *Sojourner Truth: Slave, Prophet, Legend* (1993)—have fostered debate over the authenticity of her most famous address, the "A'n't I a woman?" speech delivered at the 1851 woman's rights convention held in Akron, Ohio. Arguing that the 1851 account published in its coverage of the convention by the *Anti-Slavery Bugle*, an abolitionist newspaper, be regarded as more reliable than Frances Dana Gage's "Reminiscences," first published in 1863 and later reprinted in the *History of Woman Suffrage* (1882), Painter has challenged scholars to reconsider how Truth, and by extension black feminism itself, is represented in accounts of woman's rights specifically and American "first-wave" feminism generally. Despite questions regarding its accuracy, Gage's "Reminiscences" has long been the most anthologized, most readily available, and widely read account. Consequently, Truth remains famous for a question she may, in fact, never have uttered:

> Every eye was fixed on this almost Amazon form, which stood nearly six feet high…. [R]aising herself to her full height, and her voice to a pitch like rolling thunder, she asked, "And a'n't I a woman? Look at me! Look

at my arm! (and she bared her right arm to the shoulder, showing her tremendous muscular power). I have ploughed, and planted, and gathered into barns, and no man could head me! And a'n't I a woman? I could work as much and eat as much as a man—when I could get it—and bear de lash as well! And a'n't I a woman? I have borne thirteen chilern, and seen 'em mos' all sold off to slavery, and when I cried out with my mother's grief, none but Jesus heard me! And a'n't I a woman?" (Cady Stanton *et al.* 1969[1882], I: 116).

No other account of Truth's address reports her baring her arm, and no other account notes her ever asking "an't I a woman?" despite Gage's recollection that she asked this famous question no less than four times. Yet, this account of Truth's speech is repeatedly anthologized and quoted as a "first" of its kind. Studies of American feminism have followed and thereby perpetuated Gage's account of the Akron convention (Lasser 1987, 344).

Consequently, Truth is understood as supporting woman's rights in an uncomplicated way, choosing gender solidarity over racial solidarity in this speech as well as in other *History of Woman Suffrage* accounts of her addresses in the 1850s and 1860s. What emerges, however, from reading accounts of her speeches in the contemporary press alongside those collected in the *History of Woman Suffrage* is a more contentious figure who repeatedly sought to intervene in what she saw as an omission of black women's concerns within the woman's rights movement. Yet Truth's reputation continues to circulate not only as *the* black feminist of the nineteenth century for many people, but, even for those more informed, as unique among her contemporaries. In fact, as we can see from reading the documents included here, Truth shared with other black feminists a concern for black civil rights and an interest in universal suffrage while negotiating critical relationships to central American reform movements like abolition, woman's rights, and temperance.

Sojourner Truth, then, illustrates central issues for understanding African American feminism as it intersects with white American feminism. Histories and studies of the latter tend to position African American feminists as secondary figures when they are included at all. For example, while we may know that certain black feminists were present at and even addressed white feminist gatherings, the archives documenting those events at times do not mention these women or fail to present what positions they took on the issues then being discussed.[2] When African American feminists are included in accounts of important gatherings, their complex work is often reduced, as was Truth's, to an unproblematic advocating of woman's rights.

In Truth's case, this is the result of taking the *History of Woman Suffrage* as both artefact and authoritative record of that struggle. Gage's account of Truth's Akron speech has been accorded institutional significance within the American woman's rights movement by virtue of its inclusion in this multi-volume set, whose editors aimed to amass "an arsenal of facts...[for] a faithful history...written by its actors...[and so] nearer the soul of the subject" (Cady Stanton *et al.* 1969[1882], I: 7-8). *The History of Woman Suffrage*, as feminist artefact and "an archive in itself" (Hersch 1978, 72), continues to determine the historical record of American woman suffrage. Yet what it perpetuates is the representation of African American feminists as lone figures who neither interacted with one another in an existing and well-established black feminist culture nor drew upon the history of such a culture for their own work. For many, then, Truth has become a distinctive, lone figure and one of the very few nineteenth-century black feminists of whom they are aware.

Alongside the position African American feminists are given in historical narratives of first wave American feminism is the equally important consideration of how histories of African American feminism have documented this politics and its advocates. Most studies of black feminisms in the United States have tended to privilege events of the late nineteenth century and focus on the black women's club movement as the apex of black feminist organizing because it fostered national autonomous organizations and was the prime mobilizer in black women's struggle for the vote. Elsa Barkley Brown contends that such studies have created two central misconceptions of early black feminism: first, that the turn of the century was "the height of black women's participation in politics," and second, that black women's emergence in politics is "tied to external factors" like the disenfranchisement of black men or "vitriolic attacks" on black female morality (Barkley Brown 1994, 137). Consequently, the autonomous, and often national, African American woman's organization is emphasized as the emergence or height of black feminism when it is, in fact, neither. The result is to omit a significant history of black women's documented work within their communities and the reform networks with which they affiliated.[3] As Stephanie Shaw has noted, the Colored Women's League (1892) "was a coalition of 113 organizations" and the National Federation of African-American Women (1895) "of 85 organizations." Shaw cites these organizations to remind readers that "when these two federations combined in 1896 to form the National Association of Colored Women, the inclination and impetus for black women to form a collective was more than a few years old" (Shaw 1995, 433-34). A national federation of black women's clubs was far from a "first" in black feminist collectivity as Shaw documents by citing the mutual benevolent associations that were established as early as the 1820s and 1830s.

In addition to such a temporal privileging of the turn of the century, work to document the development of black feminism has tended to set the North in opposition to the South, to focus on central figures, or to concentrate on individual reform movements. A number of historians and literary critics have produced groundbreaking studies of early African American feminist politics and black women's political culture without which an anthology like this would not be possible. However, that early work, which established the field of black women's history, focused primarily on particular movements like abolition,[4] the Black Baptist Women's Convention,[5] suffrage,[6] and the black women's club movement and organized reform.[7] This may give readers the impression that black feminists tended to contribute to a single reform movement even though, as the readings that follow illustrate, many began activist work as abolitionists, became women's rightists, and worked all along for reforms addressing the particular concerns of the black women in the communities in which they lived and worked. Studies that have been published since, and that work to draw together a variety of political organizations and discourses in which black women participated, largely confine their scope to particular regions, consequently polarizing rather than comparing the North and South.[8] And the tendency to focus on central figures of early black feminist politics—Sojourner Truth, Frances Harper, Ida B. Wells, Mary Church Terrell, Maria Stewart, and Mary Ann Shadd Cary[9]—positions them as singular figures rather than considering them within the networks in which they worked. The "great woman" is isolated, then, as though her feminist activism was an individual achievement largely independent of an existing black feminist community. Questioning why these "greats" have achieved that status even though they were part of a much larger critical mass of black feminism, how black feminisms were both responsive to local needs yet also part of a larger politic, and the ways in which individual black feminists worked across a number of reforms, together offers us a complex context in which to understand early black feminisms and the varied publics black feminists addressed.

The readings offered in this anthology not only give a sense of early black feminism across regions, movements, and organizations, but they also include both lesser known black feminists and their more famous contemporaries. Early black feminism's rich complexity in its locations, arguments, and rhetorics are evident throughout. African American women, as these documents attest, established female benevolent and literary societies, voiced views on emigration and colonization, and contested intimidation tactics such as rape and lynching. They also negotiated competing and often conflicting demands within interracial reform movements like abolition, woman's rights, and temperance, as well as within organizations like the black church, making documents that offer insight into those unique demands that are key to understanding the subtlety of black feminist arguments. Indeed, African American feminists pursued varied rhetorics, ranging from advocating domestic and maternal feminism to promoting the black nationalist principles of communal unity and economic self-sufficiency. Finally, as these documents make clear, African American feminists were also keenly attuned to opening useful venues to black feminist voices—from the pulpit and platform to the press—and urged the women who followed them to continue this important work.

African American feminists in the early nineteenth century established a tradition of arguing that the advancement of "the race" was directly linked to the status of African American women. Across the nineteenth and into the twentieth century, black feminists pursued a remarkable array of politics to advance black women's interests, accessed and actively created political networks to forward these goals, and achieved national as well as international recognition for their efforts and causes. That they undertook such work despite considerable personal risk to themselves or in the face of considerable demands on their commitments to family and community is a testament to their belief that they could make a difference in the lives of black women and in their communities. While early black feminism was by no means uniform, it sustained and developed distinctive rhetorics and politics that cohered around that central focus—the role and position of African American women within community and nation. In some of this work black feminists formed their own collectives, yet they also participated in reform networks that were predominantly white and in predominantly black male political networks within their communities. Early black feminism is arguably unique in the ways in which it negotiated competing claims from the publics it addressed and sought to motivate for change, publics that had class, racial, and gender interests that might differ from and at times effectively silence the politics African American women were advancing. But advance they did.

Notes

1. In 1619 the first 20 captive Africans were brought to Jamestown, Virginia, by a Dutch slaver and sold as servants.

2. For example, Rosalyn Terborg-Penn notes that "Mary Ann Shadd Cary

wrote the NWSA [National Woman Suffrage Association] in 1876 on behalf of ninety-four Black women from the District of Columbia...request[ing] that their names be enrolled in the July 4th centennial autograph book as signers of the Woman's Declaration of Sentiments, which called for the immediate enfranchise-ment of American women. Although the editors of the *History of Woman Suffrage* made note of the letter, the names of the black women were not included. Hence they remain anonymous" (Terborg-Penn 1998, 41).

3. We must always remember that attending to *documented* black feminist work will mean we have only a partial picture of African American feminism. This may be the only view collections such as this can offer, given their limited ability to document oral culture and its work, for example.

4. See Yee 1992; Yellin and Van Horne 1994; and Yellin 1990.

5. Higginbotham 1993.

6. Terborg-Penn 1998; Gordon and Collier-Thomas 1997.

7. Carby 1987; Salem 1990; Knupfer 1996.

8. Neverdon-Morton 1989; Higginbotham 1993; Peterson 1995; Knupfer 1996.

9. See, for example, Painter 1996; Mabee and Mabee Newhouse 1993; Boyd 1994; Foster 1990; McMurray 1998; Schechter 2001; Thompson 1990; Washington Jones 1990; Richardson 1987; Beardin and Butler 1977; Rhodes 1998.

I

Roots of Reform
and Early African American
Feminism

African American women sought to open the church to women's voices and concerns, thereby challenging the church hierarchy. These women are notable for the attention they drew to their search for control over the black female body through service to God; for their varied claims to authority through appeals to an inner voice, spiritual eye, or divine "call" to public voice; and for their travels, which acted to circumvent attempts to silence them and gave them access to a wider community. Their writings, and writings about them, are key to understanding not only early African American feminism but the roots of American reform movements. As Jean Humez has noted, "historians of the great social reform movements of the nineteenth century have shown that ultimately political liberationist movements like abolitionism and feminism were deeply rooted in the successive layers of religious enthusiasm that spread out over the northeastern United States in the first four decades of the century" (1981, 2).

Despite institutional sanctions against their licensing or ordination, African American women were active in the nineteenth and early twentieth centuries as preachers, exhorters, evangelists, and missionaries. The itinerant preaching of women like Jarena Lee, Sojourner Truth, Julia Foote, and Zilpha Elaw, and the revivalist and evangelical work of women like Amanda Berry Smith and Reverend Annie E. Brown document African American women's defiance of open hostility and attempts to limit, if not prevent, their work. Often taking their messages to whomever would receive them, they addressed men and women, whites and blacks, at camp meetings, in churches, in streets and alleyways, and in private homes. Studies of these

1

women tend to characterize their position as marginalized given that institutional positions were denied them for much of the nineteenth century (see, for example Peterson 1995; Andrews 1986, 1-22). Certainly, many of them labored outside religious institutional structures and those who were successful in their efforts to be ordained experienced their inclusion within it as tenuous. Yet these women arguably reached more potential converts outside the church's formal structure than they would have had they been licensed by a denomination or given a pastorate.

Both the Second Great Awakening and the Holiness revival movement of the nineteenth century defined American religious life, converting thousands of people organized denominations did not reach, and reclaiming "backsliders" who had strayed from the church. These movements provided numerous opportunities for African American women to preach, exhort, and evangelize. Where opportunities were not readily available, they made their own, traveling even into the dangerous Southern slave states to reach their audiences. It should be stressed that the church was, and continues to be, central to African American political life. Noting that nineteenth-century African Americans were drawn to revivals and camp meetings for their sense of social solidarity, E. Franklin Frazier both cites the ability of people to vote within churches to elect church officers and identifies the church as one of the only arenas in which individuals might "achieve distinction and status" (1974, 49) as markers of the church's centrality to African American political life. C. Eric Lincoln and Lawrence Mamiya add that the black church has been key to social cohesion among African Americans (1990, 92). Consequently, struggles that African American preaching women undertook to improve women's and African Americans' access to both black and mixed churches, and to freedom of religious worship, were highly political struggles.

As the documents collected in the first section of this chapter attest, African American feminism in the church went beyond preaching and evangelizing to include the work of women such as Maria Stewart, who utilized a "social gospel" to forward her feminist politics. Taken together, these documents indicate the labors of black feminists in several areas of religious life and the church as institution, mark the centrality of religious enthusiasm as the bedrock for social reforms like abolition, and reveal the religious inflections in African American politics during the nineteenth century that many scholars identify as social gospel. That African American feminists were locating themselves within religious communities or creating their own, all the while regarding them as publics for a feminist politics, underlines the centrality of religious revivalism to early black feminism.

African American preaching women not only advocated the right of a woman to preach, but, like their black feminist sisters who took up abolition, spoke against slavery in the antebellum period, despite the danger of doing so. In an important sense, their preaching must be understood as abolitionist, feminist, and, of course, religious. Given that link between religious enthusiasm and reform, this chapter moves from women and the church to a focus on early African American female organizing through the female benevolent and literary societies of the Northeast, as well as on African American women working in the abolition movement. African American abolitionists such as Mary Ann Shadd Cary, Ellen Craft, Sarah Mapps Douglass, Frances Harper, Sarah Parker Remond, and Sojourner Truth, among others, worked in a variety of locations to speak on behalf of enslaved African Americans. Free African Americans in the Northeast, who formed the backbone of black participation in abolition, understood their material condition as inextricably linked to that of their enslaved brothers and sisters. Discrimination against African Americans in employment markets, education, social venues, and transportation was enabled by the legal tenet that black skin was the mark of slavery. Free blacks saw that black civil rights could not be achieved while slavery continued to be legal in the United States. The women who spoke and appeared on anti-slavery platforms and who participated in abolition societies and voluntary associations understood and experienced this link in their daily lives.

Whether they were fugitive slaves themselves, as was Ellen Craft; or freeborn, as were Frances Harper, Sarah Parker Remond, and Mary Ann Shadd Cary; or emancipated slaves, as was Sojourner Truth, when black female abolitionists addressed the predominately white and bourgeois audiences of the anti-slavery movement they were frequently put in the position of embodying those "victims" of slavery for whom they spoke. White abolitionists declared a greater interest in former slaves as "slavery's silent argument" than in those men and women offering a political argument for abolition and black civil rights themselves. The positioning of African Americans as symbols within the abolitionist movement was further exacerbated by the growth of what is now called "feminist abolitionism," or the increased participation of white women in anti-slavery politics and their use of slavery as a metaphor for woman's condition in a nascent feminist movement both in the United States and abroad in Britain. When Sarah Parker Remond appeared before American, and later British, Scottish, and Irish audiences, in the 1840s and 1850s, she was soliciting and managing what could be competing political sympathies.

The 1850s, in particular, were active years for women in the anti-slavery cause and saw the development of women's rights agitation historically attributed to women's participation in abolition. From this intersection of

3

woman's rights and abolition, the woman as slave trope—in use as early as the mid-1820s—grew in popularity so as to become virtually commonplace. Jean Fagan Yellin has documented that American anti-slavery women used the image of the female supplicant slave in multiple ways: alternately "addressing and avoiding issues of race, sexual conformity, and patriarchal definitions of true womanhood," white female abolitionists favored two distinct appeals that either "picture[ed] themselves as chain-breaking liberators" of enslaved black women or "as enchained slaves[, themselves,] pleading for their own liberty," which they subsequently asserted in order to become "free" (1989, 25).

By the time Sarah Parker Remond appeared before her first abolitionist audiences in the late 1840s and early1850s, American feminist abolitionists and woman's rights advocates were well versed in the analogy that had become an identification—woman as sister slave. However, she was not the only black feminist working in abolition to negotiate the circulation of "slave" as symbol. Sojourner Truth's work in abolition and the woman's rights movement, as documented by selections in this chapter and Chapter 5, offers insight into how African American women managed the demand to be a symbol of suffering—the slave's or woman's—while still articulating their political positions and demands. Reading across accounts of these very different self-presentations or representations in the press, their different uses of existing appeals and rhetorics and their shared focus on keeping African American rights and freedoms at the center of political discourse offer us a fascinating glimpse of complicated and daring black feminist work.

Perhaps the first black female traveling lecturer for the Maine Anti-Slavery Society, Frances Ellen Watkins Harper's work in abolition is, in important ways, different from that of Remond and Truth.[1] Harper's fame as an abolitionist was established in the United States, while Remond's work comes through reports in the British press, where she achieved greater success than while lecturing in her homeland. Like Truth, Harper had to negotiate the largely segregated abolitionist movement; similarly, she frequently sought out black communities and gave speeches in black churches. They were the most famous black female abolitionists of their day, but they differed in a very important respect—Truth was illiterate, while Harper became a successful writer, whose *Poems on Miscellaneous Subjects*, published in 1854, sold some 10,000 copies by 1857. Harper is recognized as a radical abolitionist whose politics went beyond moral suasion to include Free Produce politics and aiding fugitives on the Underground Railroad even after she became a widowed mother. Like Truth, Harper remained active in reform politics after the end of the Civil War, becoming a leader in suffrage agitation, the American Equal Rights Association, and the Woman's Christian

Temperance Union. She also worked extensively in Reconstruction efforts in the South and, as did Truth, for the freedmen and freedwomen there.

In an important sense, work like Frances Harper's was built on the efforts of black feminists who organized literary and mutual benefit societies, such as the African Dorcas Association;[2] literary societies in major cities in the Northeast; and female and "mutual" benefit, charitable, or benevolent societies. By 1830 Philadelphia could claim some 80 mutual benefit societies organized by African Americans, many of them established by African American women. These were venues for black women to continue their active support for their communities, but they were also sources of sustained mutual support. Other female benevolent or mutual benevolent societies effectively provided a form of insurance for working African American women who joined and contributed a membership fee, thereby creating a fund upon which they could draw if they found themselves in need. They also pooled what resources they could to support the sick and others in need in their communities. Still other societies focused on the needs of fugitive slaves, such as the Toronto Ladies Association for the Relief of Destitute Colored Fugitives. Given Maria Stewart's important feminist black nationalist work in the early 1830s linking the labour of working black women to the political advancement of "the race," these benevolent societies must be regarded as offering immediate material assistance as well as political promise to their communities.

The African American female literary societies worked in related ways, offering immediate outlets for black women's creative and political writing, acceptable venues to discuss concerns affecting the community and women within it, and an important sense of women's collectivity. Elizabeth McHenry argues that such societies provided free African Americans "with opportunities to practice and perform literacy and allowed them to experiment with voice and self-representation in ways that approximated the ideals of civic participation" (2002, 56). Indeed, it was the Female Literary Association of Philadelphia that first drew William Lloyd Garrison's attention to the writing skills and political views of African American women in the early 1830s, and it is credited with influencing him to establish *The Liberator*'s "Ladies Department" in order to share the addresses read at their "mental feasts" with his readers. The importance of these literary societies cannot be underestimated: Maria Stewart is believed to have presented her *Productions* at Garrison's *Liberator* offices after seeing him as a potential "sympathizer" because of his interest in the literary productions and debates emerging from these societies. Stewart's first public address in Boston was to just such an organization at their invitation—the Afric-American Female Intelligence Society.

Finally, African American female associations established for mutual support also proved to be effective sites in which women tried on leadership roles, taking what they learned and practiced into abolition. Such was the case for Clarissa Lawrence, who once led the Colored Female Religious and Moral Society of Salem, founded in 1818 with a mandate to write about and discuss the conditions of enslaved African American women. Lawrence also held a leadership role in the Salem Female Anti-Slavery Society, a racially mixed organization founded on June 4, 1834. It had formed from the reorganization of the Female Anti-Slavery Society of Salem, a black female anti-slavery society founded in 1832 to promote the welfare of African Americans generally. In important ways, mutual benevolent associations and literary societies fostered the all-black female anti-slavery societies, societies that were clearly foundational and sustaining for black female abolitionists who also worked in interracial abolition efforts. For example, Sarah Mapps Douglass maintained membership in both the racially mixed Philadelphia Female Anti-Slavery Society, founded in 1833, and in the Women's Association of Philadelphia, an all-black association founded in 1848 (Yee 1992, 111).

WOMEN AND THE CHURCH

Maria W. Stewart, "Cause for Encouragement." *The Liberator,* 14 July 1832

By a lady of color.
For the Liberator.
CAUSE FOR ENCOURAGEMENT.
*Composed upon hearing the Editor's account
of the late Convention in Philadelphia.*[3]

O, who can be discouraged from persevering in the paths of virtue, and the ways of well-doing? Where is the soul amongst us that is not fired with a holy ambition? Has not every one a wish to excel in order to encourage those benevolent hearts who are making every exertion in our behalf—whose prayers are ascending up before the majesty on high, like holy incense—and whose tears are beginning to flow at Afric's woes? Many have desired to hear those things, which we hear, and have not heard them; and to see those things that we see, and have not seen them.

The day-star from on high is beginning to dawn upon us, and Ethiopia will soon stretch forth her hands unto God.[4] These Anti-Slavery Societies, in my opinion, will soon cause many grateful tears to flow, and many desponding hearts to bound and leap for joy.

And is it the applause of men that has prompted these benevolent ones to take their lives in their hands, as it were, to plead our cause before the great and powerful? Ah, no! it is that holy religion (which is held in derision and contempt by many) whose precepts will raise and elevate us above our present condition, and cause our aspirations to ascend up in unison with theirs, and become the final means of bursting the bands of oppression.

Who have been the greatest and most powerful men since the first foundations of the earth were laid? Those who have been the most eminent for their piety and virtue. Upon what was America founded? Upon religion and pure principles. O, America, America! thou land of my birth! I love and admire thy virtues, as much as I abhor and detest thy vices; and I am in hopes that thy stains will soon be wiped away, and thy cruelties forgotten. O, ye southern slaveholders! we will no longer curse you for your wrongs; but we will implore the Almighty to soften your hard hearts towards our brethren, and to send them a speedy deliverance.

What has caused the downfal [sic] of nations, kings and empires? Sin, that abominable thing which God hates. Why has the Almighty commissioned the destroying angel to execute the fierceness of his anger upon the inhabitants of the earth? Because they have made light of the name of the Lord, and forgotten the rock of their salvation. Why is it that churches and societies are not more flourishing among us? Because too much self-will and prejudice exists. Shall we, for a moment, persist in a course that will dampen the zeal of our benefactors? On the other hand, shall we not convince them that our souls respond with theirs? Do you say, how can we? In a thousand ways, I reply. 1st. In promoting, encouraging and holding each other up by the hand; and, secondly, in preserving our lips from slander and our tongues from deceit. It is high time for us to elevate ourselves by some meritorious acts. And would to God that the advocates of freedom might perceive a trait in each one of us, that would encourage their hearts and strengthen their hands.

Many bright and intelligent ones are in the midst of us; but because they are not calculated to display a classical education, they hide their talents beneath a napkin. I should rejoice to behold my friends or foes far exceed my feeble efforts. I should be happy to discern amongst them patterns worthy of imitation, and become proud to acknowledge them as my superiors. O, how I long for the time to come when I shall behold our young men anxious to inform their minds on moral and political subjects—ambitious to become distinguished men of talents—view them standing pillars in the church, qualifying themselves to preach the everlasting gospel of our Lord Jesus Christ—becoming useful and active members in society, and the future hopes of our declining years.

Finally, it appears to me, at times, as though eternity would be too short for me to admire and adore that Being who first directed my inexperienced footsteps to the abode of piety and virtue, where I was early taught to look upon vice with abhorrence and disgust. And could I now receive my choice, I would prefer moral worth and excellence of character to the wealth of the Indies, or the gold of Peru.

Jarena Lee, Excerpts from *The Life and Religious Experiences of Jarena Lee, a Coloured Lady, Giving an Account of her Call to Preach the Gospel*. Philadelphia: For the author, 1836

And it shall come to pass...that I will pour out my Spirit upon all flesh; and your sons, and your *daughters* shall prophecy.
Joel ii. 28

I was born February 11th, 1783, at Cape May, state of New Jersey. At the age of seven years I was parted from my parents, and went to live as a servant maid, with a Mr. Sharp, at the distance of about sixty miles from the place of my birth.

My parents being wholly ignorant of the knowledge of God, had not therefore instructed me in any degree in this great matter. Not long after the commencement of my attendance on this lady, she had bid me do something respecting my work, which in a little while after, she asked me if I had done, when I replied, Yes—but this was not true.

At this awful point, in my early history, the spirit of God moved in power through my conscience, and told me I was a wretched sinner. On this account so great was the impression, and so strong were the feelings of guilt, that I promised in my heart that I would not tell another lie.

But notwithstanding this promise my heart grew harder, after a while, yet the spirit of the Lord never entirely forsook me, but continued mercifully striving with me, until his gracious power converted my soul.

The manner of this great accomplishment was as follows: In the year 1804, it so happened that I went with others to hear a missionary of the Presbyterian order preach. It was an afternoon meeting, but few were there, the place was a school room; but the preacher was solemn, and in his countenance the earnestness of his master's business appeared equally strong, as though he were about to speak to a multitude.

At the reading of the Psalms, a ray of renewed conviction darted to my soul. These were the words, composing the first verse of the Psalms for the service:

Lord, I am vile, conceived in sin,
Born unholy and unclean.
Sprung from man, whose guilty fall
Corrupts the race, and taints us all.[5]

This description of my condition struck me to the heart, and made me to feel in some measure, the weight of my sins, and sinful nature. But not knowing how to run immediately to the Lord for help, I was driven of Satan, in the course of a few days, and tempted to destroy myself.

There was a brook about a quarter of a mile from the house, in which there was a deep hole, where the water whirled about among the rocks; to this place it was suggested, I must go and drown myself.

At the time I had a book in my hand; it was on a Sabbath morning, about ten o'clock; to this place I resorted, where on coming to the water I sat down on the bank, and on my looking into it; it was suggested, that drowning would be an easy death. It seemed as if some one was speaking to me, saying put your head under, it will not distress you. But by some means, of which I can give no account, my thoughts were taken entirely from this purpose, when I went from the place to the house again. It was the unseen arm of God which saved me from self murder.

But notwithstanding this escape from death, my mind was not at rest—but so great was the labour of my spirit and the fearful oppressions of a judgment to come, that I was reduced as one extremely ill. On which account a physician was called to attend me, from which illness I recovered in about three months.

But as yet I had not found him of whom Moses and the prophets did write, being extremely ignorant: there being no one to instruct me in the way of life and salvation as yet. After my recovery, I left the lady, who during my sickness, was exceedingly kind, and went to Philadelphia. From this place I soon went a few miles into the country, where I resided in the family of a Roman Catholic. But my anxiety still continued respecting my poor soul, on which account I used to watch my opportunity to read in the Bible; and this lady observing this, took the Bible from me and hid it, giving me a novel in its stead—which when I perceived, I refused to read.

Soon after this I again went to the city of Philadelphia; and commenced going to the English Church, the pastor of which was an Englishman, by the name of Pilmore, one of the number, who at first preached Methodism in America, in the city of New York.[6]

But while sitting under the ministration of this man, which was about three months, and at the last time, it appeared that there was a wall between me and a communion with that people, which was higher than I could possibly see over, and seemed to make this impression upon my mind, *this is not the people for you.*

But on returning home at noon I inquired of the head cook of the house respecting the rules of the Methodists, as I knew she belonged to that society, who told me what they were; on which account I replied, that I should not be able to abide by such strict rules not even one year;—however, I told her that I would go with her and hear what they had to say.

The man who was to speak in the afternoon of that day, was the Rev. Richard Allen, since bishop of the African Episcopal Methodists in America.[7] During the labors of this man that afternoon, I had come to the conclusion, that this is the people to which my heart unites, and it so happened, that as soon as the service closed he invited such as felt a desire to flee the wrath to come, to unite on trial with them—I embraced the opportunity. Three weeks from that day, my soul was gloriously converted to God, under preaching, at the very outset of the sermon. The text was barely pronounced, which was: "I perceive thy heart is not right in the sight of God,"[8] when there appeared to *my* view, in the centre of the heart *one* sin; and this was *malice*, against one particular individual, who had strove deeply to injure me, which I resented. At this discovery I said, *Lord* I forgive *every* creature. That instant, it appeared to me, as if a garment, which had entirely enveloped my whole person, even to my fingers ends, split at the crown of my head, and was stripped away from me, passing like a shadow, from my sight—when the glory of God seemed to cover me in its stead.

That moment, though hundreds were present, I did leap to my feet, and declare that God, for Christ's sake, had pardoned the sins of my soul. Great was the ecstasy of my mind, for I felt that not only the sin of *malice* was pardoned, but all other sins were swept away together. That day was the first when my heart had believed, and my tongue had made confession unto salvation—the first words uttered, a part of that song, which shall fill eternity with its sound, was *glory to God.* For a few moments I had power to exhort sinners and to tell of the wonders and of the goodness of him who had clothed me with *his* salvation. During this, the minister was silent, until my soul felt its duty had been performed, when he declared another witness of the power of Christ to forgive sins on earth, was manifest in my conversion.

From the day on which I first went to the Methodist church, until the hour of my deliverance, I was strangely buffetted by that enemy of all righteousness—the devil.

I was naturally of a lively turn of disposition; and during the space of time from my first awakening until I knew my peace was made with God, I rejoiced in the vanities of this life, and then again sunk back into sorrow.

For four years I had continued in this way, frequently labouring under the awful apprehension, that I could never be happy in this life. This persuasion was greatly strengthened, during the three weeks, which was the last of Satan's power over me, in this peculiar manner: on which account, I had come to the conclusion that I had better be dead than alive. Here I was again tempted to destroy my life by drowning; but suddenly this mode was changed, and while in the dusk of the evening, as I was walking to and fro in the yard of the house, I was beset to hang myself, with a cord suspended from the wall enclosing the secluded spot.

But no sooner was the intention resolved on in my mind, than an awful dread came over me, when I ran into the house; still the tempter pursued me. There was standing a vessel of water—into this I was strongly impressed to plunge my head, so as to extinguish the life which God had given me. Had I have done this, I have been always of the opinion that I should have been unable to have released myself; although the vessel was scarcely large enough to hold a gallon of water. Of me may it not be said, as written by Isaiah, (chap. 65, verses 1,2.) "I am sought of them that asked not for me; I am found of them that sought me not." Glory be to God for his redeeming power, which saved me from the violence of my own hands, from the malice of Satan, and from eternal death; for had I have killed myself, a great ransom could not have delivered me; for it is written—"No murderer hath eternal life abiding in him."[9] How appropriately can I sing—

Jesus sought me, when a stranger,
Wandering from the fold of God;
He to rescue me from danger,
Interposed his precious blood.[10]

But notwithstanding the terror which seized upon me, when about to end my life, I had no view of the precipice on the edge of which I was tottering, until it was over, and my eyes were opened. Then the awful gulf of hell seemed to be open beneath me, covered only, as it were, by a spider's web, on which I stood. I seemed to hear the howling of the damned, to see the smoke of the bottomless pit, and to hear the rattling of those chains, which hold the impenitent under clouds of darkness to the judgment of the great day.

I trembled like Belshazzar,[11] and cried out in the horror of my spirit, "God be merciful to me a sinner." That night I formed a resolution to pray;

which, when resolved upon, there appeared, sitting in one corner of the room, Satan, in the form of a monstrous dog, and in a rage, as if in pursuit, his tongue protruding from his mouth to a great length, and his eyes looked like two balls of fire; it soon, however, vanished out of my sight. From this state of terror and dismay, I was happily delivered under the preaching of the Gospel as before related.

This view, which I was permitted to have of Satan, in the form of a dog, is evidence, which corroborates in my estimation, the Bible account of a hell of fire, which burneth with brimstone, called in Scripture the bottom-less pit; the place where all liars, who repent not, shall have their portion; as also the Sabbath breaker, the adulterer, the fornicator, with the fearful, the abominable, and the unbelieving, this shall be the portion of their cup.

This language is too strong and expressive to be applied to any state of suffering in *time*. Were it to be thus applied, the reality could no where be found in human life; the consequence would be, that *this* scripture would be found a false testimony. But when made to apply to an endless state of perdition, in eternity, beyond the bounds of human life, then this language is found not to exceed our views of a state of eternal damnation [...]

Although at this time, when my conviction was so great, yet I knew not that Jesus Christ was the Son of God, the second person in the adorable trinity. I knew him not in the pardon of my sins, yet I felt a consciousness that if I died without pardon, that my lot must inevitably be damnation. If I would pray—I knew not how. I could form no connexion of ideas into words; but I knew the Lord's prayer; this I uttered with a loud voice, and with all my might and strength. I was the most ignorant creature in the world; I did not even know that Christ had died for the sins of the world, and to save sinners [...]

But the Lord led me on; being gracious, he took pity on my ignorance; he heard my wailings, which had entered into the ear of the Lord of Sabaoth.[12] Circumstances so transpired that I soon came to a knowledge of the being and character of the Son of God, of whom I knew nothing.

My strength had left me. I had become feverish and sickly through the violence of my feelings, on which account I left my place of service to spend a week with a coloured physician, who was a member of the Methodist society, and also to spend this week in going to places where prayer and supplication was statedly made for such as me.

Through this means I had learned much, so as to be able in some degree to comprehend the spiritual meaning of the text, which the minister took on the Sabbath morning, as before related, which was, "I perceive thy heart is not right in the sight of God." Acts, chap. 8, verse 21.

This text, as already related, became the power of God unto salvation to me, because I believed. I was baptized according to the direction of our Lord, who said, as he was about to ascend from the mount, to his disciples, "Go ye into all the world and preach my gospel to every creature, he that believeth and is baptized shall be saved."[13] I have now passed through the account of my conviction, and also of my conversion to God; and shall next speak of the blessing of sanctification.[14]

A time after I had received forgiveness flowed sweetly on; day and night my joy was full, no temptation was permitted to molest me [...]

I continued in this happy state of mind for almost three months, when a certain coloured man, by name William Scott, came to pay me a religious visit. He had been for many years a faithful follower of the Lamb; and he had also taken much time in visiting the sick and distressed of our colour, and understood well the great things belonging to a man of full stature in Christ Jesus.

In the course of our conversation, he inquired if the Lord had justified my soul. I answered, yes. He then asked me if he had sanctified me. I answered, no; and that I did not know what that was. He then undertook to instruct me further in the knowledge of the Lord respecting this blessing.

He told me the progress of the soul from a state of darkness, or of nature, was threefold; or consisted in three degrees, as follows:—First, conviction for sin. Second, justification from sin. Third, the entire sanctification of the soul to God. I thought this description was beautiful, and immediately believed in it. He then inquired if I would promise to pray for this in my secret devotions. I told him, yes. Very soon I began to call upon the Lord to show me all that was in my heart, which was not according to his will. Now there appeared to be a new struggle commencing in my soul, not accompanied with fear, guilt, and bitter distress, as while under my first conviction for sin; but a labouring of the mind to know more of the right way of the Lord. I began now to feel that my heart was not clean in his sight [...]

By the increasing light of the Spirit, I had found there yet remained the root of pride, anger, self-will, with many evils, the result of fallen nature. I now became alarmed at this discovery, and began to fear that I had been deceived in my experience. I was now greatly alarmed, lest I should fall away from what I knew I had enjoyed; and to guard against this I prayed almost incessantly, without acting faith on the power and promises of God to keep me from falling. I had not yet learned how to war against temptation of this kind. Satan well knew that if he could succeed in making me disbelieve my conversion, that he would catch me either on the ground of complete despair, or on the ground of infidelity. For if all I had passed through was to go for nothing, and was but a fiction, the mere ravings of a disordered mind, then I would naturally be led to believe that there is nothing in religion at all.

From this snare I was mercifully preserved, and led to believe that there was yet a greater work than that of pardon to be wrought in me. I retired to a secret place (after having sought this blessing, as well as I could, for nearly three months, from the time brother Scott had instructed me respecting it) for prayer, about four o'clock in the afternoon. I had struggled long and hard, but found not the desire of my heart. When I rose from my knees, there seemed a voice speaking to me, as I yet stood in a leaning posture—"Ask for sanctification." When to my surprise, I recollected that I had not even thought of it in my whole prayer. It would seem Satan had hidden the very object from my mind, for which I had purposely kneeled to pray. But when this voice whispered in my heart, saying, "Pray for sanctification," I again bowed in the same place, at the same time, and said, "Lord *sanctify* my soul for Christ's sake?" That very instant, as if lightning had darted through me, I sprang to my feet, and cried, "The Lord has sanctified my soul!" There was none to hear this but the angels who stood around to witness my joy—and Satan, whose malice raged the more. That Satan was there, I knew; for no sooner had I cried out, "The Lord has sanctified my soul," than there seemed another voice behind me, saying, "No, it is too great a work to be done." But another spirit said, "Bow down for the witness—I received it—*thou art sanctified!*"[15] The first I knew of myself after that, I was standing in the yard with my hands spread out, and looking with my face toward heaven. I now ran into the house and told them what had happened to me, when, as it were, a new rush of the same ecstasy came upon me, and caused me to feel as if I were in an ocean of light and bliss.

During this, I stood perfectly still, the tears rolling in a flood from my eyes. So great was the joy, that it is past description. There is no language that can describe it, except that which was heard by St. Paul, when he was caught up to the third heaven, and heard words which it was not lawful to utter.[16]

MY CALL TO PREACH THE GOSPEL.

Between four and five years after my sanctification, on a certain time, an impressive silence fell upon me, and I stood as if some one was about to speak to me, yet I had no such thought in my heart. But to my utter surprise there seemed to sound a voice which I thought I distinctly heard, and most certainly understood, which said to me, "Go preach the Gospel!" I immediately replied aloud, "No one will believe me." Again I listened, and again the same voice seemed to say, "Preach the Gospel; I will put words in your mouth, and will turn your enemies to become your friends."

At first I supposed that Satan had spoken to me, for I had read that he could transform himself into an angel of light, for the purpose of deception. Immediately I went into a secret place, and called upon the Lord to know if he had called me to preach, and whether I was deceived or not; when there appeared to my view the form and figure of a pulpit, with a Bible lying thereon, the back of which was presented to me as plainly as if it had been a literal fact.

In consequence of this, my mind became so exercised that during the night following, I took a text, and preached in my sleep. I thought there stood before me a great multitude, while I expounded to them the things of religion [...] Two days after, I went to see the preacher in charge of the African Society,[17] who was the Rev. Richard Allen, the same before named in these pages, to tell him that I felt it my duty to preach the gospel [...] He replied by asking, in what sphere I wished to move in? I said, among the Methodists. He then replied, that a Mrs. Cook, a Methodist lady, had also some time before requested the same privilege; who it was believed, had done much good in the way of exhortation, and holding prayer meetings; and who had been permitted to do so by the verbal license of the preacher in charge at the time. But as to women preaching, he said that our Discipline knew nothing at all about it—that it did not call for women preachers.[18] This I was glad to hear, because it removed the fear of the cross—but no sooner did this feeling cross my mind, than I found that a love of souls had in a measure departed from me; that holy energy which burned within me, as a fire, began to be smothered. This I soon perceived.

O how careful ought we to be, lest through our by-laws of church government and discipline, we bring into disrepute even the word of life. For as unseemly as it may appear now-a-days for a woman to preach, it should be remembered that nothing is impossible with God. And why should it be thought impossible, heterodox, or improper, for a woman to preach? seeing the Saviour died for the woman as well as the man.

If a man may preach, because the Saviour died for him, why not the woman? seeing he died for her also. Is he not a whole Saviour, instead of a half one? as those who hold it wrong for a woman to preach, would seem to make it appear.

Did not Mary *first* preach the risen Saviour, and is not the doctrine of the resurrection the very climax of Christianity—hangs not all our hope on this, as argued by St. Paul? Then did not Mary, a woman, preach the gospel? for she preached the resurrection of the crucified Son of God.

But some will say, that Mary did not expound the Scripture, therefore, she did not preach, in the proper sense of the term. To this I reply, it may be that the term *preach*, in those primitive times, did not mean exactly what

15

it is now *made* to mean; perhaps it was a great deal more simple then, than it is now:—if it were not, the unlearned fishermen could not have preached the gospel at all, as they had no learning.

To this it may be replied, by those who are determined not to believe that it is right for a woman to preach, that the disciples, though they were fishermen, and ignorant of letters too, were inspired so to do. To which I would reply, that though they were inspired, yet that inspiration did not save them from showing their ignorance of letters, and of man's wisdom; this the multitude soon found out, by listening to the remarks of the envious Jewish priests. If then, to preach the gospel, by the gift of heaven, comes by inspiration solely, is God straitened; must he take the man exclusively? May he not, did he not, and can he not inspire a female to preach the simple story of the birth, life, death, and resurrection of our Lord, and accompany it too, with power to the sinner's heart. As for me, I am fully persuaded that the Lord called me to labour according to what I have received, in his vineyard. If he has not, how could he consistently bear testimony in favour of my poor labours, in awakening and converting sinners?

In my wanderings up and down among men, preaching according to my ability, I have frequently found families who told me that they had not for several years been to a meeting, and yet, while listening to hear what God would say by his poor coloured female instrument, have believed with trembling—tears rolling down their cheeks, the signs of contrition and repentance towards God. I firmly believe that I have sown seed, in the name of the Lord, which shall appear with its increase at the great day of accounts, when Christ shall come to make up his jewels [...]

THE SUBJECT OF MY CALL TO PREACH RENEWED

It was now eight years since I had made application to be permitted to preach the gospel, during which time I had only been allowed to exhort,[19] and even this privilege but seldom [...] During this time, I had solicited of the Rev. Bishop Richard Allen, who at this time had become Bishop of the African Episcopal Methodists in America, to be permitted the liberty of holding prayer meetings in my own hired house, and of exhorting as I found liberty, which was granted me. By this means, my mind was relieved, as the house was soon filled when the hour appointed for prayer had arrived [...]

But to return to the subject of my call to preach. Soon after this, as above related, the Rev. Richard Williams was to preach at Bethel Church, where I with others were assembled. He entered the pulpit, gave out the hymn, which was sung, and then addressed the throne of grace; took his text, passed through the exordium,[20] and commenced to expound it. The text he took is in Jonah, 2d chap. 9th verse, — "Salvation is of the Lord." But as he proceeded to explain, he seemed to have lost the spirit; when in the same instant, I sprang, as by an altogether supernatural impulse, to my feet, when I was aided from above to give an exhortation on the very text which my brother Williams had taken.

I told them that I was like Jonah; for it had been then nearly eight years since the Lord had called me to preach his gospel to the fallen sons and daughters of Adam's race, but that I had lingered like him, and delayed to go at the bidding of the Lord, and warn those who are as deeply guilty as were the people of Ninevah.

During the exhortation, God made manifest his power in a manner sufficient to show the world that I was called to labour according to my ability, and the grace given unto me, in the vineyard of the good husbandman.

I now sat down, scarcely knowing what I had done, being frightened. I imagined, that for this indecorum, as I feared it might be called, I should be expelled from the church. But instead of this, the Bishop rose up in the assembly, and related that I had called upon him eight years before, asking to be permitted to preach, and that he had put me off; but that he now as much believed that I was called to that work, as any of the preachers present. These remarks greatly strengthened me, so that my fears of having given an offence, and made myself liable as an offender, subsided, giving place to a sweet serenity, a holy job of a peculiar kind, untasted in my bosom until then.

The next Sabbath day, while sitting under the word of the gospel, I felt moved to attempt to speak to the people in a public manner, but I could not bring my mind to attempt it in the church. I said, Lord, anywhere but here. Accordingly, there was a house not far off which was pointed out to me, to this I went. It was the house of a sister belonging to the same society with myself. Her name was Anderson. I told her I had come to hold a meeting in her house, if she would call in her neighbours. With this request she immediately complied. My congregation consisted of but five persons. I commenced by reading and singing a hymn, when I dropped to my knees by the side of a table to pray. When I arose I found my hand resting on the Bible, which I had not noticed till that moment. It now occurred to me to take a text. I opened the Scripture, as it happened, at the 141st Psalm, fixing my eye on the 3d verse, which reads: "Set a watch, O Lord, before my mouth, keep the door of my lips." My sermon, such as it was, I applied wholly to myself, and added an exhortation. Two of my congregation wept much, as the fruit of my labour this time. In closing I said to the few, that if any one would open a door, I would hold a meeting the next sixth-day evening; when one answered that her house was at my service. Accordingly I went, and God made manifest his power among the people.

Some wept, while others shouted for joy. One whole seat of females, by the power of God, as the rushing of a wind, were all bowed to the floor at once, and screamed out. Also a sick man and woman in one house, the Lord convicted them both; one lived, and the other died. God wrought a judgment—some were well at night, and died in the morning. At this place I continued to hold meetings about six months. During that time I kept house with my little son, who was very sickly. About this time I had a call to preach at a place about thirty miles distant, among the Methodists, with whom I remained one week, and during the whole time, not a thought of my little son came into my mind; it was hid from me, lest I should have been diverted from the work I had to, to look after my son [...]

I now returned home, found all well; no harm had come to my child, although I left it very sick. Friends had taken care of it which was of the Lord. I now began to think seriously of breaking up housekeeping, and forsaking all to preach the everlasting Gospel. I felt a strong desire to return to the place of my nativity, at Cape May, after an absence of about fourteen years [...] I proceeded on as opportunities offered, toward where my mother lived. When within ten miles of that place, I appointed an evening meeting. There were a goodly number came out to hear. The Lord was pleased to give me light and liberty among the people. After meeting, there came an elderly lady to me and said, she believed the Lord had sent me among them; she then appointed me another meeting there two weeks from that night. The next day I hastened forward to the place of my mother, who was happy to see me, and the happiness was mutual between us. With her I left my poor sickly boy, while I departed to do my Master's will. In this neighbourhood I had an uncle, who was a Methodist, and who gladly threw open his door for meetings to be held there [...]

The week following, I had an invitation to hold a meeting at the Court House of the County, when I spoke from the 53d chap, of Isaiah, 3d verse. It was a solemn time, and the Lord attended the word; I had life and liberty, though there were people there of various denominations [...] This day I spoke twice, and walked six miles to the place appointed. There was a magistrate present, who showed his friendship, by saying in a friendly manner, that he had heard of me [...] When the meeting was over, he invited me to preach in a schoolhouse in his neighbourhood, about three miles distant from where I then was [...] This day I walked six miles, and preached twice to large congregations, both in the morning and evening. The Lord was with me, glory be to his holy name. I next went six miles and held a meeting in a coloured friend's house, at eleven o'clock in the morning, and preached to a well behaved congregation of both coloured and white. After service I again walked back, which was in all twelve miles in the same day [...] On fourth-day,[21] after this, in compliance with an invitation received by note, from the same magistrate who had heard me at the above place, I preached to a large congregation, where we had a precious time: much weeping was heard among the people. The same gentleman, now at the close of the meeting, gave out another appointment at the same place, that day week [...]

From this place I next went to Dennis Creek meeting house, where at the invitation of an elder, I spoke to a large congregation of various and conflicting sentiments, when a wonderful shock of God's power was felt, shown everywhere by groans, by sighs, and loud and happy amens. I felt as if aided from above. My tongue was cut loose, the stammerer spoke freely; the love of God, and of his service, burned with a vehement flame within me—his name was glorified among the people.

But here I feel myself constrained to give over, as from the smallness of this pamphlet I cannot go through with the whole of my journal, as it would probably make a volume of two hundred pages; which, if the Lord be willing, may at some future day be published.[22] But for the satisfaction of such as may follow after me, when I am no more, I have recorded how the Lord called me to his work, and how he has kept me from falling from grace, as I feared I should. In all things he has proved himself a God of truth to me; and in his service I am now as much determined to spend and be spent, as at the very first. My ardour for the progress of his cause abates not a whit, so far as I am able to judge, though I am now something more than fifty years of age.

As to the nature of uncommon impressions, which the reader cannot but have noticed, and possibly sneered at in the course of these pages, they may be accounted for in this way: It is known that the blind have the sense of hearing in a manner much more acute than those who can see: also their sense of feeling is exceedingly fine, and is found to detect any roughness on the smoothest surface, where those who can see can find none. So it may be with such as [I] am, who has never had more than three months schooling; and wishing to know much of the way and law of God, have therefore watched the more closely the operations of the Spirit, and have in consequence been led thereby. But let it be remarked that [I] have never found that Spirit to lead me contrary to the Scriptures of truth, as I understand them. "For as many as are led by the Spirit of God are the sons of God." —Rom. viii. 14.

I have now only to say, May the blessing of the Father, and of the Son, and of the Holy Ghost, accompany the reading of this poor effort to speak well of his name, wherever it may be read. AMEN.

Zilpha Elaw, Excerpts from *Memoirs of the Life, Religious Experiences, Ministerial Travels and Labours of Mrs. Zilpha Elaw, An American Female of Colour: Together with Some Account of the Great Religious Revivals in America*. London: T. Dudley, 1846

[...] Soon after my return [from a camp meeting in 1821 where Elaw received her "call" to preach], I laid my case in reference to my call to the work of the ministry before the ministers; and they greatly encouraged me to proceed, and to preach wherever and whenever opportunities offered. They saw no impropriety in it, and therefore advised me to go on and do all the good I could. I first broached the subject to Mr. John Potts, the beloved brother who preached at the camp-meeting on the morning of the day on which the heavenly commission was delivered unto me; and I obtained the approbation and sanction of all the ministers and of the society. But some of the members of our class soon began to betray a little jealousy, lest I should rise into too great estimation; for a prophet is not without honour, save in his own country;[23] and they began to discover many faults and imperfections in me; for three years previously there had not been a single jarring string amongst us; and nothing could be done without my opinion being first given; in every thing I suited them exactly, and we were a very loving and happy band;[24] but after I commenced the work of the ministry, I was a person of no account, and ever had been; and I became so unpopular, that all our coloured class abandoned me excepting three. Like Joseph, I was hated for my dreams; and like Paul, none stood with me.[25] This treatment, however painful, by no means damped my ardour in the work to which I had been called. I still continued in my Master's work, and great crowds assembled every Lord's day to hear me: the Lord was with me and strengthened me in my feeble labours; the number of white brethren and sisters who flocked to my ministry increased daily; the work prospered amazingly; and thus I had gone on for two months before my husband knew any thing about it; for he never went to a place of worship. At last the tidings came to his ears, and were tauntingly disclosed by one who said to him, "Josh, your wife is a preacher"; this important announcement he met with a direct negative; but when he returned home, he asked me if it was true; and I informed him that it was. "Well," said he, "I'll come and hear you, if I come barefoot"; at these words my heart leaped for joy; and I indulged in sanguine hopes that he might thereby be converted to God. He came according to his word; and I think that conviction of the sinfulness of his state strong fastened on his conscience, for he became much troubled in mind: he was also apprehensive that I should become a laughing-stock for the people; and this also grieved him considerably: sometimes he said

to me, "Now child, we are undone" it appeared to him so strange and singular a thing, that I should become a public speaker; and he advised me to
decline the work altogether, and proceed no further. I was very sorry to see
him so much grieved about it; but my heavenly Father had informed me
that he had a great work for me to do; I could not therefore descend down
to the counsel of flesh and blood, but adhered faithfully to my commission;
and very soon after, all my friends who had forsaken me, returned to me
again, for they perceived that God was with me; and many were added to
our numbers, whom I hope to meet in the realms of immortality.

My poor husband's health about this time began visibly to decline; and
his disorder soon settled into an intractable consumption [...] The fatal hour
came at last when the brittle thread of life snapped asunder, and his spirit
fled to an invisible world. This mournful event took place on the 27th day
of January, 1823 [...] After my dear husband was buried, and I had become
a little settled, instead of submitting myself in all things to be led by the
Spirit, I rather leaned to my own understanding, and procured a situation
of servitude for my little girl, and another for myself, judging these the best
means I could adopt for the liquidation of my debts; and I remained in
service until my health was so impaired that I was compelled to relinquish
it; nor did the blessing of my heavenly Father appear to prosper this course;
for I was constantly obliged to be under medical treatment, and yet grew
worse and worse. I therefore left my situation, and went back to my house,
which I had still reserved in case I should want it. I then opened a school,
and the Lord blessed the effort, and increased the number of my pupils, so
that I soon had a nice little school; many of the Society of Friends came and
visited it, and assisted me with books and other necessaries for it. They were
also much pleased with the improvement of the children; and when any
strangers came to visit Burlington, they introduced them to me; and it was
gratifying to many of them to see a female of colour teaching the coloured
children, whom the white people refused to admit into their seminaries
and who had been suffered formerly to run about the streets for want of a
teacher. The pride of a white skin is a bauble of great value with many in
some parts of the United States, who readily sacrifice their intelligence to
their prejudices, and possess more knowledge than wisdom. The Almighty
accounts not the black races of man either in the order of nature or spiritual capacity as inferior to the white; for He bestows his Holy Spirit on, and
dwells in them as readily as in persons of whiter complexion: the Ethiopian
eunuch was adopted as a son and heir of God; and when Ethiopia shall stretch
forth her hands unto him,[26] their submission and worship will be graciously accepted. This prejudice was far less prevalent in that part of the country
where I resided in my infancy; for when a child, I was not prohibited from any

school on account of the colour of my skin. Oh! That men would outgrow their nursery prejudices and learn that "God hath made of one blood all the nations of men that dwell upon all the face of the earth." Acts Xvii.26.

But my mind was not long at rest in this situation; for the remembrance of the commission which I had received from the Lord very strongly impressed me; and as the Lord had said, "Thou must preach the gospel, and thou must travel far and wide," so He was about to bring it to pass, but I knew not in what manner. I was not yet out of debt; and with an empty exchequer, I felt myself but ill adapted to set out on an excursion for preaching the gospel [...] My peace again flowed as a river on a calm summer's day; and I began to draw my school to a close. About three weeks prior to the time appointed for the dismission of my scholars, some friends who resided in the direction my mind was disposed to take, and with whom I had been previously acquainted, came to Burlington; and they, together with some of my dear people thought it advisable for me to accompany them on their return; but I saw no possibility of doing this, because they were about to take their departure before I could arrange my affairs, and receive the accounts due to me at the end of the current quarter. I therefore informed my kind friend that I should not be ready to go with him; but he insisted upon it, and enforced it with many arguments [...] I returned home, and my little daughter seeing the tears flowing down my cheeks, said to me, "Now, mother, what is the matter?" for she was aware of the great anxiety of mind I had so long been labouring under, and said all she could to comfort me; and added, "If I were you, I should not mind what any person said, but I should go just as I had arranged to go, and do not think any thing about me, for I shall do very well." [...] I took my little girl, and placed her under the care of a dear relative of mine, and proceeded on my way to the City of Philadelphia, commenced my Master's business, and strange to relate, when I arrived in that large city, every one appeared to be acquainted with my situation. I preached in a great many chapels, and every congregation voluntarily made a collection for my aid; and every person at whose house I visited, gave me something for my journey. Oh! how astonishing was this to me. I had been for several years striving to provide myself with necessary supplies for my Master's work, and without success; nor did I ever think of obtaining any money in my travels. It never occurred to me that I should receive a single penny in this work; but when I was willing, I ought to say—made willing to go just as I was, as the apostles of old, without purse or scrip, then the Lord made my way straight before me, and dealt bountifully with me; then was that blessed promise verified, "Seek ye the kingdom of God, and His righteousness, and all other things shall be added unto you" [Matt. 6:33]. In the first three weeks

22

I obtained every particle that I wanted, and abundance of silver to proceed on my journey with[....]

Thus I left my child and ventured on my journey, not knowing whither I should go. From Philadelphia I started for New York; [...] and there the Lord rendered my ministry a blessing to many precious souls—glory be to His name. I was absent from home seven months; and when I returned I was able to meet my creditors and pay my debts, which was an unspeakable indulgence. Hallelujah. Praise the Lord.

I returned home in April, 1828, and remained there a few days. During my stay at home, I was one day exercised with devout contemplations of God, and suddenly the Spirit came upon me, and a voice addressed me, saying, "Be of good cheer, and be faithful; I will yet bring thee to England and thou shall see London, that great city, and declare my name there." I looked round to ascertain from whence and from whom the voice proceeded, but no person was near me; my surprise was so great that my very blood seemed to stagnate and chill in my veins: it was evidently the Spirit of the Lord whose I am, and whom I serve, who had spoken to me; and my soul responded to His word, saying, "The will of the Lord be done in and by me on earth, as it is by His servants in Heaven." My mind was at this time very much perplexed as to what was the will of God concerning me: I was in doubt as to what I ought to do; but, after a few days, I took my journey again to Philadelphia, with the intention of visiting the southern or slave-holding states of America; here I saw my dear daughter, and remained with my friends during some few weeks; but the confusion of my mind still continued, and whenever I opened a Bible, wherever I visited, as well as at my apartments, the book of the prophet Jonah was perpetually presented before me. I mentioned to my friends the uncertainty of my mind as to what the Lord required me to do, the propriety of a voyage to England, and my repeatedly opening in the Bible at the book of Jonah; and they assured me that if it was God's will that I should then visit England, He would make it appear, and smooth the way for me in His own good time. I therefore rested upon this assurance; and while I yet abode in Philadelphia, I dreamed one night, that I saw two ships cleared out of the docks there, bound for England, and I was not on board either of them. I then concluded that the time for my journey to England had not yet come; and being now satisfied on this matter, I started off for the southern territories of the United States, where slavery is established and enforced by law. When I arrived in the slave states, Satan much worried and distressed my soul with the fear of being arrested and sold for a slave, which their laws would have warranted, on account of my complexion and features.[27] On one occasion, in particular, I had been preaching to a coloured congregation, and had exhorted them impressively to quit themselves as men approved of God, and to maintain and witness a good profession of their faith before the world, &c. I had no sooner sat down, than Satan suggested to me with such force, that the slave-holders would speedily capture me, as filled me with fear and terror. I was then in a small town in one of the slave states; and the news of a coloured female preaching to the slaves had already been spread widely throughout the neighbourhood; the novelty of the thing had produced an immense excitement and the people were collecting from every quarter, to gaze at the unexampled prodigy of a coloured female preacher. I was sitting in a very conspicuous situation near the door, and I observed, with very painful emotions, the crowd outside, pointing with their fingers at me, and saying, "that's her," "that's her"; for Satan strongly set before me the prospect of an immediate arrest and consignment by sale to some slave owner. Being very much alarmed, I removed from my seat to a retired part of the room, where, becoming more collected, I inquired within myself, "from whence cometh all this fear?" My faith then rallied and my confidence in the Lord returned, and I said, "get thee behind me Satan, for my Jesus hath made me free." My fears instantly forsook me, and I vacated my retired corner, and came forth before all the people again; and the presence and power of the Lord became greatly manifested in the assembly during the remainder of the service. At the earnest request of the friends, I consented to preach there again on the following Lord's-day morning, which I accordingly did. Some of the white brethren in connexion with the Methodist Society were present on that occasion; at the conclusion thereof, they introduced themselves to me, and wished me to preach for them in the afternoon; to which I agreed; and they obtained permission of the authorities to open and use the courthouse; and therein I obtained a very large auditory; and God gave forth proofs that my ministry was from Him, in giving me many seals to it on that day; thus was I relieved from my fearful forebodings, and pursued my course with increased energy, rejoicing in the prosperity and success with which the Almighty crowned my efforts.

After this, I visited Baltimore in the State of Maryland and attended a conference of the coloured brethren, by whom I was very kindly received; a large field of labour was provided, and a great and effectual door of utterance opened to me by the Lord. After labouring there for some weeks, I proceeded to the City of Washington, the capital of the United States, and the seat of government: here also I laboured with much success; many souls obtaining the knowledge of salvation by the remission of their sins, with the gift of the Holy Spirit, through the instrumentality of so feeble an earthen vessel. I continued my travels southward into the State of Virginia, and arrived at the City of Alexandria, where the Lord rendered my labours effectual to the conversion of many from darkness to light, and from the power of Satan unto God. I abode there two months, and was an humble agent, in the Lord's hand, of arousing many of His heritage to a great revival; and the weakness and incompetency of the poor coloured female but the more displayed the excellency of the power to be of God. There were some among the great folks whom curiosity induced to attend my ministry; and this formed a topic of lively interest with many of the slave holders, who thought it surpassingly strange that a person (and a female) belonging to the same family stock with their poor debased, uneducated, coloured slaves, should come into their territories and teach the enlightened proprietors the knowledge of God; and more strange still was it to some others, when in the spirit and power of Christ, that female drew the portraits of their characters, made manifest the secrets of their hearts, and told them all things that ever they did. This was a paradox to them indeed: for they were not deficient of pastors and reverend divines, who possessed all the advantages of talents, learning, respectability and worldly influence, to aid their religious efforts; and yet the power of truth and of God was never so manifest in any of their agencies, as with the dark coloured female stranger, who had come from afar to minister amongst them [...] I became such a prodigy to this people, that I was watched wherever I went; and if I went out to tea with any of the friends, the people would flock around the house where I was; and as soon as they judged that the repast was finished, they came in and filled the house, and required me to minister to them the word of life, whether I had previously intended to preach or not [...]

It is true, that in the ordinary course of Church arrangement and order, the Apostle Paul laid it down as a rule, that females should not speak in the church, nor be suffered to teach; but the Scriptures make it evident that this rule was not intended to limit the extraordinary directions of the Holy Ghost, in reference to female Evangelists, or oracular sisters; nor to be rigidly observed in peculiar circumstances. St. Paul himself attests that Phoebe was a servant or deaconess of the Church at Cenchrea; and as such was employed by the Church to manage some of their affairs; and it was strange indeed, if she was required to receive the commissions of the Church in mute silence, and not allowed to utter a syllable before them. The Apostle John wrote his second epistle to a Christian lady, as a matron of eminence and authority; exhorting her believing children by her, and bidding her to prove the doctrines of those who visited her in the capacity of Christian teachers: honourable mention is made of many other Christian females who promoted the cause of Jesus; and Paul wished every assistance to be given to those women who laboured with him in the Gospel. Tryphena laboured with Tryphosa in the Lord; mention is made of the services of many of the sisters of Nereus, of the mother of Rufus, many others are also very respectfully referred to by St. Paul.[28] The prophet Joel predicted that God would pour His Spirit on His handmaids, and that they should prophecy as well as His servants; and this prophecy, Peter, on the day of Pentecost, asserted was fulfilled;[29] and if so, the Christian dispensation has for its main feature the inspirations of the holy prophetic Spirit, descending on the handmaids as well as on the servants of God; and thus qualifying both for the conversion of men, and spread of the Gospel. Priscilla took upon herself the work of a teacher, when, in conjunction with her husband Aquila, she expounded to Apollos the way of God more perfectly;[30] the four virgin daughters of Philip the Evangelist,[31] were prophetesses or exhorters, probably assisting their father in his evangelic labours: being prophetesses or exhorters, the work in which they were employed was prophecy or exhortation; and those brethren certainly err, who fetter all and every ecclesiastical circumstance, and even the extraordinary inspirations of the Holy Spirit with the regulations given by the apostle to a church, the brethren of which extensively possessed the gift of utterance, and were therefore in no need of female speakers; and a Church, too, which owing to its disorders and excesses, required the most stringent rules for its proper regulation [...]

In 1837, when on a visit to some religious friends, one morning, I saw a remarkable vision; I appeared to be in a strange place and conversing with a stranger, when three enormous balls of fire came perpendicularly over my head, and each of them exploded and burst at the same moment: I instantly appeared to fall to the ground; but was caught up by an unseen hand, and placed upon an animal, which darted with me through the regions of the air, with the velocity of lightning, and deposited me inside the window of an upper chamber. I there heard the voice of the Almighty, saying, "I have a message for her to go with upon the high seas, and she will go." This occurrence took place just three years prior to my departure from America.

[...] Many were the proofs besides those related in this work, that the Lord gave me of His purpose that I should come to England; and being now many hundreds of miles distant from my daughter, and feeling that the Lord's time had arrived, I wrote to apprise her thereof, and shortly after returned homewards as far as New York, where I attended the anniversary of the abolition society: many of the speakers on that occasion came over to England to attend the great anti-slavery meeting in Exeter Hall.[32] I then returned home; and was very affectionately received by my dear daughter; and made all possible dispatch in preparations for my departure.

The parting moment was painful in the extreme; for my daughter, and her two dear little boys, were entwined in the strongest affections of my heart; but I durst not disobey Him who had said unto me, as He had said unto Abraham, "Get thee out from thy country, and from thy kindred, and from thy father's house, unto a land that I will show thee."[33] On the 10th of June 1840, I rose from the bed on which I had laid for the last time; the recollection of that bitter morning even now suffuses my eyes with tears, and interrupts the delineations of my pen: the morning was calm, our minds resigned and peaceful, and we took, and held each other's hand, in silence; which was at length broken by my daughter, who said, "Mother, we part now, but I think we shall yet meet again; the will of the Lord be done, and God be with thee." At nine o'clock a.m., I bade farewell to those dear ties, and started for New York, where I tarried until the 1st July; and then I took the steam-boat to go to the ship Philadelphia....

On the 23rd day of July, we were cheered with the sight of land; and on the 24th, we came to anchor off Falmouth, where most of the cabin passengers left us. On the evening of the 25th, we came safely into the London Docks: this was on a Saturday; and on the morning of the Lord's-day, I first set my foot on British ground. [...] Ere this work meets the eye of the public, I shall have sojourned in England five years: and I am justified in saying, that my God hath made my ministry a blessing to hundreds of persons; and many who were living in sin and darkness before they saw my coloured face, have risen up to praise the Lord, for having sent me to preach His Gospel on the shores of Britain; numbers who had been reared to maturity, and were resident in localities plentifully furnished with places of worship and ministers of the gospel, and had scarcely heard a sermon in their lives, were attracted to hear the coloured female preacher, were inclosed in the gospel net, and are now walking in the commandments and ordinances of the Lord. I have travelled in several parts of England, and I thank God He has given me some spiritual children in every place wherein I have laboured [...] My reader may perceive that I have not been an idle spectator in my Heavenly Master's cause. During my sojourn in England, I have preached considerably more than a thousand sermons. I have expended all my means in travels of no little extent and duration; devoted my time, employed the energies of my spirit, spent my strength and exhausted my constitution in the cause of Jesus; and received of pecuniary supplies and temporal remunerations in comparison with my time and labours a mere pittance, altogether inadequate to shield me from a thousand privations, hardships, targetfires, vexatious anxieties and deep afflictions, to which my previous life was an utter stranger [...]

Let me exhort my dear Christian friends of every name and denomination, by no means to omit any possible attendance on the means of grace, which are intended for their growth in the divine life and image; that they may not only hold fast where to they have attained, but become filled with the life and power, and display the perfection of the Christian religion; being the children of the resurrection, the sons of God, and receive an abundant entrance into the everlasting kingdom of our Lord and Saviour Jesus Christ. Slumbering virgins, the Bridegroom cometh! Rouse, timely to the midnight cry. I exhort all Christians, believing that there is but one church of Jesus Christ in this wilderness; and I trust she will soon come forth as the morning, leaning on her beloved, fair as the moon, clear as the sun, and terrible as a bannered army. May all who are of the household of faith stand fast in the liberty wherewith Christ has made them free. Dear brethren, the time is short, it is ominous, and it is perilous: be steadfast, unmoveable, always abounding in the work of the Lord. Be not carried about with every wind of doctrine; at the same time, reject not, nor fight against any statement of the Scriptures of truth, but with all confidence, aptitude and simplicity, as little children, receive and adopt all their inspired instructions. Mark, I beseech you, the signs of the times; they are awfully portentous: Christ's words are every where fulfilling, "Because iniquity shall abound, the love of many shall wax cold. Perilous times are verging upon us: He has asked the question, when the Son of man cometh will He find faith on the earth?"[34] Alas, of outward profession there is abundance; but of true faith, a melancholy dearth. May we be prepared to answer this question for ourselves, by keeping our faith in continual exercise.

I have now furnished my readers with an outline of my religious experience, ministerial labours and travels, together with some of the attendant results, both on the continent of America and in England: these humble memoirs will doubtless continue to be read long after I shall have ceased from my earthly labours and existence. I submit them, dear Christian reader, to thy attentive consideration, and commend this little volume and each of its readers to the blessing of the adorable God, the Father, Son and Holy Spirit. Amen.

Julia Foote, Excerpts from _A Brand Plucked From the Fire. An Autobiographical Sketch_. Cleveland, OH: W.F. Schneider, 1879

VII
MY CONVERSION

I was converted when fifteen years old. It was on a Sunday evening at a quarterly meeting. The minister preached from the text: "And they sung as it were a new song before the throne, and before the four beasts and the elders, and no man could learn that song but the hundred and forty and four thousand which were redeemed from earth." Rev.xiv.3.

As the minister dwelt with great force and power on the first clause of the text, I beheld my lost condition as I never had done before. Something within me kept saying, "Such a sinner as you are can never sing that new song." No tongue can tell the agony I suffered. I fell to the floor, unconscious, and was carried home. Several remained with me all night, singing and praying. I did not recognize any one, but seemed to be walking in the dark, followed by some one who kept saying, "Such a sinner as you are can never sing that new song." Every converted man and woman can imagine what my feelings were. I thought God was driving me on to hell. In great terror I cried: "Lord, have mercy on me, a poor sinner!" The voice which had been crying in my ears ceased at once, and a ray of light flashed across my eyes, accompanied by a sound of far distant singing; the light grew brighter and brighter, and the singing more distinct, and soon I caught the words: "This is the new song—redeemed, redeemed!" I at once sprang from the bed where I had been lying for twenty hours, without meat or drink, and commenced singing: "Redeemed! redeemed! glory! glory!" Such joy and peace as filled my heart, when I felt that I was redeemed and could sing the new song. Thus was I wonderfully saved from eternal burning […]

X

DISOBEDIENCE, BUT HAPPY RESULTS

Finally, I did something I never had done before: I deliberately disobeyed my mother. I visited these old saints, weeping as though my heart would break. When I grew calm, I told them all my troubles, and asked what I must do to get rid of them. They told me that sanctification was for the young believer, as well as the old. These words were a portion in due season. After talking a long time, and they had prayed with me, I returned home, though not yet satisfied.

I remained in this condition more than a week, going many times to my secret place of prayer, which was behind the chimney in the garret of our house. None but those who have passed up this way know how wretched every moment of my life was. I thought I must die. But truly, God does make his little ones ministering angels—sending them forth on missions of love and mercy. So he sent that dear old mother in Israel to me one fine morning in May. At the sight of her my heart seemed to melt within me, so unexpected, and yet so much desired was her visit. Oh, bless the Lord for sanctified men and women!

There was no one at home except the younger children, so our coming together was uninterrupted. She read and explained many passages of Scripture to me, such as, John xvii; 1 Thess.iv.3; v.23; 1Cor.vi. 9-12; Heb.ii.11; and many others—carefully marking them in my Bible. All this had been as a sealed book to me until now. Glory to Jesus! the seals were broken and light began to shine upon the blessed Word of God as I had never seen it before.

The second day after that pilgrim's visit, while waiting on the Lord, my large desire was granted, through faith in my precious Saviour. The glory of God seemed almost to prostrate me to the floor. There was, indeed, a weight of glory resting upon me. I sang with all my heart,

> This is the way I long have sought,
> And mourned because I found it not.[35]

Glory to the Father! glory to the Son! and glory to the Holy Ghost! who hath plucked me as a brand from the burning, and sealed me unto eternal life. I no longer hoped for glory, but I had the full assurance of it. Praise the Lord for Paul-like faith! "I am crucified with Christ: nevertheless, I live; yet not I, but Christ liveth in me."[36] This, my constant prayer, was answered, that I might be strengthened with might by his Spirit in the inner man; that being rooted and grounded in love, I might be able to comprehend with all saints what is the length, and breadth, and heighth [sic], and depth, and to know the love of Christ which passeth knowledge, and be filled with all the fullness of God.

I had been afraid to tell my mother I was praying for sanctification, but when the "old man"[37] was cast out of my heart, and perfect love took possession, I lost all fear. I went straight to my mother and told her I was sanctified. She was astonished, and called my father and told him what I had said. He was amazed as well, but said not a word. I at once began to read to them out of my Bible, and to many others, thinking, in my simplicity, that they would believe and receive the same blessing at once. To the glory of God, some did believe and were saved, but many were too wise to be taught by a child—too good to be made better.

From this time, many, who had been my warmest friends, and seemed to think me a Christian, turned against me, saying I did not know what I was talking about—that there was no such thing as sanctification and holiness in this life—and that the devil had deluded me into self-righteousness. Many of them fought holiness with more zeal and vigor than they did sin. Amid all this, I had that sweet peace that passeth all understanding springing up within my soul like a perennial fountain—glory to the precious blood of Jesus!

The King of heaven and earth
Deigns to dwell with mortals here [...][38]

XVII
MY CALL TO PREACH THE GOSPEL

For months I had been moved upon to exhort and pray with the people,
in my visits from house to house; and in meetings my whole soul seemed
drawn out for the salvation of souls. The love of Christ in me was not limited. Some of my mistaken friends said I was too forward, but a desire to
work for the Master, and to promote the glory of his kingdom in the salvation of souls, was food to my poor soul.

When called of God, on a particular occasion, to a definite work, I said,
"No, Lord, not me." Day by day I was more impressed that God would
have me work in his vineyard. I thought it could not be that I was called
to preach—I, so weak and ignorant. Still, I knew all things were possible
with God, even to confounding the wise by the foolish things of this earth.
Yet in me there was a shrinking.

I took all my doubts and fears to the Lord in prayer, when, what seemed
to be an angel, made his appearance. In his hand was a scroll, on which were
these words: "Thee have I chosen to preach my Gospel without delay." The
moment my eyes saw it, it appeared to be printed on my heart. The angel
was gone in an instant, and I, in agony, cried out, "Lord, I cannot do it!" It
was eleven o'clock in the morning, yet everything grew dark as night. The
darkness was so great that I feared to stir [...]

From that day my appetite failed me and sleep fled from my eyes. I
seemed as one tormented. I prayed, but felt no better. I belonged to a band
of sisters[39] whom I loved dearly, and to them I partially opened my mind.
One of them seemed to understand my case at once, and advised me to do
as God had bid me, or I would never be happy here or hereafter. But it
seemed too hard—I could not give up and obey.

One night as I lay weeping and beseeching the dear Lord to remove this
burden from me, there appeared the same angel that came to me before,
and on his breast were these words: "You are lost unless you obey God's
righteous commands." I saw the writing, and that was enough. I covered
my head and awoke my husband, who had returned a few days before. He
asked me why I trembled so, but I had not power to answer him. I
remained in that condition until morning, when I tried to arise and go
about my usual duties, but was too ill. Then my husband called a physician,
who prescribed medicine, but it did me no good.

I had always been opposed to the preaching of women, and had spoken against it, though, I acknowledge, without foundation. This rose before me like a mountain, and when I thought of the difficulties they had to encounter, both from professors and non-professors, I shrank back and cried, "Lord, I cannot go!"

The trouble my heavenly Father has had to keep me out of the fire that is never quenched, he alone knoweth. My husband and friends said I would die or go crazy if something favorable did not take place soon. I expected to die and be lost, knowing I had been enlightened and had tasted the heavenly gift. I read again and again the sixth chapter of Hebrews.

XVIII
HEAVENLY VISITATIONS AGAIN

Nearly two months from the time I first saw the angel, I said that I would do anything or go anywhere for God, if it were made plain to me. He took me at my word, and sent the angel again with this message: "You have I chosen to go in my name and warn the people of their sins." I bowed my head and said, "I will go, Lord."

That moment I felt a joy and peace I had not known for months. But strange as it may appear, it is not the less true, that, ere one hour had passed, I began to reason thus: "I am elected to preach the Gospel without the requisite qualifications, and, besides, my parents and friends will forsake me and turn against me; and I regret that I made a promise." At that instant all the joy and peace I had felt left me, and I thought I was standing on the brink of hell, and heard the devil say: "Let her go! let her go! I will catch her." Reader, can you imagine how I felt? If you were ever snatched from the mouth of hell, you can, in part, realize my feelings.

I continued in this state for some time, when, on a Sabbath evening— ah! that memorable Sabbath evening—while engaged in fervent prayer, the same supernatural presence came to me once more and took me by the hand. At that moment I became lost to everything in this world. The angel led me to a place where there was a large tree, the branches of which seemed to extend either way beyond sight. Beneath it sat, as I thought, God the Father, the Son, and the Holy Spirit, besides many others, whom I thought were angels. I was led before them: they looked me over from head to foot, but said nothing. Finally, the Father said to me: "Before these people make your choice, whether you will obey me or go from this place to eternal misery and pain." I answered not a word. He then took me by the hand to lead me, as I thought, to hell, when I cried out, "I will obey thee, Lord!" He then pointed my hand in different directions, and asked if I would go there. I replied, "Yes, Lord." He then led me, all the others following, till we came to a place where there was a great quantity of water, which looked like silver, where we made a halt. My hand was given to Christ, who led me into the water and stripped me of my clothing, which at once vanished from sight. Christ then appeared to wash me, the water feeling quite warm.

During this operation, all the others stood on the bank, looking on in profound silence. When the washing was ended, the sweetest music I had ever heard greeted my ears. We walked to the shore, where an angel stood with a clean, white robe, which the Father at once put on me. In an instant I appeared to be changed into an angel. The whole company looked at me with delight, and began to make a noise which I called shouting.[40] We all marched back with music. When we reached the tree to which the angel first led me, it hung full of fruit, which I had not seen before. The Holy Ghost plucked some and gave me, and the rest helped themselves. We sat down and ate of the fruit, which had a taste like nothing I had ever tasted before. When we had finished, we all arose and gave another shout. Then God the Father said to me: "You are now prepared, and must go where I have commanded you." I replied, "If I go, they will not believe me." Christ then appeared to write something with a golden pen and golden ink, upon golden paper. Then he rolled it up, and said to me: "Put this in your bosom, and, wherever you go, show it, and they will know that I have sent you to proclaim salvation to all." He then put it into my bosom, and they all went with me to a bright, shining gate, singing and shouting. Here they embraced me, and I found myself once more on earth.

When I came to myself, I found that several friends had been with me all night, and my husband had called a physician, but he had not been able to do anything for me. He ordered those around me to keep very quiet, or to go home […]

XIX
PUBLIC EFFORT—EXCOMMUNICATION

From this time the opposition to my lifework commenced, instigated by the minister, Mr. Beman.[41] Many in the church were anxious to have me preach in the hall, where our meetings were held at that time, and were not a little astonished at the minister's cool treatment of me. At length two of the trustees got some of the elder sisters to call on the minister and ask him to let me preach. His answer was: "No; she can't preach her holiness stuff here, and I am astonished that you should ask it of me." The sisters said he seemed to be in quite a rage, although he said he was not angry.

There being no meeting of the society on Monday evening, a brother in the church opened his house to me, that I might preach, which displeased

Mr. Beman very much. He appointed a committee to wait upon the brother and sister who had opened their doors to me, to tell them they must not allow any more meetings of that kind, and that they must abide by the rules of the church, making them believe they would be excommunicated if they disobeyed him. I happened to be present at this interview, and the committee remonstrated with me for the course I had taken. I told them my business was with the Lord, and wherever I found a door opened I intended to go in and work for my Master.

There was another meeting appointed at the same place, which I, of course, attended; after which the meetings were stopped for that time, though I held many more there after these people had withdrawn from Mr. Beman's church.

I then held meetings in my own house; whereat the minister told the members that if they attended them he would deal with them, for they were breaking the rules of the church. When he found that I continued the meetings, and that the Lord was blessing my feeble efforts, he sent a committee of two to ask me if I considered myself a member of his church. I told them I did, and should continue to do so until I had done something worthy of dismembership.

At this, Mr. Beman sent another committee with a note, asking me to meet him with the committee, which I did. He asked me a number of questions, nearly all of which I have forgotten. One, however, I do remember: he asked if I was willing to comply with the rules of the discipline. To this I answered: "Not if the discipline prohibits me from doing what God has bidden me to do; I fear God more than man." Similar questions were asked and answered in the same manner. The committee said what they wished to say, and then told me I could go home. When I reached the door, I turned and said: "I now shake off the dust of my feet as a witness against you. See to it that this meeting does not rise in judgment against you."[42]

The next evening, one of the committee came to me and told me that I was no longer a member of the church, because I had violated the rules of the discipline by preaching.

When this action became known, the people wondered how any one could be excommunicated for trying to do good. I did not say much, and my friends simply said I had done nothing but hold meetings. Others, anxious to know the particulars, asked the minister what the trouble was. He told them he had given me the privilege of speaking or preaching as long as I chose, but that he could not give me the right to use the pulpit, and that I was not satisfied with any other place. Also, that I had appointed meeting on the evening of his meetings, which was a thing no member had a right to do. For these reasons he said he had turned me out of the church.[43]

Now, if the people who repeated this to me told the truth—and I have no doubt but they did—Mr. Beman told an actual falsehood. I had never asked for his pulpit, but had told him and others, repeatedly, that I did not care where I stood—any corner of the hall would do. To which Mr. Beman had answered: "You cannot have any place in the hall." Then I said: "I'll preach in a private house." He answered me: "No, not in this place; I am stationed over all Boston." He was determined I should not preach in the city of Boston. To cover up his deceptive, unrighteous course toward me, he told the above falsehoods.

From his statements, many erroneous stories concerning me gained credence with a large number of people. At that time, I thought it my duty as well as privilege to address a letter to the Conference,[44] which I took to them in person, stating all the facts. At the same time I told them it was not in the power of Mr. Beman, or any one else, to truthfully bring anything against my moral or religious character—that my only offence was in trying to preach the Gospel of Christ—and that I cherished no ill feelings toward Mr. Beman or any one else, but that I desired the Conference to give the case an impartial hearing, and then give me a written statement expressive of their opinion. I also said I considered myself a member of the Conference, and should do so until they said I was not, and gave me their reasons, that I might let the world know what my offence had been.

My letter was slightingly noticed, and then thrown under the table. Why should they notice it? It was only the grievance of a woman, and there was no justice meted out to women in those days. Even ministers of Christ did not feel that women had any rights which they were bound to respect.

XX
WOMEN IN THE GOSPEL

Thirty years ago there could scarcely a person be found, in the churches, to sympathize with any one who talked of Holiness.[45] But, in my simplicity, I did think that a body of Christian ministers would understand my case and judge righteously. I was, however, disappointed.

It is no little thing to feel that every man's hand is against us, and ours against every man, as seemed to be the case with me at this time; yet how precious, if Jesus but be with us. In this severe trial I had constant access to God, and a clear consciousness that he heard me; yet I did not seem to have that plenitude of the Spirit that I had before. I realized most keenly that the closer the communion that may have existed, the keener the suffering of the slightest departure from God. Unbroken communion can only be retained by a constant application of the blood which cleanseth.

Though I did not wish to pain any one, neither could I please any one only as I was led by the Holy Spirit. I saw, as never before, that the best men were liable to err, and that the only safe way was to fall on Christ, even though censure and reproach fell upon me for obeying his voice. Man's opinion weighed nothing with me, for my commission was from heaven, and my reward was with the Most High.

I could not believe that it was a short-lived impulse or spasmodic influence that impelled me to preach. I read that on the day or Pentecost was the Scripture fulfilled as found in Joel ii.28, 29; and it certainly will not be denied that women as well as men were at that time filled with the Holy Ghost, because it is expressly stated that women were among those who continued in prayer and supplication, waiting for the fulfillment of the promise. Women and men are classed together, and if the power to preach the Gospel is short-lived and spasmodic in the case of women, it must be equally so in that of men; and if women have lost the gift of prophecy, so have men.

We are sometimes told that if a woman pretends to a Divine and thereon grounds the right to plead the cause of a crucified Redeemer in public, she will be believed when she shows credentials from heaven; that is, when she works a miracle. If it be necessary to prove one's right to preach the Gospel, I ask of my brethren to show me their credentials, or I can not believe in the propriety of their ministry.

But the Bible puts an end to this strife when it says: "There is neither male nor female in Christ Jesus."[46] Philip had four daughters that prophesied, or preached. Paul called Priscilla, as well as Aquila, his "helper," or, as in the Greek, his "fellow-laborer." Rom.xv.3; 23Cor.viii.23; Phil.ii.5; 1Thess.iii.2. The same word, which, in our common translation, is now rendered a "servant of the church," in speaking of Phoebe (Rom.xix.1), is rendered "minister" when applied to Tychicus. Eph.vi.21. When Paul said, "Help those women who labor with me in the Gospel," he certainly meant that they did more than to pour out tea.[47] In the eleventh chapter of First Corinthians Paul gives directions, to men and women, how they should appear when they prophesy or pray in public assemblies; and he defines prophesying to be speaking to edification, exhortation and comfort.

I may further remark that the conduct of holy women is recorded in Scripture as an example to others of their sex. And in the early ages of Christianity many women were happy and glorious in martyrdom. How nobly, how heroically, too, in later ages, have women suffered persecution and death for the name of the Lord Jesus.

In looking over these facts, I could see no miracle wrought for those women more than in myself.

Though opposed, I went forth laboring for God, and he owned and blessed my labors, and has done so wherever I have been until this day. And while I walk obediently, I know he will, though hell may rage and vent its spite.

XXI
THE LORD LEADETH—LABOR IN PHILADELPHIA

As I left the Conference, God wonderfully filled my heart with his love, so that, as I passed from place to place, meeting one and another of the ministers, my heart went out in love to each of them as though he had been my father; and the language of 1Pet.i.7, came forcibly to my mind: "The trial of our faith is much more precious than of gold that perisheth, though it be tried by fire." Fiery trials are not strange things to the Lord's anointed [...]

While in Philadelphia, attending the Conference, I became acquainted with three sisters who believed they were called to public labors in their Master's vineyard. But they had been so opposed, they were very much distressed and shrank from their duty. One of them professed sanctification. They had met with more opposition from ministers than from any one else.

After the Conference had adjourned, I proposed to these sisters to procure a place and hold a series of meetings. They were pleased with the idea, and were willing to help if I would take charge of the meetings. They apprehended some difficulty, as there had never been a meeting there under the sole charge of women. The language of my heart was:

Only Thou my Leader be
And I still will follow Thee.

Trusting in my Leader, I went on with the work. I hired a large place in Canal street, and there we opened our meetings, which continued eleven nights, and over one Sabbath. The room was crowded every night—some coming to receive good, others to criticise, sneer, and say hard things against us.

One of the sisters left us after a day or two, fearing that the Church to which she belonged would disown her if she continued to assist us. We regretted this very much, but could only say, "An enemy hath done this."[48]

These meetings were a time of refreshing from the presence of the Lord. Many were converted, and a few stepped into the fountain of cleansing.

Some of the ministers, who remained in the city after the Conference, attended our meetings, and occasionally asked us if we were organizing a new Conference, with a view of drawing out from the churches. This was simply to ridicule our meeting.

We closed with a love-feast,[49] which caused such a stir among the ministers and many of the church-members, that we could not imagine what the end would be. They seemed to think we had well nigh committed the unpardonable sin [...]

Dear sisters, who are in the evangelistic work now, you may think you have hard times; but let me tell you, I feel that the lion and lamb are lying down together, as compared with the state of things twenty-five or thirty years ago. Yes, yes; our God is marching on. Glory to his name! [...]

XXVIII
A WORD TO MY CHRISTIAN SISTERS

DEAR SISTERS: I would that I could tell you a hundredth part of what God has revealed to me of his glory, especially on that never-to-be-forgotten night when I received my high and holy calling. The songs I heard I think were those which Job, David and Isaiah speak of hearing at night upon their beds, or the one of which the Revelator says "no man could learn."[50] Certain it is, I have not been able to sing it since, though at times I have seemed to hear the distant echo of the music. When I tried to repeat it, it vanished in the dim distance. Glory! glory! glory to the Most High!

Sisters, shall not you and I unite with the heavenly host in the grand chorus? If so, you will not let what man may say or do, keep you from doing the will of the Lord or using the gifts you have for the good of others. How much easier to bear the reproach of men than to live at a distance from God. Be not kept in bondage by those who say, "We suffer not a woman to teach," thus quoting Paul's words,[51] but not rightly applying them. What though we are called to pass through deep waters, so our anchor is cast within the veil, both sure and steadfast? Blessed experience! I have had to weep because this was not my constant experience. At times, a cloud of heaviness has covered my mind, and disobedience has caused me to lose the clear witness of perfect love [...]

Those who are wholly sanctified need not fear that God will hide his face, if they continue to walk in the light even as Christ is in the light. Then they have fellowship with the Father and the Son, and become of one Spirit with the Lord. I do not believe God ever withdraws himself from a soul which does not first withdraw itself from him, though such may abide under a cloud for a season, and have to cry: "My God! my God! why hast thou forsaken me?"[52]

[...] Dear sisters in Christ, are any of you also without understanding and slow of heart to believe, as were the disciples? Although they had seen their Master do many mighty works, yet, with change of place or circumstances, they would go back upon the old ground of carnal reasoning and

38

unbelieving fears. The darkness and ignorance of our natures are such, that, even after we have embraced the Savior and received his teaching, we are ready to stumble at the plainest truths! Blind unbelief is always sure to err; it can neither trace God nor trust him. Unbelief is ever alive to distrust and fear. So long as this evil root has a place in us, our fears can not be removed nor our hope confirmed.

Not till the day of Pentecost did Christ's chosen ones see clearly, *or* have their understandings opened; and nothing short of a full baptism of the Spirit will dispel our unbelief. Without this, we are but babes—all our lives are often carried away by our carnal natures and kept in bondage; whereas, if we are wholly saved and live under full sanctifying influence of the Holy Ghost, we cannot be tossed about with every wind, but, like an iron pillar or a house built upon a rock, prove immovable. Our minds will then be fully illuminated, our hearts purified, and our souls filled with the pure love of God, bringing forth fruit to his glory [...]

XXX
HOW TO OBTAIN SANCTIFICATION

[...] How is sanctification to be obtained? An important question. I answer, by faith. Faith is the only condition of sanctification. By this I mean a faith that dies out to the world and every form of sin; that gives up the sin of the heart; and that believes, according to God's promise, he is able to perform, and will do it now—doeth it now.

Why not yield, believe, and be sanctified now—now, while reading? "Now is the day of salvation."[53] Say: "Here, Lord, I will, I do believe; thou hast said now—now let it be—now apply the blood of Jesus to my waiting, longing soul."

> Hallelujah! 'tis done!
> I believe on the Son;
> I am saved by the blood
> Of the crucified One.[54]

Now, dear reader, I conclude by praying that this little work may be blessed of God to your spiritual and everlasting good. I trust also that it will promote the cause of holiness in the Church.

Now, unto Him who is able to do exceeding abundantly, above all that we ask or think, according to the power that worketh in us; unto Him be glory in the church by Christ Jesus throughout all ages, world without end. Amen.

FEMALE BENEVOLENT AND LITERARY SOCIETIES

Maria W. Stewart, "An Address Delivered Before the Afric-American Female Intelligence Society of Boston.[55] By Mrs. Maria W. Stewart." *The Liberator*, 28 April 1832

The frowns of the world shall never discourage me, nor its smiles flatter me; for with the help of God, I am resolved to withstand the fiery darts of the devil, and the assaults of wicked men. The righteous are as bold as a lion, but the wicked flee when no man pursueth. I fear neither men nor devils; for the God in whom I trust is able to deliver me from the rage and malice of my enemies, and from them that rise up against me. The only motive that has prompted me to raise my voice in your behalf, my friends, is because I have discovered that religion is held in low repute among some of us; and purely to promote the cause of Christ, and the good of souls, in the hope that others more experienced, more able and talented than myself, might go forward and do likewise. I expect to render a strict, a solemn, and an awful account to God for the motives that have prompted me to exertion, and for those with which I shall address you this evening.

What I have to say, concerns the whole of us as Christians and as a people; and if you will be so kind as to give me a hearing this once, you shall receive the incense of a grateful heart.

The day is coming, my friends, and I rejoice in that day, when the secrets of all hearts shall be manifested before saints and angels, men and devils. It will be a great day of joy and rejoicing to the humble followers of Christ, but a day of terror and dismay to hypocrites and unbelievers. Of that day and hour knoweth no man, no, not even the angels in heaven, but the Father only.[56] The dead that are in Christ shall be raised first. Blessed is he that shall have a part in the first resurrection. Ah, methinks I hear the finally impenitent crying, "Rocks and mountains! fall upon us, and hide us from the wrath of the Lamb, and from him that sitteth upon the throne!"[57]

> High on a cloud our God shall come
> Bright thrones prepare his way;
> Thunder and darkness, fire and storm
> Lead on the dreadful day.[58]

Christ shall descend in the clouds of heaven, surrounded by ten thousand of his saints and angels, and it shall be very tempestuous round about him, and before him shall be gathered all nations, and kindred, and tongues and people; and every knee shall bow, and every tongue confess;[59] they also that pierced him shall look upon him, and mourn. Then shall the King separate the righteous from the wicked, as a shepherd divideth the sheep from the goats, and shall place the righteous on his right, and the wicked upon his left.[60] Then, says Christ, shall be weeping, and wailing, and gnashing of teeth, when ye shall see Abraham and the prophets, sitting in the kingdom of heaven, and ye yourselves thrust out. Then shall the righteous shine forth in the kingdom of their Father as the sun. He that hath ears to hear, let him hear.[61] The poor despised followers of Christ will not then regret their sufferings here; they shall be carried by angels into Abraham's bosom, and shall be comforted; and the Lord God shall wipe away their tears. You will then be convinced before assembled multitudes, whether they strove to promote the cause of Christ, or whether they sought for gain or applause. "Strive to enter in at the strait gate; for many, I say unto you, shall seek to enter it, and shall not be able.[62] For except your righteousness shall exceed the righteousness of the Scribes and Pharisees, ye shall in no wise enter into the kingdom of Heaven."[63]

Ah, methinks I see this people lying in wickedness; and as the Lord liveth, and as your souls live, were it not for the few righteous that are to be found among us, we should become as Sodom unto Gomorrah. Christians have too long slumbered and slept; sinners stumbled into hell, and still are stumbling, for the want of Christian exertion; and the devil is going about like a roaring lion, seeking whom he may devour. And I make bold to say, that many who profess the name of Christ at the present day, live so widely different from what becometh the Gospel of our Lord Jesus Christ, that they cannot and they dare not reason to the world upon righteousness and judgment to come.

Be not offended because I tell you the truth; for I believe that God has fired my soul with a holy zeal for his cause. It was God alone who inspired my heart to publish the Meditations thereof; and it was done with pure motives of love to your souls, in the hope that Christians might examine themselves, and sinners become pricked in their hearts. It is the word of God, though men and devils may oppose it. It is the word of God; and little did I think that any of the professed followers of Christ would have frowned upon me, and discouraged and hindered its progress.

Ah, my friends, I am speaking as one who expects to give account at the bar of God; I am speaking as a dying mortal to dying mortals. I fear there are many who have named the name of Jesus at the present day, that strain at a gnat and swallow a camel; they neither enter in to the kingdom of heaven themselves, nor suffer others to enter in. They would pull the motes out of their brother's eye, when they have a beam in their own eye.[64] And were our blessed Lord and Saviour, Jesus Christ, upon the earth, I believe he would say of many that are called by his name, "O, ye hypocrites, ye generation of vipers, how can you escape the damnation of hell."[65]

I have enlisted in the holy warfare, and Jesus is my captain; and the Lord's battle I mean to fight, until my voice expire in death. I expect to be hated of all men, and persecuted even unto death, for righteousness and the truth's sake.

A few remarks upon moral subjects, and I close. I am a strong advocate for the cause of God, and for the cause of freedom. I am not your enemy, but a friend both to you and to your children. Suffer me, then, to express my sentiments but this once, however severe they may appear to be, and then hereafter let me sink into oblivion, and let my name die in forgetfulness.

Had the ministers of the gospel shunned the very appearance of evil; had they faithfully discharged their duty, whether we would have heard them or not; we should have been a very different people from what we now are; but they have kept the truth as it were hid from our eyes, and have cried, "Peace, Peace!" when there was no peace; they have plastered us up with untempered mortar, and have been as it were blind leaders of the blind.

It appears to me that there are no people under the heavens, so unkind and so unfeeling towards their own, as are the descendants of fallen Africa. I have been something of a traveller in my day; and the general cry among the people is, "Our own color are our greatest opposers"; — and even the whites say that we are greater enemies towards each other, than they are towards us. Shall we be a hissing and a reproach among the nations of the earth any longer! Shall they laugh us to scorn forever? We might become a highly respectable people; respectable we now consider ourselves, but we might become a highly distinguished and intelligent people. And how? In convincing the world, by our own efforts, however feeble, that nothing is wanting on our part but opportunity. Without these efforts, we shall never be a people, nor our descendants after us.

But God has said, that Ethiopia shall stretch forth her hands unto him. True, but God uses means to bring about His purposes; and unless the rising generation manifest a different temper and disposition towards each other from what we have manifested, the generation following will never be an enlightened people. We this day are considered as one of the most degraded races upon the face of the earth. It is useless for us any longer to sit with our hands folded, reproaching the whites; for that will never elevate us. All the nations of the earth have distinguished themselves, and have shown forth a noble and gallant spirit. Look at the suffering Greeks! Their proud souls revolted at the idea of serving a tyrannical nation, who were no better than themselves, and perhaps not so good. They made a mighty effort and arose: their souls were knit together in the holy bonds of love and union: they were united, and came off victorious. Look at the French in the late revolution! no traitors amongst them, to expose their plans to the crowned heads of Europe! "Liberty or Death!" was their cry. And the Haytians [sic], though they have not been acknowledged as a nation, yet their firmness of character and independence of spirit have been greatly admired, and high applauded. Look at the Poles, a feeble people! They rose against three hundred thousand mighty men of Russia; and though they did not gain the conquest, yet they obtained the name of gallant Poles. And even the wild Indians of the forest are more united than ourselves. Insult one of them, and you insult a thousand. They also have contended for their rights and privileges, and are held in higher repute than we are.

And why is it, my friends, that we are despised above all the nations upon the earth? Is it merely because our skins are tinged with a sable hue? No, nor will I ever believe that it is. What then is it? Oh, it is because that we and our fathers have dealt treacherously with one another, and because many of us now possess that envious and malicious disposition, that we had rather die than see each other rise an inch above a beggar. No gentle methods are used to promote love and friendship among us, but much is done to destroy it. Shall we be a hissing and a reproach amongst the nations of the earth any longer? Shall they laugh us to scorn forever?

Ingratitude is one of the worst passions that reigns in the human breast; it is this that cuts the tender fibres of the soul; for it is impossible for us to love those who are ungrateful towards us. "Behold," says that wise man, Solomon, counting one by one, "a man have I found in a thousand, but a woman among all those have I not found."

I have sometimes thought, that God had almost departed from among us. And why? Because Christ has said, if we say we love the Father, and we hate our brother, we are liars, and the truth is not in us; and certainly if we were the true followers of Christ, I think we could not show such a disposition towards each other as we do—for God is all love.

A lady of high distinction among us, observed to me, that I might never expect your homage. God forbid! I ask it not. But I beseech you to deal with gentleness and godly sincerity towards me; and there is not one of you, my dear friends, who has given me a cup of cold water in the name of the Lord, or soothed the sorrows of my wounded heart, but God will bless you, not only you, but your children for it. Cruel indeed, are those that indulge such an opinion respecting me as that.

Finally, I have exerted myself both for your temporal and eternal welfare, as far as I am able; and my soul has been so discouraged within me, that

I have almost been induced to exclaim, "Would to God that my tongue hereafter might cleave to the roof of my mouth, and become silent forever!" and then I have felt that the Christian has no time to be idle, and I must be active, knowing that the death cometh, in which no man can work —and my mind has raised to such an extent, that I will willingly die for the cause that I have espoused—for I cannot die in a more glorious cause than in the defence of God and his laws.

O woman, woman! upon you I call; for upon your exertions almost entirely depends whether the rising generation shall be any thing more than we have been or not. O woman, woman! your example is powerful, your influence great; it extends over your husbands and over your children, and throughout the circle of your aquaintance. Then let me exhort you to cultivate among yourselves a spirit of christian love and unity, having charity one for another, without which all our goodness is as sounding brass, and as a tinkling cymbal.[66] And, O, my God, I beseech thee to the nations of the earth may hiss at us no longer! O suffer them not to laugh us to scorn forever!

Sarah Mapps Douglass, "Mental Feasts." *The Liberator*, 21 July 1832

It gives us great pleasure to learn that the excellent suggestion made by our brother Jocelyn of New-Haven,[67] to a number of respectable colored females in Philadelphia, during his late visit to that city, in regard to their holding a Mental Feast monthly, has been by them carried into effect. He proposed that they should meet alternately at their own dwellings, for the purpose of moral and religious meditation, conversation, reading and speaking, sympathising over the fate of the unhappy slaves, improving their own minds, &c. &c.; and, in order to make the meeting truly a *Mental* Feast and unburthensome to the entertainer, that the visiters [sic] should receive the simplest fare. We hope something of the kind will be attempted by the colored females of this city, and in other places. The following extract of a letter from a lady who was invited to attend the meeting alluded to, we think will prove interesting to our readers:

"Soon after all were quietly seated, a short address, prepared for the occasion, was read by the authoress, (Sarah Douglass) a copy of which is herewith sent: it speaks its own praise, therefore comment from me is unnecessary. The fifty-fourth beautiful and encouraging chapter of Isaiah was then read. After sitting a short time under a solemn and impressive silence that ensued the reading of the chapter, one of the company vocally petitioned our heavenly Father for a continuance of his favor, &c. The remainder of the evening was occupied principally by their severally reading and relating affecting slave tales, calculated to bring forcibly into view the deplorable situation of our fellow-creatures at the south—both the oppressor and oppressed. This interesting interview was closed with singing an appropriate hymn. The precious covering which was spread around bespoke that divine goodness was near; and I am bound to believe that He graciously condescends to regard, in a very peculiar manner, the sincere attempts made by this greatly, injured people to serve, Him, the true and living God. Ah! does He not design to raise from among them a peculiar people for his own praise? Methinks he does. Whether it will be separately by themselves, or collectively with white people, I will not at present presume to say."

ADDRESS

MY FRIENDS—MY SISTERS:

How important is the occasion for which we have assembled ourselves together this evening, to hold a feast, to feed our never-dying minds, to excite each other to deeds of mercy, words of peace; to stir up in the bosom of each, gratitude [to] God for his increasing goodness, and feeling of deep sympathy for our brethren and sisters, who are in this land of christian light and liberty held in bondage, the most cruel degrading—to make their cause our own!

An English writer has said, "We must feel deeply before we can act rightly; from that absorbing, heart-rending compassion for ourselves springs a deeper sympathy for others, and from a sense of our weakness and our own upbraidings arises a disposition to be indulgent, to forbear, to forgive."[68] This is my experience. One short year ago, how different were my feelings on the subject of slavery! It is true, the wail of the captive sometimes came to my ear in the midst of my happiness, and caused my heart to bleed for his wrongs; but, alas! the impression was as evanescent as the early cloud and morning dew. I had formed a little world of my own, and cared not to move beyond its precincts. But how was the scene changed when I beheld the oppressor lurking on the border of my own peaceful home![69] I saw his iron hand stretched forth to seize me as his prey, and the cause of the slave became my own. I started up, and with one mighty effort threw from me the lethargy which had covered me as a mantle for years; and determined, by the help of the Almighty, to use every exertion in my power to elevate the character of my wronged and neglected race. One year ago, I detested the slaveholder; now I can pity and pray for him. Has not this been your experience, my sisters? Have you not felt as I have felt upon this thrilling subject? My heart assures me some of you have.

45

Anonymous, "Address to the Female Literary Association of Philadelphia, On their First Anniversary: By A Member."
The Liberator, 13 October 1832[70]

My Friends—One year has now elapsed since the formation of this association; a year filled with the most interesting events in which friends have augmented, and the most gratifying and astonishing progress been made in intellectual improvement and in the virtues of the heart. A year fraught with blessings; for while a malignant disorder has stalked through our city,[71] tearing asunder the most tender ties, leaving children orphans and parents childless, it has not (except in a few instances) been allowed to enter our dwellings, and in no instance has death ensued, and though neighbors and friends have fallen around us, like the chilling blasts of autumn, we have been preserved. Does not gratitude for these important blessings demand renewed exertions on our part to strict performance of duty? Do not the numerous instances of sudden death we have witnessed loudly proclaim, "Be ye also ready"?

To continue this association will be one way of showing our gratitude and of aiding the cause. I presume none of you doubt this; if there is one here so skeptical, I would repeat to her a remark made by our unflinching advocate[72]—Every effort you make in this way, said he, helps to unbind the fetters of the slave; and if she still doubts I would tell her that as the free people of color become virtuous and intelligent, the character and condition of the slave will also improve. I would bid her if she wishes the enfranchisement of her sisters, to sympathise in their woes, to rehearse their wrongs to her friends on every occasion, always remembering that our interests are one, that we rise or fall together; and that we can never be elevated to our proper standing while they are in bondage. Too long has it been the policy of our enemies to persuade us that we are a superior race to the slaves, and that our superiority is owing to a mixture with the whites. Away with this idea, cast it from you with the indignation it deserves, and dare to assert that the black man is equal by nature with the white, and that slavery and not his color has debased him. Yet dare to tell our enemies, that with the powerful weapons of religion and education, we will do battle with the host of prejudice which surround us, satisfied that in the end we shall be more than conquerors. My sisters, let me exhort you then to perseverance, by it great things have been effected; indeed, there are few things which perseverance, joined to a sense of duty may not accomplish. By perseverance the great Demosthenes was enabled to overcome a natural defect in his pronunciation, so great, that on his first attempt to speak in public, he was hissed: to rid himself of it, he built a vault where he might practice without disturbance. His efforts were crowned with the most brilliant success, he became the first orator of the age, and his eloquence was more dreaded by Philip than all the fleets and armies of Athens. By perseverance Hannibal passed the Alps in the depth of winter, with an army of 140,000 men. By perseverance some of you have already warred successfully with sloth, that inveterate foe to intellectual advancement. By perseverance Benjamin Franklin and a host of worthies rose superior to obscure birth and early disadvantages, and acquired lasting fame in the various departments of literature and the mechanic arts, and we may do the same.

Think that the eyes of our friends are upon us, they who have forsaken all they held dear on earth to plead our cause, are looking to us to uphold their hands, shall we disappoint them? Think of the groans, the tears of your enslaved sisters, and rouse up every slumbering energy and again go forward in the path of duty and improvement, adopting Perseverance as your motto, and the difficulties of the way will vanish like clouds before the morning sun. As often as this dear evening shall return evince, by your attendance here, that you love literature, that you love your people, and that nothing shall be wanting on your part to elevate them.
Philadelphia, Sept. 25th, 1832.

ABOLITION

Sarah Forten ["Magawisca"], "The Abuse of Liberty."
The Liberator, 26 March 1831

I know no evil under the wide-spread canopy of Heaven, so great as the abuse of man's liberty; and no where has this vice a more extensive sway, than in this boasted land of Philanthropy, that offers to every white man the right to enjoy life, liberty, and happiness. I say every white man, because those who cannot shew a fair exterior (no matter what be the noble qualities of their mind,) are to be robbed of the rights by which they were endowed by an all-wise and merciful Creator, who, in his great wisdom, cast a sable hue over some of the "lords of creation." And does it follow, that those are to be loaded with ignominy, crushed by the galling chain of slavery, and degraded even to the level of the brute? Is it because their skins are black, that they are to be deprived of every tender tie that binds the heart of man to earth? Is it for this unalterable cause, that they are to bow beneath the lash, and with a broken, bleeding heart, enrich the soil of the pale faces? Yet it is no less true than infamous, that this monstrous vice has been suffered to pursue its course in the breasts of so many of our noble countrymen. It is a lamentable fact, that they can with remorseless hearts rush like fiends into the retirement of a happy, unsuspecting family, and with an unshaken hand, tear the unconscious husband from his tender wife, and the helpless babe from its mother's breast. And is *he* a happy man, who can thus, without a shudder,—yes, without a sigh, plant the thorn of misery where once contentment reigned? No—there is no state of life so anxious as his; he lives contrary to the dictates of conscience; he is in constant dread lest they, whom he unjustly condemns to bondage, will burst their fetters, and become oppressors in their turn.—And is it the insatiable thirst for mammon that has blinded our countrymen? and the glitter of paltry gold that has made them so callous to their immortal safety?

Oh, that the scales of error might fall from their eyes, that they might clearly behold with what rapidity that little stream they first introduced into their country, has spread itself! It will soon expand into a mighty river, that will ere long overwhelm them in its dark abyss. Awake from your lethargy; exert every nerve; cast off the yoke from the oppressed; let the bondmen go free; and cry unto your offended God to send freedom with its strong battlements to impede the progress of this raging flood;—I say, cry unto Him for aid; for can you think He, the Great Spirit, who created all men free and equal—He, who made the sun to shine on the black man as well as on the white, will always allow you to rest tranquil on your downy couches? No,—He is just, and his anger will not always slumber. He will wipe the tear from Ethiopia's eye; He will shake the tree of liberty, and its blossoms shall spread over the earth.
MAGAWISCA.[73]
Philadelphia, March 14, 1831.

Sarah Mapps Douglass ["Zillah"], "A Mother's Love." *The Liberator*, 28 July 1832

By a young lady of color.
For the Liberator.

A MOTHER'S LOVE.
"All our passions change
With changing circumstances; rise or fall,

48

> Dependent on their object; claim returns;
> Live on reciprocation and expire
> Unfed by hope. A mother's fondness reigns
> Without a rival, and without an end."

And dost thou, poor slave, feel this holy passion? Does thy heart swell with anguish, when thy helpless infant is torn from thy arms, and carried thou knowest not whither? when thou hast no hope left that thou shalt ever see his innocent face again? Yes, I know thou dost feel all this.

I well remember conversing with a liberated slave, who told me of the many hardships she had to encounter while in a state of captivity. At one time, after having been reaping all the morning, she returned at noon to a spring near her master's home to carry water to some hired laborers. At this spring her babe was tied; she had not been allowed to come near it since sunrise, the time at which it was placed there; her heart yearned with pity and affection for her boy, and while she kneeled at the spring and dipped the water with one hand, she drew her babe to her aching bosom with the other. She would have fed it from this fountain, troubled and almost dried with grief; but, alas! This consolation was denied her. Her cruel mistress observed her from the window where she was sitting, and immediately ran to her, and seizing a large stick beat her cruelly upon her neck and bosom, bidding her begone to her work. Poor creature! rage at her mistress almost emboldened her to return the blow; she cared not for herself, but when she reflected that her child would probably be the sufferer, maternal tenderness triumphed over every other feeling, and she again tied her child, and returned to the labors of the field.

American Mothers! can you doubt that the slave feels as tenderly for her offspring as you do for yours? Do your hearts feel no throb of pity for her woes? Will you not raise your voices, and plead for her emancipation—her immediate emancipation?

At another time when assisting her mistress to get dinner, she dropped the skin of a potato in what she was preparing. The angry woman snatched the knife from her hand, and struck her with it upon her bosom! My countenance expressed as much horror at this account, that I believe the poor woman thought I doubted her veracity. Baring her aged bosom, "Look," said she, "my child here, is the scar"—and I looked and wept that woman should have so forgot her gentle nature. Soon after this, she was sold to another person, and at his death freed. She then went to reside in a neighboring city. Her old mistress, after a series of misfourtunes, was reduced almost to beggary, and bent her weary footsteps to the same city: and would you believe it, reader? She sent for the woman she had so cruelly wronged,

[margin note: appeal to white women]

to come and assist her. Her friends persuaded her not to go; but she, noble creature! woman-like, weeping that a lady should be so reduced, obeyed the call, and went upon her as faithfully as if she had been her dearest friend.

Calumniators of my despised race, read this and blush.

Lucy Stanton, "A Plea for the Oppressed." *Oberlin Evangelist,* 17 December 1850

When I forget you, Oh my people, may my tongue cleave to the roof of my mouth, and may my right hand forget her cunning! Dark hover the clouds. The Anti-Slavery pulse beats faintly. The right of suffrage is denied. The colored man is still crushed by the weight of oppression. He may possess talents of the highest order, yet for him is no path of fame or distinction opened. He can never hope to attain those privileges while his brethren remain enslaved. Since, therefore, freedom of the slave and the gaining of our rights, social and political, are inseparably connected, let, all the friends of humanity plead for those who may not plead their own cause.

Reformers, ye who have labored long to convince man that happiness is found alone in doing good to others, that humanity is a unit, that he who injures one individual wrongs the race;—that to love one's neighbor as one's self is the sum of human virtue—ye that advocate the great principles of Temperance, Peace, and Moral Reform, will you not raise your voice in behalf of these stricken ones!—will you not plead the cause of the Slave?

Slavery is the combination of all crime. It is War.

Those who rob their fellow-men of home, of liberty, of education, of life, as really war against them as though they cleft them down upon the bloody field. It is intemperance; for there is an intoxication when the fierce passions rage in man's breast, more fearful than the madness of the drunkard, which if let loose upon the moral universe would sweep away everything pure and holy, leaving but the wreck of man's nobler nature. Such passions does Slavery foster—yea, they are a part of herself. It is full of pollution. Know you not that to a slave, virtue is a sin counted worthy of death? that many, true to the light within, notwithstanding the attempts to shut out the truth, feeling that a consciousness of purity is dearer than life, have nobly died? Their blood crieth to God, a witness against the oppressor.

Statesmen, you who have bent at ambition's shrine, who would leave your names on the page of history, to be venerated by coming generations as among those of the great and good, will you not advocate the cause of the down-trodden, remembering that the spirit of liberty is abroad in the land! The precious seed is sown in the heart of the people, and though the fruit does not appear, the germ is there, and the harvest will yet be gathered. Truly is this an age of reform. The world is going on, not indeed keeping pace with the rapid tread of its leaders, but none the less progressing. As the people take a step in one reform, the way is prepared for another. Now while other evils in man's social and political condition are being remedied, think you that Slavery can stand that searching test—an enlightened people's sense of justice? Then speak the truth boldly; fear not loss of property or station. It is a higher honor to embalm your name in the hearts of a grateful people than to contend for the paltry honors of party preferment.

Woman, I turn to thee. Is it not thy mission to visit the poor? to shed the tear of sympathy? to relieve the wants of the suffering? Where wilt thou find objects more needing sympathy than among the slaves?

Mother, hast thou a precious gem in thy charge, like those that make up the Savior's jewels? Has thy heart, trembling with its unutterable joyousness, bent before the throne of the Giver with the prayer that thy child might be found in his courts? Thou hast seen the dawning of intelligence in its bright eye, and watched with interest the unfolding of its powers. Its gentle, winning ways have doubly endeared it to thee. Death breathes upon the flower, and it is gone. Now thou canst feel for the slave-mother who has bent with the same interest over her child, whose heart is entwined around it even more firmly than thine own around thine, for to her it is the only ray of joy in a dreary world. She returns weary and sick at heart from the labors of the field; the child's beaming smile of welcome half banishes the misery of her lot. Would she not die for it? Ye who know the depths of a mother's love, answer! Hark! strange footsteps are near her dwelling! The door is thrown rudely open! Her master says—"There is the woman!" She comprehends it all—she is sold! From her trembling lips escape the words—"my child!" She throws herself at the feet of those merciless men, and pleads permission to keep her babe, but in vain. What is she more than any other slave, that she should be permitted this favor? They are separated.

Sister, have you ever had a kind and loving brother! How often would he lay aside his book to relieve you from some difficulty! How have you hung upon the words of wisdom that he uttered! How earnestly have you studied that you might stand his companion—his equal. You saw him suddenly stricken by the destroyer. Oh! how your heart ached!

There was a slave-girl who had a brother kind and noble as your own. He had scarcely any advantages: yet stealthily would he draw an old volume from his pocket, and through the long night would pore over its contents. His soul thirsted for knowledge. He yearned for freedom, but free-soil was far away. That sister might not go; he staid with her. They say that slaves do not feel for or love each other; I fear that there are few brothers with a pale face who would have stood that test. For her he tamed the fire of his eye, tolled for that which profited him not, and labored so industriously that the overseer had no apology for applying the lash to his back. Time passed on: that brother stood in his manhood's prime as tenderly kind and as dearly beloved as ever. That sister was insulted;—the lash was applied to her quivering back; her brother rushed to save her! He tore away the fastenings which bound her to the whipping post, he held her on his arm—she was safe. She looked up, encountered the ferocious gaze of the overseer, heard the report of a pistol, and felt the heart's blood of a brother gushing over her. But we draw the veil.

Mother, sister, by thy own deep sorrow of heart; by the sympathy of thy woman's nature, plead for the downtrodden of thy own, of every land. Instill the principles of love, of common brotherhood, in the nursery, in the social circle. Let these be the prayer of thy life.

Christians, you whose souls are filled with love for your fellow men, whose prayer to the Lord is, "Oh! that I may see thy salvation among the children of men!" Does the battle wax warm! dost thou faint with the burden and heat of the day! Yet a little longer; the arm of the Lord is mighty to save those who trust in him. Truth and right must prevail. The bondman shall go free. Look to the future! Hark! the shout of joy gushes from the heart of earth's freed millions! It rushes upward; the angels on heaven's outward battlement catch the sound on their golden lyres, and send it thrilling through the echoing arches of the upper world. How sweet, how majestic, from those starry isles float those deep inspiring sounds over the ocean of space! Softened and mellowed they reach earth, filling the soul with harmony, and breathing of God—of love—and of universal freedom.

Frances Ellen Watkins Harper, "The Colored People in America." *Poems on Miscellaneous Subjects*. Boston: J.B. Yerrinton and Son, 1854. 38–40

Having been placed by a dominant race in circumstances over which we have had no control, we have been the butt of ridicule and the mark of oppression. Identified with a people over whom weary ages of degradation have passed, whatever concerns them, as a race, concerns me. I have noticed among our people a disposition to censure and upbraid each other, a disposition which has its foundation rather, perhaps, in a want of common sympathy and consideration, than mutual hatred or other unholy passions. Born to an inheritance of misery, nurtured in degradation, and cradled in

Figure 1.1: Frances Harper

oppression, with the scorn of the white man upon their souls, his fetters upon their limbs, his scourge upon their flesh, what can be expected from their offspring, but a mournful reaction of that cursed system which spreads its baneful influence over body and soul; which dwarfs the intellect, stunts its development, debases the spirit, and degrades the soul? Place any nation in the same condition which has been our hapless lot, fetter their limbs and degrade their souls, debase their sons and corrupt their daugh-
rape ters; and, when the restless yearnings for liberty shall burn through heart and brain—when, tortured by wrong and goaded by oppression, the hearts that would madden with misery, or break in despair, resolve to break their thrall, and escape from bondage, then let the bay of the bloodhound and the scent of the human tiger be upon their track;—let them feel that, from the ceaseless murmur of the Atlantic to the sullen roar of the Pacific, from the thunders of the rainbow-crowned Niagara to the swollen waters of the

53

Mexican gulf, they have no shelter for their bleeding feet, or resting place for their defenceless heads;—let them, when nominally free, feel that they have only exchanged the iron yoke of oppression for the galling fetters of a vitiated public opinion;—let prejudice assign them the lowest places and the humblest positions, and make them "hewers of wood and drawers of water"—let their income be so small that they must from necessity bequeath to their children an inheritance of poverty and a limited education; and tell me, reviler of our race! censurer of our people! if there is a nation in whose veins runs the purest Caucasian blood, upon whom the same causes would not produce the same effects; whose social condition, intellectual and moral character, would present a more favorable aspect than ours ? But there is hope; yes, "blessed be God!" for our down-trodden and despised race. Public and private schools accommodate our children; and in my own southern home, I see women whose lot is unremitted labor, saving a pittance from their scanty wages to defray the expense of learning to read.[74] We have papers edited by colored editors, which we may consider an honor to possess, and a credit to sustain.[75] We have a church that is extending itself from east to west, from north to south, through poverty and reproach, persecution and pain. We have our faults, our want of union and concentration of purpose; but are there not extenuating circumstances around our darkest faults—palliating excuses for our most egregious errors? and shall we not hope, that the mental and moral aspect which we present is but the first step of a mighty advancement, the faintest coruscations [sic] of the day that will dawn with unclouded splendor upon our down-trodden and benighted race, and that ere long we may present to the admiring gaze of those who wish us well, a people to whom knowledge has given power, and righteousness exaltation?

Frances Ellen Watkins Harper, "Could we trace the record of every human heart…" *National Anti-Slavery Standard,* **23 May 1857**

NEW YORK CITY ANTI-SLAVERY SOCIETY
FOURTH ANNIVERSARY

The Fourth Anniversary of this Society was held at the City Assembly Rooms, on Wednesday evening, May 13th, and was well attended […]

SPEECH OF MISS WATKINS

Could we trace the record of every human heart, the aspirations of every immortal soul, perhaps we would find no man so imbruted and degraded that we could not trace the word liberty either written in living characters upon the soul or hidden away in some nook or corner of the heart. The law of liberty is the law of God, and is antecedent to all human legislation. It existed in the mind of Deity when He hung the first world upon its orbit and gave it liberty to gather light from the central sun.

Some people say, set the slaves free. Did you ever think, if the slaves were free, they would steal everything they could lay their hands on from now till the day of their death—that they would steal more than two thousand millions of dollars (applause)? Ask Maryland, with her tens of thousands of slaves, if she is not prepared for freedom, and hear her answer: "I help supply the coffee-gangs of the South." Ask Virginia, with her hundreds of thousands of slaves, if she is not weary with her merchandise of blood and anxious to shake the gory traffic from her hands, and hear her reply: "Though fertility has covered my soil, though a genial sky bends over my hills and vales, though I hold in my hand a wealth of water-power enough to turn the spindles to clothe the world, yet, with all these advantages, one of my chief staples has been the sons and daughters I send to the human market and human shambles" (applause). Ask the farther South, and all the cotton-growing States chime in, "We have need of fresh supplies to fill the ranks of those whose lives have gone out in unrequited toil on our distant plantations."

A hundred thousand new-born babes are annually added to the victims of slavery; twenty thousand lives are annually sacrificed on the plantations of the South. Such a sight should send a thrill of horror through the nerves of civilization and impel the heart of humanity to lofty deeds. So it might, if men had not found out a fearful alchemy by which this blood can be transformed into gold. Instead of listening to the cry of agony, they listen to the ring of dollars and stoop down to pick up the coin (applause).

But a few months since a man escaped from bondage and found a temporary shelter almost beneath the shadow of Bunker Hill.[76] Had that man stood upon the deck of an Austrian ship, beneath the shadow of the house of the Hapsburgs, he would have found protection. Had he been wrecked upon an island or colony of Great Britain, the waves of the tempest-lashed ocean would have washed him deliverance. Had he landed upon the territory of vine-encircled France and a Frenchman had reduced him to a thing and brought him here beneath the protection of our institutions and our laws, for such a nefarious deed that Frenchman would have lost his citizenship in France. Beneath the feebler light which glimmers from the Koran, the Bey of Tunis would have granted him freedom in his own dominions. Beside the ancient pyramids of Egypt he would have found liberty, for the soil laved by the glorious Nile is now consecrated to freedom. But from Boston harbour, made memorable by the infusion of three-penny taxed tea, Boston in its proximity to the plains of Lexington and Concord, Boston almost beneath the shadow of Bunker Hill and almost in sight of Plymouth Rock, he is thrust back from liberty and manhood and reconverted into a chattel. You have heard that, down South, they keep bloodhounds to hunt slaves. Ye bloodhounds, go back to your kennels; when you fail to catch the flying fugitive, when his stealthy tread is heard in the place where the bones of the revolutionary sires repose, the ready North is base enough to do your shameful service (applause).[77]

Slavery is mean, because it tramples on the feeble and weak. A man comes with his affidavits from the South and hurries me before a commissioner; upon that evidence *ex parte* and alone he hitches me to the car of slavery and trails my womanhood in the dust. I stand at the threshold of the Supreme Court and ask for justice, simple justice. Upon my tortured heart is thrown the mocking words, "You are a negro; you have no rights which white men are bound to respect" (loud and long-continued applause)! Had it been my lot to have lived beneath the Crescent instead of the Cross, had injustice and violence been heaped upon my head as a Mohammedan woman, as a member of a common faith, I might have demanded justice and been listened to by the Pasha, the Bey or the Vizier; but when I come here to ask for justice, men tell me, "We have no higher law than the Constitution" (applause).

But I will not dwell on the dark side of the picture. God is on the side of freedom; and any cause that has God on its side, I care not how much it may be trampled upon, how much it may be trailed in the dust, is sure to triumph. The message of Jesus Christ is on the side of freedom, "I come to preach deliverance to the captives, the opening of the prison doors to them that are bound."[78] The truest and noblest hearts in the land are on the side of freedom. They may be hissed at by slavery's minions, their names cast out as evil, their characters branded with fanaticism, but O,

To side with Truth is noble when we share her humble crust
Ere the cause bring fame and profit and it's prosperous to be just.[79]

May I not, in conclusion, ask every honest, noble heart, every seeker after truth and justice, if they will not also be on the side of freedom. Will you not resolve that you will abate neither heart nor hope till you hear the death-knell of human bondage sounded, and over the black ocean of slavery shall be heard a song, more exulting than the song of Miriam[80] when it floated o'er Egypt's dark sea, the requiem of Egypt's ruined hosts and the anthem of the deliverance of Israel's captive people (great applause)?

[We have not attempted to give a full report of Miss Watkins's speech.]

Figure 1.2: Sojourner Truth

Sojourner Truth, "Pro-Slavery in Indiana." *The Liberator*, 15 October 1858

SILVER LAKE, Kosciusko Co., Ind.,
October 1, 1858

FRIEND W.L.GARRISON:

Sojourner Truth, an elderly colored woman, well known throughout the Eastern States, is now holding a series of anti-slavery meetings in Northern Indiana.[81] Sojourner comes well recommended by H.B. Stowe, yourself, and others, and was gladly received and welcomed by the friends of the slave in this locality. Her progress in knowledge, truth and righteousness is very remarkable, especially when we consider her former low estate as a slave. The border-ruffian[82] Democracy of Indiana, however, appear to be jealous and suspicious of every anti-slavery movement. A rumor was immediately circulated that Sojourner was an imposter; that she was, indeed, a man disguised in women's clothing. It appears, too, from what has since transpired, that they suspected her to be a mercenary hireling of the Republican party.[83]

At her third appointed meeting in this vicinity, which was held in the meeting-house of the United Brethren, a large number of Democrats and other pro-slavery persons were present. At the close of the meeting, Dr. T.W. Strain, the mouthpiece of the slave Democracy, requested the large congregation to "hold on," and stated that a doubt existed in the minds of many persons present respecting the sex of the speaker, and that it was his impression that a majority of them believed the speaker to be a man. The doctor also affirmed (which was not believed by the friends of the slave) that it was for the speaker's special benefit that he now demanded that Sojourner submit her breast to the inspection of some of the ladies present, that the doubt might be removed by their testimony. There were large numbers of ladies present, who appeared to be ashamed and indignant at such a proposition. Sojourner's friends, some of whom had not heard the rumor, were surprised and indignant at such ruffianly surmises and treatment. Confusion and uproar ensued, which was soon suppressed by Sojourner, who, immediately rising, asked them why they suspected her to be a man. The Democracy answered, "Your voice is not the voice of a woman, it is the voice of a man, and we believe you are a man." Dr. Strain called for a vote, and a boisterous "Aye" was the result. A negative vote was not called for. Sojourner told them that her breasts had suckled many a white babe, to the exclusion of her own offspring; that some of those white babies had grown to man's estate; that, although they had sucked her colored breasts, they were, in her estimation, far more manly than they (her persecutors) appeared to be; and she quietly asked them, as she disrobed her bosom, if they, too, wished to suck! In vindication of her truthfulness, she told them that she would show her breast to the whole congregation; that it was not to her shame that she uncovered her breast before them, but to their shame. Two young men (A. Badgely and J. Horner) stepped forward while Sojourner exposed her naked breast to the audience. One of the Democrats present cried out, "Why, it does look like an old sow's teat." I heard a Democrat say, as we were returning home from meeting, that Dr. Strain had, previous to the examination, offered to bet forty dollars that Sojourner was a man! So much for the physiological acumen of a western physician.

As "agitation of thought is the beginning of wisdom," we hope that Indiana will yet be redeemed.

Your's, truly, for the slave,
WILLIAM HAYWARD.

Figure 1.3: Sarah Parker Remond

Sarah Parker Remond. Three Lectures (1859)

1. "Lecture on American Slavery by a Colored Lady." *Warrington Times*, 29 January 1859

We announced last week, that a lecture would be given on Slave life in America, by Miss Remond, a colored lady, who has recently arrived in this country from America. From the notices we had observed of Miss Remond, in the Liverpool papers, we had fortified ourselves with the belief that this lady was a person of no ordinary character, and certainly her lecture of Monday night in no way disappointed our expectations. We believe the design of Miss Remond is to make a tour through England with a view to awaken the public mind as to the evils of slavery, and to ask Englishmen to endorse propositions protesting against American slavery, as a blot on the civilized world [...] Miss Remond is one of the best female lecturers we have heard; her gentle and easy manner, combined with an animated and intelligent countenance, rivets the attention of her auditors; the character of her language in which she clothes her thoughts is oftentimes not of an ordinary character, and, spoken with a pure accent, and in the voice of a fine modulating nature, when declaiming on the wrongs and indignities heaped upon her race, she is often eloquent and thrilling. We think we may venture to say that the Music Hall was never so packed before. Not a foot of standing room could be obtained in any part of the building [...] Great numbers of most respectable people were thus debarred entrance. We think that the gentlemen making the arrangements would have acted more wisely had they issued tickets, and thus have secured a few seats for the better class of people who were almost entirely excluded, or a small charge would have effected the object.

[...] MISS REMOND commenced by thanking the audience for their kind manifestations towards her, and said that though she was 3,000 miles from home, and from loved ones, yet she felt that a common sympathy should unite all, for was not God their father, and were they not all brethren? She was there that evening as the representative of a race that was stripped of every right and debarred from every privilege—a race which was deprived of the protection of the law, and the glorious influences of religion, and all the strong ties and influences of social life. She was there as the representation of a race, which, in the estimation of American law, had no rights which the white man was bound to respect, and for what? For no other reason than that they were of a different complexion from the majority of American citizens. And this infamous doctrine had the sanction of the established courts of law in that country.[84] Nine judges of the supreme court of America had met together and given this decision. Five of them were slave holders, and were educated in the belief that black men and women were made for no other purpose than to be slaves. The other four were from Northern States where slavery did not exist; but only two of the four lifted their hands against this iniquitous decision. They thus established a law which would disgrace any country in any age—a law which would receive, and deserved to receive, the execration of the civilized world.

60

(Applause.) And yet in that boasted America, only two out of nine of the judges of the country lifted their hand against it! She would remind her audience that in 16 of the 31 States slavery did not exist by law; but in those States there were half a million, perhaps more, honourable men and women—descendants of the African race, varying in complexion from black to white, and yet these men and women in either of the 16 States where slavery was prohibited, were deprived of every privilege as citizens. They were, in one respect, just as much deprived of these rights before this decision was given; but this had given the final blow to any faint hope that existed, and now, throughout the 31 states, the black people found that this law was irrevocable, and must be obeyed—not the slightest chance appeared of alteration. She would tell them in America politics were corrupt. (Hear, hear.) It would be uninteresting to an English audience to state the mass of corruptions that underlaid the whole system of American government; but no one who read the newspapers of America could be ignorant of this fact. Let them look at the filibustering expeditions that were constantly fitted out to ravage other States, and no notice being taken of them by the government.[85] The government did not take any measures to suppress—not even to mitigate the horrors of the slave trade; and numberless other points there were which she could not in the limited time touch on; but they all knew sufficient to be aware that American politics were corrupt. But she would tell them that the American churches were infinitely more corrupt than American politics. (Hear, hear.) The American churches were responsible for many of the worst features that existed in regard to the slavery of the African population. When that infamous decision was given that was before mentioned, the church did not set their face against it, but tamely said with the pro-slavery party at the north, "we must obey the law. It is necessary for the public safety that we should obey the law." But if there was an attempt made to pass a law in favour of the negro, there was no movement on their parts, or sympathy shown towards it. Thus the laws of America stood condemned—for they were insincere and inconsistent. Miss Remond then alluded to the disabilities of the negro population in various States. There was not an hotel in Boston but one that would receive a coloured man or woman. In Massachusetts there had been an improvement within the last five years. Black men and women were allowed to ride in the omnibuses. This had been effected by a few who had determined to stand by the weak; but the majority stood aside. These few individuals had renovated the public sentiment to the extent mentioned. But in New York and Philadelphia, if a coloured individual were ready to sink in the street through exhaustion, not a single omnibus would take him in. When they took into consideration that the American people, beyond all others, were making greater professions of liberty than any other nation; and then besides, any 4th of July to hear their Declaration of Independence, and the speeches that were made, when they heard all this, and looked a little farther, they saw in that same America an iron despotism crushing out the intellect, aye, the very souls of men and women, made but little lower than the angels! She should like to tell how 17,000 free northern men, called free-soil men, submitted to the dictum of the 347,000 slaveholders who lived south of Mason and Dixon's line,[86] but time would fail her. But these 347,000 usurped the real power and guidance of the state; the executive, legislative, judicial, religious, educational, and social influences of the country were all controlled by the advocates of slavery. She appeared there that evening as she had before said, the representative of a down-trodden and greatly injured race, and when she realized her position, and the inadequacy of her efforts, she felt almost overpowered and overwhelmed, for what tongue could describe the horrors of American slavery? Who could give the faintest idea of what the slave mother suffered? She would not spend a moment of the precious time she had to occupy in endeavouring to prove that slavery was a sin—that would be an insult to their understanding—an insult to their hearts. That God gave the right of liberty, and the right to pursue happiness as they listed, no one before her would question—nor that a right so sacred no one could take from another without infringing the higher law of God; therefore, they believed that every man and woman who dared to take from another a right so sacred, was a usurper of freedom, and should receive the indignation of every honest heart, and that the moral feeling of mankind should be arrayed against the sinner and the sin. Miss Remond then touchingly related the case of Margaret Garner,[87] who determined to be free or die in the attempt. She was born a slave, and had suffered in her own person the degradation that a woman could not mention. She got as far as Cincinnati with her children. Cincinnati —the queen of the west—that city excelled by no other except New York. There she stood amidst magnificent temples dedicated to God on either hand, but no sympathy or help was afforded her. The slaveholder found her; as he appeared at the door she snatched up a knife and slew her first-born child, but before the poor frenzied creature could proceed further in her dread object, the hand of the tyrant was on her, when she called to the grandmother of the children to kill the others, as she preferred to return them to the bosom of God rather than they should be taken back to American slavery. Above all sufferers in America, American women who were slaves lived in the most pitiable condition. They could not protect themselves from the licentiousness which met them on every hand—they could not protect their honour from the tyrant. There were slaveholders everywhere in that country. There were no morals there; no genuine regard for womanhood or manhood. The slaveholders south of Mason and Dixon's line were as low in the scale of morals as it was possible to conceive; and Margaret Garner would rather that her children should suffer death than be left in the hands of such beings as she had been describing. The courts decided that Margaret Garner must be returned to slavery under the Fugitive Slave Law — a law which had disgraced America so much, and which could find no parallel in history, ancient or modern. But the counsel of Margaret Garner had told her (the lecturer) that he could have raised 10,000 dollars if he could have rescued her from the hands of the tyrant, but the slave-holder said there was not enough money in Cincinnati to purchase his chattel! She was a thing! (Deep sensation.) Yes, every slave below Mason and Dixon's line was a thing! "Ah!" continued Miss Remond, in deep and thrilling tones, "what is slavery? who can tell? In the open market place women are exposed for sale — their persons not always covered. Yes, I can tell you English men and women, that women are sold into slavery with cheeks like the lily and the rose, as well as those that might compare with the wing of the raven. They are exposed for sale, and subjected to the most shameful indignities. The more Anglo-Saxon blood that mingles with the blood of the slave, the more gold is poured out when the auctioneer has a woman for sale, because they are sold to be concubines for white Americans. They are not sold for plantation slaves." Miss Remond then dwelt on the discountenance such a system demanded from Christians, and to which the Christian churches of America were indifferent. She did not say that there were not churches which did not sanction American slavery. It must be understood when she spoke of American churches she included all sections, Episcopalians, Wesleyans, Baptists, &c. She would read to them the law relating to the nominally free coloured population below Mason and Dixon's line. The statute was then read, which virtually prohibited any discussion on slavery, or it might be construed into an offence, for which the punishment was not less than three years of imprisonment with hard labour, or more than twenty-one years.[88] She was there that evening to ask English men and women to send forth their indignant protest against this glaring system. Black men and women were treated worse than criminals for no other reason than because they were black. "Liberty or death" was the motto of the American slave; and there were from 30,000 to 40,000 who had escaped into Canada in spite of the overwhelming obstacles that presented themselves. These men and women had taken their lives in their hand, and by the assistance of the Friend's underground railroad, they had got safe away. After further allusion to the disgraceful recreancy of the American churches, Miss Remond observed, it was sometimes said, "why don't the black man take the liberty of which he has been deprived by the cruel despot?" Ah! the spirit of revenge was forming—it was coming upwards in the breast of the slave, and she related circumstances which had revealed this to her. There were insurrections taking place constantly on the plantations, and the masters had to go about armed. This spirit of revenge would increase, and unless something occurred to free them from the thraldom, it was impossible to see the end of it. But she believed in the efficacy of preaching. She believed in appealing to that high moral feeling which every man's heart could appreciate—viz., the idea of love of God and man which was implanted in the heart of every man—for who had not felt these emotions in their breast?—and until that man had got to the utmost depth of moral debasement she believed there was a chance of reaching his conscience. This was the opinion of the American anti-slavery party;[89] they had faith in great principles—in the eternal law of right. The Americans believed that if the slaves were educated they would throw off the yoke; therefore slave education was prohibited, and at the north where there were free coloured people they were not allowed to enter on any store or any business beyond the lowest position, and they were excluded from the privilege of learning any mechanical trade. Miss Remond related that lately the Rev. Dr. Taylor had shot one of his wife's negroes for insubordination, and she then recited a piece from Shakespeare, showing the nature of revenge, as displayed by Shylock, and asked was it strange that these feelings appeared in the breast of the slave who lived a life without hope; and it had been laid down by all statesmen that such an existence brought despair. There was known no despair like that of the slave. The case of the slave was desperate. Ignorant the oppressor had made him, and had determined to keep him so; therefore if the spirit of revenge did come uppermost she could not censure them for it. If any class of persons in this world had a right to take their freedom by force it was the slaves. Miss Remond further illustrated the debased state of the American Churches by relating how the Rev. Dudley Tyng,[90] a man of rare ability and powers, and of pro-slavery views, was dismissed from one of the principal churches of Cincinnati, simply because he opposed the extension of slavery into Kansas, and a minister appointed to succeed him who owned 100 slaves. The church lent their names to the disruption of the most sacred ties, and a Baptist Church had lately given out the abominable doctrine that if the master sells the wife of a slave, he would be at liberty to take another wife, and vice versa. The noble conduct of England in wiping away slavery from her dominions was then noticed, and Miss Remond warned Englishmen against the insidious attempts made by Americans by sophistry and other means to disarm all opposition from the public opinion of this country. Let them not allow 347,000 despots of America even by the shadow of a shade, to contaminate their minds. Let not English merchants if they sold their goods sell their principles. God forbid that ever an English heart should lend a sincere throb to American despotism in this 19th century! (Enthusiastic cheers.) The result of American slavery was this, that the great American republic was destined to be sundered. She thanked God for it. It would be severed, and no power could save it unless a sentiment could be created in the northern mind which would overrule the antagonism of the south. The work would go on. God, love, and truth would prevail. She concluded by saying that in the City of Washington if a slave landed there that night, and could not prove his freedom through a stone wall a number of inches thick, he was cast into prison, and after a certain length of time placed on the auction block and sold to the highest bidder to pay his gaol fees! They were misrepresented by the American press, and that was one reason why they were bound to represent themselves. They shut up every avenue—every means was denied them by which knowledge could be gained—and then they turned round and said "You are an inferior race, and have no rights which a white man is bound to respect." Admitting they were an inferior race—which she did not—granting all their oppressors said on the matter to be correct—it was still their duty if they laid claims to the name of Christians and the name of humanity to protect them because they were weak. If a mother had a daughter or son who was weaker than his fellows, did she neglect and oppress them on that account, or did she not rather by all the means which God had given her succour and support by increased solicitude and affection such a one? Therefore they were wished that evening to give her race their sympathy, and to express their moral indignation, against American despotism. Miss Remond then sat down amidst the most enthusiastic cheering, after speaking an hour and a quarter.

2. "A Second Lecture by Miss Remond." *Warrington Times*, reprinted in *The Liberator* 11 March 1859

According to announcement, Miss Remond, the American colored lady, appeared again in the Music Hall, on Monday evening last. To permit the attendance of many who were excluded from the other meeting, a small charge was made for admission, but the room was pretty well filled notwithstanding—indeed it appeared to be crowded at the farther end. A further acquaintance with Miss Remond justifies the commendations we passed on her last week. The lecture was not, as many had anticipated, a repetition of her former one. The matter was of quite a new character, although, of course, a few facts were necessarily repeated.

The Worshipful the [sic] MAYOR occupied the chair, and remarked that he should say nothing as regarded that evening's lecture by Miss Remond. He should leave it entirely in her hands, which he felt quite sure he might do safely. One thing he might say in which they all participated, and that was, that if there was a subject on which the people of England were unanimous, it was on the question of slavery. (Cheers.) [...] Another thing he would remark was, that it was a lady going to lecture. However common this might be on the other side of the water, it was an uncommon thing in this country. And perhaps it was as it ought to be. We in England all looked to the past—we all looked to antiquity, and prided ourselves on the habits of the past; and it had not been a habit to admit ladies prominently into public, still he could never forget that we have a lady on the throne; and that we had admitted our ladies in the classes of our universities; we had given them prizes for the best poems, and we held them in the first rank in works of literature, and really we had done almost everything, except letting them appear before the public to speak. He did not think himself, however, there was anything, the slightest, approaching to indecorousness in a lady addressing her remarks to the public, nor that their friend was not justified tonight in appearing before them, and he had very great pleasure in recommending her as a proper person to hold up before them the evils of American slavery.

MISS REMOND then commenced her lecture by thanking the audience for their kind manifestations on her behalf, as her appearance had been the signal for loud cheering. She thanked them from the depths of an overflowing soul, and from a grateful heart, for their willingness to allow her to present the claims of the bondman and bondwoman of America before them. She must present her stand-point, which would be this, that she should endeavor to say for the slave what she would wish that he or she would say for her were she the victim upon the plantations, as they were, in their stead. When she stated the fact that in the United States of America sixteen hundred million dollars were invested in the bone, blood, and sinews of men and women,[91] was it not a sufficient reason why some advocate should present the claims of these oppressed ones on all and every occasion? After alluding to the exclusive monopoly which the slaveholders held in every department of government in America, Miss Remond said she was not there to speak of America in disparaging terms, because she was herself an American born upon its soil, in the free State of Massachusetts. She then contrasted the North with the South. In the North, where no slave labor existed, all was intelligence, energy, and industry. And there were free schools in every town and village, and the poorest child, unless it happened to be black, could obtain a good education. In the State of Massachusetts even colored children now received their education on equal terms with the white children, but that was the only State, she believed. But in the South free schools were deemed a nuisance; even the poor white population was deprived of an education as well as the slave. She then commented on the Fugitive Slave Law, which the people of the North refused to obey, owing to its infamous nature. The slaveholders said it must be obeyed, but still the great heart of New England rebelled, till Daniel Webster, the greatest of New England statesmen, said it must be obeyed.[92] Thus Daniel Webster set aside the great authority of Black-stone,[93] who was professed to be the guide of all jurisprudence in the United States. She then related instances of a fearful nature where this Fugitive Slave Law had been put in operation, and then said that she asked them as English men and women in the land of Clarkson and Wilber-force[94] — as the people who still kept before the world the high standard which those great men raised — with a determination of soul, to send their Christian and moral sympathy across the Atlantic, and say to those tyrants — "Give up those men and women, and restore to them those God-given rights, and as far as you can, atone to them for the great injury you have inflicted on them." It was false that this Fugitive Slave Law, as asserted by man, was a dead letter. If a slave were found in the Northern States, the parties sheltering him would be obliged to give him up. She read one or two instances to prove the horrible torture inflicted on the slaves. They could pick up a Southern newspaper at almost any time, and find accounts of this nature — of the mutilated forms of men and women, slave mothers torn from their children, fathers separated from their loved ones, and every conceivable enormity. White children were not always safe. They were kid-napped and their faces plastered, and sold, if possible. As for the children of free colored people, they were often taken up in the night, and never heard of afterwards. Under this Fugitive Slave Law, men could take colored peo-ple before the Courts, and they had only to swear they were their slaves, and they were allowed to take them away. They were told that they must not agitate in England. But that was an injunction which they should not obey, and England she was sure would not acquiesce in it. There were often great test questions raised in England. They were, at first, supported by individual influence, before the heart of the people took hold of them. Therefore, they would ask England for the exertion of her moral power in the cause of the slaves, and this she believed would have its due weight on the people of America. She did not wish the English people to sympathize with her as the representative of a down-trodden race, and then sit quietly and silently down, and do nothing, but she wished them on every occasion in old England, to utter their protest in public and private, whenever an opportunity presented, against American despotism. Whenever they came into contact with an American, let them do so, for Americans loved liberty, but only for themselves. A slaveholder in Boston was received into the best circles, and treated as though he was superior, because he had men and women in his possession; and she related the return the Northerners obtained for this treatment if they happened to go South, and dared to hint their disapprobation of slavery. There was not a man in any governmental department throughout America that was not favorable to slavery, even down to the smallest postmaster.

At the conclusion of her remarks, Miss Remond was very warmly applauded.

3. "The Lecture at the Lion Hotel." *Warrington Times*, reprinted in *The Liberator*, 11 March 1859

On Wednesday, Miss Remond attended at twelve o'clock at the Red Lion Hotel to address a few words chiefly to the ladies [...] Miss Remond then spoke, and her remarks chiefly bore on the sufferings and indignities which were perpetrated on her sisters in America, and the fearful amount of licentiousness which everywhere pervaded the Southern States. This fact would be best realized when she stated that there were 800,000 mulattoes in the Southern States of America—the fruits of licentiousness—bringing nothing but desolation in the hearts of the mother who bore them, and it ought to have brought shame to the fathers; but there was no respect for morality while the ministers of the gospel and statesmen of the south did not set an example which even their slaves could follow. She preferred, however, giving them unquestionable facts instead of personal statements which she might offer, and to this end read several extracts from books, all proving that the system of slavery and the immorality it engenders is eating out the vitals of the country, and destroying domestic happiness, not only amongst the subject race, but amongst the families of slaveholders. She then read graphic a description of a young and beautiful girl at a slave sale. The auctioneer was offered 1,000 dollars for her at first. He then expatiated on the superior education she possessed, and 600 dollars more were offered, and lastly he commented on the religious and moral principles she held, when she rose to 2,000 dollars, at which she was knocked down. Thus 1,000 dollars were paid for her blood, bone, and sinew, 600 for her improved intellect, and 400 more for the profession of the religion of God! Miss Remond further treated her subject, and in concluding said she intended to have said more, but her strength failed her.

At the conclusion, Mrs. ASHTON advanced towards Miss Remond, and after addressing her in a few most affectionate sentiments, said she felt proud to acknowledge her as a sister, and she, in common with her sex present, entertained the most heartfelt sympathy with her in the object she proposed to herself to endeavour to carry out. As a slight expression of their sympathy and esteem, she begged, on the part of the ladies of Warrington, to present her with a watch, on which was inscribed, "Presented to S.P. Remond by Englishwomen, her sisters, in Warrington. February 2nd, 1850."

MISS REMOND was so taken by surprise at this manifestation of feeling towards her that her utterance was for some moments prevented by her emotions. At length she said, I do not need this testimonial. I have been received here as a sister by white women for the first time in my life. I have been removed from the degradation which overhangs all persons of my complexion; and I have felt most deeply that since I have been in Warrington and in England that I have received a sympathy I never was offered before. I had therefore no need of this testimonial of sympathy, but I receive it as the representative of my race with pleasure. In this spirit I accept it, and I believe I shall be faithful to that race now and for ever.

Sarah Parker Remond, "Miss Remond in Manchester." *The Anti-Slavery Advocate* 34.2 (1 October 1859): 274–75

A meeting was held at the Athenaeum[95] on this subject, on Wednesday evening last, September 17th, the Mayor of Manchester (Ivie Mackie, Esq.) presiding. The lecture hall was densely crowded by a highly respectable audience, and many hundreds were necessarily refused admission. The principal speakers were: Miss Remond, a coloured lady, from Salem, Massachusetts, United States; Rev. S.J. May, a veteran abolitionist, from Syracuse, New York; Rev. F. Bishop, Chesterfield; Rev. S.A. Steinthal, Liverpool; Henry Vincent, Esq.; Rev. Dr. Beard; and Messrs. Shuttleworth, Ollernshaw, Nelson, and others.

The Mayor opened the meeting and introduced Miss Remond.

Miss Remond, having stated the subject of her lecture, remarked that she appeared as the agent of no society—speaking simply on her own responsibility, of her own knowledge and experience;[96] but that in feeling and in principle she was identified with the ultra-abolitionists of America. She continued:—Although the Anti-slavery enterprise was begun some thirty years ago, the evil is still present—and I am glad to see them here, for

north v.
south again

theme

it is important that they should understand this subject,—I shall briefly explain that there are thirty-two states, sixteen of which are free, and sixteen slave states. The free states are in the north. The political feelings in the north and south are essentially different, so is the social life. In the north, democracy, not what the Americans call democracy, but the true principle of equal rights, prevails—I speak of the white population, mind—wealth is abundant; the country, in every material sense, flourishes. In the south, aristocratic feelings prevail, labour is dishonourable, and five millions of poor whites live in the most degrading ignorance and destitution, I might dwell long on the miserable condition of these poor whites, the indirect victims of slavery; but I must go on to speak of the four millions of slaves. The slaves are essentially *things*, with no rights, political, social, domestic, or religious; the absolute victims of all but irresponsible power. For the slave there is no home, no love, no hope, no help; and what is life without hope? No writer can describe the slave's life; it cannot be told; the fullest description ever given to the world does but skim over the surface of this subject. You may infer something of the state of society in the southern States, when I tell you there are eight hundred thousand mulattoes, nine-tenths of whom are the children of white fathers, and these are constantly sold by their parents, for the slave follows the condition of the mother. Hence we see every shade of complexion amongst the slaves, from the blackest African hue to that of women and men in whose cheeks the lily and the rose vie for predominance. To describe to you the miserable poor whites of the south, I need only quote the words of Mr. Helper, a southerner, in his important work on slavery, and the testimony also of a Virginian gentleman of my acquaintance. The five millions of poor whites are almost in as gross a state of ignorance as Mrs. Stowe's Topsy, in "Uncle Tom's Cabin." The free coloured people of the northern States are, for no crime but merely the fact of complexion, deprived of all political and social rights. Whatever wealth or eminence in intellect or refinement they may attain to, they are treated as outcasts; and white men and women who identify themselves with them are sure to be insulted in the grossest manner. I do not ask your political interference in any way. This is a moral question. Even in America the Abolitionists generally disclaim every other ground but the moral and religious one on which this matter is based. You send missionaries to the heathen. I tell you of professing Christians practising what is worse than any heathenism on record. How is it that we have come to this state of things, you ask? I reply, the whole power of the country is in the hands of the slaveholders. For more than thirty years we have had a slaveholding President, and the slave power has been dominant. The consequence has been a series of encroachments, until now at last the slave trade is re-opened and all but

70

legitimised in America. It was a sad backward step when England last year fell into the trap laid by America, and surrendered the right of search. Now slavers ply on the seas which were previously guarded by your ships. We have, besides, an international slave trade. We have states where, I am ashamed to say, men and women are reared like cattle, for the market. When I walk through the streets of Manchester, and meet load after load of cotton, I think of those eighty thousand cotton plantations on which was grown the one hundred and twenty-five millions of dollars' worth of cotton which supplies your market, and I remember that not one cent of that money ever reached the hands of the labourers. The whole army and navy of the United States are pledged to pursue and shoot down the poor fugitives, who, panting for liberty, fly to Canada, to seek the security of the British flag. All denominations of Christians are guilty of sustaining or defending slavery. Even the Quakers must be included in this rule. Now I ask for your sympathy and your influence. Give us the power of your public opinion — it has great weight in America. Words spoken here are read there as no words written in America are read. Lord Brougham's[97] testimony on the 1st of August resounded through America; your Clarkson and your Wilberforce are names of strength to us. I ask you, raise the moral public opinion until its voice reaches the American shores. Aid us thus until the shackles of the American slave melt like dew before the morning sun. I ask for especial help from the women of England. Women are the worst victims of the slave power. I am met on every hand by the cry, "Cotton! cotton!" I cannot stop to speak of cotton while men and women are being brutalised.[98] But there is an answer for the cotton cry too, and the argument is an unanswerable one. Before concluding, I shall give you a few passages from the laws of the slave states. By some of these laws, free coloured people may be arrested in the discharge of their lawful business; and, if no papers attesting their freedom be found on them, they are committed to jail; and if not claimed within a limited time, they may be sold to pay the jail fees. By another law any person who speaks at the bar, bench, on the stage, or in private, to the slaves, so as to excite insurrection, or brings any paper or pamphlet of such nature into the state, shall be imprisoned for not less than three or more than twenty-one years, or shall suffer death as the judge decides. I could read such laws for hours, but I shall only add that in Maryland there is at present a minister in prison, condemned for ten years, because a copy of "Uncle Tom's Cabin" was found in his possession. The laws are equally severe against teaching a slave to read — against teaching even the name of the good God. In conclusion, Miss Remond made another powerful appeal for sympathy and help.

Notes

1. Frances Smith Foster notes she was appointed to this position sometime in 1854 after she moved from Philadelphia to Boston and then on to New Bedford, Massachusetts, where she began her lecturing career. Harper would later leave Maine, return to Philadelphia, and lecture throughout the Northeast in the late 1850s, at times as a lecturer for the Pennsylvania Anti-Slavery Society and at times as a member of the Ohio State Anti-Slavery Society (Foster 1990, 11, 15).

2. The African Dorcas Association, formed in New York City in 1828, supported the Free African Schools network in Boston and New York, and provided care for black children.

3. Stewart refers to the Second Annual Convention for the Improvement of the Free People of Color in these United States, held in Philadelphia in 1832 and conducted by African American organizers and supporters of immediate abolition ("Garrisonianism"). The convention addressed concerns of trade, labor (especially mechanical), and the education of young black men, as well as cooperation between white and black abolitionist movements and organizations. It was attended and addressed by William Lloyd Garrison, editor of *The Liberator* and one of the founders of the American Anti-Slavery Society. See: *Minutes and Proceedings* 1832.

4. Psalms 68:31. Black preachers and leaders had used this phrase to rally their communities since the late eighteenth century.

5. Psalms 51:2.

6. Joseph Pilmore (1739-1825), born in Yorkshire, left in 1769 to bring Methodism to Philadelphia and became the first Methodist preacher in that city.

7. Born a slave in 1760, Richard Allen (1760-1831), along with Reverend Absalom Jones, decided in 1787 to form the Free African Society, a non-denominational religious mutual aid society for the black community. From this society grew the African Church of Philadelphia. In 1794, Allen founded Bethel, the "Mother" church of the African Methodist Episcopal Church (AME), the first independent black denomination. In 1816, he was elected its first bishop.

8. Acts 8:21.

9. 1 John 3:15.

10. Methodist hymn, "Come Thou Fount of Every Blessing," written by Robert Robinson in 1757.

11. Daniel 5:1-4.

12. James 5:4.

13. Mark 16:15-16.

14. Women led the Holiness movement beginning with Sarah Lankford's "house church" in 1835, or the "Tuesday Meetings for the Promotion of Holiness," which extended with Lankford's sister Phoebe Worrall Palmer's Tuesday meetings to become the Palmer movement (Dieter 1980, 26-27). Holiness stressed the

importance of public testimony of one's attainment of grace and held that after conversion, the second experience of grace, spiritual perfection or sanctification, was necessary for salvation. As Jean Humez defines it, conversion or justification was the "conviction that [one's] sins were forgiven and [one] was 'made just' through Christ's love." Sanctification, the second state of grace or blessedness, was the experience of "full freedom from 'intentional sin,'" a "second, higher, heart-felt experience of divine grace" (1981, 5). Further on in her spiritual autobiography, Lee describes these as three, not two stages: conviction, justification, and sanctification.

15. For preaching black women, regardless of denomination, the experience of sanctification was paramount and drew many to Holiness revivals and camp meetings. An early Methodist teaching, sanctification, or "perfection," became popularized through the camp meetings and revivals of the Second Great Awakening and the interdenominational Holiness movement. Significantly, sanctification was seen as a class-inflected spiritual belief and practice within the AME church. A growing middle-class institution under Bishop Daniel Payne, the AME church at mid-century sought to promote a "respectable" image of African Americans, one that rose above the "lower class" at the expense of some long-lived elements of religious worship, such as the spirituals, sanctification, and ecstatic forms of worship.

16. 2 Corinthians 12:2.

17. The Free African Society, precursor of the AME church.

18. In his annotation of Lee's spiritual autobiography, Andrews documents that the Wesleyan Methodist doctrine "did not allow the formal ordination of women as preachers, although Wesley himself was willing to admit unofficially of 'exceptions' to this rule." Until the AME church drafted its own *Doctrines and Discipline* in 1817, it followed the articles of the Methodist Episcopal church (1986, 239, n. 8).

19. Andrews defines the position: "Exhorters occupied the lowest position in the church's preaching hierarchy and had to have permission before addressing individual congregations. They could lead Sunday school classes and prayer meetings, but in formal church services they usually spoke at the sufferance of the presiding minister and only in response to the biblical text that he had selected" (1986, 14). An exhorter is also defined as "a person who encourages through personal testimony ... [and] is examined and licensed by the Quarterly Conference" of the AME ("Ministry of the AME Church").

20. The introduction.

21. Lee notes that after her conversion she followed the practice of Quakers in calling the Sabbath seventh-day. Fourth-day would be Thursday.

22. Lee originally had 1,000 copies of her *Life and Religious Experience* printed and distributed at camp meetings, organizational meetings, and on the street. In 1839, one year before she joined the American Anti-slavery Society, she had another 1,000 copies printed; in 1849 she printed an expanded version, *Religious Experience*

and Journal of Mrs. Jarena Lee, which contained her notes about where she traveled to preach, the distances she covered, and the scriptures on which she based her sermons.

23. Matthew 13:57.

24. Female praying bands were a Methodist tradition, but Daniel Payne singled out the "extravagant" worship styles and practices of largely female "praying and singing bands" in 1841 and again in the 1870s after he had become bishop of the AME church. These were elements he sought to get rid of as the church institutionalized. Jean Humez notes that praying bands formed an entry point for women into preaching: "Predominantly or entirely female 'praying bands' were an early and continuing phenomenon of black Methodism in America and were the original unit of the Holiness movement.... [T]estifying to spiritual experience in these small groups, meeting weekly at the homes of their members, encouraged substantial numbers of devout black Methodist women to think of preaching to larger audiences. In these relatively intimate, highly participatory, democratic religious gatherings, in the familiar private world of women friends, spiritual talents and speaking skills were developed and protected" (1981, 6).

25. Genesis 37:1-5; 2 Timothy 4:16.

26. Psalm 68:31.

27. Elaw would have been constrained by both Black Codes and the 1793 *Fugitive Slave Act*. The Codes, as Jocelyn Moody documents, included forbidding "African Americans' public assembly... racially integrated worship services... [and also] forbade any colored minister, as well as any colored people belonging to another state, from entrance there" unless they were slaves or servants (2001, 42).

28. Romans 16.

29. Acts 2:16-18.

30. Acts 18:24-26.

31. Acts 21:9.

32. Elaw refers to the Great Anti-Slavery Meeting of 1841 in Exeter Hall.

33. Genesis 12:1.

34. Matthew 24:12.

35. From "Jesus my all to heav'n is gone," a Calvin hymn.

36. Galatians 2:20.

37. Romans 6:6.

38. From "Forsaking All For The True Light," a sixteenth-century German hymn.

39. A praying band; see note 24.

40. Enthusiastic worship styles included "shouting," a descendant of the ring shout practiced by enslaved African Americans. Shouting was condemned in the early nineteenth century by Methodist, Presbyterian, and Baptist revivalists as "sinful." Black Methodists were also critical of "shouting," with both Richard Allen and Daniel Payne condemning it; Payne favored excommunicating those who practiced it. Holiness believers, however, approved of shouting and "getting happy,"

while the black Baptists kept it in their tradition despite its link to sanctification (Sobel 1988, 142).

41. Foote's own minister at AME Zion Church in Boston, Jehiel Beman. Beman was the son of a slave and became a minister in the AME Zion Church of Middletown, Connecticut in 1830 (the third AME Zion Church founded). When the AME Zion Church of Boston was founded in 1838, Beman was sent to be its first minister. He returned to Middletown in 1844. Throughout his years with the church, Beman was active in anti-slavery, moral reform, temperance, and black male suffrage efforts. Significantly, in 1840 he was one of five men appointed to revise the AME *Discipline*, which governed the church through the rules, regulations, and procedures it established. See James 1997, 133-57.

42. Mark 6:11; Luke 9:5.

43. Foote's experience was part of the larger opposition to ordaining women as preachers within the AME church when, in the 1840s, motions to ordain women began to be debated and defeated at AME General Conferences. In 1845, the church instituted education qualifications as one way to police who could appeal for ordination. In 1858 it sought to contain women's preaching by reaffirming the roles of exhorter, missionary, and evangelist as those suitable and open to women. By the 1880s, the role of "evangelist of conference" was supported for women because it limited their preaching to special worship on a one-time-only or limited basis. See Dodson 1981; and Angell 1996.

44. According to the official AME church website: "The General Conference is the supreme body of the African Methodist Episcopal Church. It is composed of the Bishops, as ex-officio presidents, according to the rank of election, and an equal number of ministerial and lay delegates, elected by each of the Annual Conferences and the lay Electoral Colleges of the Annual Conferences.... The General Conference meets quadrennialy (every four years), but may have extra sessions in certain emergencies." See < http://www.ame-church.com/about-us/structure.php>. It is more likely that Foote made appeal not to the General Conference, but to her District Conference, given that she claims to consider herself a member of the body she appeals to.

45. See note 14. Holiness attracted women because it so highly valued personal testimony which "gave many a ... woman the authority and power to speak out 'as the Holy Spirit led her'" (Dieter 1980, 42). Holiness also "had a particularly strong appeal for black women" likely because, as Humez speculates, attaining sanctification, a feeling of "complete personal security[,] ... could be of great psychological value for a woman who had to deal daily with white racism" (1981, 5). Even though Holiness was Methodist in origin, it was an interdenominational revivalist movement that spread through the private and domestic Tuesday meetings held in homes as well as through public revivals and camp meetings. By the mid-nineteenth century, Tuesday meetings were common in "the major cities of the east and

west," camp meeting reporters were giving accounts of sanctifications as well as "the more usual conversions" as "increasingly common" experiences at revivals, and Holiness had moved to a more public arena through "inter-denominational evangelism" (Dieter 1980, 45, 48).

46. Galatians 3:28.

47. Phil. 4:3.

48. Matthew 13:28.

49. *AMEC Book of Worship* defines love feasts as "devotional services, not sacraments such as Holy Communion or Baptism, that are customarily observed to spiritually prepare the church for Holy Communion. Love Feasts may be conducted by the Pastor, a class leader, or the Pastor's appointee" (1984, 40). "In the early church," a love feast was "a meal eaten together as a sign of Christian affection and cordiality, also called AGAPE. Water and bread are used" (1984, 235).

50. John the Revelator, Revelation 14:1-3.

51. 1 Corinthians 14:34.

52. Matthew 27:46.

53. 2 Corinthians 6:2.

54. Philip Bliss, "Hallelujah, 'Tis Done."

55. The Afric-American Female Intelligence Society of Boston was founded in September 1831. It was a benevolent society that sponsored political lectures and discussions, and provided health insurance and other forms of social welfare to its members and the wider African American community. According to its constitution, its goals were "the diffusion of knowledge, the suppression of vice and immorality, and…[the] cherishing [of] such virtues as will render us happy and useful to society" (quoted in McHenry 2002, 69). Initially the Society was rather hostile in its reception of Stewart; her outspokenness and ambitious political agenda appeared too active for its modestly progressive members who adhered to more traditional roles and ideals of femininity. See Richardson 1987. Harry Reed notes that the society "rented halls and sponsored lectures by William Lloyd Garrison" and others; promoted "abolitionist debates, dramatic readings, fund-raising" and the establishment of "reading rooms, and other community welfare projects"; but "did not itself participate in public debates or lectures" (1994, 77-78). Shirley Yee notes that Boston black women were also active abolitionists, helping to organize the interracial Boston Female Anti-Slavery Society in 1833: "At least eleven black women participated in the Boston Female Anti-Slavery Society, including Susan Paul, Louisa Nell, and Nancy Prince" (1992, 90).

56. Matthew 24:36.

57. Revelation 6:16.

58. Watts, Hymn 649.

59. Romans 14:11.

60. Matthew 25:32, 33.

61. Matthew 13:9.

62. Luke 13:24.

63. Matthew 5:20.

64. Matthew 7:3.

65. Matthew 23:33.

66. I Corinthians 13:1.

67. Simeon Jocelyn was a white abolitionist who studied ministry at Yale, became the first pastor of a black congregation at the "Temple Street" Church in New Haven, and acted as a "conductor" on the Underground Railroad.

68. Anna Brownell Jameson's *The Diary of an Ennuyée* (Colburn, 1826). See <http://www.gutenberg.org/files/18049/18049-h/18049-h.htm>.

69. The *Fugitive Slave Act* of 1793 criminalized assisting the escape of a slave; fined those who sheltered a fugitive $500; and established a legal mechanism by which escaped slaves could be seized (even in the free North), extradited, and returned to their master solely on the oral testimony of a slavecatcher that the individual was a runaway. The act prompted the emergence of a slave-capturing industry, which also jeopardized the freedom of free blacks, who were unlawfully seized and sold into slavery in the South. Pennsylvania responded with an 1820 statute, "An act to prevent kidnapping," and with the *Pennsylvania Fugitive Slave Act* of 1826, titled "An act to give effect to the provisions to the constitution of the United States, relative to fugitives of labor, for the protection of free people of color, and to prevent kidnapping." See Leslie 1952, 429–45.

70. The Female Literary Association of Philadelphia was founded in the fall of 1831. Its members included Sara Mapps Douglass (secretary) and Sarah Forten (whose pseudonyms were Ada and Magawisca). The association had their constitution printed in *The Liberator* (3 December 1832); see <http://www.primary research.org/bh/liberator/show.php?file=350.jpg&id=350>. As Garrison apprised his readers in June 1832, the members of this association met every Tuesday "for the purpose of mutual improvement in moral and literary pursuits. Nearly all of them write, almost weekly, original pieces, which are put anonymously into a box, and afterward criticized by a committee" (*The Liberator* 16 June 1832). The Female Literary Association of Philadelphia became a model for future "self-improvement" societies such as the Edgeworth Literary Association (c.1834) and the Female Minervan Association (1834), both of Philadelphia. Elizabeth McHenry notes that the largest black women's literary societies in the 1830s and 1840s "consisted of about thirty members" (2002, 332, n.92).

71. The "malignant disorder" to which the writer refers is likely the cholera epidemic that spread through Philadelphia from July to October 1832, claiming 935 lives.

72. William Lloyd Garrison.

73. Sarah Forten drew her pseudonym "Magawisca" from a character of the same name in Catherine Maria Sedgwick's *Hope Leslie; or Early Times in Massachusetts*

(1827), who was the daughter of a Pequot chieftain. *Hope Leslie* (White, Gallaher, and White, 1827) initially sold 2,000 copies. The novel was reissued in 1842, 1862, and 1872. See Bell 2000, 100; McHenry 2002, 63-64.

74. Schools that educated African American children in the North in the mid-1850s included those in Pennsylvania, New York, Massachusetts, Rhode Island, Indiana, Illinois, Ohio, and Maine (Horton and Horton 1997, 150-54). In the South, little formal education for African Americans was available at the time, as most states had passed laws prohibiting teaching slaves to read or write, with frequent conviction and punishment of violators. However, some slaves were educated by their owners, often for the advantages offered by a literate slave. Southern states with the largest black populations had the most stringent prohibitions against their education until such laws were rescinded after emancipation. Lexington, Kentucky opened a small school for black children in 1830, and an underground school operated in Savannah, Georgia for 30 years. Most educational institutions in the South were self-organized and clandestine. An estimated 4,354 black children in the South were enrolled in school in 1850. See: "Black Self-Help Educational Efforts" <http://academic.udayton.edu/race/04needs/education06.htm>.

75. There were approximately 40 black periodicals in circulation in the 1840s and early 1850s. Papers in circulation at the time with a substantial black readership, or edited by and written for blacks, included *The Liberator* (Boston 1831), *Colored American* (Boston 1837), *Anti-Slavery Herald* (Boston 1838), *Clarksonian* (Hartford 1843), *L'Album Litteraire, Journal des Jeunes Gens* (New Orleans 1843), *African Methodist Episcopal Review* (1841), *Impartial Citizen* (Boston 1850), and the *Christian Recorder* (Philadelphia 1852). See Cooper 2007; Pride and Wilson 1997; and McHenry 2002.

76. Harper refers to Anthony Burns, an escaped slave from Virginia who was captured by slave-hunters in Boston in 1854. He was arrested and remanded to slavery in Virginia, outraging abolitionists and the more general Boston community, which was becoming increasingly hostile towards the enforcement of the 1850 *Fugitive Slave Act*. Abolitionist plans to free Burns from prison and bring him to safety were frustrated when President Pierce deployed federal artillery and marines to take him to the ship on which he was to return to enslavement. Abolitionists sustained injuries and a US marshall was killed during the ensuing struggle.

77. Harper is rousing her audience with an indictment of the *Fugitive Slave Act* of 1850. In response to the weakening of the 1793 *Fugitive Slave Law* (which was rarely enforced) and resulting from the Compromise of 1850, the *Fugitive Slave Act* required federal marshals and other officials to arrest any suspected runaway slave on only the claimant's sworn testimony of ownership as evidence. Those who refused this duty (as well as anyone who assisted a runaway slave) were subject to possible imprisonment and a $1,000 fine. The act made the citizens and institutions

of the free North complicit in enforcing the South's slave law. Abolitionists were thus forced to choose between breaking the law or acting against their conscience.

78. Barnes 1838, 224.

79. James Russell Lowell, "The Present Crisis," 1844.

80. The Song of Miriam, Exodus 15:20-21.

81. As Painter notes, "Truth was a big enough draw to convene a series of meetings on her own in Indiana" by the 1850s (1996, 138).

82. "Border-ruffians" were seen to be poor, white, pro-slavery activists from border states (especially the free Kansas territory) who advocated admission to the Southern Union.

83. Republicans and their supporters were often black sympathizers and abolitionists, and at this meeting Truth was suspected to be a hired mouthpiece paid to spread support of the Republican Party.

84. Harper is referring to *Dred Scott v Sanford* (1856), a Supreme Court case in which Dred Scott, a slave, unsuccessfully sued for his freedom. The Dred Scott case raised the issue of a slave's free status while in a free state; Congress had not asserted whether a slave was free once setting foot on northern soil. The Supreme Court decision ruled that people of African descent, whether bound or free, could never be American citizens and that Congress had no authority to prohibit slavery in federal territories. The decision further polarized the North and South division over slavery and arguably violated the Missouri Compromise, as it suggested that a Southern slave owner could purchase slaves in a slave state, then transport them to a free state without losing his ownership rights.

85. Remond refers here to the attempted Latin American incursions of the 1850s. General Narciso Lopez planned to invade Cuba in 1849 to foment a revolution against Spain but his expedition was broken up by federal authorities before it set sail. John A. Quitman, a Mississippi politician, organized a Cuban expedition in 1853 but abandoned his plans when President Franklin Pierce withdrew his support and approval. William Walker, of Tennessee, led three expeditions into Central America and established himself as dictator of Nicaragua from 1855 to 1857, while he sought to form a Central American federation. He was executed by a Honduran firing squad in 1860. From 1859 to 1860, a Virginian physician, George Bickly, organized the Knights of the Golden Circle, a paramilitary group, to annex Mexico, but the Knights disbanded before they even reached Mexico (Ripley *et al.* 1991, I: 442, n. 4).

86. Remond, like other American abolitionists, charges that pro-slavery interests exerted significant influence and power in the Kansas territory, which elected a pro-slavery territorial legislature in 1855 through electoral fraud. Free-state settlers then created a territorial government and submitted an antislavery constitution to voters, who approved it by a strong majority. Pro-slavery forces sacked Lawrence

in May 1856, destroying the free-state government, and wrote a pro-slavery constitution the following year that was approved in a fraudulent referendum. Voters rejected it in January 1858, but President James Buchanan submitted it to Congress; the House of Representatives then rejected it and called for a third referendum. Though it was soundly defeated, Kansas was not admitted as a free state until 1861 (Ripley *et al.* 1991, I: 442-43, n. 6).

87. Margaret Garner attempted to kill her children following her family's failed escape from slavery. The house in which they took refuge in Cincinnati, Ohio, was under siege by her master, two of his friends, three deputies, and several other men, comprising a posse of eleven; as gunfire erupted, Garner slit the throat of her two-year-old daughter, Mary, attempted to kill her two sons, Tom and Sam (ages six and four), and her nine-month-old daughter Cilla. Garner became an abolitionist *cause célèbre*, as her case focused attention on the "horrors" of slavery and the *Fugitive Slave Act*. Even though her lawyer attempted to have her tried for murder, a capital crime that would override her master's attempt to have her remanded to slavery as a fugitive, he was unsuccessful. For information regarding the popularity of the Garner case among American abolitionists see Weisenburger 1998. Remond, herself, discussed Garner's case with Garner's lawyer, John Joliffe.

88. Remond would have been referring to the legislation many Southern states enacted prohibiting "inflammatory" anti-slavery language and discussions of slavery.

89. The American Anti-Slavery Society.

90. Frances Harper published a poem entitled "The Dismissal of Tyng" in the *National Anti-Slavery Standard* on November 29, 1856. Tyng, who was pastor of the Church of the Epiphany in Philadelphia at the time, preached an anti-slavery sermon on June 29, 1856. He was immediately censured for his political views and subsequently resigned. Remond goes on to refer to William Prentiss, a slaveholding Episcopal clergyman who replaced Tyng (Ripley *et al.* 1991, I: 443-44, n. 13 and 14).

91. Remond is using a stock phrase of anti-slavery speeches in her reference to blood, bone, and sinew.

92. Daniel Webster was a New England Statesman, twice Secretary of State (1841-43 and 1850-52), a constitutional lawyer, and a Federalist. He spoke in opposition to universal suffrage, arguing that power naturally follows property; supported the Compromise of 1850, which included the *Fugitive Slave Act*; and was bitterly attacked by his abolitionist constituents for what was perceived as betrayal and treachery.

93. William Blackstone (1723-80) was an English jurist and professor, and author of the analytic treatise on British common law, *Commentaries on the Laws of England* (1765-69). *Commentaries* served as the primary source of pre-revolutionary American common law.

94. Thomas Clarkson (1760-1846) was a British abolitionist and campaigner against the British slave trade. In 1786 he published "An essay on the slavery and

commerce of the human species, particularly the African, translated from a Latin Dissertation which was honoured with the first prize in the University of Cambridge, for the year 1785," which garnered the support of many like-minded abolitionists, politicians, scholars, and anti-slavery campaigners. Clarkson conducted interviews and gathered evidence of the cruel treatment of Africans brought to Britain on slave ships, which he published in a number of widely circulated pamphlets and essays. William Wilberforce (1759-1833) was a British politician, philanthropist, and abolitionist. A leader of the parliamentary campaign against the slave trade (Committee for the Abolition of the Slave Trade), he put forth propositions for abolition, drawing largely from Clarkson's *Essay on the Impolicy of the African Slave Trade* and the evidence Clarkson outlined of the appalling and inhuman conditions of the Middle Passage. Together Clarkson and Wilberforce were the mobilizing force behind the national abolitionist movement in Britain.

95. The Athenaeum was designed by Sir Charles Barry in 1836-37. It became an established club promoting culture and education among the working classes and contained a library and reading and newsroom facilities. In 1854 the library contained nearly 3,000 volumes, all but 600 of which were destroyed in a fire in 1856. It was rebuilt in 1857, and its collection founded the Manchester Public Library. Significant figures, such as Charles Dickens, Benjamin Disraeli, and Richard Cobden, spoke at its first annual general meeting, addressing issues of poverty and education.

96. Frequently, Remond opened her lectures by identifying herself as the "representative of a race" rather than as the "agent" of an anti-slavery society. This can be read as an attempt to eschew schisms within the abolitionist community, an "independence" that R.J.M. Blackett identifies as key to the success of African American abolitionists in Britain (1986, 42).

97. Henry Peter Brougham (1778-1868) was a British writer, scientist, politician (Whig), and abolitionist. He served as Lord Chancellor from 1830 to 1834 and passed the *Slavery Abolition Act* of 1833, which abolished slavery throughout the British Empire. Brougham was a member of the Anti-Slavery Society, along with Clarkson and Wilberforce.

98. Cotton textiles from greater Manchester were traded for slaves in West Africa throughout the eighteenth century. After the British abolished the slave trade in 1807 and slavery in 1834, they continued to import slave-grown raw cotton from the Southern states. Industry in Manchester was further linked to slavery through cotton mills, trade, production, and other economic transactions involving American cotton. Manchester was also home to a large abolitionist community and supporters of anti-slavery efforts, including a petition with over 2,000 signatures in support of the *Slave Trade Abolition Bill* in 1806.

2

Feminist Black Nationalism

This chapter focuses on African American feminist contributions to the political concerns of the black community. These documents show us that African American women shared black nationalism's concern for African American self-sufficiency, community solidarity, emigration and colonization, and education. Yet, importantly, they also focused on the position of women within this politics and their condition as affected by the changes it advocated. The writings and speeches of Maria Stewart are central to understanding feminist black nationalism's links to black feminism in the church, since Stewart's work attests to the fact that for African Americans "the nation is imagined not alongside religion but precisely *through* the precepts of black Christianity.... [O]ut of black religious life emerged a conception of black national identity" (Glaude 2000, 6). Clearly, Stewart aimed to take a central position in the black political debates of her day. She urged the free black community to pursue a program of economic self-help in the form of a store selling "dry goods and ... groceries,"[1] and a program of political self-interest. Even as the black national convention movement and the black press were targeting African American women as the objects of moral concern, Stewart focused on their mental and material elevation through their own economic solidarity. And given that education was a long-held value that African Americans linked to freedom, she effectively made the African American woman key to the liberation of "the race" from both slavery in the South and menial labor in the North with her stress on the importance of women's mental elevation.

Stewart's opposition to colonization, registered in her Franklin Hall lecture, should be considered alongside the writings on colonization and emigration by women such as Mary Ann Shadd Cary, Frances Harper, and Sojourner Truth. And Stewart's strong advocacy of education provides an important precursor to the writings of Frances Harper on education in the 1850s and 1860s, as well as the later work of feminists such as Anna Julia Cooper, Anna Holland Jones, Gertrude Mossell, and Josephine Turpin Washington.

In addition to being the first American woman to take to the public platform, an abolitionist, and an early promoter of feminist black nationalism, Maria Stewart was also the first African American feminist journalist, deliberately using *The Liberator*, William Lloyd Garrison's paper, to reach a wider audience than her speeches could. In Stewart's career, then, we see the press as central to African American feminism's growing "publicness"; the connections between the church, abolition, and black nationalism in black feminist politics; as well as black feminism's agitation for improved education and employment opportunities for black women and men and its concern for black women's position in debates over emigration and colonization.

The black press rivaled only the church in its centrality to nineteenth-century African American political culture and the black community. Fostered by the black convention movement, the 11 national conventions held in the Northeast between 1830 and 1861 were frequently led by editors of the black press; they formulated an organized response to American racism. Early African American papers printed convention resolutions, pursued the political agenda set there, and worked to unite free Northern blacks (Glaude 2000, 17). It was not by chance that Maria Stewart took her political message to the press as well as the platform, nor coincidental that African American women journalists, like Mary Ann Shadd Cary, promoted journalism as an important profession for black women and used the press to forward a feminist politics.

Stewart's and Shadd Cary's work are important precursors to black feminist journalism on black women's labor and employment opportunities, particularly those they sought in the urban North by migrating. While writings on labor employment in this chapter evidence a black feminist advocacy of employment opportunities for both black men and women, and also include the work of labor activist and socialist, Lucy Parsons, black feminist writing on migration is also of interest. The documents in the final section of this chapter address the growing public attention to the material conditions and employment opportunities of black women who were migrating North in sufficient numbers to constitute a "concern" at the turn into the twentieth century. Estimates suggest that African American migration to the North virtually tripled between 1910 and 1920. In the two decades before this Great Migration, black women journalists advocated for the migrant woman, rather than pathologized her, in a bid for black middle-class respectability in the eyes of white Americans. This tendency is distinctive in their work and is available here alongside Fannie Barrier Williams's piece in *Charities* that was part of a larger discourse presenting migrant women as "contagion."

EMIGRATION AND COLONIZATION

Sojourner Truth, "Lecture by Sojourner Truth." *National Anti-Slavery Standard*, 10 December 1853

A respectable audience of coloured people assembled at their church, in Anthony-st., last evening to listen to an address from a woman of their race, named Sojourner Truth. Pendant from the pulpit cushion was a banner of white satin, on which was inscribed:

> Am I not a Woman and a Sister?[2]
> [Kneeling figure of a woman with uplifted hands.]
> How long, O, Lord! How long.
> A million and a half of American Women in chains.
> Shall we heed their wrongs?
> Will not a righteous God be avenged upon
> such a nation as this?

At 8 o'clock. Sojourner arose and asked some person present who possessed the spirit of prayer to give utterance to it. An elderly coloured man responded to her invitation.

Mrs. Truth commenced her discourse by singing a hymn beginning with

> I am pleading for my people,
> A poor, down-trodden race.[3]

After the hymn was finished, she detailed much of her practical experience as a slave. Some twenty-five years have elapsed since she received her freedom,[4] but the brutality of the Dutch family, whose slave she was,[5] had not been effaced by time. In her heathen despair she used to pray to God that he would kill all the white people. She prayed to God, but she did not know what or who the Divine being was. In her mind he was like Napoleon or General Washington. When her soul was lighted by the influx of celestial love, her nature changed: where she had before showered curses she called down blessings. She went on to talk of the condition of the coloured people and their prospects. They were gradually being thrust out from every menial occupation by their white brethren: but she believed this was ominous of a better future. They were being prepared for some great change that would take place ere long. She was decidedly opposed to the colonization project: they must stay, and a short time would show that that was the best course.[6] — When the coloured people were waiters, and did all the common and lower kinds of work, the streets were clean, the servants scraped the dirt from the corners, swept out the gutters and half-way across the streets. Now, white folk clean boots, wait at table, lie about lazy and beg cold victuals. The coloured people did that sometimes too — but not to keep boarders on it. [Laughter.] Well, in those times, twenty-five or thirty years ago, the streets were kept nice and clean without costing the people a penny. Now the white people have taken it in hand, the dirt lies in the streets till it gets too thick, and flies all about into the shops and people's eyes, and then they sift water all over it, and make it into mud, and that's what they do over and over again, without ever dreaming of such an easy thing as taking it away. In the course of time it becomes too thick, and too big a nuisance and then they go to work right straight off with picks and crow bars, and pull up the stones above the dirt and then go on again. [Laughter] Not long ago nobody but coloured people were coachmen and barbers, but now they have white Pompeys with the livery coats on and poor black Pompey goes to the wall. My coloured brothers and sisters, there's a remedy for this: where I was lately lecturing out in Pennsylvania, the farmers wanted good men and women to work their farms on shares for them. Why can't you go out there? — and depend upon it, in the course of time you will get to be independent.[7] She asked the audience to review the history of the past fifty years, and although the course was slow, the coloured had vastly improved and that menial position to which nature seemed to have consigned them was rapidly being changed for the better. How long ago was it that a coloured woman could address a white audience of a thousand people, and be listened to with respectful attention? These things were signs of the times. The papers rarely recorded crimes committed by her race, though they often teemed with those committed against them. She hoped her people would thus continue to put the white people to the blush. Mrs. Truth is something of a reformer in her way. She commented somewhat severely on the modern style of preaching the Gospel. The parsons went away into Egypt among the bones of dead Pharoahs and mummies, and talked about what happened thousands of years ago, but quite forgot that the living present around them teemed with the sternest realities. Many of the churches were big lumbering things, covering up costly space and doing good to no one. While many of the citizens of this metropolis were living in low dens and sky-lighted garrets, these immense buildings, which would comfortably lodge them, were about one-third filled once in the week, and for the other six days allowed to lie unoccupied and a dead loss. And then the preachers, too, came in for a share of her satire. Big Greek crammed mouthing men, who, for many a long century had been befogging the world and getting its affairs into the most terrible snarl and confusion, and then when women came in to their assistance, cried "shame on women!" They liked the fat and easy work of preaching and entangling too well not to feel alarmed when women attempt to set matters aright. She conceived that women were peculiarly adapted to fill the talking professions, and men should no longer unsex themselves by leaving the plow and the plane, for the pulpit and the platform.[8] She hoped all of her sex would set to work and drag the world right side up, disentangle it from the snarl which men have willfully got it into, and set matters in general aright, and then keep them so. They could only do this by being united and resolutely putting their shoulders to the wheel.

After her address she did a considerable business in the way of selling the first part of her life, done up in some 120 pages, 12 mo., to support the remainder.[9] — *Tribune.*

Mary Ann Shadd Cary, "The Humbug of Reform." *The Provincial Freeman*, 27 May 1854

"This is a great age," we are often told, and undeniably it is; great in moral progress—great in the inventive genius displayed, and great in the facilities it offers to invest vice with the semblance of virtue.

The disposition to make black appear white is the most prominent feature of the times. It is not confined to projects of doubtful propriety either; but is as true of the most necessary reforms as of other, and less important projects.—We pass over the different schemes for this great purpose or the other, which are, in some degree, made to contribute their quota to the general fund of deception, and come at once to the most important movement now engrossing the attention of the people of America—the Abolition question. This project which has for its object the emancipation of the slave, is not an exception.

It is a difficult matter for an American to take a liberal view on subjects involving the interests of colored Americans, disconnected from the selfishness of *individual* gain, personal or pecuniary. The position assumed by the majority who oppose Negro Slavery, is, that it works positive evil to the

Figure 2.1: Mary Ann Shadd Cary

white classes, and, for our own profit, it should be abolished; the inherent wickedness of the system is lost to sight, but "*our*" interests as white *freemen*, may not be subserved by its continuance.

All around, we hear much of Anti-Slavery.—Men now have a measure of *glory* in being Abolitionists, since the thought of security against "any more ebony additions on this continent," is prevailing, the thousands who flock to the standard, are only required to use the Shibboleth Abolition, in order to be received into the household of Anti-Slavery faith; such prose-lytes are not to be relied upon, much less should they be tolerated as ortho-dox on a subject of such great importance. Some of the most miraculous changes of the present time, have been wrought among them, first, *violent-ly* in favor of freedom for the poor negro, and as quick, and with no per-ceptible intermediate change, as decidedly in favor of his expatriation or his continuance in servitude. A man in haste to be popular sets out with the opinion that Slavery is encroaching upon his rights—at once a love for all men is announced, but, as there is an intervening obstacle in his progress, the brotherhood of the race is a "fixed fact": there is a surplus of affection-ate consideration for the black brother; wondrous things are to be done for him, and that in the twinkling of an eye.

In fact, being so blind that he cannot see to advantage, the seeing must be done for him. He cannot hear either, except that which has first been tried, and found to be safe for his delicate organs; the consequence is, that after many "convictions" and "opinions."—a puzzle induced by his decidedly progressive course, in spite of the tutoring and watching he gets, he is thought to be just what his barefaced oppressors have all along asserted of him—"an undesirable part of the *free* population." The land of his forefathers would be the best country for him; could it only be "fixed up a bit," —say a few missions and some republics; at all events, America is wanted for those whom Sojourner Truth delights in calling the "Shaxon race."[10]

Why is it that many reflecting men will not be influenced by appeals when made to them by popular reformers, but that their free principles will out, although they cautiously try to conceal them? Sensible people will not allow themselves to be caught up with the chaff of an empty profession, made by men calling themselves abolitionists, who, in addition to this, wrangle about this trifle or the other, connected with their particular creed, and so lose sight of the shadow of their aim.

We are an abolitionist—we do not want the slave to remain in his chains a second; whether the master gets paid or not, is a point of no importance to us whatever; strictly speaking, however, he has no claim to him and should not, therefore, have pay for that to which he has no shadow of right!

We go further, we want that the colored man should live in America—should "plant his tree" deep in the soil, and whether he turns white, or his neighbors turn black by reason of the residence, is of no moment. He must have his rights—must not be driven to Africa, nor obliged to stay in the States if he desires to go elsewhere. We confess to their views as objectionable, as we knew them to be, but this does not close our eyes against the "humbug" connected with this abolition reform, some phases of which would cause a worm-eating New Hollander to hide his head from very disgust.

Mary Ann Shadd Cary, "A Voice of Thanks." *The Liberator*, 29 November 1861

Wm. Lloyd Garrison, Esq.

Dear Sir—Could the friends of freedom know the effect that a good word timely spoken in behalf of the fleeing slave has upon the colored residents in this country, and the deep gratitude they feel for your many acts of kindness and your solicitude, and, above all, for that sterling, out-spoken sentiment—as true in its services to them, and in its results upon their destiny, as the needle is to the tempest-tossed mariner—I think there would be more faith in the colored people as a responsible moral element, necessary component of the anti-slavery forces, destined now and in the future to enter largely into the moral and political make-up of this continent. I say this continent, because, the importance of islands and other continents admitted,[11] as far as it goes, whatever newfangled theories may be afloat about our destiny as colored native Americans away from here, and out in an island any where, we, at least, realize the truth, that the masses have a fixed destiny here, and we do not believe, and do not intend, that it must always be as the substratum of the body politic.

There are certain plain land-marks by means of which we come to this conclusion, and upon which the beams of this new policy of our removal from the continent to Hayti [sic] break like Samson's withes.[12]

I am led to this train of thought by a very noticeable, and, to us, very important paragraph in your remarks in reply to the letter of friend Hiram Wilson,[13] in the last *Liberator*, wherein you say: "Although it is probable that the number of fugitives, seeking freedom and safety in Canada, will be somewhat diminished for the present; still, there is reason to believe that many of them will go there this winter," &c. &c.

For this gleam of the old light—this stray beam from the old beacon so well known to our people, we give you sincerest thanks. This says, as plain as English can, that the well-worn friends of the refugee[14] and contraband[15] are not to be turned aside, by every wind of doctrine, from the long-established custom of aiding them to settle upon this free soil, without, in their extremity, either attempting to bias their imperfectly formed judgments against Canada[16] and America generally, or joining in the now seeking-to-be popular cry that they must leave the country because of the hatred to pursue them as the cause of the war, when the stupid among them know that the slave-holder, not the poor slave, is the cause, and that once he and his system are crushed out, the cause will have been destroyed, and America must become a desirable country for the masses.

Pointed and easily understood paragraphs as your own say plainly enough, that the Abolitionists of America, who labored and suffered long ago, do not join in the crusade against the colored people, but are right upon this question of residence on this continent for the colored men of the land. There has of late been much silence upon this point—so much, that now the new emigration scheme, about which Mr. Higginson[17] wrote, and for which others work, is thought by many to have absorbed all the Anti-Slavery of the United States worth having.

I have often thought that there was a misapprehension somewhere of the relation in which the refugees here stand to the cause proper.

It is a debatable question with some, whether or not, after being once helped to Canada, they are any longer connected with the Anti-Slavery polity. Some are out-spoken, and say that any consideration of the fugitive in

Canada is not Anti-Slavery work; others, less sincere, regard this Canada as a vast poaching-ground for negro game, from which they may get the material for experiment in the islands without loss to the cause, and certainly without loss to the experiment makers. A few there are who are honest in believing that they would profit by removal to the British islands.

That you do not share the views of the two first, I infer from your recommendation for "local provision" in behalf of the refugees, should the contingencies of travel make it necessary. This explicit acknowledgment of it, as Anti-Slavery work, is subject of congratulation here.

The institution of slavery has despoiled the colored man of America wofully; the injury done to him intellectually, physically, morally, is not of his seeking; those, therefore, whose sympathies do not care to reach beyond your geographical boundaries, and who choose to forget his perils and the difficulties which he must encounter in his new position by reason of former deprivations in slavery, yet scruple not when here, to arouse prejudice by deprecating further emigration of fugitives and contrabands to the Canadas, clearly forfeit the right to the confidence of the colored Canadian, and must not complain, if they do not command his respect.

The fugitives in Canada, though assuming new and important political relations to this government[18]—relations not to be trifled with by every theorizer, who, upon a flying or discursive visit, may hope to sharpen his axe upon their instability and credulity—have keen sympathies for friends and kindred left behind; their better selves remember *for ever* the friends who helped them on, and aid others with help when needed here: they divide to the last their morsel with the wayfarer when he escapes, and they gladly welcome and will welcome the many you may send the coming winter, whether to St. Catharines or this western section.[19] They hail also every organized and responsible society for the necessary relief of the really deserving, as in earnest of the ever kind regards of long-tried friends; and your endorsement of Fugitive Aid Societies,[20] under proper auspices and limitations, must, as I hear that the one at St. Catharines does, receive their grateful acknowledgments and fullest approbation.

Frances Ellen Watkins Harper, "Mrs. Frances E. Watkins Harper on the War and the President's Colonization Scheme." *Christian Recorder*, 27 September 1862

Let me refer to the great topic of the day—the war. You ask my opinion, I think, in one of your letters. To me the times are gloomy, and though I stand not in the valley of vision,[21] and my lips neither tremble nor thrill with the prophet's ecstasy or agony, yet if I can read the fate of this republic by the lurid light that gleams around the tombs of buried nations, where the footprints of decay have lingered for centuries, I see no palliation of her guilt that justifies the idea that the great and dreadful God will spare her in her crimes,[22] when less favored nations have been dragged from their places of pride and power, and their dominion swept away like mists before the rising sun. Heavy is the guilt that hangs upon the neck of this nation, and where is the first sign of national repentance? The least signs of contrition for the wrongs of the Indian or the outrages of the negro? As this nation has had glorious opportunities for standing as an example to the nations leading the van of the world's progress, and inviting the groaning millions to a higher destiny; but instead [of] that she has dwarfed herself to slavery's base and ignoble ends, and now, smitten of God and conquered by her crimes, she has become a mournful warning, a sad exemplification of the close connextion [sic] between national crimes and national judgment.

This lesson she should have learned amid the wrecks of ancient empires, buried beneath the weight of their crimes. She should have learned it from Egypt, seared with the wrath of God, and weeping over her first-born and her dead. She should have read it on the tombstone of proud Babylon, who said in her fancied security, I sit a queen and shall see no sorrow, when destruction was preparing its mines beneath her feet, and ruin brooding over her head. You wonder at the blindness of the nation in refusing the negro's aid, in rejecting the services of men acquainted with both the enemy and the country, who might have, ere this, led their stumbling feet to victory. I am not surprised. It looks as if the nation, stultified by its crimes, with the loss of its moral power, had also parted with its mental perceptions.

The North, if I understand her position aright, lacks one great element of success, and that is enthusiasm. In this battle she lacks the enthusiasm of love and the fanaticism of hate. The South has the latter—a terrible fanaticism that has given vigor to their arms and strength to their labors. If the age would only give another Peter, the hermit,[23] to set every heart to throbbing with a hatred of oppression and a love of freedom, then we might witness another crusade, not to rescue the sepulcher of our once dead Savior, but temples of a living Christ, from the great Mausoleum of American oppression.

The country needs a leader, high and strong, and bold and brave: his heart the home of great and noble purposes, who would count the greatest victory worse than a shameful defeat if resubjugation of the South should only mean a reconstruction of the Union on its old basis.

As to the colonization scheme, give yourself no uneasiness. If Jeff. Davis does not colonize Lincoln out of Washington, let him be thankful. The President's dabbling with colonization[24] just now suggests to my mind the idea of a man almost dying with a loathsome cancer and busying himself about having his hair trimmed according to the latest fashion. I anticipate no fresh trouble to our people from this new movement. Let the President be answered firmly and respectfully, not in the tones of supplication and entreaty, but of earnestness and decision, that while we admit the right of every man to choose his home, that we neither see the wisdom nor expediency of our self-exportation from a land which has been in a measure enriched by our toil for generations, till we have a birth-right on the soil, and the strongest claims on the nation for that justice and equity which has been withheld from us for ages—ages whose accumulated wrongs have dragged the present wars that overshadow our head. And even were we willing to go, is the nation able to part with us? What Christian land under heaven is able to part with four millions of its laboring population? And should this country ever emerge from this dreadful war, with its resources diminished, its strength crippled, and industry paralyzed, will it not want our labor to help rebuild the ravages of war and the wastes of carnage? Did not cruel persecutions drive from Spain and France some of their best workmen and artisans, and what has been the result? All the gold gathered from the new world, that glittered in the coffers of Spain, have not saved her from decay, and does not France, till this hour, miss the strong current of Protestant blood from their veins.

O, be hopeful, my friend! Upon our side of the controversy stands God himself, and this gives us a solemn and sublime position. A people thus situated may lift up their heads and take courage in the hope of a sure and speedy redemption.

Elizabeth J. Jennings, "Thoughts on Colonization." *Pacific Appeal*, 29 November 1862

New Bedford, Nov. 1, 1862.

Mr. Editor—The colonization of the negro race in this country, seems always to rise in the mind of the Anglo-Americans whenever there is any discussion on the slavery question, for one single feature in this problem is, colonize the free men and that will rid us of the incubus slaver. Thirty years ago, there was a grand move made by the leading men of this country, to send us, the Africo-Americans, to the land of our forefathers.[25] In this movement, the learned and professedly holy joined heart and hand. Singular as it may appear, the church has ever been afraid, with few noble exceptions, to speak out on this subject; yet she is ever ready to join any party and cast her influence in favor of colonizing the free blacks. The clergy will preach and pray for its success, aye, and aid by their money also. The great minds of the country have written lengthy articles; the statesmen have made thrilling speeches, showing forth to their delighted and deeply interested auditors how impossible it was to remain here, and how necessary it was that we should remove to Africa. We have been able to show the world that impossibilities can be overcome. We are yet here and apparently as well to do as any other class of citizens.

What has been accomplished by our statesmen and clergy is the planting of a small colony on the western coast of Africa, which we suppose fully demonstrates the fact which was needed that the African race is capable of self-government. The Republic of Liberia is a fixed fact,[26] and we would say, all hail Liberia, for every effort of this kind does add one more stone to the building of the temple of universal democracy.

But with all the eloquence of our Ciceros, the prayers of the church and the gold of millionaires, our fathers said, The more you talk and work, the more we won't go. They, simple souls, could not see the advantage of leaving the home of their birth for the comforts in the wilds of Africa; they could not comprehend what benefit the enslaved would derive from this great and glorious scheme so they calmly shook their grave and venerable heads, and said, Sires, we cannot see it in that light. And now, we of this generation are compelled to acknowledge the same shortsightedness. During the past quarter of a century the coals have been kindled; a slight light would arise to let us know that the fire was not out, but we have maintained our ground.

Few have not proved faithful who started with us. During our struggle they spoke bold words, words that warmed our hearts for the conflict. They said to our would-be friends, This is our home; we know no other; here we will live, and here we will die, and here our ashes will remain until the resurrection morn. They have been allured, the current has been too strong, or the golden temptation too great, and they have gone out. Still we can claim a unity, on this question, unparalleled.

But while our progress, as a people, has been slow, yet we know it to be sure. The hill difficulty is a weary one to ascend, yet we have moved on and upward. Thanks to our large imitative faculties, we have partaken of the refinement of one more favored class. We have in some measure educated ourselves. By the perseverance and the assistance of our true friends, the way has been opened in many States for our children to receive an English education; aye, in many instances, the halls of science have been opened, and our sons can feast at the same board with the great minds of the country.

94

We have even seen the churches open their doors, and allow us to enter on terms of equality, and partake of the good things that God has provided for his children. There are many large and heavy boulders on the road, yet we do not despair. We have progressed, considering, that every step we have taken we have been compelled to bring 4,000,000 of the enslaved with us.

We have reason to thank God and take courage. From the uneasiness just now manifested by some persons whose ever-smiling and hopeful countenance has buoyed us on our journey of life, we fear they are weary of waiting. Remember, those who work can afford to wait.

In our next article we may have a word to say, concerning our Government and its administration.

EDUCATION

Maria W. Stewart, "Mrs. Steward's Essays." *The Liberator*, 7 January 1832

A few weeks since, we alluded to an excellent little tract, published at this office, entitled, "Religion and the pure principles of morality the sure foundation on which we [the people of color] must build," by Mrs. Maria W. Steward [sic], a colored lady of this city.[27] We give the following spirited extract:

"I am of a strong opinion, that the day on which we unite, heart and soul, and turn our attention to knowledge and improvement, that day the hissing and reproach amongst the nations of the earth against us will cease.[28] And even those who now point at us with the finger of scorn, will aid and befriend us. It is of no use for us to sit with our hands folded, hanging our heads like bulrushes, lamenting our wretched condition; but let us make a mighty effort and arise; and if no one will promote or respect us, let us promote and respect ourselves.

The American ladies have the honor conferred on them, that by prudence and economy in their domestic concerns, and their unwearied attention in forming the minds and manners of their children, they laid the foundation of their becoming what they now are. The good women of Wethersfield, Connecticut, toiled in the blazing sun, year after year, weeding onions, then sold the seed and procured money enough to erect them a house of worship; and shall we not imitate their examples, as far as they are worthy of imitation? Why cannot we do something to distinguish ourselves, and contribute some of our hard earnings that would reflect honor upon our memories, and cause our children to arise and call us blessed? Shall it any longer be said of the daughters of Africa, they have no ambition, they have no force? By no means. Let every female heart become united, and let us raise a fund ourselves; and at the end of one year and a half, we might be able to lay the corner-stone for the building of a High School, that the higher branches of knowledge might be enjoyed by us;[29] and God would raise us up and enough to aid us in our laudable designs. Let each one strive to excel in good housewifery, knowing that prudence and economy are the road to wealth. Let us not say, we know this, or we know that, and practise nothing; but let as practise what we do know.

How long shall the fair daughters of Africa be compelled to bury their minds and talents beneath a load of iron pots and kettles?[30] Until union, knowledge and love begin to flow amongst us. How long shall a mean set of men flatter us with their smiles, and enrich themselves with our hard earnings,—their wives' fingers sparkling with rings, and they themselves laughing at our folly? Until we begin to promote and patronize each other. Shall we be a by-word among the nations any longer? Shall they laugh us to scorn forever? Do you ask, what can we do? Unite, and build a store of your own, if you cannot procure a license. Fill one side with dry goods, and the other with groceries.[31] Do you ask, where is the money? We have spent more than enough for nonsense, to do what building we should want. We have never had an opportunity of displaying our talents, therefore the world thinks we know nothing. And we have been possessed of by far too mean and cowardly a disposition, though I highly disapprove of an insolent or impertinent one. Do you ask the disposition I would have you possess? Possess the spirit of independence. The Americans do, and why should not you? Possess the spirit of men, bold and enterprising, fearless and undaunted. Sue for your rights and privileges. Know the reason that you cannot attain them. Weary them with your importunities. You can but die, if you make the attempt; and we shall certainly die if you do not. The Americans have practiced nothing but head work these 200 years, and we have done their drudgery. And is it not high time for us to imitate their examples and practise head-work too, and keep what we have got, and get what we can? We need never to think that any body is going to feel interested for us, if we do not feel interested for ourselves. That day we, as a people, hearken unto the voice of the Lord our God, and walk in his ways and ordinances, and become distinguished for our ease, elegance and grace, combined with other virtues,—that day the Lord will raise us up, and enough to aid and befriend us, and we shall begin to flourish.

Frances Ellen Watkins Harper, "Letter from Miss Watkins." *Anti-Slavery Bugle*, 21 May 1859

Wilberforce Institute.[32]

Respected Friend: My last letter for the Bugle was dated Pittsburg.[33] Since then I have returned to Ohio, and been lecturing almost constantly ever since I left Pittsburgh. My last meeting there was in Lafayette Hall. It was not very large but quite interesting. Madame Picolomi was there, and of course, a source of attraction.[34] However, there were some earnest hearts who could turn from the charms of the enchantress to listen to the cries of the enslaved, who were not only willing to hear anti slavery truth but lend their co-operation.

Among those who lent a helping hand I would mention Rev. Mr. Peck and Tibbs, and Mrs. Lauretta Smith at whose home I was kindly and hospitably entertained. As you were present at my meeting in Salem it will be no news to you to tell you of the respectable size of the audience notwithstanding the inclemency of the weather. — Since then I have lectured twice in Salineville, where I was kindly entertained at Mrs. Bracken's, I have spoken twice in Columbus, three times in Delaware, once in Springfield, but none of these meetings were very largely attended. Last week I held a number of meetings in Cincinnati, one in Elder Sheldon's and one in Rev. Mr. Colver's church. I spoke on Life and existence in Mr. Sheldon's church, and on Slavery and its allies in Mr. Colver's church. The last meeting was pretty well attended. I have had good meetings in Xenian [sic] not withstanding the insanity of negro hatred that has existed there; the last meeting was in Theological Hall before the colored Lyceum of Xenia.[35]

I am now at Wilberforce. The Wilberforce institution is an institution of learning under the auspices of the Methodist Episcopal church. It is beautifully situated in one of the loveliest spots of Ohio, and is in a flourishing condition, — it numbers about 98 scholars, and is under the care of President Reust of New England, and has four other teachers including the music teacher. They have one of the finest school rooms I ever saw, light, airy and commodious, and an excellent play ground for the children. The scholars are from various parts of the Union, I think possibly more than a third from the South. They have a lyceum here and a literary paper, written but not printed. They hold discussions on various questions, some of the teachers joining with them. They have been discussing the disunion question, or rather I think the question before them was, whether it was better or best to dissolve the Union, than admit any more Slave States.

I came in rather late last night to hear all the speaking on the subject, but the decision I understood was against the Union. I like these discussions, they awaken thought, and will surely help carry on a revolution in public opinion favorable to universal freedom.

You have probably heard by this time of the shameful refusal of the Wesly [sic] chapel of Cincinnati[36] to admit the colored Sabbath school children with the white children, because of the outlawed blood in their veins. Other children might enter their temple, and lift their hands in prayer to a common Father, but these poor children of a pariah race, might not kneel with them and call God their father. From hundreds of youthful lips might ascend songs of praise, but these dark browed children might not mingle in their songs, nor join in their strains. And yet these men who smote our children with this cruel repulse, can prate about bringing children to Christ. The Christ of Calvary was kind, and took little children in his arms and blessed them; these men repulse the children of a despised race and forbid them entering their sacred (?) fane. The Christ of Judea was merciful and good, and taught the law of love, these men trample on the brotherhood of man and shake hands with cruelty and crime. Once a year on Easter the Russian serf may embrace his master, or the master embrace him, and say "Christ has risen for us." The poorest Mahometan may kneel beside his richest brethren, saying "God is God and Mahomet is his prophet." But professed Christians can thrust aside the children who they say are bought with the same price and redeemed with the same blood; can treat them as the outcasts of humanity and the Pariahs of mankind. There was something so mean and cruel in the deed. It was cruel to both races, cruel to teach the white children such lessons of selfish hypocricy [sic], cruel to teach our children such barbarity and practical Atheism.

I have spoken in Dr. Colver [sic] church in Cincinnati and expect to speak in some more of the churches next week, and I may earnestly thank God if he will only give me power to expose this act of shameful infidelity to God and man; this act in keeping with the practical Atheism of part of the American church, who uphold a system of concrete, concentrated and intense blasphemy, which treads upon the divine in woman, and tramples upon the image of God in man.

Katie S. Campbell, "Our Educational Interests." *New National Era*,[37] 12 June 1873

Shall we educate ourselves, or shall others educate us? is a question which should be awakened in the mind of every intelligent young man and woman in the AME Church.

We can never be on a par with the so-called *superior* race, until we place *ourselves* there; and the only way to do this, is to educate ourselves up to the standard to which our more favored brethren of a paler hue have already attained; this we can very easily do, by uniting upon the single idea of educating ourselves. I say educating ourselves, because when we are educating others we are educating ourselves. If a congregation educates a man for the ministry, and that man returns to labor among them, in every sermon that he preaches, in every lecture that he delivers, in every conversation with his people, he imparts to them a portion of the education which he has received. In all intercourse with the learned, as ministers or teachers, in business or social relations, we receive a portion of the knowledge which they possess.

Now we want—not only want, but must have—an educated ministry; must have competent teachers in our schools, we want men of business—lawyers, doctors, mechanics, merchants—but they must be educated up to the highest standard. We already have Senators and Representatives in Congress; we want more. When those who are now there shall have reached the close of the term for which they were elected, we want others ready to take their places, and we want them to be men of the highest erudition, men who can compete with the most intelligent; who can stand an argument with the most learned.

All these things we want, but it requires work to get them; and more, it requires unity. We can do but little unless we are united. "United we stand; divided we fall."

Thinking over this subject a short time ago, this idea suggested itself to the writer, (which she venture [sic] to bring before the readers of the *Recorder*,[38] if haply some one more able may enlarge upon it). Why should not the young people in each of our churches establish among themselves a society to help educate those who may wish to prepare themselves for a profession, and yet who are unable to give themselves such a training as they need; and also to help carry on schools for the purpose of giving them the proper discipline.

Our own college, we believe, can give such a training as is needed to any one preparing for any of the professions, but money is needed to carry it on; it must have an efficient corps of teachers, and the proper kind of apparatus, &c. All this can be easily accomplished, if we would only set our heads and hearts to the work, and then would we do away with the necessity of our young men and women going to white colleges to prepare for their various vocations, and we should have the rich reward of feeling that our ministers and teachers, and others, are being educated in our own school, by our own teachers. Then those who think we are unable to manage institutions for ourselves will be compelled to give back before the facts themselves, when presented before them, and those who now look down upon us with scorn, would then look at us with respect.

Shall this be done? or shall we every year lose men of talent, because others say to them, come to us and we will educate you.

Shall we not rather say to them ourselves, if you have not the means to get the training you wish, apply to us, and we will give you all that you need?

We ought to have more schools belonging to our Church. Other denominations have them, the Catholics have day schools in connection with their churches—why should not we?

We ought to have a school in each Conference district. There are efforts being made, in some parts of the connection, to establish such schools—by the active operation of some such project as I have mentioned, several such schools could easily be established, and kept in good working order, in connection with Wilberforce.

Who will be the first to go to work without delay? What church will first say, we have a plan in operation, to forward the educational interest of our church?

Philadelphia, May 29th, 1873.

Anna Julia Cooper, "The Higher Education of Women." *The Southland*[39] 2.2 (April 1891): 186-202. Reprinted in *A Voice from the South*

In the very year of our century, the year 1801, there appeared in Paris a book by Silvain Marechal,[40] entitled "Shall Woman learn the Alphabet." The book proposes a law prohibiting the alphabet to women, and quotes authorities weighty and various, to prove that the woman who knows the alphabet has already lost part of her womanliness. The author declares that women can use the alphabet only as Moliere predicted they would in spelling out the verb *amo*; that they have no occasion to peruse Ovids Ars Amoris, since that is already the ground and limit of their intuitive furnishing; that Madame Guion would have been far more adorable had she remained a beautiful ignoramus as nature made her; that Ruth, Naomi, the Spartan women, the Amazons, Penelope, Andromache, Lucretia, Joan of Arc, Petrarch's Laura, the daughters of Charlemagne, could not spell their names; while Sappho, Aspasia, Madame de Maintenon and Madame de Staël could read altogether too well for their good: finally that if women were once permitted to read Sophocles and work with logarithms, or to nibble at any side of the apple of knowledge there would be an end forever to their sewing on buttons and embroidering slippers.

Figure 2.2: Anna Julia Cooper

Please remember this book was published at the *beginning* of the Nineteenth Century. At the end of its first third, (in the year 1833) one solitary college in America decided to admit women within its sacred precincts,[41] and organized what was called a "Ladies' Course" as well as the regular B.A. or Gentlemen's course.

It was felt to be an experiment—a rather dangerous experiment—and was adopted with fear and trembling by the good fathers, who looked as if they had been caught secretly mixing explosive compounds and were guiltily expecting every moment to see the foundations under them shaken and rent and their fair superstructure shattered into fragments.

But the girls came and there was no upheaval. They performed their tasks modestly and intelligently. Once in a while one or two were found choosing the gentlemen's course. Still no collapse, and the dear, careful, scrupulous, frightened old professors were just getting their hearts out of their throats and preparing to draw one good free breath, when they found they would have to change the names of those courses; for there were as many ladies in the gentlemen's course as in the ladies', and a distinctly Ladies' Course, inferior in scope and aim to the regular classical course, did not and could not exist.

Other colleges gradually fell in line and to-day there are one hundred and thirty-five in the United States alone offering the degree of B.A. to women, and sending out yearly into the arteries of this nation a warm, rich flood of strong, brave, active, energetic, well-equipped, thoughtful women— women quick to see and eager to help the needs of this needy world—women who can think as well as feel, and who feel none the less because they think —women who are none the less tender and true for the parchment scroll they bear in their hands—women who have given a deeper, richer, nobler and grander meaning to the word "womanly" than any one-sided mascu- line definition could ever have suggested or inspired—women whom the world has long waited for in pain and anguish till the complement of that masculine influence which has for almost fourteen centuries dominated it, should be at last added to its forces and allowed to permeate its thought.

Since the idea of order and subordination succumbed to barbarian brawn and brutality in the fifth century, the civilized world has been like a child brought up by his father. It has needed the great mother heart to teach it to be pitiful, to love mercy, to succor the weak and to care for the lowly.

Whence came this apotheosis of greed and cruelty? Whence this sneak- ing admiration we all have for bullies and prizefighters? Whence the self- congratulation of "dominant" races, as if "dominant" meant "righteous" and carried with it a title to inherit the earth? Whence the scorn of so-called weak or unwarlike races and individuals, and the very comfortable assur- ance that it is their manifest destiny to be wiped out as vermin before this advancing civilization? As if the possession of the Christian graces of meek- ness, non-resistance and forgiveness, were incompatible with a civilization professedly based on Christianity!

The world of thought under the predominant man-influence, unmolli- fied and unrestrained by its complementary force, would become like Daniel's fourth beast: "dreadful and terrible, and *strong* exceedingly"; "it had great iron teeth; it devoured and brake in pieces, and stamped the residue with the feet of it,"[42] and the most independent of us find ourselves ready at times to fall down and worship this incarnation of Power.

Mrs. Mary A. Livermore,[43] a woman whom I can mention only to admire and reverence, came near shaking my faith a few weeks ago in my theory of the thinking woman's mission to put in the tender and sympathetic chord in nature's grand symphony.

She was dwelling on the Anglo-Saxon genius for power and his contempt for weakness, and described a scene in San Francisco which she had witnessed.

The incorrigible animal known as the American Small-boy, had pounced upon a simple, unoffending Chinaman, who was taking home his work, and had emptied the beautifully laundried contents of his basket into the ditch. "And," said she, "when that great man stood there and blubbered before that crowd of lawless urchins, to any one of whom he might have taught a lasting lesson with his two fists, *I didn't much care!*"

This is said like a man! It grates harshly. It smacks of the worship of the beast. It is contempt for weakness, and taken out of its setting it seems to contradict my theory. It either shows that one of the highest exponents of the Higher Education can be at times untrue to the instincts I have ascribed to the thinking woman and to the contribution she is to add to the civilized world, or else the influence she wields upon our civilization may be potent without being necessarily and always direct and conscious. The latter is the case. Her voice may strike a false note, but her whole being is musical with the vibrations of human suffering. Her tongue may parrot over the cold conceits that some man has taught her, but her heart is aglow with sympathy and loving kindness, and she cannot be true to her real self without giving out these elements into the forces of the world.

As in the case of individuals, we are constantly and inevitably, whether we are conscious of it or not, giving out our real selves into our several little worlds, inexorably adding our own true ray to the flood of starlight, quite independently of our professions and our masquerading; so in the world of thought, the influence of thinking woman far transcends her feeble declamation and may seem at times even opposed to it.

A visitor in Oberlin once said to the lady principal, "Have you no rabble in Oberlin? How is it? I see no police here and yet the streets are as quiet and orderly as if there were an officer of the law standing on every corner."

Mrs. Johnston replied, "Oh yes; there are vicious persons in Oberlin just as in other towns—*but our girls are our police.*"

With from five to ten hundred pure-mind young women threading the streets of the village every evening unattended, vice must slink away, like frost before the rising sun: and yet I venture to say there was not one in a hundred of those girls who would not have run from a street brawl as she would from a mouse, and who would not have declared she could never stand the sight of blood and pistols.

There is then, a real and special influence of woman. An influence subtle and often involuntary, an influence so infinitely interwoven in, so intricately interpenetrated by the masculine influence of the time that it is often difficult to extricate the delicate meshes and analyze and identify the closely clinging fibers. And yet without this influence—so long as woman sat with bandaged eyes and manacled hands, fast bound in the clamps of ignorance and inaction, the world of thought moved in its orbit like the revolutions of the moon; with one face, the man's face always out, so that the spectator could not distinguish whether it was disc or sphere.

Now I claim that it is the prevalence of the Higher Education among women, the making it a common everyday affair for women to reason and think and express their thought, the training and stimulus which enable and encourage women to administer to the world the bread it needs as well as the sugar it cries for; in short it is the transmitting the potential forces of her soul into dynamic factors that has given symmetry and completeness to the world's agencies. So only could it be consummated that Mercy (the lesson she teaches) and Truth (the task man has set himself) should meet together: that righteousness, or "*rightness*" (man's ideal) and *peace* (its necessary other half) should kiss each other.

We must thank the general enlightenment and independence of woman (which we may now regard as a *fait accompli*) that both these forces are now at work in the world and it is fair to demand from them for the twentieth century a higher type of civilization than any attained in the nineteenth. Religion, science, art, economics, have all needed the feminine flavor; and literature, the expression of what is permanent and best in all of these, may be guarded at any time to measure the strength of the feminine ingredient. You will not find theology consigning infants to lakes of unquenchable fire long after women have had a chance to grasp, master, and wield its dogmas. You will not find science annihilating personality from the government of the Universe and making of God an ungovernable, unintelligible, blind, destructive physical force; you will not find jurisprudence formulating as an axiom the absurdity that man and wife are one, and that one the man—that a married woman may not hold or bequeath her property save as subject to her husband's direction; you will not find political economists declaring that the only possible adjustment between laborers and capitalists is that of selfishness and rapacity—that each must get all he can and keep all that he gets, while the world cries *laissez faire* and the lawyers explain, "it is the beautiful working of the law of supply and demand" in fine you will not find the law of love shut out from the affairs of men after the feminine half of the world's truth is completed.

Nay, put your ear now close to the pulse of the time. What is the keynote of the literature of these days? What is the banner cry of all the activities of the last half decade? What is the dominant seventh which is to add richness and tone to the final cadences of this century and lead by a grand modulation into the triumphant harmonies of the next? Is it not compassion, for the poor and unfortunate, and, as Bellamy has expressed it, "indignant outcry against the failure of the social machinery as it is, to ameliorate the miseries of men!"[44]

When went there by an age, when so much time and thought, so much money and labor were given to God's poor and God's invalids, the lowly and unlovely, the sinning as well as the suffering—homes for inebriates and homes for lunatics, shelter for the aged and shelter for babes, hospitals for the sick, props and braces for the falling, reformatory prisons and prison reformatories, all show that a "mothering" influence from some source is leavening the nation.

Now please understand me. I do not ask you to admit that these benefactions and virtues are the exclusive possession of women, or even that women are their chief and only advocates. It may be a man who formulates and makes them vocal. It may be, and often is, a man who weeps over the wrongs and struggles for the amelioration: but that man has imbibed those impulses from a mother rather than from a father and is simply materialising and giving back to the world in tangible form the ideal love and tenderness, devotion and care that have cherished and nurtured the helpless period of his own existence.

All I claim is that there is a feminine as well as a masculine side to truth; that these are related not as inferior and superior, not as better and worse, not as weaker and stronger, but as complements—complements in one necessary and symmetric whole: That as the man is more noble in reason, so the woman is more quick in sympathy. That as he is indefatigable in pursuit of abstract truth, so is she in caring for the interests by the way—striving tenderly and lovingly, that not one of the least of these "little ones" should perish. That while, we not unfrequently see women who reason, we say, with the coolness and precision of a man, and men as considerate of helplessness as a woman, still there is a general consensus of mankind that the one trait is essentially masculine and the other is peculiarly feminine. That both are needed to be worked into the training of children, in order that our boys may supplement their virility by tenderness and sensibility, and our girls may round out their gentles [sic] by strength and self-reliance. That as both are alike necessary in giving symmetry to the individual, so a nation or a race will degenerate into mere emotionalism on the one hand, or bullyism on the other if dominated by either exclusively; lastly and most emphatically, that the feminine factor can have its proper effect only through woman's development and education so that she may fitly stamp her force on the forces of her day and add her modicum to the riches of the world's thought.

> For woman's cause is man's: they rise or sink
> Together, dwarfed or godlike, bond or free:
> For she that out of Lethe scales with man,
> The shining steps of nature, shares with man
> His nights, his days, moves with him to one goal
> If she be small, slight natured, miserable,
> How shall men grow?
> ★ ★ ★ Let her make herself her own
> To give or keep, to live and learn and be
> All that not harms distinctive womanhood.
> For woman is not undeveloped man
> But diverse: could we make her as the man
> Sweet love were slain; his dearest bond is this,
> Not like to like, but like in difference.
> Yet in the long years liker must they grow;
> The man be more of woman, she of man;
> He gain in sweetness and in moral height,
> Nor lose the wrestling thews that throw the world;
> She mental breadth, nor fail in childward care,
> Nor lose childlike in the larger mind;
> Till at the last she set herself to man,
> Like perfect music unto noble words.[45]

Now you will argue, perhaps, and rightly, that higher education for women is not a modern idea, and that, if that is the means of setting free and invigorating the long desired feminine force in the world, it has already had a trial and should, in the past, have produced some of these glowing effects. Sappho, the bright, sweet singer, of Lesbos, "the violet-crowned, pure, sweetly, smiling Sappho" as Alcaeus calls her, chanted her lyrics and poured forth her soul nearly six centuries before Christ, in notes as full and free, as passionate and eloquent as did ever Archilochus or Anacreon.

Aspasia, that earliest queen of the drawing-room, a century later ministered to the intellectual entertainment of Socrates and the leading wits and philosophers of her time. Indeed to her is attributed, by the best critics, the authorship of one of the most noted speeches ever delivered by Pericles.

Later on, during the Renaissance period, women were professors in mathematics, physics, metaphysics, and the classic languages in Bologna,

Pavia, Padua, and Brescia. Olympia Fulvia Morata, of Terrara, a most interesting character, whose magnificent library was destroyed in 1553 in the
Invasion of Schweinfurt by Albert of Bradenburg, had acquired a most
extensive education. It is said that this wonderful girl gave lectures on classical subjects in her sixteenth year and had even before that written several very remarkable Greek and Latin poems, and what is also to the point,
she married a professor at Heidelburg and became a help–meet for him.

It is true then that the higher education for women—in fact the highest that the world has ever witnessed—belongs to the past; but we must
remember that it was possible, down to the middle of our own century,
only to a select few; and that the fashions and traditions of the times were
all against it. There were not only no stimuli to encourage women to make
the most of their powers and to welcome their development as a helpful
agency in the progress of civilization, but their little aspirations, when they
had any were chilled and snubbed in embryo and any attempt at thought
was received as a monstrous usurpation of man's prerogative.

Lessing declared that "the woman who thinks is like the man who puts
on rouge—ridiculous," and Voltaire in his coarse, flippant way used to say,
"Ideas are like beards—women and boys have none." Dr Maginn remarked,
"We like to hear a few words of sense from a Woman sometimes, as we do
from a parrot—they are so unexpected!" and even the pious Fenelon taught
that virgin delicacy is almost as incompatible with learning as with vice.

That the average woman retired before these shafts of wit and ridicule
and even gloried in her ignorance is not surprising. The Abbe Choisi it is
said praised the Duchesse de Fontanges as being pretty as an angel and silly
as a goose, and all the young ladies of the court strove to make up in folly
what they lacked in charms. The ideal of the day was that "women must be
pretty, dress prettily, flirt prettily; and not be too well informed"; that it was
the *summum bonum* of her earthly hopes to have, as Thackery puts it, "all the
fellows battling to dance with her"; that she had no God-given destiny, no
soul with unquenchable longings and inexhaustible possibilities—no work
of her own to do and give to the world—no absolute and inherent value,
no duty to self, transcending all pleasures that may be demanded of a mere
toy: but that her value was purely a relative one and to be estimated as are
the fine arts—by the pleasure they give. "Woman, wine and song as the
world's best gifts to man," were linked together in praise with as little
thought of this first saying, "What doest thou," as that the second and third
should declare, "We must be about our Father's business."[46]

Men believe, or pretended to believe, that the great law of self development was obligatory on their half of the human family only; that while it
was the chief end of man to glorify God and put his five talents to the

exchangers, gaining thereby other five, it was, or ought to be, the sole end of woman to glorify man and wrap her one decently away in a napkin, retiring into "Hezekiah Smith's lady during her natural life and Hezekiah Smith's relict on her tombstone"; that higher education was incompatible with the shape of the female cerebrum, and that even if it could be acquired it must inevitably unsex woman destroying the lisping, clinging, tenderly help-less, and beautifully dependent creatures whom men would so heroically think for and so gallantly fight for, and giving in their stead a formidable race of blue stockings with corkscrew ringlets and other spinster propensities.

But these are 18th century ideas.

We have seen how the pendulum has swung across our present centu-ry. The men of our time have asked with Emerson, "that woman only show us how she can best be served," and woman has replied: the chance of the seedling and of the animalcule is all I ask—the chance for growth and self-development, the permission to be true to the aspirations of my soul without incurring the blight of your censure and ridicule.

"Audetque viris concurrere virgo."[47]

In soul-culture woman at last dares to contend with men, and we may cite Grant Allen (who certainly cannot be suspected of advocating the unsex-ing of woman) as an example of the broadening effect of this contest on the ideas at least of the men of the day. He says in his Plain Words on the Woman Question, recently published:[48]

"The position of woman was not [in the past] a position which could bear the test of nineteenth-century scrutiny. Their education was inade-quate, their social state was humiliating, their political power was nil, their practical and personal grievances were innumerable; above all their rela-tions to the family—to their husbands, their children, their friends, their property—was simply insupportable."

And again: "As a body we 'Advanced men' are I think prepared to recon-sider, and to reconsider fundamentally, without prejudice or preconception, the entire question of the relations between the sexes. We are ready to make any modifications in those relations which will satisfy the woman's just aspiration for personal independence, for intellectual and moral develop-ment; for physical culture, for political activity, and for a voice in the arrangement of her own affairs, both domestic and national."

Now this is magnanimous enough, surely; and quite a step from 18th-century preaching, is it not? The higher education of Woman has certain-ly developed the men;—let us see what it has done for the woman.

Matthew Arnold during his last visit to America in 82 or 83, lectured before a certain co-educational college in the West. After the lecture he remarked to a lady professor that the young women in his audience he noticed, "paid as close attention as the men, *all the way through* [.]" This led, of course, to a spirited discussion of the higher education for women, during which he said to his enthusiastic interlocutor, eyeing her philosophically through his English eyeglass: "But—eh—don't you think it—eh—spoils their *chawnces*, you know!"

Now as to the result to woman, this is the most serious argument ever urged against the higher education. If it interferes with marriage, classical training has a grave objection to weigh and answer.

For I agree with Mr. Allen at least on this one point, that there must be marrying and giving in marriage even till the end of time.

I grant you that intellectual development, with the self-reliance and capacity for earning a livelihood which it gives, renders woman less dependent on the marriage relation for physical support (which, by the way, does not always accompany it). Neither is she compelled to look to sexual love as the one sensation capable of giving tone and relish, movement and vim to the life she leads. Her horizon is extended. Her sympathies are broadened and deepened and multiplied. She is in closer touch with nature. Not a bud that opens, not a dew drop, not a ray of light, not a cloud-burst or a thunderbolt but adds to the expansiveness and zeal of her soul. And if the sun of an absorbing passion be gone down, still 'tis night that brings the stars. She has remaining the mellow, less obtrusive, but none the less enchanting and inspiring light of friendship, and into its charmed circle she may gather the best the world has known. She can commune with Socrates about the *daimön* he knew and to which she too can bear witness; she can revel in the majesty of Dante, the sweetness of Virgil, the simplicity of Homer, the strength of Milton. She can listen to the pulsing heart throbs of passionate Sappho's encaged soul, as she beats her bruised wings against her prison bars and struggles to flutter out into Heaven's aether, and the fires of her own soul cry back as she listens: "Yes; Sappho, I know it all; I know it all." Here is communion without suspicion; friendship without misunderstanding; love without jealousy.

We must admit then that Byron's picture, whether a thing of beauty or not, has faded from the canvas of to-day.

"Man's love," he wrote, "is of man's life a thing apart,
'Tis woman's whole existence.
Man may range the court, camp, church, the vessel and the mart,
Sword, gown, gain, glory offer in exchange.
Pride, fame, ambition to fill up his heart—

And few there are whom these cannot estrange.
Men have all these resources, we but one —
To love again, and be again undone."[49]

This may have been true when written. *It is not true today.* The old, sub-jective, stagnant, indolent and wretched life for woman has gone. She has as many resources as men, as many activities beckon her on. As large pos-sibilities swell and inspire her heart.

Now, then does it destroy or diminish her capacity for loving?

Her standards have undoubtedly gone up. The necessity of speculating in "chawnces" has probably shifted. The question is not now with the woman "How shall I so cramp, stunt, simplify and nullify myself as to make me eligible to the honor of being 'shallowed up' into some little man?" but the problem, I trow, now rests with the man as to how he can develope [sic] his God-given powers as to reach this ideal of a generation of women who demand the noblest, grandest and best achievements of which he is capa-ble, and this surely is the only fair and natural adjustment of the chances. Nature never meant that the ideals and standards of the world should be dwarfing and minimizing ones, and the men should thank us for requiring of them the richest fruits which they can grow. If it makes them work, all the better for them.

As to the adaptability of the educated woman to the marriage relation, I shall simply quote from that excellent symposium of learned women that appeared recently under Mrs. Armstrong's signature in answer to the "Plain Words" of Mr. Allen, already referred to. "Admitting no longer any ques-tion as to their intellectual equality with the men whom they meet, with the simplicity of conscious strength, they take their place beside the men who challenge them and fearlessly face the result of their actions. They deny that their education in any way unfits them for the duty of wifehood and maternity or primarily renders these conditions any less attractive to them than to the domestic type of woman. On the contrary, they hold that their knowledge of physiology makes them better mothers and house-keepers; their knowledge of chemistry makes them better cooks; while from their training in other natural sciences and in mathematics, they obtain an accuracy and fair-mindedness which is of great value to them in dealing with their children or their employees."

So much for their willingness. Now the apple may be good for food and pleasant to the eyes and a fruit to be desired to make one wise. Nay, it may even assure you that it has no aversion whatever to being bitten. Still, if you do not like the flavor all these recommendations are nothing. Is the intel-lectual woman *desirable* in the matrimonial market?

This I cannot answer. I must confess my ignorance. I am no judge of such things. I have been told that strong-minded women could be, when they thought it worth their while, quite endurable, and judging from the number of female names I find in college catalogues with double patronymics, I surmise that quite a number of men are willing to put up with them.

Now I would that my task ended here. Having shown that a great want of the world in the past has been a feminine force; that that force can have its full effect only through the untrammelled development of woman; that such development, while it gives her to the world and to civilization, does not necessarily remove her from the home and fireside; finally, that while past centuries have witnessed sporadic instances of this higher growth, still it was reserved for the latter half of the nineteenth century to render it common and general enough to be effective. I might close with a glowing prediction of what the twentieth century may expect from this heritage of twin forces—the masculine battered and toil-worn as a grim veteran after centuries of warfare, but still strong, active and vigorous, ready to help with his hard-won experience the young recruit rejoicing in her newly found freedom, who so confidently places her hand in his with mutual pledges to redeem the age's.

And so the twain upon the skirts of Time,
Sit side by side, full-summed in all their powers,
Dispensing harvest, sowing the To-be,
Self-reverent each and reverencing each.[50]

With a view of enlightenment on the point, as the achievement of the century for the higher education of the colored women, I wrote a few days ago to the Colleges which admit women and asked how many Colored women had completed the B.A. course in each during its entire history. These are the figures returned: Fisk leads the way with twelve; Oberlin next with five; Ann Arbor, Wellesley and Wilberforce three each; Livingstone two; Atlanta one; Howard, as yet, none.

I then asked the principal of the Washington High School how many out of the large number of female graduates from his school had chosen to go forward and take a collegiate course. He replied that but one had ever done so, and she is now at Cornell.[51]

Others ask questions too, sometimes, and I was asked a few years ago by a white friend, "How is it that the men of your race seem to outstrip the women in mental attainment?" "Oh," I said, "so far as it is true, the men, I suppose, from the life they lead, gain more by contact, and so far as it is only apparent, I think the women are more quiet. They don't feel called to mount a barrel and harangue by the hour every time they imagine they have produced an idea."

But I am sure there is another reason which I did not at that time see fit to give. The atmosphere, the standards, the requirements of our little world do not afford any special stimulus to female development.

It seems hardly a gracious thing to say, but it strikes me as true, that while our men seem thoroughly abreast of the times on almost every other subject, when they strike the woman question they drop back into sixteenth century logic. They leave nothing to be desired generally in regard to gallantry and chivalry, but they actually do not seem sometimes to have outgrown that old contemporary of chivalry—the idea that women may stand on pedestals or live in doll-houses, (if they happen to have them) but they must not furrow their brows with thought or attempt to help men tug at the great questions of the world. I fear the majority of colored men do not yet think it worth while that women aspire to higher education. Not many will subscribe to the "advanced" ideas of Grant Allen already quoted. The three R's, a little music and a good deal of dancing, a first rate dress-maker and a bottle of magnolia balm, are quite enough generally to render charming any woman possessed of tact and the capacity of worshipping masculinity.

My readers will pardon my illustrating my point and also giving a reason for the fear that is in me by a little bit of personal experience. When a child I was put into a school near home that professed to be normal and collegiate, i.e., to prepare teachers for colored youth, furnish candidates for the ministry, and offer collegiate training for those who should be ready for it. Well, I found after a while that I had a good deal of time on my hands. I had devoured what was put before me, and, like Oliver Twist, was looking around to ask for more. I constantly felt (as I suppose many an ambitious girl has felt) a thumping from within unanswered by any beckoning from without. Class after class was organized for these ministerial candidates (many of them men who had been preaching before I was born). Into every one of these classes I was expected to go, with the sole intent, I thought at the time, of enabling the dear old principal, as he looked from the vacant countenances of his sleepy old class over to where I sat, to get off his solitary pun— his never-failing pleasantry, especially in hot weather—which was, as he called out "Any one!" to the effect that "*any* one" then meant "*Annie* one."

Finally a Greek class was to be formed. My inspiring preceptor informed me that Greek had never been taught in the school, but that he was going to form a class *for the candidates for the ministry*, and if I liked I might join it. I replied—humbly I hope, as became the female of the human species— that I would like very much to study Greek, and that I was thankful for the opportunity, and so it went on. A boy, however meager his equipment and shallow his pretensions, had only to declare a floating intention to study

112

theology and he could get all the support, encouragement and stimulus he needed, be absolved from work and invested beforehand with all the dignity of his far away office. While a self-supporting girl had to struggle on by teaching in the summer and working after school hours to keep up with her board bills, and actually to fight her way against positive discouragements to the higher education, till one such girl one day flared out and told the principal "the only mission opening before a girl in his school was to marry one of those candidates." He said he didn't know but it was. And when at last that same girl announced her desire and intention to go to college it was received with about the same incredulity and dismay as if a brass button on one of those candidate's coats had propounded a new method for squaring the circle or trisecting the arc.

Now this is not fancy. It is a simple unvarnished photograph, and what I believe was not in those days exceptional in colored schools, and I ask the men and women who are teachers and co-workers for the highest interests of the race, that they give the girls a chance! We might as well expect to grow trees from leaves as hope to build up a civilization or a manhood without taking into consideration our women and the home life made by them, which must be the root and ground of the whole matter. Let us insist then on special encouragement for the education of our women and special care in their training. Let our girls feel that we expect something more of them than that they merely look pretty and appear well in society. Teach them that there is a race with special needs which they and only they can help; that the world needs and is already asking for their trained, efficient forces. Finally, if there is an ambitious girl with pluck and brain to take a higher education, encourage her to make the most of it. Let there be the same flourish of trumpets and clapping of hands as when a boy announces his determination to enter the lists, and then as you know that she is physically the weaker of the two, don't stand from under and leave her to buffet the waves alone. Let her know, that your heart is following her, that your hand, though she sees it not, is ready to support her. To be plain, I mean let money be raised and scholarships be founded in our colleges and universities for self-supporting, worthy young women, to offset and balance the aid that can always be found for boys who will take theology.

The earnest well trained Christian young woman, as a teacher, as a home-maker, as wife, mother, or silent influence even, is as potent a missionary agency among our people as is the theologian; and I claim that at the present stage of our development in the South she is even more important and necessary.

Let us then, here and now, recognize this force and resolve to make the most of it—not the boys less, but the girls more.

Nannie Helen Burroughs, "Industrial Education—Will it Solve the Negro Problem."[52] *Colored American Magazine* 7.4 (March 1904): 188-90

The Negro problem is a problem of color, and not of fitness. Industrial education is not a skin changer, and could not, therefore, solve a problem that is but skin deep. By industrial education I take it that you mean the development of that part of the mental and physical man that will respond to all or some special phase of manual labor. Industrial education will solve but one phase of the problem, and the Negro must have all phases of the problem solved in order to secure the key to the situation.

Before anyone can assume that industrial education alone will solve the Negro problem it must be proved first that the Negro's mind, feelings, tastes, habit, interest and enthusiasm naturally adapt him to this particular branch of learning. This being proved, systematic development and cultivation along industrial lines would make him the man intended by his Creator. But it has yet to be shown that the Negro is outside of the law of evolution, and needs a special law for his development. Since he is within the pale, and it has taken all kinds of education to solve the problem of other races within those confines, it will take the same kinds of education to make him a better man and a better citizen, the same man and the same citizen, equal to any, inferior to none.

Secondly, it must be shown that the Negro can do everything else well except manual labor, and with this happy adjunct his salvation along all lines will be complete. It must also be shown that he cannot simultaneously attain two kinds of education. For if he can, the law of economics would suggest that he do so. The Negro is surely not the one-talent fellow of Bible fame, and the demand should not be made upon him to yield a one-talent result. God used the same constructive timber in making Ham that He used in making Shem and Japheth, and His "whosoever will" Gospel will reclaim the one as quickly and as surely as it will the other.

Those who outline a specific course of study and attempt to confine him to one field of labor must remember that his capacity, his ability, his ambition is as varied as to quality and quantity as the capacity and the ability of each individual of any other race, and the educators of the Negro race must prepare to meet the demands of individual inclinations, feelings and tastes, as far as it is possible.

It has never been shown that the Negro's mental power must be cast in an industrial mould in order to fully respond to the biddings of his mind and the pleadings of his heart; nor have we evidence to show that the Negro makes a better citizen and a better man with an industrial education than with any other kind; nor has the Negro any evidence that an industrial education will secure for him an even brake [sic] in the race of life. Is the Negro to spend years fitting himself as a laborer of skill, and then be forced to work for unskilled prices or starve? Can any race be saved morally, spiritually, intellectually, and industrially, by directing its energies along one line? Verily, verily, I say unto you, unless the Negro is saved, not in part but wholly, he cannot see the kingdom of earth nor reign therein.[53] The very best thing, as I see it, is for him to do as he has been doing for the past thirty years—take his chances and follow the other race in every avocation from the bootblack to the college chair, from the coal cart to congress halls.

It takes as much and as many kinds of education to solve the Negro problem as it took and is now taking to solve the white man's problem. It takes as much education to make the Negro a man as to make the white man a man. To say that it takes less would be to say that the Negro by creation is superior. A well educated Negro is worth as much to any community as a well educated white man, and wherever he has been given a chance to prove his worth, his loyalty, or his manhood at home or abroad, he has never been found wanting. If the Negro can be made a good citizen by having one kind of education, a white man can also, and this enormous expenditure of government funds and gifts of philanthropists for all branches of learning is useless. In the educational world as elsewhere the Negro asks no special favor nor any specific remedy to cure his malady. He asks that the same laws protect him, the same facilities be offered him, and the same chances be given him as other men, and he will move up to the flag, and will not ask that the flag be brought back to him.

If industrial education will save the ignorant Negro, the same gospel will save the ignorant white man, and you have only to look around to see that one is as bad off as the other, and it is the salvation of all its citizens at which this republic must aim.

General education is as necessary for the formation of character and correct notions of life as general exercise is essential to systematic physical growth. The reformation of any people is not abiding unless the mass of that people build upon the broad, general platform of individual preparation along general educational lines. Then, if there is in that mass those in whom the love of the classics extinguishes all other loves, they should have seats in the best colleges in the land, and to keep them from these colleges because the mass cannot go would be as criminal as to incase a prospective giant, and make a pygmy of him, or to dwarf one child because the other one cannot grow.

The Negro, as a mass, is neither fitted by creation nor can he be fitted by training, to ply at one profession or trade. There are thousands of

Negroes, who would make first-class professional men who couldn't farm, shoe horses, or invent a device as an improvement to the hay-mower if the race problem is never solved. There are hundreds of Negro women who would make first-class clerks, stenographers, book-keepers, musicians, and teachers, who couldn't maintain themselves by cooking, washing, ironing, sewing and working on a farm if the race problem were never solved.

A large per cent of any race comes under the laboring class. There need be no special legislation, discussion nor training to put them there. Circumstances over which they have no control put them there, and necessity which knows no law keeps them there. The Negro is not an exception to this rule.

The Negro must write some books for himself. They must not all be upon one subject. The Negro must make some music for himself, and all must not sing along the same line.

The Negro must do some high thinking for himself, but all must not think the same lay.

Industrial education alone would never have produced our Bannaker, our Douglass, our Bruce, our Langstone, our Blyden, our Scarborough, our Fortune, our Roscoe Conkling Bruce, nor our Booker T. Washington.[54] Had these bright lights, that have helped to illumine the hall of fame, marched by any other route than by the one they traveled, they would have perished in the middle-passage.

The progress of the Negro has been rapid and pleasing because all have not hoed corn and picked cotton. While some have been in the field, others have been at the desk. While some have been at the anvil, others have been in the college chair.

At what trade did Frederick Douglass work to become one of the greatest orators the world has ever heard? At what trade did Booker T. Washington work to build Tuskegee? What trade did Roscoe Conkling Bruce ply to march off with the honors of Harvard? At what trades have the thousands of teachers, preachers, doctors, and lawyers worked to open up the understandings, save the souls, and give ease to the enfeebled bodies of the thousands who have come unto them?

Have not these men and women, from Phyllis Wheatly[55] and Frederick Douglass to the last leader in any calling, been great factors in the solution of the race problem?

If the Negro had tried all other kinds of education and failed, I might say, try industrial education; but he has not been found wanting in any of the branches of knowledge nor incompetent in any calling, but to the admiration of his friends and to the humiliation and regret of his enemies, he started in the School of Adversity and never stopped until he stood as Valedictorian of Harvard, and has yet to be heard to say, "My cup runneth over."

If the object of the American people is to make the Negro a better man and thus a better citizen, he must be dealt with as a man, and given a man's chance to choose for himself such callings as appeal to him individually.

Why talk about a Negro problem when he has not propounded a single question to the American people as to his ability to do or to be. He has never asked whether he could learn reading, writing, spelling, arithmetic, geography, history, Latin, Greek, geometry, physics, music, painting, drawing, medicine, or law. He has never asked which would be the more conducive to his growth and happiness in this country, hoeing corn or studying a little science from a book. He has never asked if he may stay here or take ship for another clime. He has never asked whether he is a man or a missing link. He read in the Bible that "out of one blood God hath made all nations for to dwell upon the face of the earth" and he said, "that means me, too." It has never been a question, therefore, with him as to where he came from, where he belongs, or where he is going, for he believed this Bible assertion, and felt that since he came from where other races came, must dwell where other races dwell, that with like course of action, he would go where other races go.

> You may talk about the Negro,
> You may make his faults infinite
> But you cannot turn a wheel,
> That the Negro isn't in it.

Fannie Barrier Williams, "Industrial Education — Will it Solve the Negro Problem." *Colored American Magazine* 7.7 (July 1904): 491-95

Industrial Education is a much overworked term. Among the colored people, at least, it has caused no end of confusion of ideas and absurd conclusions as to what is the best kind of education for the masses of the people. Scarcely any subject, since emancipation, has been talked about and discussed as this one subject of Industrial Education. All sorts and conditions of people have their opinion as to the merits and demerits of this kind of education, and have been curiously eager to give expression to such opinions in the public press, in the pulpit and on the rostrum. Among these thinkers, writers, and speakers there are many who know absolutely nothing about the question, and there are others whose academic training has

Figure 2.3: Fannie Barrier Williams

given them a fixed bias against any sort of mental training which does not include as a *sine qua non* the "humanities." On the other hand, there are those among the advocates of Industrial Education who insist that nothing else will solve the race problem. So the discussion goes on from one extreme to the other, with more or less earnestness and noise, truth and falsehood, sense and nonsense.

With the exception of occasional personalities and vindictive misrepresentations, this widespread discussion of the principles of Industrial Education has added enormously to the general interest in the subject of education for the colored and white people of the South. More than any other man, Dr. Booker T. Washington has made the subject of education in the South one of paramount interest to all the people. The helpful agencies that have been created and developed by this new propaganda of the training of the brawn as well as the brain of the people are quite beyond calculation. Industrial Education has long since ceased to be a theory. The discussion as to whether or not this kind of education is best for the Negro race may go on indefinitely; but, in the meantime, the industrial system of education has taken deep root in the needs of the people.

But what is this Industrial Education? The following are some of the answers given, by persons who ought to know better: "To teach the Negro how to work hard"; "to teach the Negro how to be a good servant and forever hewers of wood and drawers of water"; "to teach the Negro how to undervalue his manhood rights."

It is scarcely necessary to say that Industrial Education is immeasurably more than anything contained in these definitions. In the term Industrial Education, the emphasis is always upon education. Mathematics, drawing, chemistry, history, psychology, and sociology go along with the deft handling of the carpenter's and engineer's tools, with the knowledge of farming, dairying, printing, and the whole range of the mechanical arts. To the students in the industrial or manual training schools, their education means more than the mere names of the various trades imply. The carpenter has been given the foundation training by which he may well aspire to become an architect, the printer a publisher, the engineer a manufacturer, and the trained farmer a prosperous land owner. It can be readily seen that, by this kind of training, occupations that were once considered mere drudgery have become enlarged and ennobled by the amount of intelligence put into them. It was once thought that no one outside of the professions and other well deserved occupations needed to be educated. The tradesman or mechanic was not expected to know anything beyond the more or less skillful handling of his cash book or tools. An educated mechanic was the exception. Farming without the knowledge of forestry, dairying and the many other things that enter into the farmer's life, was regarded as drudgery.

What was true of masculine occupations was equally true of woman in the whole range of her special occupations and domestic concerns. It was thought that the only occupations for which women needed any sort of training were those which fitted her for the parlor and "society." Piano playing was an accomplishment; cooking and housekeeping, drudgery. A woman's apron was a badge of servility, and the kitchen a place not to be frequented by ladies. Poor woman! How narrow was her sphere! How wide the distance between the sphere of her every day home usefulness and the accomplishments of the "lady!" How different since the newer education has enlarged our sense of values. A new dignity has been added to the occupations that concern our health, our homes and our happiness. Through the influence of schools of domestic science, cooking has become a profession; the trained nurse divides honors with the physician, and the dressmaker and the milliner, by proper training, have become artists. In fact, Industrial training has dignified everything it has touched. It is not only banishing drudgery from the workshop and the home, but is widening the opportunities for talents of all kinds. There can be no such thing as caste in the everyday work of life, if that work is under the direction and control of trained intellects. Whether we do our share of the world's work with the pen or with the tool, in the office or in the shop, in the broad green acres on the hill slopes, or in the senate hall, the question is always, the same—how much intelligence and character do you bring to your work? We believe that it is not too much to say that this is the spirit, the purpose and the result of Industrial Education.

Yet there are those who oppose this kind of education, as if it meant exactly the opposite of all this. It must be said that in a good deal of this opposition there is a curious blending of ignorance, envy and perversity. The best that can be said of those who think they are sincere is that they represent a belated conception of the higher and larger functions of education.

It should be stated in passing that nearly all of the most competent educators of the country, including presidents of the leading universities, believe in the Washington idea of Industrial Education, for white as well as colored people. That the idea has the encouragement and support of the best thought of the day is witnessed by the large number of industrial, polytechnical and agricultural schools that have been built and developed in the Northern states during the past ten or twelve years. These schools are always over crowded by white students. It is very difficult to keep a white boy in a high school long enough to enable him to graduate, but he will remain in a manual training school without persuasion. A leading professor in the Chicago University recently stated to his class, that Booker T. Washington must always be regarded as the true leader of American education in its largest sense. The conception as to what is real and fundamental in education, has become so broadened that even the great universities are enlarging their curricula so as to include schools of technology. Such being the sphere and purpose and resulting possibilities of industrial education, can it be right or just to urge it as especially suited to the condition of the colored people?

It is claimed by the academician that the Negro is not essentially different from any other people, and, therefore, he should not be singled out for any special kind of education. We certainly all like to believe that the Negro is as good as any one else, but the important fact remains that the Negro is essentially different from any other race amongst us in the conditions that beset him. Just what these conditions are every intelligent Negro knows and feels. Among these conditions are illiteracy and restricted opportunities for the exercise of his talents and tastes. To multitudes of colored people illiteracy is a continuous night without a single ray of light. Inability to read and write is the least of his deficiencies; the ignorance of what to do to help himself and his kind is the pitiful thing. Any system of education that does not, in its helpful effect, reach from the school house back to the cabin is of small value in solving the race problem. The crying need of the multitude is, "Can you show me how to live, — how to raise more and better crops, — how to hold and use the benefits of my labor, — how to own and keep the land that I have earned over and over again by my labor, — how to appreciate the value of the earth's bounties and turn them into the currents of commerce? Any system of education that cannot give direct and helpful answer to this wail of despair, to this confession of incompetency and helplessness, falls far short of effectiveness. Industrial education aims to reach these conditions. It first aims to bring the benighted masses into conscious relationship with their own environments. It comes to teach these despairing people how to work out their own salvation by the tools and instrumentalities that are indigenous to their habitations. If agriculture must, for a long time to come, be the chief occupation of our people, then let their education for a long time to come be inclusive of all that which makes for thrift and intelligence in husbandry. If engineers, carpenters, plumbers, printers, wagon-makers, brick-makers, electricians, and other artisans are needed to build up and develop the rich resources of the communities in which they must live, is it not wise to train our own people to do all of this work so masterfully as to give them a monopoly against all others? It has been predicted already that the colored people will some day own the South, but this ownership can be realized only by the exercise of thrift, character and practical intelligence that can be gained in the best of the industrial schools.

It is not the contention of this article that Industrial Education must be the limit of education for colored people. We believe with Dr. Rankin, of Howard University, that "any system of education for the Negro that does not open to him the golden gate of the highest culture will fail on the ethical and spiritual side." At the same time the creators of wealth, — the great captains of industry, who are the real builders of communities, — have been those who wrought intelligently with their hands. The demand for colored artisans of all kinds, is always in excess of the supply. The supply of lawyers, doctors and ministers and other professions, always exceeds the demand. The race is not only poor in the resources and means of wealth, but poor also in the practical intelligence that creates wealth.

It will prove an inmeasurable [sic] blunder if we shall now lack the foresight to provide for our young men and women the kind of training that will enable them to do everything in the line of industries that will equip them to become the real builders of the future greatness of the South. If by our neglect the master mechanics and skilled laborers of other races must be called into the South to do this work, the Negro will be relegated to a position of hopeless servitude.

The advocates of industrial education are laying the foundation broad and deep for the future as well as providing for the present. They are wisely seeking to widen the Negro's sphere of usefulness. They realize the danger of equipping young Colored men and women for occupations from which they are excluded by an unyielding prejudice. They are aiming to teach our aspiring young people that the positions and occupations from which they are now barred are not more honorable or more remunerative than those which they are permitted to enter, if they but carry the proper training and intelligence into those occupations. It teaches that the prizes of life lie along every pathway in which intelligence and character walk arm in arm. A professional man is not better than a mechanic unless he has more intelligence. An intelligent blacksmith is worth more to a community than an incompetent doctor, a hungry lawyer or an immoral minister.

The time is coming, aye, is now here, when a colored graduate from a school of domestic science will be more honored and better paid than are many white women who now hold the positions colored women cannot enter. The time is coming when there will be no excuse for a colored young woman to remain in soul-destroying idleness, because she cannot obtain a clerkship. She can be trained in an industrial school for positions that she can fill and still be socially eligible among those who make "society." An increasing respect is being shown to the young man or Woman who is brave enough to learn a trade and follow it with pride and honor. The graduate from an industrial school finds a place awaiting him or her with a good salary. The graduates from Dr. Jones's Cooking School, in Richmond, Va., receive from $14 to $16 per week, while the untrained cook receives $5 per week. The graduates from Provident Hospital and Training School receive from $15 to $25 per week for their services; the untrained nurse not more than $6 per week. These instances are fair examples of how direct and immediate is the value of industrial training added to individual worth. These schools are every day creating new opportunities for honorable and well paid employment. The graduates of schools of this kind are seldom mendicants for employments. They have won their independence and their efficiency is a part of the good in every community in which they live and work.

The graduates of Hampton, Tuskegee and other industrial schools are the advance guard of efficiency and conquest. They touch more sides of the life of a community than any other class of our educated people. Rich and poor, black and white, prejudiced and unprejudiced, those who dread "Negro

122

domination" and those who expect it, must all at one time or another ask for the service of the best trained artisan in the community. Along every pathway of material progress in that great undeveloped country south of the Ohio, we will soon begin to read all sorts of evidences of what industrial education has done for these black builders of a new empire of power.

The heroic efforts of Dr. Washington and others to furnish a system of education that shall be of the greatest good to the greatest number, should not and does not discourage what is called the higher education. In their tastes and aptitudes our young men and women are like those of other races. The doors of the universities are always open to the few who have the gifts and tastes for scholarship. The passion for higher education has not seemed to diminish as a consequence of the development of industrial schools. Every year witnesses a large number of Negro graduates from the best universities of the country. Many of these college graduates find their way down to Tuskegee, proving that Dr. Washington insists upon giving his Tuskegee students the advantage of studying under the best educated Negroes in the country.

The colored people are entitled to the best possible education that this country can afford, but this education should fit them for the life they must live. It should give as much encouragement to the would-be mechanic and agriculturist as to the would-be teacher, the lawyer or other professions. It should be the special aim to reach helpfully the lives of the thousands who live under conditions peculiarly their own and different from that of any other people.

These schools should educate their graduates toward and not away from the people. The evidence of this kind of education should make itself felt in every honorable relationship that the Negro bears to his community and to his government. Such an education will make the Negro efficient, self-respecting, proud, brave and proof against every prophecy of evil that would consign him to a destiny of "hopeless inferiority."

Josephine B. Bruce, "What Has Education Done for Colored Women." *Our Woman's Number. The Voice of the Negro* 1.7 (July 1904): 294-98

A question of so great importance cannot be answered without serious reflection. Evidence is not wanting to show that our educated colored women have risen to some eminence in the world. In any considerable community into which one may go, will be found colored women of education who have gained distinction as teachers, as leaders in philanthropic work, as temperance advocates, as church workers, and in many other lines of activity which require ability and endurance, education and character. While all this and more is true it seems to me that we have arrived at a stage when we must seek for the evidences of general growth due to education below the level of the exceptional woman, however numerous they may be. The ranks of the exceptional women must be constantly recruited, in order that the influence they now exert may be a continuing force; and herein is another reason for the importance of seeking for an answer to the pregnant question, "What has education done for Colored Women?"

In order to be definite and clear, I propose to take facts from several scientific investigations which have been conducted with intelligence and skill, without prejudice, by trained sociologists, and shall endeavor to present as briefly as possible conclusions which these social studies in widely scattered communities have developed.

While from locality to locality the condition of the Negro population varies in notable degree, being here vastly lower and there a little lower, and in many places indubitably higher, nevertheless, after extended enquiry and years of critical observation, I am convinced that the Negro population of Farmville, Virginia, may be taken to represent medium conditions generally. Farmville is rather centrally located in Virginia, and the Negroes in this locality live a separate and in most respects an independent group life. They live in sections to themselves, they have their separate schools, separate churches, separate social organizations. They live upon their own land mostly. Their contact with the whites is purely in a business relation.

But with the habit of dependence upon one another which is fostered by separation in school life, social and church life, is growing the disposition toward economic independence, resulting in the establishment of Negro business enterprises, which are rapidly absorbing Negro patronage. The fact of special significance to which I wish to call attention is that the enterprising members of this social group and those who exert the greatest influence have all had some advantages of education; many of the younger ones have been sent away to school. This educated class, as we may designate them, are in every way people of exemplary lives. They form the highest of the three social strata which are distinctly marked in this community, moral first, and then education and means being the lines of cleavage. They possess and practice the highest virtues. They own their own homes and farms, carrying on in many instances independent businesses, and are thrifty, aspiring and progressive. The general trend of the community is upward, and its general life is wholesome.

The special significance of this showing which I have condensed in few words is evident, when it is remembered that here slavery flourished until the Emancipation Proclamation freed the slave; that the community is still rural, and its inhabitants are removed from the great centers of educational effort and opportunity; and yet they have attained, with meagre advantages, unto the wholesome things of life.

The women who are responsible for good homes, good morals, and good society are fullfilling their mission faithfully. As Dr. DuBois says, "No black girl of this town can transgress the moral law without being shut off from the best class of people, and looked at askance by ordinary folks."[56] And certainly this is a sound test of the community's moral integrity. As a result of this discrimination there has grown up in Farmville an agreeable social and religious life, dominated by worthy ideals, and destined to exert a wide and beneficent influence.

In tragic contrast with conditions in Farmville where the Negroes avail themselves of the educational opportunities offered, are conditions in Calumet, Louisiana,[57] where the school term is four months and compulsory attendance not required. The consequent difference in morality is appalling, there being at Calumet, one is tempted to think, no such thing as the monogamic family. Hardly fifty per cent of the population are legally married, and then the marriage vow is not respected. Only ten per cent of the children of school age attend school for the four months of its session, and seventy per cent of the entire colored population are illiterate, with a large proportion of the remaining thirty per cent being able to write very poorly their own names, and to read signs which they usually recognize by their shape. This pathetic condition may be traced directly to the absence of proper educational facilities.

From these Southern communities we will turn to one in the State of Ohio. The city selected for this study was Xenia,[58] one [of] the oldest towns in the State, for the reason that here a considerable group of Negroes have settled in one section, many of them representing the second and third generations of freemen, the descendants of run-away slaves.

Life in this community was necessarily under somewhat different circumstances. Freely the Negroes have been permitted to persue [sic] the tenor of their way, unrestricted by either political, social, or economic conditions. The spirit which actuated their forebears in risking all for freedom was a lofty one, and must have produced a marked influence upon the younger generations proceeding from the brave spirits of their progenitors, engendering a hopeful and enterprising attitude.

An emphatic expression of this disposition to proceed forward in the race of life is furnished in the establishment of Wilberforce University in

1856. The African Methodist Episcopal Church presides over its destinies, and its faculty is composed entirely of Negroes. Life in Xenia centers largely around the University and its public schools,—the High School in particular, which accomplishes a great deal of extension work in the community through its regular courses of lectures on the live subjects of the day, as well as upon literary and historical subjects.

Since the war, Xenia very naturally became for Negroes a refuge. Many of the poor and illiterate, flying from the ills they knew, found their way to Xenia; being moneyless and unskilled, they are still struggling upward slowly. The presence of this class has brought about the sifting process, the separation of the chaff and the wheat, so that today there exist in Xenia well defined social distinctions. To the highest grade belong the educated people whose lives are above reproach, men and women of refinement and gentle breeding, who set the standard for their community. This class almost without exception own their own homes and maintain themselves as preachers, as teachers, often in independent businesses, or as managers of industrial enterprises.

There has been another marked advance which is becoming noticable [sic] among educated colored people and is distinctly observable here. It is the fact that the Negro home is rapidly assuming the position designed for it. It is distinctly becoming the center of social and intellectual life; it is building up strength and righteousness in its sons and daughters, and equipping them for the inevitable battles of life which grow out of the struggle for existence. This higher and purer family life is creating a more effective and influential church, and thus these two great social and moral forces are making, in no uncertain way, a strong righteous community in Xenia.

As the mother in the home, as the woman teacher in the school room, and the woman in the church set the standards for the multitude, so the women in Xenia (not unaided by their brethren) with their education, refinement and aspirations are building up a community which well serves as an example of what education does for Negro womanhood.

Now let us go from the quiet sequestered shades of an Ohio town to St. Louis, a large, noisy, bustling city in the central west and learn, if we can, something of the Negro in cosmopolitan atmosphere.

The Negro in St. Louis is not a strange feature, having been identified with life there almost from the founding of the city. A census of 1799 gives a total population of 925, of whom 601 were whites, 56 were free Negroes, and 268 were slaves. A fact worthy to be noted here is that free Negroes increased much faster than the enslaved. At the beginning of the century they constituted 17 per cent of the colored population, in 1850 they formed one third of it, and in 1860 they numbered over one-half of the colored population. Thus, in St. Louis Negroes have lived under a set of circumstances quite different from either of the other cases already considered. In a limited article it is impossible to follow the gradual growth and development covering a century of time. What is attempted is to trace results of a long struggle in present conditions. In a question which so inextricably involves men and women, it is difficult to separate the woman problem from the general problem, and especially so in this community where men and women have stood shoulder to shoulder and accomplished so much.

As is usual among educated colored women, a large number of them are engaged in teaching in St. Louis. In most cases they have been carefully prepared for their work; many have received in addition to training in the home schools the higher training in colleges, and have brought earnestness and high purpose to their work. The liberal education which they have enjoyed has developed and strengthened the ideals which have ennobled their lives, and these ideals the teacher is interpreting and fixing in the minds of the youths who form the school constituency. The colored schools of St. Louis whose teaching force is almost wholly colored, are perhaps at once the arena for the display of the possibilities of the capable Negro teacher, and his power to direct and mould the rising generation of colored youth in an environment of contending forces, such as large cities constantly present. The Kindergarten School, which is a considerable feature in educational circles in St. Louis, attracts women of rare equipment, who have done great credit to themselves, their profession and their race.

There are many well to do Negroes in St. Louis who occupy and own beautiful homes, presided over by wives and mothers, who, because of intelligence, wisely rear and direct the trend of their own children, and are by direct effort raising the moral standard in the community about them. They have gone freely into philanthropic work, evincing the broad spirit which their own opportunities for self improvement have developed, and growing along side is the feeling of increasing responsibility to undertake the tasks of assisting the unfortunate by establishing and maintaining a hospital, an orphan's home, a day nursery, a home for women and girls who come to the city seeking employment, and a rescue home for girls. They also have in active operation temperance societies, with their many lines of endeavor, such as visiting the jail and work houses, conducting sewing schools in the slum districts, visiting the needy and sick. Besides there are many other means of extending charity that does not content itself with simply giving alms, but requires thought and self-sacrifice and devotion to purpose. The men of St. Louis are to be found in the professions and in independent business; they have their Young Men's Christian Associations, their debating societies, and preacher, teacher and layman join hands in the steady march forward, not unmindful of their laggard brothers in the rear.

If I were to go to the slums of St. Louis and relate the conditions there, I should indeed present a sorry picture, as well as a most unfair and one sided one. All cities have their slum districts where the wayward and vicious naturally gravitate. But slum districts simply emphasize the strange inequalities which exist under American civilization. The problems of poverty and crime and work are yet unsolved.

It may be said that the Negroes in St. Louis live mostly in unsanitary houses in unattractive neighborhoods. Conditions in the past and present have tended to this sort of segregation; but there is very definite evidence that there is and for some time has been a strong effort to overcome this tendency. That the effort has been successful has been again and again demonstrated, and today you find Negroes of education, refinement and means occupying homes owned by them in the most desirable parts of the city. There would without doubt be a great many more thus situated but for the antagonism that is met from residents in white neighborhoods, and the additional fact that from the masses of people only a comparatively small number emerge, because the masses of people are untrained for the merciless competitions of city life, and are ruthlessly restricted to the lower forms of labor.

In addition to all the favorable data at hand, much more might be added to the credit of the educated colored woman. The achievements of numberless individual women of nobly useful lives all over the country might be cited, but to bring to light the results of community improvement due to the influence of educated women, working together with their educated brothers, is perhaps an effective method of proving the case of the educated colored woman. At least I believe so.

LABOR AND EMPLOYMENT

Maria W. Stewart, "Lecture. Delivered at the Franklin Hall, Boston, September 21st, 1832. By Mrs. Maria W. Stewart."
The Liberator, **17 November 1832**

Why sit ye here and die? If we say we will go to a foreign land, the famine and the pestilence are there, and there we shall die. If we sit here, we shall die. Come let us plead our cause before the whites: if they save us alive, we shall live—and if they kill us, we shall but die.

Methinks I heard a spiritual interrogation—"Who shall go forward, and take off the reproach that is cast upon the people of color? Shall it be a woman?" And my heart made this reply—"If it is thy will, be it even so, Lord Jesus!"

I have heard much respecting the horrors of slavery; but may Heaven forbid that the generality of my color throughout these United States should experience any more of its horrors than to be a servant of servants, or hewers of wood and drawers of water![59] Tell us no more of southern slavery; for with few exceptions, although I may be very erroneous in my opinion, yet I consider our condition but little better than that.[60] Yet, after all, methinks there are no chains so galling as those that bind the soul, and exclude it from the vast field of useful and scientific knowledge. O, had I received the advantages of an early education, my ideas would, ere now, have expanded far and wide; but, alas! I possess nothing but moral capability—no teachings but the teachings of the Holy Spirit.

I have asked several individuals of my sex, who transact business for themselves, if providing our girls were to give them the most satisfactory references, they would not be willing to grant them an equal opportunity with others? Their reply has been—for their own part, they had no objection; but as it was not the custom, were they to take them into their employ, they would be in danger of losing the public patronage.

And such is the powerful force of prejudice. Let our girls possess whatever amiable qualities of soul they may; let their characters be fair and spotless as innocence itself; let their natural taste and ingenuity be what they may; it is impossible for scarce an individual of them to rise above the condition of servants. Ah! why is this cruel and unfeeling distinction? Is it merely because God has made our complexion to vary? If it be, O shame to soft, relenting humanity! "Tell it not in Gath! publish it not in the streets of Askelon!"[61] Yet, after all, methinks were the American free people of color to turn their attention more assiduously to moral worth and intellectual improvement, this would be the result: prejudice would gradually diminish, and the whites would be compelled to say, unloose those fetters!

> Though black their skins as shades of night
> Their hearts are pure—their souls are white.

Few white persons of either sex, who are calculated for anything else, are willing to spend their lives and bury their talents in performing mean, servile labor. And such is the horrible idea that I entertain respecting a life of servitude, that if I conceived of their [sic] being no possibility of my rising above the condition of servant, I would gladly hail death as a welcome messenger. O, horrible idea, indeed! to possess noble souls aspiring after *today?*

high and honorable acquirements, yet confined by the chains of ignorance and poverty to lives of continual drudgery and toil. Neither do I know of any who have enriched themselves by spending their lives as house-domestics, washing windows, shaking carpets, brushing boots, or tending upon gentlemen's tables. I can but die for expressing my sentiments: and I am as willing to die by the sword as the pestilence—for I am a true born American—your blood flows in my veins, and your spirit fires my breast.

I observed a piece in the *Liberator* a few months since, stating that the colonizationists had published a work respecting us, asserting that we were lazy and idle. I confute them on that point. Take us generally as a people, we are neither lazy nor idle; and considering how little we have to excite or stimulate us, I am almost astonished that there are so many industrious and ambitious ones to be found—although I acknowledge, with extreme sorrow, that there are some who never were and never will be serviceable to society. And have you not a similar class among yourselves?

Again—It was asserted that we were "a ragged set, crying for liberty." I reply to it, the whites have so long and so loudly proclaimed the theme of equal rights and privileges, that our souls have caught the flame also, ragged as we are. As far as our merit deserves, we feel a common desire to rise above the condition of servants and drudges. I have learnt, by bitter experience, that continual hard labor deadens the energies of the soul, and benumbs the faculties of the mind; the ideas become confined, the mind barren, and, like the scorching sands of Arabia, produces nothing—or like the uncultivated soil, brings forth thorns and thistles.

Again, continual and hard labor irritates our tempers and sours our dispositions; the whole system becomes worn out with toil and fatigue; nature herself becomes almost exhausted, and we care but little whether we live or die. It is true, that the free people of color throughout these United States are neither bought nor sold, nor under the lash of the cruel driver; many obtain a comfortable support; but few, if any, have an opportunity of becoming rich and independent; and the enjoyments we most pursue are as unprofitable to us as the spider's web or the floating bubbles that vanish into air. As servants, we are respected; but let us presume to aspire any higher, our employer regards us no longer. And were it not that the King eternal has declared that Ethiopia shall stretch forth her hands unto God,[62] I should indeed despair.

I do not consider it derogatory, my friends, for persons to live out to service. There are many whose inclination leads them to aspire no higher; —and I would highly commend the performance of almost anything for an honest livelihood; but where constitutional strength is wanting, labor of this kind, in its mildest form, is painful. And doubtless many are the prayers that

130

have ascended to Heaven from Afric's daughters for strength to perform their work. Oh, many are the tears that have been shed for the want of that strength! Most of our color have dragged out a miserable existence of servitude from the cradle to the grave. And what literary acquirement can be made, or useful knowledge derived, from either maps, books, or charts, by those who continually drudge from Monday morning until Sunday noon? O, ye fairer sisters, whose hands are never soiled, whose nerves and muscles are never strained, go learn by experience! Had we had the opportunity that you have had, to improve our moral and mental faculties, what would have hindered our intellects from being as bright, and our manners from being as dignified as yours? Had it been our lot to have been nursed in the lap of affluence and ease, and to have basked beneath the smiles and sunshine of fortune, should we not have naturally supposed that we were never made to toil? And why are not our forms as delicate, and our constitutions as slender, as yours? Is not the workmanship as curious and complete? Have pity upon us, have pity upon us, O ye who have hearts to feel for other's woes; for the hand of God has touched us. Owing to the disadvantages under which we labor, there are many flowers among us that are

> —born to bloom unseen,
> And waste their fragrance on the desert air.[63]

My beloved brethren, as Christ has died in vain for those who will not accept his offered mercy, so will it be vain for the advocates of freedom to spend their breath in our behalf, unless with united hearts and souls you make some mighty efforts to raise your sons and daughters from the horrible state of servitude and degradation in which they are placed. It is upon you that woman depends; she can do but little besides using her influence; and it is for her sake and yours that I have come forward and made myself a hissing and a reproach among the people;[64] for I am also one of the wretched and miserable daughters of the descendants of fallen Africa. Do you ask, —Why are you wretched and miserable? I reply, look at many of the most worthy and most interesting of us doomed to spend our lives in gentlemen's kitchens. Look at our young men, smart, active and energetic, with souls filled with ambitious fire; if they look forward, alas! what are their prospects? They can be nothing but the humblest laborers, on account of their dark complexions; hence many of them lose their ambition, and become worthless. Look at our middle-aged men, clad in their rusty plaids and coats;—in winter, every cent they earn goes to buy their wood and pay their rents; the poor wives also toil beyond their strength, to help support their families. Look at our aged sires, whose heads are whitened with the

131

frosts of seventy winters, with their old wood-saws on their backs. Alas, what keeps us so? Prejudice, ignorance and poverty. But ah! methinks our oppression is soon to come to an end; yea, before the Majesty of heaven, our groans and cries have reached the ears of the Lord of Sabaoth.[65] As the prayers and tears of Christians will avail the finally impenitent nothing; neither will the prayers and tears of the friends of humanity avail us anything, unless we possess a spirit of virtuous emulation within our breasts. Did the pilgrims, when they first landed on these shores, quietly compose themselves and say, "The Britons have all the money and all the power, and we must continue their servants forever?" Did they sluggishly sigh and say, "Our lot is hard—the Indians own the soil, and we cannot cultivate it?" No —they first made powerful efforts to raise themselves, and then God raised up those illustrious patriots, Washington and Lafayette, to assist and defend them. And, my brethren, have you made a powerful effort? Have you prayed the legislature for mercy's sake to grant you all the rights and privileges of free citizens, that your daughters may rise to that degree of respectability which true merit deserves, and your sons above the servile situations which most of them fill?

Lucy Parsons, "Mrs. Parson's Lecture [I am an anarchist...]." *The Kansas City Journal*, 21 December 1886

Kump's hall was packed to its utmost capacity last night by anarchists, Knights of Labor,[66] workingmen, loafers and those drawn thither by curiosity. Mrs. Lucy Parsons, wife of the condemned anarchist, A.R. Parsons, had been announced to speak in the hall at 8 o'clock, and promptly at the hour she stepped upon the platform. Her appearance was the signal for uproarious applause, which continued for a few minutes. Dr. William H. Hammond presided over the meeting and introduced the speaker. "I am an anarchist [...] I suppose you came here, the most of you, to see what a real, live anarchist looks like. I suppose some of you expected to see me with a bomb in one hand and a flaming torch in the other, but are disappointed at seeing neither. If such has been your ideas regarding an anarchist, you deserved to be disappointed. Anarchists are peaceable, law abiding people. What do anarchists mean when they speak of anarchy? Webster gives the term two definitions—chaos and the state of being without political rule. We cling to the latter definition. Our enemies hold that we believe only in the former.

"Do you wonder why there are anarchists in this country, in this great land of liberty, as you love to call it? Go to New York. Go through the byways and alleys of that great city. Count the myriads starving; count the multiplied thousands who are homeless; number those who work harder than slaves and live on less and have fewer comforts than the meanest slaves. You will be dumbfounded by your discoveries, you who have paid no attention to these poor, save as objects of charity and commiseration [sic]. They are not objects of charity, they are the victims of the rank injustice that permeates the system of government, and of political economy that holds sway from the Atlantic to the Pacific. Its oppression, the misery it causes, the wretchedness it gives birth to, are found to a greater extent in New York than elsewhere. In New York, where not many days ago two governments united in unveiling a statue of liberty, where a hundred bands played that hymn of liberty, 'The Marseillaise.' But almost its equal is found among the miners of the West, who dwell in squalor and wear rags, that the capitalists, who control the earth that should be free to all, may add still further to their millions! Oh, there are plenty of reasons for the existence of anarchists.

"But in Chicago they do not think anarchists have any right to exist at all. They want to hang them there, lawfully or unlawfully. You have heard of a certain Haymarket meeting. You have heard of a bomb. You have heard of arrests and of succeeding arrests effected by detectives.[67] Those detectives! There is a set of men—nay, beasts—for you! Pinkerton detectives! They would do anything. I feel sure capitalists wanted a man to throw that bomb at the Haymarket meeting and have the anarchists blamed for it. Pinkerton could have accomplished it for him. You have heard a great deal about bombs. You have heard that the anarchists said lots about dynamite. You have been told that Lingg made bombs. He violated no law. Dynamite bombs can kill, can murder, so can Gatling guns. Suppose that bomb had been thrown by an anarchist. The constitution says there are certain inalienable rights, among which are a free press, free speech and free assemblage. The citizens of this great land are given by the constitution the right to repel the unlawful invasion of those rights. The meeting at Haymarket square was a peaceable meeting. Suppose, when an anarchist saw the police arrive on the scene, with murder in their eyes, determined to break up that meeting, suppose he had thrown that bomb; he would have violated no law. That will be the verdict of your children. Had I been there, had I seen those murderous police approach, had I heard that insolent command to disperse, had I heard Fielden say, 'Captain, this is a peaceable meeting,' had I seen the liberties of my countrymen trodden under foot, I would have flung the bomb myself. I would have violated no law, but would have upheld the constitution.

"If the anarchists had planned to destroy the city of Chicago and to massacre the police, why was it they had only two or three bombs in hand? Such was not their intention. It was a peaceable meeting. Carter Harrison, the mayor of Chicago, was there. He said it was a quiet meeting. He told Bonfield to send the police to their different beats. I do not stand here to gloat over the murder of those policemen. I despise murder. But when a ball from the revolver of a policeman kills it is as much murder as when death results from a bomb.

"The police rushed upon that meeting as it was about to disperse. Mr. Simonson talked to Bonfield about the meeting. Bonfield said he wanted to do the anarchists up. Parsons went to the meeting. He took his wife, two ladies and his two children along. Toward the close of the meeting, he said, 'I believe it is going to rain. Let us adjourn to Zeph's hall.' Fielden said he was about through with his speech and would close it at once. The people were beginning to scatter about, a thousand of the more enthusiastic still lingered in spite of the rain. Parsons, and those who accompanied him started for home. They had gone as far as the Desplaine's street police station when they saw the police start at a double quick. Parsons stopped to see what was the trouble. Those 200 policemen rushed on to do the anarchists up. Then we went on. I was in Zeph's hall when I heard that terrible detonation. It was heard around the world. Tyrants trembled and felt there was something wrong.

"The discovery of dynamite and its use by anarchists is a repetition of history. When gun-powder was discovered, the feudal system was at the height of its power. Its discovery and use made the middle classes. Its first discharge sounded the death knell of the feudal system. The bomb at Chicago sounded the downfall of the wage system of the nineteenth century. Why?

Because I know no intelligent people will submit to despotism. The first means the diffusion of power. I tell no man to use it. But it was the achievement of science, not of anarchy, and would do for the masses. I suppose the press will say I belched forth treason. If I have violated any law, arrest me, give me a trial, and the proper punishment, but let the next anarchist that comes along ventilate his views without hindrance.

"Well, the bomb exploded, the arrests were made and then came that great judicial farce, beginning on June 21. The jury was impaneled. Is there a Knight of Labor here? Then know that a Knight of Labor was not considered competent enough to serve on that jury. 'Are you a Knight of Labor?' 'Have you any sympathy with labor organizations?' were the questions asked each talisman. If an affirmative answer was given, the talisman was bounced. It was not are you a Mason, a Knight Templar? O, no! [Great applause.] I see you read the signs of the times by that expression. Hangman Gary, miscalled judge, ruled that if a man was prejudiced against the defendants, it did not incapacitate him for serving on the jury. For such a man, said Hangman Gary, would pay closer attention to the law and evidence and would be more apt to render a verdict for the defense. Is there a lawyer here? If there is he knows such a ruling is without precedent and contrary to all law, reason or common sense.

"In the heat of patriotism the American citizen sometimes drops a tear for the nihilist of Russia. They say the nihilist can't get justice, that he is condemned without trial. How much more should he weep for his next door neighbor, the anarchist, who is given the form of trial under such a ruling.

"There were 'squealers' introduced as witnesses for the prosecution. There were three of them. Each and every one was compelled to admit they had been purchased and intimidated by the prosecution. Yet Hangman Gary held their evidence as competent. It came out in the trial that the Haymarket meeting was the result of no plot, but was caused in this wise. The day before the wage slaves in McCormick's factory had struck for eight hours labor, McCormick, from his luxurious office, with one stroke of the pen by his idle, be-ringed fingers, turned 40,000 men out of employment. Some gathered and stoned the factory. Therefore they were anarchists, said the press. But anarchists are not fools; only fools stone buildings. The police were sent out and they killed six wage slaves. You didn't know that. The capitalistic press kept it quiet, but it made a great fuss over the killing of some policemen. Then these crazy anarchists, as they are called, thought a meeting ought to be held to consider the killing of six brethren and to discuss the eight hour movement. The meeting was held. It was peaceable. When Bonfield ordered the police to charge those peaceable anarchists, he hauled down the American flag and should have been shot on the spot.

"While this judicial farce was going on the red and black flags were brought into court, to prove that the anarchists threw the bomb. They were placed on the walls and hung there, awful specters before the jury. What does the black flag mean? When a cablegram says it was carried through the streets of a European city it means that the people are suffering—that the men are out of work, the women starving, the children barefooted. But, you say, that is in Europe. How about America? The Chicago *Tribune* said there were 80,000 men in that city with nothing to do. Another authority said there were 10,000 barefooted children in midwinter. The police said hundreds had no place to sleep or warm. Then President Cleveland issued his Thanksgiving proclamation and the anarchists formed in procession and carried the black flag to show that these thousands had nothing for which to return thanks. When the Board of Trade, that gambling den, was dedicated by means of a banquet, $20 a plate, again the black flag was carried, to signify that there were thousands who couldn't enjoy a 2 cent meal.

"But the red flag, the horrible red flag, what does that mean? Not that the streets should run with gore, but that the same red blood coursed through the veins of the whole human race. It meant the brotherhood of man. When the red flag floats over the world the idle shall be called to work. There will be an end of prostitution for women, of slavery for man, of hunger for children.

"Liberty has been named anarchy. If this verdict is carried out it will be the death knell of America's liberty. You and your children will be slaves. You will have liberty if you can pay for it. If this verdict is carried out, place the flag of our country at half mast and write on every fold, 'shame.' Let our flag be trailed in the dust. Let the children of workingmen place laurels in the brow of these modern heroes, for they committed no crime. Break the two fold yoke. Bread is freedom and freedom is bread."

The address was frequently interrupted with applause and cheers. At the conclusion, the following resolutions were adopted by the meeting:

"Be it resolved by this assembly that we uncompromisingly condemn the great judicial farce of Chicago known as the anarchist trial, and in order to have the remnants of the fair fame of American justice, we demand a new trial for the convicted men now incarcerated in Cook county jail, Illinois.

"Resolved, further, That we condemn the dangerous and treasonable precedent inaugurated at the Haymarket meeting of police interference in peaceable meetings, and maintain that free speech and a free press are the first guarantees of liberty."

A collection was taken up for the families of the condemned anarchists, and a good business was done in the sale of the photographs and the speeches of the anarchists. Mrs. Parsons will speak at Omaha to-night.

Nannie Helen Burroughs, Corresponding Secretary, Woman's Convention Auxiliary to National Baptist Convention, Louisville, Ky.[68] "The Colored Woman and Her Relation to the Domestic Problem." *The United Negro: His Problems and His Progress. Containing the Addresses and Proceedings of the Negro Young People's Christian and Educational Congress, Held August 6–11, 1902.* **Ed. I. Garland Penn and J.W.E. Bowen. Atlanta: D.E. Luther, 1902. 324–29**

You ask what is meant by the domestic problem. It is that peculiar condition under which women are living and laboring without the knowledge of the secrets of thrift, or of true scientific methods in which the mind has been awakened, and hands made capable thereby to give the most efficient services. It is a condition of indifference on the part of our working women as to their needs as to how we may so dignify labor that our services may become indispensable on the one hand and Negro sentiment will cease to array itself against the "working girls" on the other hand. It is a question as to how we may receive for our services, compensation commensurate with the work done. The solution of this problem will be the prime factor in the salvation of Negro womanhood, whose salvation must be attained before the so-called race problem can be solved.

The training of Negro women is absolutely necessary, not only for their own salvation and the salvation of the race, but because the hour in which we live demands it. If we lose sight of the demands of the hour we blight our hope of progress. The subject of domestic science has crowded itself upon us, and unless we receive it, master it and be wise, the next ten years will so revolutionize things that we will find our women without the where-with to support themselves.

Untrained hands, however willing, will find themselves unwelcomed in the humblest homes. We may be careless about this matter of equipping our women for work in the homes, but if we are to judge from the wonderful progress that recent years has brought in the world of domestic labor we must admit that steps must be taken, and that at once, to train the hands of Negro women for better services and their hearts for purer living. All through the North white imported help is taking the place of Negro help. Where we once held forth without a thought of change we find our places filled by those of other races and climes. The people who had to have servants declared that they wanted intelligent, refined, trained help, and in the majority of cases we were not ready to give them what they needed. Our intelligent Negroes, even though they may not have bread to eat, in many cases shun service work, when the fact is evident that ignorant help is not wanted by the best class of people in this country. The more thorough and intelligent the help the better.

What will this crowding from service mean to Negro women? It will mean their degradation. Our women will sink beneath the undermining influences of insidious sloth. Industry is one of the noblest virtues of any race. The people who scorn and frown upon her must die. While little heed may have been paid to the demand for better help and the supplanting of Negro servants by Irish, Dagoes and English may have been unnoticed by all of us, yet it is time for the leaders to sound the alarm, ere we are root-ed from the places we have held for over two centuries. The time will come when we will stand as helpless as babes, as dependent as beggars, without the wherewith to sustain life, unless we meet the demands squarely.

Our women have worked as best they could without making any improvements and thus developing the service into a profession, and in that way make the calling more desirable from a standpoint of being lifted from a mere drudgery, as well as from the standpoint of compensation received.

The race whose women have not learned that industry and self-respect are the only guarantees of a true character will find itself bound by ignorance and violence or fettered with chains of poverty. There is a growing tendency among us to almost abhor women who work at service for a living. If we hold in contempt women who are too honest, industrious and independent, women whose sense of pride is too exalted to be debased by idleness, we will find our women becoming more and more slothful in this matter of supporting themselves. Our "high-toned" notions as to the kind of positions educated people ought to fill have caused many women who can not get anything to do after they come out of school to loaf rather than work for an honest living, declaring to themselves and acting it before others, that they were not educated to live among pots and pans. None of us may have been educated for that purpose, but educated women without work and the wherewith to support themselves and who have declared in their souls that they will not stoop to toil are not worth an ounce more to the race than ignorant women who have made the same declarations. Educated loafers will bear as much watching as ignorant ones. When the nobility of labor is magnified, and those who do labor respected more because of their real worth to the race, we will find a less number trying to escape the brand, "servant girl." We are not less honorable if we are servants. Fidelity to duty rather than the grade of one's occupation is the true measure of character. Every gentle virtue will go down before a people and their endeavors come to naught when they forget that the foundation stone of prosperity is toil. What matters it if we do rise from pots and pans? They tell us we came from apes and baboons, and we have made it this far. Further, if God could take a crop of apes or baboons and make beings like us He is God indeed, and we can trust Him to raise us from servants to queens. If we did come from these ungainly animals of the four-footed family, we got here nearly as soon as the people who didn't have so far to come.

What matters it if our women, by honest toil, make their way from the kitchen to places of respect and trust in the walks of life? Are they less honorable because they have been servants? Are not the women who by thrift and economy, with everything operating against them in their own race, and low wages, that mighty power before whom the poor of earth must bow, struggling for mastery, work their way to the front, more deserving of praise, more worthy of recognition and respect than scores of "parlor orna-ments" who, by methods, have maintained some social standing, and hold in contempt the "unfortunate servant girl?" There are women at service who would eat their meals off the heads of barrels or dress after the fash-ion of John the Baptist in the wilderness before they would sacrifice their high-toned moral character, simply to shine in the social world by virtue of their idleness and ability to dress well. It is not the depth from which we come, but the heights to which we soar. The incomparable water lily grows out of the slime of black lagoons, and heaven itself consists not in location but in nobility of the character of its population. It matters not where nor how lowly the station, pursue the unswerving way of industry and victory or defeat will decide our fitness for the places we seek.

Again, if we scorn women who have character and are honest enough to work to preserve it and accept into our company women who have no character and will not work to secure it, are we making the race any more moral? This pulling aside of our silken skirts at the approach of the servant women has materially affected the morals of Negro women. How many of them have abandoned honest labor in which they could have given char-acter and tone to the service rendered by our women, and to satisfy their ambitions for social recognition have resorted to idleness in order to gain the smiles of a class among us who will receive any woman who can dress well without working at service to pay for it.

Scorn the servant women? No, never. Rather scorn that class of women who have resolved not to work and hang out of doors and windows, hold up corners, or keep the neighborhood astir with demoralizing gossip. Scorn young Negro women who flirt and loiter about the streets at the sacrifice of their good name and the name of Negro womanhood. But honor and praise to the women who have learned that all labor is just as honorable, just as honest, as the person who is doing it. Have not all of us been servants? God made us all servants the very day He dismissed Adam from Eden. "By the sweat of thy brow shalt thou eat bread."[69] What mean these women who are eating bread and are not sweating, either, by scorn-ing the women who are obeying the divine injunction?

Young women from rural districts flock to great cities like New York, Chicago, Philadelphia, Boston, Baltimore and Washington in search of employment. Not only are they unprepared to serve but are woefully igno-rant of the new social conditions into which they must be thrown. The white women in these large cities conduct guilds and other organizations that employ attendants to meet the trains and be on the alert for the white servant class that may be coming in seeking work or homes. Christian homes and churches are pointed out to the newcomers. The strong arms of Christian women are thrown about them, and while they are far from home and loved ones, they have the assurance that they have friends who will be ever mindful of them and their interests.

What are the results of this wholesale abandonment of working women? Nine cases out of ten the girls who come from the country fall into the hands of ill-disposed Negro men or keepers of some "back way boarding house" of the famous "furnished rooms" character. Thousands of our women are to-day in the clutches of men of our own race who are not worth the cost of their existence. They dress well and live on the earnings of servant girls. Negro men can aid us in the solution of the problem by becoming self-supporting rather than live on the earnings of women who often get less than ten dollars per month. Not only does this increase idleness among us but weakens the moral life of women. Negro women can help solve their own problem by applying to these lazy men Horace Greeley's doctrine, "Root hog or die."

The solution of the servant girl problem, then, can only be accomplished—first, by making it possible for these girls to overcome their ignorance, dishonesty and carelessness by establishing training classes and other moral agencies in these large cities and maintaining one or more first-class schools of domestic science. Second, by employers demanding the trained help from these classes or schools and paying wages in keeping with the ability of the servant to do the work. Third, by giving to women who work, time for recreation and self-improvement. This constant all-day "go" has made service a drudgery. If servants had hours for rest and improvement, like other laborers, they would come to their work with a freshness and intelligence that is now absent.

Emphasize the importance of preparation for service work. Let Negro women who are idle find work, stick to it and use it as a stepping stone to something better. Let us cease reaching over women who are servants and have character enough for queens to queens who haven't brains and character enough for servants. By becoming exponents of the blessed principles of honesty, cleanliness and industry, Negro women can bring dignity to service life, respect and trust to themselves and honor to the race. Then in deed and in truth we can mount up as with the wings of eagles, soar above the mountains of virtue and hide our heads among the stars. If anybody is to be scorned, scorn those women who will not honestly toil to raise themselves and are pulling us from the throne of honor and virtue.

Mary Church Terrell, "What it Means to Be Colored in the Capital of the United States." *The Independent*, 24 January 1907: 181–86

[The special interest in the present article rests in the fact that it describes conditions in Washington, a city governed solely by the United States Congress. It is our only city which represents the whole country. It lies between the two sections, North and South, and it has a very large negro population. The article is timely now that Senator Foraker has brought before the Senate the dismissal without honor of the negro battalion. The writer is a colored woman of much culture and recognized standing. —EDITOR.]

Washington, D.C., has been called "The Colored Man's Paradise." Whether this sobriquet was given to the national capital in bitter irony by a member of the handicapped race, as he reviewed some of his own persecutions and rebuffs, or whether it was given immediately after the war by an ex-slave-holder who for the first time in his life saw colored people walking about like freemen, minus the overseer and his whip, history saith not. It is certain that it would be difficult to find a worse misnomer for Washington than "The Colored Man's Paradise" if so prosaic a consideration as veracity is to determine the appropriateness of a name.

For fifteen years I have resided in Washington, and while it was far from being a paradise for colored people, when I first touched these shores it has been doing its level best ever since to make conditions for us intolerable. As a colored woman I might enter Washington any night, a stranger in a strange land, and walk miles without finding a place to lay my head. Unless I happened to know colored people who live here or ran across a chance acquaintance who could recommend a colored boarding-house to me, I should be obliged to spend the entire night wandering about. Indians, Chinamen, Filipinos, Japanese and representatives of any other dark race can find hotel accommodations, if they can pay for them. The colored man alone is thrust out of the hotels of the national capital like a leper.

As a colored woman I may walk from the Capitol to the White House, ravenously hungry and abundantly supplied with money with which to purchase a meal, without finding a single restaurant in which I would be permitted to take a morsel of food, if it was patronized by white people, unless I were willing to sit behind a screen. As a colored woman I cannot visit the tomb of the Father of this country, which owes its very existence to the love of freedom in the human heart and which stands for equal opportunity to all, without being forced to sit in the Jim Crow[70] section of an electric car which starts from the very heart of the city—midway between the Capitol and the White House. If I refuse thus to be humiliated, I am cast into jail and forced to pay a fine for violating the Virginia laws. Every hour in the day Jim Crow cars filled with colored people, many of whom are intelligent and well to do, enter and leave the national capital.

As a colored woman I may enter more than one white church in Washington without receiving that welcome which as a human being I have a right to expect in the sanctuary of God. Sometimes the color blindness of the usher takes on that peculiar form which prevents a dark face from making any impression whatsoever upon his retina, so that it is impossible for him to see colored people at all. If he is not so afflicted, after keeping a colored man or woman waiting a long time, he will ungraciously show these dusky Christians who have had the temerity to thrust themselves into a temple where only the fair of face are expected to worship God to a seat in the rear, which is named in honor of a certain personage, well known in this country, and commonly called Jim Crow.

Unless I am willing to engage in a few menial occupations, in which the pay for my services would be very poor, there is no way for me to earn an honest living, if I am not a trained nurse or a dressmaker or can secure a position as teacher in the public schools, which is exceedingly difficult to do. It matters not what my intellectual attainments may be or how great is the need of the services of a competent person, if I try to enter many of the numerous vocations in which my white sisters are allowed to engage, the door is shut in my face.

From one Washington theater I am excluded altogether. In the remainder certain seats are set aside for colored people, and it is almost impossible to secure others. I once telephoned to the ticket seller just before a matinee and asked if a neat-appearing colored nurse would be allowed to sit in the parquet with her little white charge, and the answer rushed quickly and positively thru the receiver—NO. When I remonstrated a bit and told him that in some of the theaters colored nurses were allowed to sit with the white children for whom they cared, the ticket seller told me that in Washington it was very poor policy to employ colored nurses, for they were excluded from many places where white girls would be allowed to take children for pleasure.

If I possess artistic talent, there is not a single art school of repute which will admit me. A few years ago a colored woman who possessed great talent submitted some drawings to the Corcoran Art School, of Washington, which were accepted by the committee of awards, who sent her a ticket entitling her to a course in this school. But when the committee discovered that the young woman was colored they declined to admit her, and told her that if they had suspected that her drawings had been made by a colored woman they would not have examined them at all. The efforts of Frederick Douglass and a lawyer of great repute who took a keen interest in the affair were unavailing. In order to cultivate her talent this young woman was forced to leave her comfortable home in Washington and incur the expense of going to New York. Having entered the Woman's Art School of Cooper Union, she graduated with honor, and then went to Paris to continue her studies, where she achieved signal success and was complimented by some of the greatest living artists in France.

With the exception of the Catholic University, there is not a single white college in the national capital to which colored people are admitted, no matter how great their ability, how lofty their ambition, how unexceptionable their character or how great their thirst for knowledge may be.

A few years ago the Columbian Law School admitted colored students, but in deference to the Southern white students the authorities have decided to exclude them altogether.

Some time ago a young woman who had already attracted some attention in the literary world by her volume of short stories answered an advertisement which appeared in a Washington newspaper, which called for the services of a skilled stenographer and expert typewriter. It is unnecessary to state the reasons why a young woman whose literary ability was so great as that possessed by the one referred to should decide to earn money in this way. The applicants were requested to send specimens of their work and answer certain questions concerning their experience and their speed before they called in person. In reply to her application the young colored woman, who, by the way, is very fair and attractive indeed, received a letter from the firm stating that her references and experience were the most satisfactory that had been sent and requesting her to call. When she presented herself, there was some doubt in the mind of the man to whom she was directed concerning her racial pedigree, so he asked her point-blank whether she was colored or white. When she confessed the truth the merchant expressed great sorrow and deep regret that he could not avail himself of the services of so competent a person, but frankly admitted that employing a colored woman in his establishment in any except a menial position was simply out of the question.

Another young friend had an experience which, for some reasons, was still more disheartening and bitter than the one just mentioned. In order to secure lucrative employment she left Washington and went to New York. There she worked her way up in one of the largest dry goods stores till she was placed as saleswoman in the cloak department. Tired of being separated from her family she decided to return to Washington, feeling sure that, with her experience and her fine recommendation from the New York firm, she could easily secure employment. Nor was she overconfident, for the proprietor of one of the largest dry goods stores in her native city was glad to secure the services of a young woman who brought such hearty credentials from New York. She had not been in this store very long, however, before she called upon me one day and asked me to intercede with the proprietor in her behalf, saying that she had been discharged that afternoon because it had been discovered that she was colored. When I called upon my young friend's employer he made no effort to avoid the issue, as I feared he would. He did not say he had discharged the young saleswoman because she had not given satisfaction, as he might easily have done. On the contrary, he admitted without the slightest hesitation that the young woman he had just discharged was one of the best clerks he had ever had. In the cloak department, where she had been assigned, she had been a brilliant success, he said. "But I cannot keep Miss Smith in my employ," he concluded. "Are you not master of your own store?" I ventured to inquire. The proprietor of this store was a Jew, and I felt that it was particularly cruel, unnatural and cold-blooded for the representative of one oppressed and persecuted race to deal so harshly and unjustly with a member of another. I had intended to make this point when I decided to intercede for my young friend, but when I thought how a reference to the persecution of his own race would wound his feelings, the words froze on my lips. "When I first heard your friend was colored," he explained, "I did not believe it and said so to the clerks who made the statement. Finally, the girls who had been most pronounced in their opposition to working in a store with a colored girl came to me in a body and threatened to strike. 'Strike away,' said I, 'your places will be easily filled.' Then they started on another tack. Delegation after delegation began to file down to my office, some of the women my very best customers, to protest against my employing a colored girl. Moreover, they threatened to boycott my store if I did not discharge her at once. Then it became a question of bread and butter and I yielded to the inevitable—that's all. Now," said he, concluding, "if I lived in a great, cosmopolitan city like New York, I should do as I pleased, and refuse to discharge a girl simply because she was colored." But I thought of a similar incident that happened in New York. I remembered that a colored woman, as fair as a lily and as beautiful as a Madonna, who was the head saleswoman in a large department store in New York, had been discharged, after she had held this position for years, when the proprietor accidentally discovered that a fatal drop of African blood was percolating somewhere thru her veins.

Not only can colored women secure no employment in the Washington stores, department and otherwise, except as menials, and such positions, of course, are few, but even as customers they are not infrequently treated with discourtesy both by the clerks and the proprietor himself. Following the trend of the times, the senior partner of the largest and best department store in Washington, who originally hailed from Boston, once the home of Wm. Lloyd Garrison, Wendell Phillips and Charles Sumner, if my memory serves me right, decided to open a restaurant in his store. Tired and hungry after her morning's shopping a colored school teacher, whose relation to her African progenitors is so remote as scarcely to be discernible to the naked eye, took a seat at one of the tables in the restaurant of this Boston store. After sitting unnoticed a long time the colored teacher asked a waiter who passed her by if she would not take her order. She was quickly informed that colored people could not be served in that restaurant and was obliged to leave in confusion and shame, much to the amusement of the waiters and the guests, who had noticed the incident. Shortly after that a teacher in Howard University, one of the best schools for colored youth in the country, was similarly insulted in the restaurant of the same store.

In one of the Washington theaters from which colored people are excluded altogether, members of the race have been viciously assaulted several times, for the proprietor well knows that colored people have no redress for such discriminations against them in the District courts. Not long ago a colored clerk in one of the departments who looks more like his paternal ancestors who fought for the lost cause than his grandmothers, who were victims of the peculiar institution, bought a ticket for the parquet of this theater in which colored people are nowhere welcome, for himself and mother, whose complexion is a bit swarthy. The usher refused to allow the young man to take the seats for which his tickets called and tried to snatch from him the coupons. A scuffle ensued and both mother and son were ejected by force. A suit was brought against the proprietor and the damages awarded the injured man and his mother amounted to the munificent sum of one cent. One of the teachers in the Colored High School received similar treatment in the same theater.

Not long ago one of my little daughter's bosom friends figured in one of the most pathetic instances of which I have ever heard. A gentleman who is very fond of children promised to take six little girls in his neighborhood to a matinee. It happened that he himself and five of his little friends were so fair that they easily passed muster, as they stood in judgment before the ticket-seller and the ticket taker. Three of the little girls were sisters, two of whom were very fair and the other a bit brown. Just as this little girl, who happened to be last in the procession, went by the ticket taker, that argus-eyed sophisticated gentleman detected something which caused a deep, dark frown to mantle his brow and he did not allow her to pass. "I guess you have made a mistake," he called to the host of this theater party. "Those little girls," pointing to the fair ones, "may be admitted, but this one," designating the brown one, "can't." But the colored man was quite equal to the emergency. Fairly frothing at the mouth with anger he asked the ticket taker what he meant, what he was trying to insinuate about that particular little girl. "Do you mean to tell me," he shouted in rage, "that I must go clear to the Philippine Islands to bring this child to the United States and then I can't take her to the theater in the National Capital?" The little ruse succeeded brilliantly, as he knew it would. "Beg your pardon," said the ticket taker, "don't know what I was thinking about. Of course she can go in."

"What was the matter with me this afternoon, mother?" asked the little brown girl innocently, when she mentioned the affair at home. "Why did the man at the theater let my two sisters and the other girls in and try to keep me out?" In relating this incident, the child's mother told me her little girl's question, which showed such blissful ignorance of the depressing, cruel conditions which confronted her, completely unnerved her for a time.

Altho white and colored teachers are under the same Board of Education and the system for the children of both races is said to be uniform, prejudice against the colored teachers in the public schools is manifested in a variety of ways. From 1870 to 1900 there was a colored superintendent at the head of the colored schools. During all that time the directors of the cooking, sewing, physical culture, manual training, music and art departments were colored people. Six years ago a change was inaugurated. The colored superintendent was legislated out of office and the directorships, without a single exception, were taken from colored teachers and given to the whites. There was no complaint about the work done by the colored directors no more than is heard about every officer in every school. The directors of the art and physical culture departments were particularly fine. Now, no matter how competent or superior the colored teachers in our public schools may be, they know that they can never rise to the height of a directorship, can never hope to be more than an assistant and receive the meager salary therefor, unless the present regime is radically changed.

Not long ago one of the most distinguished kindergartners in the country came to deliver a course of lectures in Washington. The colored teachers were eager to attend, but they could not buy the coveted privilege for love or money. When they appealed to the director of kindergartens, they were told that the expert kindergartner had come to Washington under the auspices of private individuals, so that she could not possibly have them admitted. Realizing what a loss colored teachers had sustained in being deprived of the information and inspiration which these lectures afforded, one of the

white teachers volunteered to repeat them as best she could for the benefit of her colored co-laborers for half the price she herself had paid and the
proposition was eagerly accepted by some.

Strenuous efforts are being made to run Jim Crow street cars in the national capital. "Resolved, that a Jim Crow law should be adopted and enforced
in the District of Columbia," was the subject of a discussion engaged in last
January by the Columbian Debating Society of the George Washington
University in our national capital, and the decision was rendered in favor
of the affirmative. Representative Heflin, of Alabama, who introduced a bill
providing for Jim Crow street cars in the District of Columbia last winter,
has just received a letter from the president of the East Brookland Citizens'
Association "indorsing the movement for separate street cars and sincerely
hoping that you will be successful in getting this enacted into a law as soon
as possible." Brookland is a suburb of Washington.

The colored laborer's path to a decent livelihood is by no means smooth.
Into some of the trades unions here he is admitted, while from others he is
excluded altogether. By the union men this is denied, altho I am personally acquainted with skilled workmen who tell me they are not admitted
into the unions because they are colored. But even when they are allowed
to join the unions they frequently derive little benefit, owing to certain
tricks of the trade. When the word passes round that help is needed and
colored laborers apply, they are often told by the union officials that they
have secured all the men they needed, because the places are reserved for
white men, until they have been provided with jobs, and colored men must
remain idle, unless the supply of white men is too small.

I am personally acquainted with one of the most skilful laborers in the
hard-ware business in Washington. For thirty years he has been working for
the same firm. He told me he could not join the union and that his
employer had been almost forced to discharge him, because the union
men threatened to boycott his store if he did not. If another man could
have been found at the time to take his place he would have lost his job,
he said. When no other human being can bring a refractory chimney or
stove to its senses, this colored man is called upon as the court of last
appeal. If he fails to subdue it, it is pronounced a hopeless case at once. And
yet this expert workman receives much less for his services than do white
men who cannot compare with him in skill.

And so I might go on citing instance after instance to show the variety
of ways in which our people are sacrificed on the altar of prejudice in the
Capital of the United States and how almost insurmountable are the obstacles which block his path to success. Early in life, many a colored youth is

so appalled by the helplessness and the hopelessness of his situation in this country that in a sort of stoical despair he resigns himself to his fate. "What is the good of our trying to acquire an education? We can't all be preachers, teachers, doctors and lawyers. Besides those professions there is almost nothing for colored people to do but engage in the most menial occupations, and we do not need an education for that." More than once such remarks, uttered by young men and women in our public schools who possess brilliant intellects, have wrung my heart.

It is impossible for any white person in the United States, no matter how sympathetic and broad, to realize what life would mean to him if his incentive to effort were suddenly snatched away. To the lack of incentive to effort, which is the awful shadow under which we live, may be traced the wreck and ruin of scores of colored youth. And surely nowhere in the world do oppression and persecution based solely on the color of the skin appear more hateful and hideous than in the capital of the United States, because the chasm between the principles upon which this Government was founded, in which it still professes to believe, and those which are daily practiced under the protection of the flag, yawns so wide and deep.

Addie Hunton, "Employment of Colored Women in Chicago From a Study Made by the Chicago School of Civics and Philanthropy."[71] *The Crisis* 1.3 (January 1911): 24-25

In considering the field of employment for colored women, the professional women must be discussed separately. They admit fewer difficulties and put a brave face on the matter, but in any case their present position was gained only after a long struggle. The education is the less difficult part. The great effort is to get the work after having prepared themselves for it. The Negro woman, like her white sister, is constantly forced to choose between a lower wage or no work. The pity is that her own people do not know the colored girl needs their help nor realize how much they could do for her.

Two of the musicians found the struggle too hard and were compelled to leave Chicago. One girl of twenty-three, a graduate of the Chicago Conservatory of Music, is playing in a low concert hall in one of the worst sections of the city, from 8 in the evening till 4 in the morning. Her wages are $18 a week, and with this she supports a father and mother and younger sister.

There are from fifteen to twenty colored teachers in the public schools of Chicago. This information was obtained from the office of the superintendent, where it was said no record was kept of the number of colored teachers. When they are given such a place they are always warned that they are likely to have difficulty. As a rule they are in schools where the majority of the children are Negroes. They are in all the grades, but they say that their opportunities for promotion are equal to those of white women. Indeed, they say that there are two places where they are not discriminated against because of their color. One is in the public schools, the other is under the Civil Service Commission.

However, the professional women do not have the greatest difficulty. The real barriers are met by the women who have had only an average education—girls who have finished high school, or perhaps only the eighth grade. These girls, if they were white, would find employment at clerical and office work in Chicago's department stores, mail order houses and wholesale stores. But these positions are absolutely closed to the Negro girl. She has no choice but housework.

When the object of the inquiry was explained to one woman she said: "Why, no one wants a Negro to work for him. I'll show you—look in the newspaper." And she produced a paper with its columns of advertisements for help wanted. "See, not one person in this whole city has asked for a Negro to work for him."

A great many of the colored women find what they call "day work" most satisfactory. This means from eight to nine hours a day at some kind of housework, cleaning, washing, ironing or dusting. This the Negro women prefer to regular positions as maids, because it allows them to go at night to their families. The majority of the women who do this work receive $1.50, with 10 cents extra for carfare. There was a higher grade of day work for which the pay was $2 a day besides the carfare. This included the packing of trunks, washing of fine linen and lace curtains, and even some mending.

The records of the South Side Free Employment Agency showed that the wages of colored women were uniformly lower than those of white women. Of course, there is no way of judging of ability by records, but where the white cooks received $8 per week the Negro cooks were paid $7, and where the white maids received $6, sometimes, but not as frequently as in the case of the cooks, the Negro maid received less. One dollar and a half was paid for "day work." At the colored employment agency which is run in connection with the Frederick Douglass Center[72] they have many more requests for maids than they have girls to fill the places. Good places with high wages are sometimes offered, but the girls are more and more demanding "day work" and refusing to work by the week. At the South Side Free Employment Agency during the months of January, February and March of this year forty-two positions for colored women were found.[73]

These forty-two positions were filled by thirty-six women, some of them coming back to the office two or three times during the three months. The superintendent said it was difficult to find places for the colored women who applied, and they probably succeeded in placing only about 25 per cent of them. In the opinion of those finding the work for the girls in this office, the reason for the difficulties they encounter are the fact that they do not remain long in one place and have a general reputation for dishonesty. The fundamental cause of the discrimination by employers against them is racial prejudice either in the employer himself or in his customers.

One girl who has only a trace of colored blood was able to secure a position as salesgirl in a store. After she had been there a long time she asked for an increase in wages, such as had been allowed the white girls, but the request was refused and she was told that she ought to be thankful that they kept her at all.

In many cases, especially when the women were living alone, the earnings, plus the income from the lodgers, barely covered the rent. When they work by the day they rarely work more than four days a week. Sometimes the amount they gave as their weekly wage fell short of even paying the rent, but more often the rent was covered and a very small margin left to live on.

Such treatment has discouraged the Negro woman. She has accepted the conditions and seldom makes any real effort to get into other sorts of work. The twelfth question on the schedule, "What attempts have you made to secure other kinds of work in Chicago or elsewhere?" was usually answered by a question: "What's the use of trying to get work when you know you can't get it?"

The colored women are like white women in the same grade of life. They do not realize the need of careful training, and they do not appreciate the advantages of specialization in their work. But the Negro woman is especially handicapped, for she not only lacks training but must overcome the prejudice against her color. Of the 270 women interviewed, 43 per cent were doing some form of housework for wages, yet all evidence of conscious training was entirely lacking. This need must be brought home to them before they can expect any real advancement.

A peculiar problem presents itself in connection with the housework. Practically this is the only occupation open to Negro women, and it is also the only occupation where one is not expected to go home at night. This the Negroes insist on doing. They are accused of having no family feeling, yet the fact remains that they will accept a lower wage and live under far less advantageous conditions for the sake of being free at night. That is why the "day work" is so popular. Rather than live in some other person's home and get good wages for continued service, the colored woman prefers to live in this way. She will have a tiny room, go out as many days a week as she can get places, and pay for her room and part of her board out of her earnings, which sometimes amount to only $3 or $4.50 per week.

Occasionally laundry, sewing or hair work is done in their homes, but the day work is almost universally preferred.

Many of the Negroes are so nearly white that they can be mistaken for white girls, in which case they are able to secure very good positions and keep them as long as their color is not known.

One girl worked for a fellowship at the Art Institute. Her work was good and the place was promised her. In making out the papers she said Negro, when asked her nationality, to the great astonishment of the man in charge. He said he would have to look into the matter, but the girl did not get the fellowship.

A young man, son of a colored minister in the city, had a position in a business man's office, kept the books, collected rents, etc. He had a peculiar name, and one of the tenants remembered it in connection with the boy's father, who had all the physical characteristics of the Negro. The tenant made inquiries and reported the matter to the landlord, threatening to leave the building if he had to pay rent to a Negro. The boy was discharged.

A colored girl, who was very light colored, said that more than once she secured a place and the colored people themselves had told the employer he had a "Negro" working for him. The woman with whom she was living said: "It's true every time. The Negroes are their own worst enemies."

To summarize, the isolation which is forced upon the Negro, both in his social and his business life, constitutes one of the principal difficulties which he encounters. As far as the colored woman is concerned, as we have shown, the principal occupations which are open to her are domestic service and school teaching. This leaves a large number of women whose education has given them ambitions beyond housework, who are not fitted to compete with northern teachers and yet cannot obtain clerical work because they are Negroes. Certain fields in which there is apparently an opportunity for the colored women are little tried. For example, sewing is profitable and there is little feeling against the employment of Negro seamstresses, and yet few follow the dressmaking profession.

Without doubt, one fundamental reason for the difficulties the colored woman meets in seeking employment is her lack of industrial training. The white woman suffers from this also, but the colored woman doubly so. The most hopeful sign is the growing conviction on the part of the leading Negro women of the city that there is need of co-operation between them and the uneducated and unskilled, and that they are trying to find some practical means to give to these women the much-needed training for industrial life.

A Negro Nurse, "More Slavery at the South." *The Independent,* 25 January 1912: 196–200

[The following thrilling story was obtained by a representative of THE INDE-PENDENT specially commissioned to gather the facts. The reporting is, of course, our representative's, but the facts are those given by the nurse. — EDITOR.]

I am a negro woman, and I was born and reared in the South. I am now past forty years of age and am the mother of three children. My husband died nearly fifteen years ago, after we had been married about five years. For more than thirty years—or since I was ten years old—I have been a servant in one capacity or another in white families in a thriving Southern city, which has at present a population of more than 50,000. In my early years I was at first what might be called a "house-girl," or, better, a "house-boy." I used to answer the doorbell, sweep the yard, go on errands and do odd jobs. Later on I became a chambermaid and performed the usual duties of such a servant in a home. Still later I was graduated into a cook, in which position I served at different times for nearly eight years in all. During the last ten years I have been a nurse. I have worked for only four different families during all these thirty years. But, belonging to the servant class, which is the majority class among my race at the South, and associating only with servants, I have been able to become intimately acquainted not only with the lives of hundreds of household servants, but also with the lives of their employers. I can, therefore, speak with authority on the so-called servant question; and what I say is said out of an experience which covers many years.

To begin with, then, I should say that more than two-thirds of the negroes of the town where I live are menial servants of one kind or another, and besides that more than two-thirds of the negro women here, whether married or single, are compelled to work for a living—as nurses, cooks, washerwomen, chambermaids, seamstresses, hucksters, janitresses, and the like. I will say, also, that the condition of this vast host of poor colored people is just as bad as, if not worse than, it was during the days of slavery. Tho today we are enjoying nominal freedom, we are literally slaves. And, not to generalize, I will give you a sketch of the work I have to do— and I'm only one of many.

I frequently work from fourteen to sixteen hours a day. I am compelled by my contract, which is oral only, to sleep in the house. I am allowed to go home to my own children, the oldest of whom is a girl of 18 years, only once in two weeks, every other Sunday afternoon—even then I'm not permitted to stay all night. I not only have to nurse a little white child, now eleven months old, but I have to act as playmate or "handy-andy," not to say governess, to three other children in the home, the oldest of whom is only nine years of age. I wash and dress the baby two or three times each day; I give it its meals, mainly from a bottle; I have to put it to bed each night; and, in addition, I have to get up and attend to its every call between midnight and morning. If the baby falls to sleep during the day, as it has been trained to do every day about eleven o'clock, I am not permitted to rest. It's "Mammy, do this," or "Mammy, do that," or "Mammy, do the other," from my mistress, all the time. So it is not strange to see "Mammy" watering the lawn in front with the garden hose, sweeping the sidewalk, mopping the porch and halls, dusting around the house, helping the cook, or darning stockings. Not only so, but I have to put the other three children to bed each night as well as the baby, and I have to wash them and dress them each morning. I don't know what it is to go to church; I don't know what it is to go to a lecture or entertainment or anything of the kind; I live a treadmill life; and I see my own children only when they happen to see me on the streets when I am out with the children, or when my children come to the "yard" to see me, which isn't often, because my white folks don't like to see their servants' children hanging around their premises. You might as well say that I'm on duty all the time—from sunrise to sunrise, every day in the week. I am the slave, body and soul, of this family. And what do I get for this work—this lifetime bondage? The pitiful sum of ten dollars a month! And what am I expected to do with these ten dollars? With this money I'm expected to pay my house rent, which is four dollars, per month, for a little house of two-rooms, just big enough to turn round in; and I'm expected, also, to feed and clothe myself and three children. For two years my oldest child, it is true, has helped a little toward our support by taking in a little washing at home. She does the washing and ironing of two white families, with a total of five persons; one of these families pays her $1.00 per week, and the other 75 cents per week, and my daughter has to furnish her own soap and starch and wood. For six months my youngest child, a girl about thirteen years old, has been nursing, and she receives $1.50 per week but has no night work. When I think of the low rate of wages we poor colored people receive, and when I hear so much said about our unreliability, our untrustworthiness, and even our vices, I recall the story of the private soldier in a certain army who, once upon a time, being upbraided by the commanding officer because the heels of his shoes were not polished, is said to have replied: "Captain, do you expect all the virtues for $13 per month?"

Of course, nothing is being done to increase our wages, and the way things are going at present it would seem that nothing could be done to cause an increase of wages. We have no labor unions or organizations of any kind that could demand for us a uniform scale of wages for cooks, washerwomen, nurses, and the like; and, for another thing, if some negroes did here and there refuse to work for seven and eight and ten dollars a month, there would be hundreds of other negroes right on the spot ready to take their places and do the same work, or more, for the low wages that had been refused! So that, the truth is, we have to work for little or nothing or become vagrants! And that, of course, in this State would mean that we would be arrested, tried, and despatched to the "State Farm," where we would surely have to work for nothing, or be beaten with many stripes!

Nor does this low rate of pay tend to make us efficient servants! The most that can be said of us negro household servants in the South—and I speak as one of them—is that we are to the extent of our ability willing and faithful slaves. We do not cook according to scientific principles because we do not know anything about scientific principles. Most of our cooking is done by guesswork or by memory. We cook well when our "hand" is in, as we say, and when anything about the dinner goes wrong, we simply say, "I lost my hand today!" We don't know anything about scientific food for babies, nor anything about what science says must be done for infants at certain periods of their growth or when certain symptoms of disease appear; but somehow we "raise" more of the children than we kill, and, for the most part, they are lusty chaps—all of them. But the point is, we do not go to cooking-schools nor to nurse-training schools, and so it cannot be expected that we should make as efficient servants without such training provided. And yet with our cooking and nursing, such as it is, the white folks seem to be satisfied—perfectly satisfied. I sometimes wonder if this satisfaction is the outgrowth of the knowledge that more highly trained servants would be able to demand better pay!

Perhaps some might say, if the poor pay is the only thing about which we have to complain, then the slavery in which we daily toil and struggle is not so bad after all—not by any means! I remember very well the first and last place from which I was dismissed. I lost my place because I refused to let the madam's husband kiss me. He must have been accustomed to undue familiarity with his servants, or else he took it as a matter of course, because without any lovemaking at all, soon after I was installed as cook, he walked up to me, threw his arms around me, and was in the act of kissing me, when I demanded to know what he meant, and shoved him away. I was young then, and newly married, and didn't know then what has been a burden to my mind and heart ever since: that a colored woman's virtue in this part of the country has no protection. I at once went home, and told my husband about it. When my husband went to the man who had insulted me, the man cursed him, and slapped him, and—had him arrested! The police judge fined my husband $25. I was present at the hearing, and testified on oath to the insult offered me. The white man, of course, denied the charge. The old judge looked up and said: "This court will never take the word of a nigger against the word of a white man." Many and many a time since I have heard similar stories repeated again and again by my friends; I believe nearly all white men take, and expect to take, undue liberties with their colored female servants—not only the fathers, but in many cases the sons also. Those servants who rebel against such familiarity must either leave or expect a mighty hard time, if they stay. By comparison, those who tamely submit to these improper relations live in clover. They always have a little "spending change," wear better clothes, and are able to get off from work at least once a week—and sometimes oftener. This moral debasement is not at all times unknown to the white women in these homes. I know of more than one colored woman, who was openly importuned by white women to become the mistresses of their white husbands, on the ground that they, the white wives, were afraid that, if their husbands did not associate with colored women, they would certainly do so with outside white women, and the white wives, for reasons which ought to be perfectly obvious, preferred to have their husbands do wrong with colored women in order to keep their husbands *straight!* And again, I know at least fifty places in my small town where white men are positively raising two families—a white family in the "Big House" in front, and a colored family in a "Little House" in the backyard. In most cases, to be sure, the colored women involved are the cooks or chambermaids or seamstresses, but it cannot be true that their real connection with the white men of the families is unknown to the white women of the families. The results of this concubinage can be seen in all of our colored churches and in all of our colored public schools in the South, for in most of our churches and schools the majority of the young men and women and boys and girls are light-skinned mulattoes. The real, Simon-pure, blue-gum, thick-lip, coal-black negro is passing away—certainly in the cities; and the fathers of the new generation of negroes are white men, while their mothers are unmarried colored women.

Another thing—it's a small indignity, it may be, but an indignity just the same. No white person, not even the little children just learning to talk, no white person at the South ever thinks of addressing any negro man or woman as *Mr.*, or *Mrs.*, or *Miss.* The women are called, "Cook," or "Nurse," or "Mammy," or "Mary Jane," or "Lou," or "Dilcey," as the case might be, and the men are called "Bob," or "Boy," or "Old Man," or "Uncle Bill," or "Pate." In many cases our white employers refer to us, and in our presence, too, as their "niggers." No matter what they call us—no matter what they teach their children to call us—we must tamely submit, and answer when we are called; we must enter no protest; if we did object, we should be driven out without the least ceremony, and, in applying for work at other places, we should find it very hard to procure another situation. In almost every case, when our intending employers would be looking up our record, the information would be given by telephone or otherwise that we were "impudent," "saucy," "dishonest," and "generally unreliable." In our town we have no such thing as an employment agency or intelligence bureau, and, therefore, when we want work, we have to get out on the street and go from place to place, always with hat in hand, hunting for it.

Another thing. Sometimes I have gone on the street cars or the railroad trains with the white children, and, so long as I was in charge of the children, I could sit anywhere I desired, front or back. If a white man happened to ask some other white man, "What is that nigger doing in here?" and was told, "Oh, she's the nurse of those white children in front of her!" immediately there was the hush of peace. Everything was all right, so long as I was in the white man's part of the street car or in the white man's coach as a servant—a slave—but as soon as I did not present myself as a menial, and the relationship of master and servant was abolished by my not having the white children with me, I would be forthwith assigned to the "nigger" seats or the "colored people's coach." Then, too, any day in my city, and I understand that it is so in every town in the South, you can see some "great big black burly" negro coachman or carriage driver huddled up beside some aristocratic Southern white woman, and nothing is said about it, nothing is done about it, nobody resents the familiar contact. But let that same colored man take off his brass buttons and his high hat, and put on the plain livery of an average American citizen, and drive one block down any thoroughfare in any town in the South with that same white woman, as her equal or companion or friend, and he'd be shot on the spot!

You hear a good deal nowadays about the "service pan." The "service pan" is the general term applied to "left-over" food, which in many a Southern home is freely placed at the disposal of the cook, or, whether so placed or not, it is usually disposed of by the cook. In my town, I know, and I guess in many other towns also, every night when the cook starts for her home she takes with her a pan or a plate of cold victuals. The same thing is true on Sunday afternoons after dinner—and most cooks have nearly every Sunday afternoon off. Well, I'll be frank with you, if it were not for the service pan, I don't know what the majority of our Southern colored families would do. The service pan is the mainstay in many a home. Good cooks in the South receive on an average $8 per month. Porters, butlers, coachmen, janitors, "office boys" and the like receive on an average $16 per month. Few and far between are the colored men in the South who receive $1 or more per day. Some mechanics do; as, for example, carpenters, brick masons, wheelwrights, and the like. The vast majority of negroes in my town are serving in menial capacities in homes, stores and offices. Now taking it for granted, for the sake of illustration, that the husband receives $16 per month and the wife $8. That would be $24 between the two. The chances are that they will have anywhere from five to thirteen children between them. Now, how far will $24 go toward housing and feeding and clothing ten or twelve persons for thirty days? And, I tell you, with all of us poor people the service pan is a great institution; it is a great help to us, as we wag along the weary way of life. And then most of the white folks expect their cooks to avail themselves of these perquisities [sic]; they allow it; they expect it. I do not deny that the cooks find opportunity to hide away at times, along with the cold "grub," a little sugar, a little flour, a little meal, or a little piece of soap; but I indignantly deny that we are thieves. We don't steal; we just "take" things—they are a part of the oral contract, exprest [sic] or implied. We understand it, and most of the white folks understand it. Others may denounce the service pan, and say that it is used only to support idle negroes, but many a time, when I was a cook, and had the responsibility of rearing my three children upon my lone shoulders, many a time I have had occasion to bless the Lord for the service pan!

I have already told you that my youngest girl was a nurse. With scores of other colored girls who are nurses, she can be seen almost any afternoon, when the weather is fair, rolling the baby carriage or lolling about on some one of the chief boulevards of our town. The very first week that she started out on her work she was insulted by a white man, and many times since has been improperly approached by other white men. It is a favorite practice of young white sports about town—and they are not always young, either—to stop some colored nurse, inquire the name of the "sweet little baby," talk baby talk to the child, fondle it, kiss it, make love to it, etc., etc., and in nine of ten cases every such white man will wind up by making love to the colored nurse and seeking an appointment with her.

I confess that I believe it to be true that many of our colored girls are as eager as the white men are to encourage and maintain these improper relations; but where the girl is not willing, she has only herself to depend upon for protection. If their fathers, brothers or husbands seek to redress their wrongs, under our peculiar conditions, the guiltless negroes will be severely punished, if not killed, and the white blackleg will go scot-free!

Ah, we poor colored women wage-earners in the South are fighting a terrible battle, and because of our weakness, our ignorance, our poverty, and our temptations we deserve the sympathies of mankind. Perhaps a million of us are introduced daily to the privacy of a million chambers throughout [sic] the South, and hold in our arms a million white children, thousands of whom, as infants, are suckled at our breasts—during my lifetime I myself have served as "wet nurse" to more than a dozen white children. On the one hand, we are assailed by white men, and, on the other hand, we are assailed by black men, who should be our natural protectors; and, whether in the cook kitchen, at the washtub, over the sewing machine, behind the baby carriage, or at the ironing board, we are but little more than pack horses, beasts of burden, slaves! In the distant future, it may be, centuries and centuries hence, a monument of brass or stone will be erected to the Old Black Mammies of the South, but what we need is present help, present sympathy, better wages, better hours, more protection, and a chance to breathe for once while alive as free women. If none others will help us, it would seem that the Southern white women themselves might do so in their own defense, because we are rearing their children— we feed them, we bathe them, we teach them to speak the English language, and in numberless instances we sleep with them—and it is inevitable that the lives of their children will in some measure be pure or impure according as they are affected by contact with their colored nurses.

MIGRATION

Gertrude Mossell [Mrs. N.F. Mossell], "Our Woman's Department... A Word of Counsel." New York Freeman, 13 February 1886

The aim of this column will be to promote true womanhood,[74] especially that of the African race. Suggestions as to how its usefulness may be increased will be gladly received. All success, progress or need of our women will be given prompt mention. We shall be glad also to receive for exchange or for our book table such publications as may be deemed helpful. All communications should be addressed to Mrs. N.F. Mossell, 924 Lombard Street, Philadelphia.

A WORD OF COUNSEL

Many young girls reared in the country are tempted by the promise of higher wages and a brighter life into leaving their safe and sheltered homes, crowding into our large cities, where they meet with a class of men stylish in their appearance, fluent talkers and apparently with a large amount of unoccupied time on their hands. Many girls, dazzled by their seeming superiority, willingly accept their attentions. These men are, in the majority of cases, totally unprincipled, without moral character; often their entire existence is eked out by gambling, policy playing, free lunches &c. They stand around the saloons and cigar shops part of the day, and in the evening they call on two or three girls, take tea with one, go to the theatre or opera with another at her expense, and borrow small sums of money from another, and so they manage to live an easy idle life at the expense of hardworking parents and foolish girls. Many will deny that this state of affairs exists, but that does not change the fact. One girl will accuse the other, and the men jest publicly of the matter. Now, let me assure our girls that men who spend their lives so are not fit company for pure-minded women. Should they marry such an one only misery untold can follow. Remaining idle and dissolute, they compel the wife to support herself and little ones. Better by far, less wages, less city life, and marriage with an honest, sturdy country man, willing to work and win a subsistence for his family, even though he may not possess the stylish appearance of a city dandy.

Victoria Earle Matthews, "Some of the Dangers Confronting Southern Girls in the North." *Hampton Negro Conference* 2 (July 1898): 62–69

If the majority of the girls who go North every year, understood the condition of the labor market, the estimate in which the crowds are held, who are willing to adopt any method of transportation for the sake of getting to the North, and the kind of work they must expect to do, and an inkling of the many humiliations they must put up with after they get there from their so-called friends, it is reasonable to suppose that self-respect would deter hundreds from rushing into a life that only the strongest physically, spiritually and morally can be expected to stand. But the girls don't know: they feel stifled in the dead country town. Their very nature turns scornfully from the thought of supporting themselves in the home village by raising vegetables, chickens, making honey, butter, canning fruit or vegetables, putting up pickles and such like. And yet could they spend a few weeks with me, and hear the agonized moans of many a heart broken, disgraced young creature, from whom only a few short sin-stained years of city life has taken every vestige of hope, every chance of innocent happiness—could they hear as I have heard the one cry over and over—"Oh, had I known—had I only staid down home" and seen the despair upon young faces when some sympathizing one would ask, "Why not go back?," "Go back! Never! I could not face the folks; I'd rather die." Could even some of the women see and hear these things, the condition of our people in the cities would soon change and many a life would be saved, many a home protected and blessed. But the girls don't know, it is simply a story of human nature—only "the burnt child really dreads the fire" it would seem, and until the truth is known in every town and hamlet in the South, the youth of our race, educated and uneducated alike, will pay with their bright young lives, and the sacrifice of all that is noble, not only for our ignorance, but our sinful negligence in watching over and protecting our struggling working class against the hordes of unscrupulous money-making combinations that make the study of their needs and limitations for traps in moral and human life without a parallel in this country. So successful have been the operations of certain associations for the bringing of young innocent girls from the South for immoral purposes, that all southern girls are commonly adjudged to be weak morally. And the earnest young girl leaving her home for a northern city must expect to face this. So many of the careless, unneat, untrained, shiftless class have been brought out simply as blinds and imposed upon by ladies, for the purpose of lessening the demand among honest respectable people for colored help, that the demand has greatly fallen off. Combinations can't get as much money in the way of office fees from respectable people as from the disreputable class, hence every effort is made to increase trade among the latter, even at the expense of the innocence of ignorant and unprotected young girls.

Every week, from the early spring till the late fall crowds arrive by the Southern Steamship lines. They are spoken of as "crops." A "crop" will ordinarily last about five years. There are always new recruits and the work of death and destruction goes on without let or hindrance under the very eaves of the churches as it were. Never did the words of Jeremiah, the prophet, seem more fitting than at this time and in this connection; "Yet hear the voice of the Lord oh, ye women, and let your ear receive the word of his mouth, and teach your daughter wailing and every one her neighbor lamentation. For death is come up in our palaces to cut off the children from without, and the young men from the streets."—Jere. 9, 20-21.

Many of the dangers confronting our girls from the South in the great cities of the North are so perfectly planned, so overwhelming in their power to subjugate and destroy that no woman's daughter is safe away from home. And now that this honored institution has enabled the message to come to you, no woman here can shirk without sin the obligation to study into this matter, to the end that the evil may be completely exterminated, and protection guaranteed to the lives and reputations of the generations yet to come.

In order that my meaning may be perfectly clear I will confine myself to one of the dangers confronting the southern girls, one designed expressly to make money out of their helplessness and ignorance, and of which innumerable dangers spring into existence in a way so bewildering as to make life in New York and other large centers a perfect network of moral degradation for the unknowingly unfortunate who may happen to fall into its toils. Black men and women are often the promoters of this vile scheme, but it is by no means confined to them, for an actual investigation shows as many white men will be found in it as black. The very necessities of the case demand that Afro-Americans be the figure heads at least, and the fact that men and women can be found of our race willing to aid such work but illustrates the extent of certain phases of racial deterioration.

As has been said, the sporting and otherwise disreputable class prefer green southern girls as servants. They pay higher wages and higher office fees than any other class. Their mode of living offers many inducements to untrained and inexperienced workers, considerable time, a chance to make extra money, and unrestricted opportunity for entertaining promiscuous company. Pretty girls are always in demand, but not at first as servants. In order to supply the demand made by this class of patrons safe, the interest of the public must be deflected. A general employment bureau is planned. The patronage and sympathy of the public is sought on the ground that in helping the earnest but almost despairing idle class of the south to better homes a grand work of humanity will be done. Agents are sent throughout the South. Great promises are held out to the people; many are helped, particularly those too wise to be fooled. The agent offers to send a certain number off on a certain day: he tells them that an "officer" from the "Society" will meet them and conduct them to the "office" and lodging house. Another officer will procure service places for them, and all they are to do in return is to sign a paper giving the company the right to collect their wages until traveling expenses are paid back.

As soon as they arrive in New York they find the company treats them as so many head of cattle. They are huddled in dirty ill-smelling apartments, many feeling lucky if a pallet is given them to sleep on the floor. Often girls are forced to sleep on their own clothes. The food provided is not only very scant but often of the most miserable quality. No privacy is secured to them. Men can pass out and in at will and not infrequently they sleep in the same room owing to overcrowding. Board and lodging is regularly charged against each one at regular city prices, also storage for trunks. The Society will collect wages until all debts are fully cancelled according to their reckoning. Hundreds are provided with work, and if it were merely a question of an organized body charging first class fare for second class passage, extorting illegal rates of interest, herding the good, the bad and the indifferent into regular prescribed city dens making possible contact with every phase of vicious life, not excepting petty gambling, if this were all it would be simply a matter for the courts, but this is not all.

While the girls are waiting for work they are not permitted to see any lady who may call. All particulars are given and agreements are made in the "office." A girl will be sent to a place. Should she become dissatisfied with the character of the people and refuse to remain, the agent will threaten her with court proceedings, for broken contract, etc. Thoroughly cowed, she will remain with the determination to go on her own responsibility after she has worked out her debt. She does not know that no lady will care to employ her, will trust or even tolerate her in the family after she has had such contact; the girl does not know this, she determines to get out of the agent's debt and hunt for her self the kind of work she prefers. Hundreds mean this, but daily contact with depraved characters, daily association with friends (?) whose business it is to corrupt the mind of the subject by timely comments and subtle suggestions, destroys the good intention and many go down, their day is a brief one. They drift back to the "office" and become part of another circle of wickedness and depravity. Under the guidance of the officers various camps are countenanced, that is a man will be found who is willing to pose as husband. Innocent girls, tired of waiting day in and day out around the office will be decoyed, and soon they become regular members of the camp (a couple of rooms will be rented and the girls will pose as lodgers); from operating "traveling policy" and other petty gambling schemes they drift to the street. When any one of the camp is arrested the man appears and pleads for "my wife." Probably in the course of a month he appears before the same magistrate for four or five different women, each one claimed as "wife." In turn all the women of the camp share their earnings with him. When, by their combined efforts, a young and pretty girl is ensnared all will bunch their earnings, deck her out in fine clothes and diamonds, the "husband" becomes a sort of contractor, and in due time she is entered into some "swell set." Hundreds of dollars are made in this way, and distributed among the "company," the "camp" and the officers protecting both institutions. The poor butterfly finally drifts, a mass of disease and yearning for death, to the city hospital on Blackwell's Island!—begging piteously to be recorded as coming from anywhere but where she did come from, screaming in the abandonment of despair—"O! if I had only known! If I had only known!"

By various sophistries many refined, educated girls, particularly mulattoes and fair quadroons, are secured for the diversion of young Hebrews (the identity of their offspring is easily lost among Afro-Americans). These girls are led to believe they will get permanent work in stores and public-service under the control of politics. So our "tenderloins" are filled. The public, seeing these women haunting certain portions of the city in such an unfailing stream, takes it for granted that all black people—all Afro-Americans—are naturally low. The trade which supplies southern girls as domestics to disreputable [agencies] has been carried to such an extent that many ladies refuse to employ colored help for no other reason than that they are associated in the public mind with that class, and the idea prevalent that they are "signs" or "badges" as to the whereabouts of these people. Thousands of Afro-Americans throughout the city are employed by this class and the standard of the race is gauged by them. The small percentage comparatively speaking of the refined working girls is so hopelessly small that those in charge of desirable work unhesitatingly refuse to consider the application made by a nice Afro-American girl, until public sentiment has been created in favor of employing her along with respectable white girls. In other words the public must be convinced that there is another class than is represented by the depraved class commonly met with on the streets and in certain localities. The common standard of life must be elevated. The "tenderloins" must be purified. Corrective influences must be established in the infested centers. Torches must be lighted in dark places. The sending of untrained youth into the jaws of moral death must be checked. Any girl taking her chances in the cities in this stage of our history must expect in some way to be affected by the public repute of the misguided lives led by those preceding her. Unless a girl has friends whom she and her family know are to be trusted, unless she has money enough to pay her way until she can get work, she cannot expect to be independent or free from question among careful people.

These are hard truths, but truths they are. The conditions I have tried to present are not confined to any one city; by correspondence and personal investigation I have found evidences of the system in such centres as New York, Boston, San Francisco, Chicago, and other cities of lesser note. You may ask what is to be done about this awful condition? Naturally the indignant mind would immediately suggest the bringing of the guilty ones to justice. That must be done, but not in the ordinary way. All employment systems are not necessarily combined against virtue. The wrong doers are not ignorant of the law. They know their limitations, and the loop-holes, for their legal escape is simply a question of money. It would take the absorbing interest of more lives than one to ferret out all the real responsible culprits. Then the bringing of the guilty ones to justice is likely to blast the hopes of many a girl who now sees the light, and is building again slowly the ruined castle of honor. Such should be protected. This iniquitous system has the advantage of many years headway. It cannot be overthrown in a day. Let women and girls become enlightened, let them begin to think, and stop placing themselves voluntarily in the power of strangers. Let them search into the workings of every institution under whose auspices they contemplate traveling North. If they have no means of learning somewhat of every one connected with the business represented by a traveling agent, let them stay at home, it is better to starve and go home to God morally clean, than to helplessly drag out miserable lives of remorse and pain in Northern tenderloins.

As Virginia seems to have been the starting point of the system (and its beginning dates shortly after the first honest intelligence office began operations in the South—just as soon as men saw there was money in it) it is meet that appeal should be made at this conference[75] not only on behalf of Virginia's absent daughters, but the long-suffering cruelly wronged, sadly unprotected daughters of the entire South.

Fannie Barrier Williams, "Social Bonds in the 'Black Belt' of Chicago: Negro Organizations and the New Spirit Pervading Them." *Charities* 15.1 (7 October 1905): 40-44

Frederick Douglass Center, Chicago

The last federal census showed the Negro population of Chicago to be about 35,000. The present population is estimated to be over 50,000, an increase of about forty per cent in five years. The colored people who are thus crowding into Chicago come mostly from the states of Kentucky, Tennessee, Alabama, Mississippi, Louisiana, Arkansas and Missouri.

The underlying causes are easily traceable and are mainly as follows:

1. Primarily to escape laws of race discrimination that have steadily increased during the last few years.

2. To obtain better school privileges.

3. On account of the good news circulated by the hundreds of young colored men and women who have been educated in the Chicago and Northwestern Universities and the professional schools, that Chicago offers the largest liberty to citizens of all colors and languages of all communities in the North.

4. Because of the many industrial strikes which in the last ten years have brought thousands of colored people to Chicago, either for immediate work as strike breakers, or with the prospect of employment through the opportunities for both skilled and unskilled workers. Whatever the cause, the fact remains that thousands of Negro men and women are now employed

in the stockyards and other large industrial plants, where ten years ago this would not have been thought of.

This increase of Negro population has brought with it problems that directly affect the social and economic life of the newcomers. Prevented from mingling wholly and generally with the rest of the city's population, according to their needs and deservings, but with no preparation made for segregation, their life in a great city has been irregular and shifting, with the result that they have been subject to more social ills than any other nationality amongst us. Notwithstanding the disadvantages suggested, the colored people of Chicago have shown in their efforts for self-help and self-advancement a determination that is altogether creditable.[76] While it is true that they contribute almost more than their share of the sins of the community, what they contribute in the way of restraining and correcting influences over their own lives, is much more important.

The real problem of the social life of the colored people in Chicago, as in all northern cities, lies in the fact of their segregation. While they do not occupy all the worst streets and live in all the unsanitary houses in Chicago, what is known as the "Black Belt" is altogether forbidding and demoralizing. The huddling together of the good and the bad, compelling the decent element of the colored people to witness the brazen display of vice of all kinds in front of their homes and in the faces of their children, are trying conditions under which to remain socially clean and respectable. There are some of us who are all the time breaking away from these surroundings and by purchase or otherwise are securing good homes on desirable streets. But the old and unsanitary shacks from which the good and the thrifty escape are immediately occupied by others less fortunate. For there are always too few houses to meet the demands of the newcomers.

As already suggested the colored people themselves are not indifferent to the demoralizing conditions of their environments. The organizations created and maintained by them in Chicago are numerous and touch almost every phase of our social life.

Is this passion for organization peculiar to Negro people? Whether this be answered in the affirmative or not, it is a fact that the Negro individual does not like to be alone in good works. His bent for organization is a sort of racial passion. Suggest to the average man something that ought to be, and he immediately proposes an organization. There is scarcely a thing in religion, in politics, in business, in pleasure, in education, in fighting race prejudice, or anything else desirable that is not the object of organization. A catalogue of the organizations created by colored people in this country would make a very large book, and would contain an interesting story of the many ways by which the Negro seeks to improve his condition. It is a common complaint that the Negroes will not support and protect each other in any united effort; but this is clearly not so. It is true that more of these organizations fail than succeed, but the failure is not due [to] a lack of the co-operative spirit, which is the most helpful thing in our race character. The failures are mostly due to a lack of comprehension and intelligence in working out the details. The weak point is administration. It is common for men of no training and no experience to start an organization that requires the highest order of executive ability to carry out. They will take as a model the constitution and bylaws of some well-established white organization that is prominently successful. Officers, directors and committees will be made up exactly as in the organization which is its model — this, with the utmost enthusiasm and good faith that their success is assured. The colored man who ventures to suggest to them that they cannot succeed, for various and obvious reasons, is at once branded as a "traitor to his race." The enterprise may be fore-doomed, but the result will be charged up to the failure of the people to support and sustain it.

The pathway of our progress is thickly strewn with such failures, but they do not discourage other and similar attempts. A colored man who has joined and pinned his faith to an organization that has failed, will join another society of the same kind to-morrow. It is at once pathetic and splendid to note how persistent is this faith that emancipation from the ills of poverty and ignorance and race prejudice is through co-operation. Indeed, no race of men and women feel more strongly than we do the force of that maxim that "in union there is strength."

First in importance is the Negro church. There are 25 regularly organized colored churches. This number includes 9 Methodist, 8 Baptist, 1 Catholic, 1 Episcopal, 1 Christian and 1 Presbyterian. In addition to these there are numerous missions in various parts of the "Black Belt." These churches are for the most part housed in large and modern stone and brick edifices that cost from $7,000 to $40,000 each, and have a seating capacity of from 300 to 2,000 people. Most of these churches are burdened with oppressive indebtedness, and because of this their usefulness as agents of moral up-lift is seriously handicapped. For example, the members of one of the largest have raised and paid in over $60,000 during the last five years, but the church still carries an indebtedness of over $24,000.

Despite this serious handicap of a slowly diminishing debt, the colored church is the center of the social life and efforts of the people. What the church sanctions and supports is of the first importance and what it fails to support and sanction is more than apt to fail. The Negro church historically, as to numbers and reach of influence and dominion, is the strongest factor in the community life of the colored people. Aside from the ordinary functions of preaching, prayer, class meetings and Sunday-school, the church is regarded by the masses as a sort of tribune of all of their civic and social interests. Thousands of Negroes know and care for no other entertainment than that furnished by the church. Theatres, concert halls, and art galleries mean nothing. What they fail to learn of these things in the churches remains unlearned. Nearly every night the church building is open, either for worship, or for concerts, lectures, and entertainments of all kinds. Even political meetings of the most partisan sort are not barred. The party leaders find it to their advantage, if they want to secure a large audience of colored people, to hold their meetings in the colored church. In a purely social way, the church leads in setting standards of social conduct. Weddings and receptions of all kinds, except those including dancing, are held within its walls and in this respect the church has become progressively liberal. Among other nationalities, there are Young Men's Christian Associations, Young Women's Christian Associations, social clubs, gymnasiums, university extension lecture courses, etc. The colored people, generally speaking, have none of these liberalizing and elevating influences, except as they are supplied by this single institution.

Within the last six years, the colored churches of Chicago have begun to recognise the larger social needs of the people, and as much as their intense denominationalism will permit, they are endeavoring to enlarge their influence as a factor for betterment. One of the large churches has carried on such activities as a kindergarten, a day nursery, a boys' club and reading-room, a penny savings-bank, gymnasium, a kitchen garden, mothers club and sewing school.

Nearly all of the large churches have literary clubs which have become attractive to hundreds of young colored men of intelligence. The effect has been a wider and more intelligent interest in things that concern the progressive life of the people.

In fine the colored churches must be reckoned with in every movement of a social character that aims to reach and influence life. They might do more and be more to the ever-increasing number who need guidance, social ideals, and higher moral standards, if they were less burdened with debts and an unyielding orthodoxy. The important thing, however, is that the Negro church in Chicago is becoming more and more liberal and intelligently interested and earnest in its endeavors to meet the peculiar requirements of the city Negro.

Next to the Negro church in importance, as affecting the social life of the people, are the secret orders, embracing such organizations as the

Masons, Odd Fellows, Knights of Pythias, True Reformers, the United Brotherhood (a fraternal insurance association), the Ancient Order of Foresters, and the Elks. Nearly all of these secret orders have auxiliary associations composed of women. The Masons and Odd-Fellows are strongest in point of numbers and influence. There are about fourteen lodges of Odd-Fellows and about as many of Masons. Their estimated membership is respectively 2,000 and 1,600.

The colored people believe in secret societies. I believe it is safe to say fifty per cent of the better class of Negro men are enrolled in some secret order. These affect every phase of their social life and represent the best achievements of the race in the matter of organization. In no other way is the organized Negro so reliably responsive to the requirements of his social obligations. In no other form of organization do the terms brotherhood and mutual obligations mean so much.

Thousands of dollars are paid into the treasuries of these societies every month, and it is very rare that we hear of any charge of dishonest dealings in money matters. They take care of the sick and provide for the dead with a promptness, fidelity and abundance of sympathy that is not to be found in any other form of society amongst us. The lessons of right living, of charity and truthfulness are enforced in these societies more rigidly even than in the churches.

Most of the colored men belong to more than one secret order and many belong to as many as four or five at a time and live up to their obligations in all of them. In nothing does the colored man live such a strenuous life as he does as a lodge man. The lodge, more than any other merely social organization, is a permanent and ever-increasing force.

There are other social organizations among the colored people of Chicago that are indicative of a desire for progress and improvement. For example there is one organization that supports an institution known as the "Old Folk's Home," in which some twenty-five old colored men and women are comfortably cared for and saved from eking out their existence in the dreaded almshouse.

There is a Choral Study Club composed of about one hundred young men and women under competent leadership and devoted to the study of music. A business league, composed of colored business men and women, is a part of the National Business League of which Booker T. Washington is founder and president. A physicians' club has undertaken a campaign of education at to the cause of tuberculosis and methods of prevention, together with lessons on domestic sanitation and kindred subjects.

And there are, of course, numbers of purely pleasure clubs. Love of pleasure is in good part a hopeful characteristic of the Negro people. Painfully conscious as we all are of our present position, which tends to exclude us from things that are most prized in human relationships, there is an all-pervading light-heartedness which saves us from the pessimism that must inevitably banish from the soul all hope and joy. Young men's social clubs, young women's social clubs, fellowship clubs, whist clubs and social charity clubs fill nights and holidays with laughter, song and dance.

From what has been said in describing Negro organizations it might be inferred that the colored people are quite capable of taking care of themselves and of advancing their condition in every direction. Let us be undeceived in this. In every community the Negro is practically dependent for nearly everything of importance upon the dominant race. He must live in places set apart for him, and that are often in the worst portion of the city. He must find work below his capabilities and training. He must live on the outer rim of life's advantages and pleasures. His merit, whatever it may be, is more apt to be discredited than recognized. Even though he be educated, public opinion still persists in rating him an ignorant, and treating him as such. His virtues are generally overlooked or reluctantly believed in. He is the victim of more injustice than is meted out to any other class of people. In the matter of employment, the colored people of Chicago have lost in the last ten years nearly every occupation of which they once had almost a monopoly. There is now scarcely a Negro barber left in the business district. Nearly all the janitor work in the large buildings has been taken away from them by the Swedes. White men and women as waiters have supplanted colored men in nearly all the first-class hotels and restaurants. Practically all the shoe polishing is now done by Greeks. Negro coachmen and expressmen and teamsters are seldom seen in the business districts. It scarcely need be stated that colored young men and women are almost never employed as clerks and bookkeepers in business establishments. A race that can be systematically deprived of one occupation after another becomes an easy victim to all kinds of injustice. When they can be reduced to a position to be pitied, they will cease to be respected. It is not surprising then that there has been a marked lowering of that public sentiment that formerly was liberal and more tolerant of the Negro's presence and efforts to rise.

The increase of the Negro population in Chicago, already referred to, has not tended to liberalize public sentiment; in fact hostile sentiment has been considerably intensified by the importation from time to time of colored men as strikebreakers. Then again a marked increase of crime among the Negro population has been noted in recent years. All these things have tended to put us in a bad light, resulting in an appreciable loss of friends and well-wishers.

Out of these seemingly hopeless conditions a new movement has grown that is destined to have an important bearing on the status of the Chicago Negro. The organization of the Frederick Douglass Center and the Trinity Mission Settlement are in response to these needs of the hour. The Frederick Douglass Center is unlike anything of the kind in the country. It is the outgrowth of a comprehensive study of the situation by some of the best people of the city of both races. The head and soul of the movement, Mrs. Celia Parker Woolley, is a woman who has given up social pleasures and the pursuits of culture in behalf of a people and of a problem to grapple with which requires more than ordinary patience and intelligence.

The Frederick Douglass Center is intended primarily as a center of influence for the better relationship of the white and colored races along the higher levels of mutual dependence and helpfulness. The society is incorporated under the laws of the state of Illinois. Its by-laws recite its purposes as follows:

1. To promote a just and amicable relationship between the white and colored people.
2. To remove the disabilities from which the latter suffer in their civil, political, and industrial life.
3. To encourage equal opportunity irrespective of race, color, or other arbitrary distinctions.
4. To establish a center of friendly helpfulness and influence in which to gather needful information and for mutual cooperation to the end of right living and higher citizenship.

In order to properly house the movement there has been purchased, at a cost of $5,500, a large three-story gray-stone house on Wabash avenue, near Thirty-first street. The location is adjacent to the "Black Belt" in the rear, and the white belt of aristocracy and wealth on Michigan avenue in the front. This new home for social improvement is fitted up with an attractive assembly room for meetings, a club-room and workshop for boys, a reading-room and offices and living-rooms for the head resident. Arrangements are being made for mothers' meetings in the interest of the home, men's meetings, classes in manual training, cooking and dressmaking, club work for intellectual and moral culture, and domestic employment. Lectures are also being provided for under the departments of sanitation, neighborhood improvement and civics.

Mrs. Woolley has succeeded in interesting in this new work many of the well-known people of Chicago, judges, lawyers, professors, business men and women of wealth and culture. Along with these she has the co-operation of nearly every colored man and woman of standing.

Another effort toward social betterment is the Trinity Mission. This is the beginning of a more distinct social settlement. It is located in the very heart of the "Black Belt" on Eighteenth street between State and Clark streets, a neighborhood properly called "Darkest Africa." Here there is scarcely a single ray of the light of decency. Neither church, nor school nor anything else of a helpful character can be found. The head of this enterprise is a young man, Richard R. Wright, son of President Wright, of the State Industrial School, at College, Georgia. A crèche, a reading-room and a home for working girls are being carried on and substantial encouragement has come from people who are in sympathy with the principle of settlement work.

One of the results of these new organizations is the serious view the more intelligent colored people are beginning to take of the responsibilities of city life among their people. The Negro's worth as a citizen is to be tested in the great cities of the North as nowhere else in the world—the use he makes of his opportunities here, and his strength of character in resisting the malign influences of city politics.

To summarize:

1. The colored people themselves have begun to develop a sort of civic consciousness as manifested in the tendency of the Negro church and the Negro lodge to participate more largely in efforts to improve the social condition of their people.

2. The men and women who have organized in various ways to bring about a better Chicago, as well as a larger Chicago, have begun to recognize that if the ever-increasing Negro population is treated and regarded as a reprobate race, the result will be an increase of crime and disorders of all kinds, that will grow more and more difficult to handle and regulate.

3. Recent organizations with the settlement spirit are preparing to do many things in a rational way that have never before been attempted, and to make answer to many false and harmful things that now go unchallenged. In other words, by these new movements the Negro is to be generously included in all efforts to promote civic righteousness among all the people.

Notes

1. "Mrs Steward's [sic] Essays," The Liberator 2.1 (7 January 1832).
2. The Wedgwood cameo of 1787, with a kneeling male slave and the motto

"Am I not a Man and a Brother?" was modified and adopted by British women abolitionists in 1828; their version depicted a kneeling female slave and the legend, "Am I not a Woman and a Sister?" (Midgley 1992, 97). For the circulation of this image in the United States, see Yellin 1989.

3. This was Truth's most famous song, which she sang to the tune of "Auld Lang Syne."

4. Truth was freed in 1827; see Painter 1996, 21-25 for the complexity of Truth's emancipation.

5. John Dumont purchased Truth for £70 in 1810 (she was 12 or 13 at the time); she was the Dumonts' slave for the next 16 years, during which time she married and had five children (Painter 1996, 14).

6. Colonization, or the removal of African Americans to colonies in Africa (Liberia principally), and the organizational body championing it (the African Colonization Society or ACS, founded in 1816) was opposed by Northern free blacks. They saw its slaveholder membership as aiming to "remove free blacks, the strongest voices against slavery in the nation" (Horton and Horton 1997, 188). As early as the 1830s, the ACS was quite powerful, and debates over colonization continued through the 1850s, with the black convention movement being the mobilizer for free-black opposition to colonization.

7. Truth advocated black self-sufficiency; in the late 1860s and early 1870s she agitated for the government to allocate Western land to unemployed freedpeople (Painter 1996, 234-46).

8. Truth poked fun at the nineteenth-century belief that public speaking unsexed women.

9. Truth's *Narrative* went through five editions from 1850 to 1884, and she is said to have carried copies of it with her to sell at her public appearances. Truth's first *Narrative of Sojourner Truth* was written by her amanuensis, Olive Gilbert, and published in 1850; her second narrative published in 1878 is the one referred to here (Gilbert and Titus 1991[1878]).

10. Truth frequently employed puns in her work, following a long tradition of language play by African Americans.

11. Shadd Cary alludes to the popularity of Africa and Haiti, as well as Mexico, South America, and the West Indies, as possible destinations for African Americans under the colonization scheme. By this time, black emigrationists like Martin Delaney were promoting Liberia and the Haitian Emigration Bureau was actively courting African American emigration to Haiti.

12. From the Sermon on the Mount:

"Like Samson's withes—though weak alone,

United, we shall strength impart."

13. Hiram Wilson (1803-64), studied at Oberlin Theological Seminary and observed the condition of fugitive slaves in Canada as a delegate of the American

Anti-Slavery Society. He raised funds for fugitives' education and by 1839 had established 10 schools. He founded, with James Canning Fuller and ex-slave Josiah Henson, the British-American Institute at Dawn, near Chatham, Canada West in 1841. The institute sought to integrate labor and education, introducing ex-slaves to the capitalist system in order to make them into self-sufficient freedpersons.

14. Shadd Cary was adamant that escaped slaves be referred to as "refugees" not as "fugitives." In her writings she reconfigured the fugitive slave as self-sufficient individual rather than passive victim, recasting fugitives as refugee settlers and political agents rather than violators of "duty," criminals, or vagrants, as the term "fugitive" connoted.

15. A term in common use during the Civil War, contraband or contraband of war gave escaped slaves who joined the Union Forces a new status and prevented their forced return to their former masters. The *Confiscation Act* of 1861 (August) declared that any property used by the Confederate military, including slaves, could be confiscated by Union forces. The *Act Prohibiting the Return of Slaves* (March 1862) forbade the restoring of such human seizures.

16. Shadd Cary had worked to remedy the lack of information available on Canada, as a suitable site for African American immigration, in the early 1850s with her pamphlet, *A Plea for Emigration; Or, Notes of Canada West, in its Moral, Social and Political Aspect, with Suggestions Respecting Mexico, W. Indies and Vancouver's Island, for the Information of Colored Emigrants* (1852). Shadd sold her pamphlet for 12.5 cents a copy at her appearances to help pay her way during her many lecture tours in the United States and Canada (Almonte 1998, 19).

17. Thomas Wentworth Higginson (1823-1911) was an American minister, author, abolitionist, and soldier. Higginson was a fervent supporter of John Brown and is remembered as one of the "Secret Six" abolitionists who helped Brown raise money and procure supplies for the intended slave insurrection at Harper's Ferry, West Virginia.

18. A law preventing the extradition of escaped slaves to the United States was enacted in 1849, following on an earlier act and treaty (1833, 1843) that had been challenged in individual cases brought before the courts. Shadd Cary may also be referring to those elected politicians such as Archibald McKellar, Arthur Rankin, Sir Allan McNab, Isaac Buchanan, and John Scoble who advocated for their black constituents, thereby giving their concerns and interests a voice in government (Winks 1997, 208-18).

19. Shadd Cary refers to Canada West, the western portion of the United Province of Canada from 10 February 1841 to 1 July 1867. Its boundaries were identical to those of the former Province of Upper Canada and consisted of the southern portion of what is now the Province of Ontario.

20. Fugitive aid societies established missions and schools for fugitives, procured lands, and partially financed settlements. The largest of these colonies were

the Dawn Settlement at Dresden, the Elgin Settlement at Buxton, and the Refugees Home near Windsor. In the 1850s blacks comprised "nearly 20 percent of the total population of Chatham, 25 percent of Amherstburg's and 33 percent of Colchester's" (Winks 1997, 493). The American Anti-Slavery Society, the Windsor Anti-Slavery Society, the Fugitives' Union, and the Anti-Slavery Society of Canada were among those societies offering aid and support.

21. A Puritan prayer; in her opening Harper is appealing to the origins and ideals of the republic.

22. Harper makes use of a longstanding tradition within black oratory, the black jeremiad, which focused on warning "whites... [of] the judgement that was to come for the sin of slavery" (Moses 1982, 30-31). Black feminists like Maria Stewart, Sojourner Truth, and Frances Harper used the jeremiad in their oratory.

23. Considered one of the main instigators of the First Crusade, Peter the Hermit (or Little Peter, or Peter of Amiens) roused not only knights but laborers, tradesmen, and peasants with his speeches in France and Germany. His crusade to Constantinople became known as "The People's Crusade" or "The Crusade of the Poor People."

24. One month before the Emancipation Proclamation was to go into effect, President Lincoln discussed Colonization in his Second Annual Address to Congress (1 December 1862). Lincoln proposed gradual, compensated emancipation with colonization, arguing this would be less costly than continuing the war. Before this address, Lincoln was on record as supporting colonization in a *Harper's Weekly* article of 6 September 1862 titled "The President and Slavery." Lincoln saw Liberia as a success, but advocated for colonization in South and Central America, supporting the failed projects in Chirique, Grenada and Ile-a-Vache, Haiti (Paludan 2004).

25. Jennings refers to the 1830s, the heyday of the African Colonization Society's strength, when African American leaders campaigned to diminish its influence and free African Americans called local meetings to protest African colonization and support Canadian emigration in its stead. Those debates were also pursued at the national black conventions.

26. By the 1840s, Liberia had become a financial burden on the American Colonization Society. In addition, Liberia faced political threats, chiefly from Britain, because it was neither a sovereign power nor a recognized colony of any sovereign nation. Because the United States refused to claim sovereignty over Liberia, the ACS ordered the Liberians to proclaim their independence in 1846.

27. As Marilyn Richardson documents, *Religion and the Pure Principles of Morality* first appeared as a 12-page pamphlet, published by William Lloyd Garrison and Isaac Knapp in 1831, with Stewart's name misspelled as Steward (1987, xix).

28. The black community of Boston had entered a period of political dissension come the late 1820s and early 1830s, and Stewart's calls for community soli-

darity came at what James Horton and Lois Horton call a "watershed" moment for "black identity"(1997, 191) in the North.

29. Stewart explicitly challenged the black convention movement's exclusive focus on the education of African American men, a focus that developed into the 1833 proposal of a "mechanical arts" high school and college in New Haven, Connecticut.

30. Stewart foregrounded the effective segregation in Northern labor markets of black women, who were limited mainly to domestic service and who also faced competition when a surplus of laborers brought African Americans into more serious competition with whites for employment after 1820 (Horton and Horton 1997, 165).

31. Stewart challenged the platform for black self-sufficiency promoted by the black convention movement by arguing for its achievement in the urban centers where African Americans already worked and lived, while convention delegates like Austin Steward and AME Bishop Richard Allen "urged blacks to leave the city and acquire farms," believing that the effects of racial prejudice in the North were "less potent in the country," than in the city and that through farming African Americans could "act with a degree of independence" (quoted in Horton and Horton 1997, 209). Stewart's reference to building a store as a form of self-support for black women was realized in New York City when a co-operative grocery store was established there in the early 1840s by the 100-member Female Trading Association; it sold "Dry *Groceries* of every description... cheap for cash" (quoted in Sterling 1984, 218).

32. Founded in 1856 by the Methodist Episcopal Church and Bishop Daniel Payne, Wilberforce Institute is the oldest of the 110 black universities and colleges in the United States today.

33. The *Anti-Slavery Bugle* (1845-61) was published by the Ohio American Anti-Slavery Society in New-Lisbon, Ohio. At the time Harper was writing, the *Bugle* was edited by Marius Robinson, president of the Western Anti-Slavery Society. The paper published pieces on temperance, woman's rights, and abolition; by 1859 it had achieved a "respectable" circulation of 1,400 (Painter 1996, 120). This paper covered Sojourner Truth's famous "Ain't I a Woman?" speech in 1851.

34. Madame (Marietta) Piccolomini (1834-99) was a famous soprano and the singer that first brought La Traviata out of Italy, performing the role in London, Paris, and New York.

35. Harper may be referring to the Ohio Black Laws (1804, 1807): "1)Blacks could not settle in Ohio unless within twenty (20) days a bond of $500 be paid and the signatures of two white men be secured guaranteeing his good behavior and support. 2)Blacks were excluded from serving in the militia. 3)Blacks could not attend common schools, and were exempted from paying taxes which raised funds for public schools. 4)Blacks must present a certificate of freedom in order to work

for more than one (1) hour. A fine of $10 to $50 was imposed on any person hiring a Black without a certificate, and even higher fines if the Black was an escaped slave. 5)Blacks could not testify against a white person no matter what the circumstances. 6)Blacks were not allowed on juries, nor allowed to vote or hold public office." Between 1840 and 1850, Black Ohioans held seven state political conventions to address the inequities they experienced (Gordon and Collier-Thomas 1997).

36. Wesley Chapel was a Methodist church built in 1831 in Cincinnati, Ohio. In the years before the Civil War, political rallies and anti-slavery meetings were held there frequently.

37. In 1870, Frederick Douglass began publishing the *New National Era*.

38. The *Christian Recorder*, a four-page weekly established in 1852 by the AME Church's Book Concern, was central to its mandate of increasing literacy among African Americans. The *Recorder* published creative writing, bibliographic essays, and book reviews (McHenry 2002, 130-32). Its regular departments included Religious Intelligence, Domestic News, General Items, Foreign News, Obituaries, Marriages, Notices, and Advertisements.

39. *The Southland* was a monthly founded in 1890 by Joseph C. Price, the head of Livingstone College in North Carolina. In 1891, Cooper was listed on its masthead as co-editor with S.G. Atkins.

40. Sylvain Maréchal (1750-1830) was a French essayist, poet, philosopher, and political theorist.

41. In 1833 Oberlin College opened as the first college for the joint education of men and women.

42. Daniel 7:1.

43. Mary A. Livermore (1820-1905) was a journalist, philanthropist, and lecturer active in abolition, temperance, and suffrage.

44. Edward Bellamy (1850-98) was an American author and socialist, most famous for his utopian novel, *Looking Backward*, set in the year 2000 and the third-largest bestseller of its time behind *Uncle Tom's Cabin* and *Ben Hur: A Tale of the Christ*.

45. Alfred Lord Tennyson's "The Princess" (1847).

46. Luke 2:49.

47. In Book 1, when Aeneas views the decorated walls of the temple in Carthage, he sees on it Penthesilea, *bellatrix, audetque viris concurrere virgo* (a female warrior, a maiden who dared to join in battle with men, 1: 493).

48. Grant Allen (1848-99). See Allen 1889.

49. *Don Juan* (1818-24), Canto I, stanza 194.

50. Alfred Lord Tennyson's "The Princess" (1847).

51. [Author's note] Graduated from Scientific course, June, 1890, the first colored woman to graduate from Cornell.

52. In 1903, Booker T. Washington published "Industrial Education for the Negro" in *The Negro Problem; A Series Of Articles By Representative American Negroes*

Of Today (New York: J. Pott and Co.). The collection included writings by W.E.B. DuBois, T. Thomas Fortune, Charles Chesnutt, and Paul Laurence Dunbar, but notably none by women. *The Colored American Magazine*, originally established in 1900 and edited by Pauline Hopkins from 1903 to 1904, was acquired by Washington in 1904, and its mandate shifted from its goal to "intensify the bonds of racial brotherhood" to a focus on "the doings of the race along material lines" (quoted in Fultz 1995, 98). Under Washington's control, the journal published a collection of pieces on industrial education in this issue, which included Burroughs' piece as well as articles by T. Thomas Fortune, Kelly Miller, and Washington himself.

53. Based on John 5: 24.

54. Benjamin Banneker (1731-1806) was a self-taught mathematician and astronomer. Frederick Douglass (1818-95) was the most famous black leader, escaped slave, and orator of the nineteenth century. Blanche K. Bruce (1841-98) represented Mississippi in the American Senate from 1875 to 1881, was the first black to serve a full term in the Senate, and in 1881 was appointed Register of the Treasury. John Mercer Langston (1829-97) was an American abolitionist and congressman from Virginia and was appointed inspector general of the Freedman's Bureau. Edward Wilmot Blyden (1832-1912) was of African American and Liberian descent, and an educator, writer, diplomat, and politician in Liberia and Sierra Leone; he is considered the father of pan-Africanism. William Sanders Scarborough (1852-1926) served as president of Wilberforce University between 1908 and 1920 after having been born into slavery. T. Thomas Fortune (1856-1928) was an orator, civil rights leader, journalist, writer, editor, and publisher, who founded *The New York Age*. Roscoe Conkling Bruce (1879-1950) was a Harvard valedictorian, son of Blanche K. Bruce, and advocate of industrial education; he headed the Academic Department at Tuskegee Institute from 1903 to 1906. Booker Taliaferro Washington (1856-1915) was a prominent black educator, author, and leader who advocated industrial education for African Americans and was principal of Tuskegee Institute from its founding in 1881 to his death in 1915.

55. Phillis Wheatley (1753-84) was the first published African American poet. The 1773 publication of her *Poems on Various Subjects, Religious and Moral* brought her fame, with dignitaries such as George Washington praising her work.

56. As Volume 3 of the Bulletin of the Department of Labor, W.E.B. DuBois published *The Negroes of Farmville, Virginia: A Social Study* in 1898. Bruce's statements are based on this study.

57. Bruce is drawing on J. Bradford Laws's "The Negroes of Cinclare Central Factory and Calumet Plantation, Louisiana," *Bulletin of the Department of Labor* 38 (January 1902). Laws's report "was among the most derogatory of any of the Department of Labor's black studies," and though "factually accurate, was misleading," given Laws's penchant for saying the African Americans of Cinclare and Calumet "appear to have little intellectual and little moral capacity" (Grossman 2008).

58. Bruce bases her remarks upon Richard R. Wright, Jr.'s "The Negroes of Xenia, Ohio: A Social Study," *US Bureau of Labor Bulletin* 48 (September 1903). This was the only study of a Northern African American community in the series.

59. Joshua 9:23.

60. Labor conditions were much worse for free blacks in the North, even though they migrated there for better economic opportunities: "Leonard P. Curry's perusal of city directories between 1800 and 1850 led him to conclude that 'employment opportunities for blacks were clearly superior in the Lower South cities, worst in those of New England, and better in the urban centers of the Upper South than in New York and the Lower South'" (Tate 2003, 101).

61. 2 Samuel 1:20.

62. Psalms 68:31; a passage used by black orators and preachers to create a sense of black pride (Ampadu 2007, 49).

63. Thomas Gray, "Elegy Written in a Country Churchyard," 1751.

64. Jeremiah 29:18.

65. James 5:4.

66. The Knights of Labor was founded by nine Philadelphia garment workers, led by Uriah Stephens, in 1869. It advocated an end to child and convict labor, equal pay for women, progressive income tax, and cooperative ownership of mines and factories shared by workers and employers. After 1878, the Knights of Labor accepted African American members; it had always included women but excluded Asian workers. Originally a secret society, the Knights grew in the 1870s and, under Terence Powderly, operated more like a labor union; by 1881 it voted to abolish oaths of initiation and to make its name and goals public. Though not involved in the Haymarket Riot, it nonetheless tarnished the Knights of Labor's reputation. See: "Knights of Labor," *Wikipedia, The Free Encyclopedia* <http://en. wikipedia.org/wiki/Knights_of_Labor>.

67. On 4 May 1886, following the May 1st national walkout and protest in support of an eight-hour work day, a bomb exploded at a labor protest rally in a manufacturing and wholesale district in Chicago, Illinois; Officer Mathias Degan was killed by the blast. The perpetrator is still unknown, but the event was named the Haymarket Riot. The Haymarket Eight—August Spies, Albert Parsons, Adolph Fischer, George Engel, Louis Lingg, Michael Schwab, Samuel Fielden, and Oscar Neebe—were charged with murder. Fielden and Schwab were eventually sentenced to life in prison; Lingg committed suicide on 10 November 1887, the eve of his execution; and Spies, Parsons, Fischer, and Engel were hanged on 11 November 1887. Nebee was sentenced to 15 years in prison and was pardoned along with Fielden and Schwab on June 26, 1893 by Illinois Governor John Peter Altgeld. See "The Dramas of Haymarket," an online project collaboratively produced by the Chicago Historical Society and Northwestern University at <http://www.chicagohistory.org/dramas>.

68. In 1900 the Woman's Convention, "defined as an auxiliary to the NBC [National Baptist Convention]" was formed, with a membership "more than one million strong" (Higginbotham 1993, 8).

69. Genesis 3:19.

70. Jim Crow became the term referring to discriminatory practices and laws enacted to prevent African Americans from enjoying the same rights and privileges as white Americans, often termed "separate but equal." The term Jim Crow is believed to have originated around 1830 from white minstrel performer Thomas "Daddy" Rice's song and dance, "Jump Jim Crow."

71. The Chicago School of Civics and Philanthropy, established in 1908 at Hull House, was developed jointly by settlement workers and academics in order to train social workers in social investigation methods and the systemic analysis of social issues. The CSCP joined the University of Chicago as the School of Social Service Administration in 1920.

72. Fannie Barrier Williams referred to the Frederick Douglass Center of Chicago as the black Hull House. See Deegan 2002.

73. [Author's note] 454 white women in the same time.

74. "True womanhood" was the gender identity that held sway for women in the nineteenth century; it was established through etiquette books, ladies magazines, and religious sermons. This ideology stressed "piety, purity, submissiveness and domesticity" (Welter 1976, 21).

75. Matthews published this essay in the Southern black periodical *Hampton Negro Conference*, the published proceedings of the annual Hampton conferences begun in 1897. Her closing indicates that the essay was first presented at the annual conference, likely the same year it appeared in the periodical.

76. [Author's note] The Negroes of Chicago support some 20 lawyers, as many physicians, about a dozen dentists, about 20 school teachers in the public schools, and an ever increasing number of them are carrying on successfully many small business enterprises that give employment to scores of educated young colored men and women.

3

Lynching

African American feminists used the press to challenge the racialized violence of the nadir. Originally coined by historian Rayford Logan, "the nadir" refers to the post-Reconstruction climate of violent intimidation in which African Americans were raped and lynched. Statistics on lynching at this time reveal that its justification as retribution for black male rape of white women was a popular mythology with little if any relationship to reality. The most outspoken and famous of African American anti-lynching activists, Ida B. Wells reveals that in 1892 and 1893 "not one third of the victims lynched were charged with rape, and further that the charges made embraced a range of offenses from murders to misdemeanors" (Wells 1895, 156). The nadir, commonly considered to span the late 1870s through the early twentieth century, also saw the use of Jim Crow tactics, such as discrimination on public transportation, to intimidate African Americans and keep them in "their place." Wells wrote on these practices as well, having bitten the hand of a railroad conductor who sought to physically remove her from a "whites only" car and later unsuccessfully suing the railway company for its outrage against her person. In her first pamphlet, *Southern Horrors* (1892), Wells encouraged African Americans to practice "self-help" by withholding their trade from white-owned businesses, refusing to use streetcars or the railway, withdrawing their labor, leaving Southern states where the lynch mob prevailed, and arming themselves for self-protection. Clearly her mode of "self-help" is indebted to black nationalist principles of self-sufficiency, and her astute use of the press should be considered in the context of the black feminist journalism that preceded her work.

Wells, however, not only used the press as a feminist political tool but also educated her readers in what I would call a "pedagogy of the press" as an active component of lynching and political intimidation. In her call for African American self-help, Wells stressed the importance of getting the facts before the public; in urging black papers to "print the truth," saying that they were the only papers that would do so, she was also aware that the white press was an educator of its readership. Citing cases in which the crimes "motivating" lynchings were sensationally exaggerated in the white press, she proved that such accounts both aimed to justify the mob's actions and to further incite mob violence, representing it as warranted by the extremity of such crimes. In effect, these very graphic reports taught readers a technology of lynching and extended lynching's ritualized violence. In her effective challenges to both the Southern and Northern press, Wells engaged in what we might call a counter-pedagogy to such schooling in white supremacist violence.

Drawing the attention of Isabelle Fyvie Mayo and Catherine Impey, Scottish and English activists, Wells embarked on two anti-lynching tours of Britain. Her 1893 and 1894 anti-lynching tours gained such attention from British and American journalists that a biographer dubbed her "the most discussed individual in the black press – aside from Frederick Douglass" (McMurry 1998, 189). Wells's transatlantic anti-lynching work is interesting to consider alongside Sarah Parker Remond's anti-slavery appearances some forty years earlier, particularly given their astute management of competing political interests, such as white slavery. Wells also pioneered the anti-lynching arguments other black feminists pursued, including those of the Anti-Lynching Crusaders and Mary Church Terrell. She was at times too controversial a figure for her peers, such as Frances Harper, and organizations she helped found, such as the NAACP.

Frances Ellen Watkins Harper, "Duty to Dependent Races." Transactions of the National Council of Women of the United States, Assembled in Washington, DC, February 22 to 25, 1891. Ed. Rachel Foster Avery. Philadelphia: J.B. Lippincott, 1891. 86–91

While Miss Fletcher has advocated the cause of the Indian and negro under the caption of Dependent Races,[1] I deem it a privilege to present the negro, not as a mere dependent asking for Northern sympathy or Southern compassion, but as a member of the body politic who has a claim upon the nation for justice, simple justice, which is the right of every race, upon the government for protection, which is the rightful claim of every citizen, and upon our common Christianity for the best influences which can be exerted for peace on earth and good-will to man.

Our first claim upon the nation and government is the claim for protection to human life. That claim should lie at the basis of our civilization, not simply in theory but in fact. Outside of America, I know of no other civilized country, Catholic, Protestant, or even Mahometan, where men are still lynched, murdered, and even burned for real or supposed crimes. As long as there are such cases as moral irresponsibility, mental imbecility; as long as Potiphar's wife[2] stands in the world's pillory of shame, no man should be deprived of life or liberty without due process of law. A government which has power to tax a man in peace, and draft him in war, should have power to defend his life in the hour of peril. A government which can protect and defend its citizens from wrong and outrage and does not is vicious. A government which would do it and cannot is weak; and where human life is insecure through either weakness or viciousness in the administration of law, there must be a lack of justice, and where this is wanting nothing can make up the deficiency.

The strongest nation on earth cannot afford to deal unjustly towards its weakest and feeblest members. A man might just as well attempt to play with the thunderbolts of heaven and expect to escape unscathed, as for a nation to trample on justice and right and evade the divine penalty. The reason our nation snapped asunder in 1861 was because it lacked the cohesion of justice; men poured out their blood like water, scattered their wealth like chaff, summoned to the field the largest armies the nation had ever seen, but they did not get their final victories which closed the rebellion till they clasped hands with the negro, and marched with him abreast to freedom and to victory. I claim for the negro protection in every right with which the government has invested him. Whether it was wise or unwise, the government has exchanged the fetters on his wrist for the ballot in his right hand, and men cannot vitiate his vote by fraud, or intimidate the voter by violence, without being untrue to the genius and spirit of our government, and bringing demoralization into their own political life and ranks. Am I here met with the objection that the negro is poor and ignorant, and the greatest amount of land, capital, and intelligence is possessed by the white race, and that in a number of States negro suffrage means negro supremacy? But is it not a fact that both North and South power naturally gravitates into the strongest hands, and is there any danger that a race who were deemed so inferior as to be only fitted for slavery, and social and political ostracism, has in less than one generation become so powerful that, if not hindered from exercising the right of suffrage, it will dominate over a people who have behind them ages of dominion, education, freedom, and civilization, a people who have had poured into their veins the blood of some of the strongest races on earth? More than a year since Mr. Grady said, I believe, "We do not directly fear the political domination of the blacks, but that they are ignorant and easily deluded, impulsive and therefore easily led, strong of race instinct and therefore clannish, without information and therefore without political convictions, passionate and therefore easily excited, poor, irresponsible, and with no idea of the integrity of suffrage and therefore easily bought. The fear is that this vast swarm, ignorant, purchasable, will be impacted and controlled by desperate and unscrupulous white men and made to hold the balance of power when white men are divided." Admit for one moment that every word here is true, and that the whole race should be judged by its worst, and not its best members, does any civilized country legislate to punish a man before he commits a crime?

It is said the negro is ignorant. But why is he ignorant? It comes with ill grace from a man who has put out my eyes to make a parade of my blindness—to reproach me for my poverty when he has wronged me of my money. If the negro is ignorant, he has lived under the shadow of an institution which, at least in part of the country, made it a crime to teach him to read the name of the ever-blessed Christ. If he is poor, what has become of the money he has been earning for the last two hundred and fifty years? Years ago it was said cotton fights and cotton conquers for American slavery. The negro helped build up that great cotton power in the South, and in the North his sigh was in the whir of its machinery, and his blood and tears upon the warp and woof of its manufactures.

But there are some rights more precious than the rights of property or the claims of superior intelligence: they are the rights of life and liberty, and to these the poorest and humblest man has just as much right as the richest and most influential man in the country. Ignorance and poverty are conditions which men outgrow. Since the sealed volume was opened by the crimson hand of war, in spite of entailed ignorance, poverty, opposition, and a heritage of scorn, schools have sprung like wells in the desert dust. It has been estimated that about two millions have learned to read. Colored men and women have gone into journalism. Some of the first magazines in the country have received contributions from them. Learned professions have given them diplomas. Universities have granted them professorships. Colored women have combined to shelter orphaned children. Tens of thousands have been contributed by colored persons for the care of the aged and infirm. Instead of the old slave-pen of former days, imposing and commodious are edifices of prayer and praise. Millions of dollars have flowed into the pockets of the race, and freed people have not only been able to provide for themselves, but reach out their hands to impoverished owners.

Has the record of the slave been such as to warrant the belief that permitting him to share citizenship with others in the country is inimical to the welfare of the nation? Can it be said that he lacks patriotism, or a readiness to make common cause with the nation in the hour of peril? In the days of the American Revolution some of the first blood which was shed flowed from the veins of a colored man, and among the latest words that died upon his lips before they paled in death was, "Crush them underfoot," meaning the British guards.[3] To him Boston has given a monument.[4] In or after 1812 they received from General Jackson the plaudit, "I knew you would endure hunger and thirst and all the hardships of war. I knew that you loved the land of your nativity, and that, like ourselves, you had to defend all that is most dear; but you have surpassed my hopes. I have found in you, united to all these qualities, that noble enthusiasm which impels to great deeds."[5] And in our late civil conflict colored men threw their lives into the struggle, rallied around the old flag when others were trampling it underfoot and riddling it with bullets. Colored people learned to regard that flag as a harbinger of freedom and bring their most reliable information to the Union army, to share their humble fare with the escaping prisoner; to be faithful when others were faithless and help turn the tide of battle in favor of the nation. While nearly two hundred thousand joined the Union army, others remained on the old plantation; widows, wives, aged men, and helpless children were left behind, when the master was at the front trying to put new rivets in their chains, and yet was there a single slave who took advantage of the master's absence to invade the privacy of his home, or wreak a summary vengeance on those whose "defenceless condition should have been their best defence?"

Instead of taking the ballot from his hands, teach him how to use it, and to add his quota to the progress, strength, and durability of the nation. Let the nation, which once consented to his abasement under a system which made it a crime to teach him to read his Bible, feel it a privilege as well as a duty to reverse the old processes of the past by supplanting his darkness with light, not simply by providing the negro, but the whole region in which he lives, with national education. No child can be blamed because he was born in the midst of squalor, poverty, and ignorance, but society is criminal if it permits him to grow up without proper efforts for ameliorating his condition.

Some months since, when I was in South Carolina, where I addressed a number of colored schools, I was informed that white children were in the factories, beginning from eight to ten years old, with working hours from six to seven o'clock; and one day, as a number of white children were wending their way apparently from the factory, I heard a colored man say, "I pity these children." It was a strange turning of the tables to hear a colored man in South Carolina bestowing pity on white children because of neglect in their education. Surely the world does move. When parents are too poor or selfish to spare the labor of their children from the factories, and the State too indifferent or short-sighted to enforce their education by law, then let the Government save its future citizens from the results of cupidity in the parents or short-sightedness in the State. If to-day there is danger from a mass of ignorance voting, may there not be a danger even greater, and that is a mass of "ignorance that does not vote"? If there is danger that an ignorant mass might be compacted to hold the balance of power where white men are divided politically, might not that same mass, if kept ignorant and disfranchised, be used by wicked men, whose weapons may be bombs and dynamite, to dash themselves against the peace and order of society? To-day the hands of the negro are not dripping with dynamite. We do not read of his flaunting the red banners of anarchy in the face of the nation, nor plotting in beer-saloons to overthrow existing institutions, nor spitting on the American flag. Once that flag was to him an ensign of freedom. Let our Government resolve that as far as that flag extends every American-born child shall be able to read upon its folds liberty for all and chains for none.

And now permit me to make my final claim, and that is a claim upon our common Christianity. I believe in the Christianity of the Christ of Calvary, but I cannot believe in all its saddest and most terrible perversions. They are the shadow that has followed its sunshine and hindered its unfulfilled mission. I think of organized Christianity as a stream ploughing through different strata of earth, and partaking of the nature of the soil through which it percolates. It came to Latin races, but its shadow among them was the inquisition devising its tortures and the *auto-da-fé* lighting its fires.[6] It came to Slavic people, and we have the Greek Church with a background of Anti-Semitic persecutions and the horrors of Siberian prisons. Among English-speaking races we have weaker races victimized, a discontented Ireland, and a darkest England. In America we have had an emasculated Christianity— a Protestantism shorn of protesting strength, which would sing—

"Nothing in my hands I bring,
Simply to thy cross I cling,"[7]

when it should have brought in its hands the sacrifices of justice and mercy and broken every yoke and let the oppressed go free. Degenerate Israel remaining amid the graves, with the host of abominable things in her vessels, said to those whom she rejected, "Stand by thyself. Come not near me; I am holier than thou." A degenerate Christianity sitting by the dishonored tomb of American slavery and remaining amid the graves of the dead past still virtually says to millions of God's poor children, "Stand by thyself. Come not near me, for I am whiter than thou."[8]

Underlying this racial question, if I understand it aright, is one controlling idea, not simply that the negro is ignorant; *that* he is outgrowing; not that he is incapable of valor in war or adaptation in peace. On fields all drenched with blood he made his record in war, abstained from lawless violence when left on the plantation, and received his freedom in peace with moderation. But he holds in this Republic the position of an alien race among a people impatient of a rival. And in the eyes of some it seems that no valor redeems him, no social advancement nor individual development wipes off the ban which clings to him. It is the pride of Caste which opposes the spirit of Christ, and the great work to which American Christianity is called is a work of Christly reconciliation. God has heaved up your mountains with grandeur, flooded your rivers with majesty, crowned your vales with fertility, and enriched your mines with wealth. Excluding Alaska, you have, I think, nearly three hundred millions of square miles. Be reconciled to God for making a man black, permitting him to become part of your body politic, and sharing one rood or acre of our goodly heritage. Be reconciled to the Christ of Calvary, who said, "And I, if I be lifted up, will draw all men to me,"[9] and "It is better for a man that a millstone were hanged about his neck, and he were drowned in the depths of the sea, than that he should offend one of these little ones that believe in me."[10] Forgive the early adherents of Christianity who faced danger and difficulty and stood as victors by the side of Death, who would say, "I perceive that God is no respecter of persons."[11] "If ye have respect of persons ye commit sin."[12] "There is neither Greek nor Jew, circumcision nor uncircumcision, Scythian nor Barbarian, bond nor free, but Christ is all, and in all."[13]

What I ask of American Christianity is not to show us more creeds, but more of Christ; not more rites and ceremonies, but more religion glowing with love and replete with life—a religion which will be to all weaker races an uplifting power, and not a degrading influence. Jesus Christ has given us a platform of love and duty from which all oppression and selfishness is necessarily excluded. While politicians may stumble on the barren mountains of fretful controversy and ask in strange bewilderment, "What shall we do with weaker races?" I hold that Jesus Christ answered that question nearly two thousand years since. "Whatsoever ye would that men should do to you, do you even so to them."[14] When His religion fully permeates our civilization, and moulds our national life, the drink traffic will be abolished, the Indian question answered, and the negro problem solved.

187

Ida B. Wells, *Southern Horrors: Lynch Law in All Its Phases*. New York: New York Age, 1892

PREFACE

The greater part of what is contained in these pages was published in the New York *Age* June 25, 1892,[15] in explanation of the editorial which the Memphis whites considered sufficiently infamous to justify the destruction of my paper, *The Free Speech*.[16]

Since the appearance of that statement, requests have come from all parts of the country that "Exiled," (the name under which it then appeared) be issued in pamphlet form. Some donations were made, but not enough for that purpose. The noble effort of the ladies of New York and Brooklyn Oct 5 have enabled me to comply with this request and give the world a true, unvarnished account of the causes of lynch law in the South.[17]

This statement is not a shield for the despoiler of virtue, nor altogether a defense for the poor blind Afro-American Sampsons who suffer themselves to be betrayed by white Delilahs. It is a contribution to truth, an array of facts, the perusal of which it is hoped will stimulate this great American Republic to demand that justice be done though the heavens fall.

It is with no pleasure I have dipped my hands in the corruption here exposed. Somebody must show that the Afro-American race is more sinned against than sinning, and it seems to have fallen upon me to do so. The awful death-roll that Judge Lynch is calling every week is appalling, not only because of the lives it takes, the rank cruelty and outrage to the victims, but because of the prejudice it fosters and the stain it places against the good name of a weak race.

The Afro-American is not a bestial race. If this work can contribute in any way toward proving this, and at the same time arouse the conscience of the American people to a demand for justice to every citizen, and punishment by law for the lawless, I shall feel I have done my race a service. Other considerations are of minor importance.

IDA B. WELLS.

New York City, Oct. 26, 1892.

To the Afro-American women of New York and Brooklyn, whose race love, earnest zeal and unselfish effort at Lyric Hall, in the City of New York, on the night of October 5th, 1892—made possible its publication, this pamphlet is gratefully dedicated by the author.

HON. FRED. DOUGLASS'S LETTER.

Dear Miss Wells:

Let me give you thanks for your faithful paper on the lynch abomination now generally practiced against colored people in the South. There has been no word equal to it in convincing power. I have spoken, but my word is feeble in comparison. You give us what you know and testify from actual knowledge. You have dealt with the facts with cool, painstaking fidelity and left those naked and uncontradicted facts to speak for themselves.

Brave woman! you have done your people and mine a service which can neither be weighed nor measured. If American conscience were only half alive, if the American church and clergy were only half christianized, if American moral sensibility were not hardened by persistent infliction of outrage and crime against colored people, a scream of horror, shame and indignation would rise to Heaven wherever your pamphlet shall be read.

But alas! even crime has power to reproduce itself and create conditions favorable to its own existence. It sometimes seems we are deserted by earth and Heaven—yet we must still think, speak and work, and trust in the power of a merciful God for final deliverance.

Very truly and gratefully yours,
FREDERICK DOUGLASS.

Cedar Hill, Anacostia, DC, Oct. 25, 1892.

CHAPTER I
THE OFFENSE

Wednesday evening May 24th, 1892, the city of Memphis was filled with excitement. Editorials in the daily papers of that date caused a meeting to be held in the Cotton Exchange Building; a committee was sent for the editors of the "Free Speech" an Afro-American journal published in that city, and the only reason the open threats of lynching that were made were not carried out was because they could not be found. The cause of all this commotion was the following editorial published in the "Free Speech" May 21st, 1892, the Saturday previous.

Eight negroes lynched since last issue of the "Free Speech"[:] one at Little Rock, Ark., last Saturday morning where the citizens broke (?) into the penitentiary and got their man; three near Anniston, Ala., one near New Orleans; and three at Clarksville, Ga., the last three for killing a white man, and five on the same old racket—the new alarm about raping white women. The same programme of hanging, then shooting bullets into the lifeless bodies was carried out to the letter.

Nobody in this section of the country believes the old thread[-]bare lie that Negro men rape white women. If Southern white men are not careful, they will over-reach themselves and public sentiment will have a reaction; a conclusion will then be reached which will be very damaging to the moral reputation of their women.

"The Daily Commercial" of Wednesday following, May 25th, contained the following leader:

Those negroes who are attempting to make the lynching of individuals of their race a means for arousing the worst passions of their kind are playing with a dangerous sentiment. The negroes may as well understand that there is no mercy for the negro rapist and little patience with his defenders. A negro organ printed in this city, in a recent issue publishes the following atrocious paragraph: "Nobody in this section of the country believes the old thread-bare lie that negro men rape white women. If Southern white men are not careful they will over-reach themselves, and public sentiment will have a reaction; and a conclusion will be reached which will be very damaging to the moral reputation of their women."

The fact that a black scoundrel is allowed to live and utter such loathsome and repulsive calumnies is a volume of evidence as to the wonderful patience of Southern whites. But we have had enough of it.

There are some things that the Southern white man will not tolerate, and the obscene intimations of the foregoing have brought the writer to the very outermost limit of public patience. We hope we have said enough."

The "Evening Scimitar" of same date copied the "Commercial's" editorial with these words of comment: "Patience under such circumstances is not a virtue. If the negroes themselves do not apply the remedy without delay it will be the duty of those whom he has attacked to tie the wretch who utters these calumnies to a stake at the intersection of Main and Madison Sts., brand him in the forehead with a hot iron and perform upon him a surgical operation with a pair of tailor's shears."

Acting upon this advice, the leading citizens met in the Cotton Exchange Building, the same evening, and threats of lynching were freely indulged, not by the lawless element upon which the deviltry of the South is usually saddled—but by the leading business men, in their leading business centre. Mr. Fleming, the business manager and owning a half interest

[in] the "Free Speech," had to leave town to escape the mob, and was afterwards ordered not to return; letters and telegrams sent me in New York where I was spending my vacation advised me that bodily harm awaited my return. Creditors took possession of the office and sold the outfit, and the "Free Speech" was as if it had never been!

The editorial in question was prompted by the many inhuman and fiendish lynchings of Afro-Americans which have recently taken place and was meant as a warning. Eight lynched in one week and five of them charged with rape! The thinking public will not easily believe freedom and education more brutalizing than slavery, and the world knows that the crime of rape was unknown during four years of civil war, when the white women of the South were at the mercy of the race which is all at once charged with being a bestial one.

Since my business has been destroyed and I am an exile from home because of that editorial, the issue has been forced, and as the writer of it I feel that the race and the public generally should have a statement of the facts as they exist. They will serve at the same time as a defense for the Afro-American Sampsons who suffer themselves to be betrayed by white Delilahs.

The whites of Montgomery, Ala., knew J.C. Duke sounded the keynote of the situation—which they would gladly hide from the world, when he said in his paper, "The Herald," five years ago: "Why is it that white women attract negro men now more than in former days! There was a time when such a thing was unheard of. There is a secret to this thing, and we greatly suspect it is the growing appreciation of white Juliets for colored Romeos." Mr. Duke, like the *Free Speech* proprietors, was forced to leave the city for reflecting on the "honah" of white women and his paper suppressed; but the truth remains that Afro-American men do not always rape (?) white women without their consent.

Mr. Duke, before leaving Montgomery, signed a card disclaiming any intention of slandering Southern white women. The editor of the "Free Speech" has no disclaimer to enter, but asserts instead that there are many white women in the South who would marry colored men if such an act would not place them at once beyond the pale of society and within the clutches of the law. The miscegenation laws of the South only operate against the legitimate union of the races; they leave the white man free to seduce all the colored girls he can, but it is death to the colored man who yields to the force and advances of a similar attraction in white women. White men lynch the offending Afro-American, not because he is a despoiler of virtue, but because he succumbs to the smiles of white women.

CHAPTER II
THE BLACK AND WHITE OF IT

The "Cleveland Gazette" of January 16, 1892, publishes a case in point. Mrs. J.S. Underwood, the wife of a minister of Elyria, Ohio, accused an Afro-American of rape. She told her husband that during his absence in 1888, stumping the State for the Prohibition Party, the man came to the kitchen door, forced his way in the house and insulted her. She tried to drive him out with a heavy poker, but he overpowered and chloroformed her, and when she revived her clothing was torn and she was in a horrible condition. She did not know the man but could identify him. She pointed out William Offett, a married man, who was arrested and, being in Ohio, was granted a trial.

The prisoner vehemently denied the charge of rape, but confessed he went to Mrs. Underwood's residence at her invitation and was criminally intimate with her at her request. This availed him nothing against the sworn testimony of a minister's wife, a lady of the highest respectability. He was found guilty, and entered the penitentiary, December 14, 1888, for fifteen years. Some time afterwards the woman's remorse led her to confess to her husband that the man was innocent.

These are her words: "I met Offett at the Post Office. It was raining. He was polite to me, and as I had several bundles in my arms he offered to carry them home for me, which he did. He had a strange fascination for me, and I invited him to call on me. He called, bringing chestnuts and candy for the children. By this means we got them to leave us alone in the room. Then I sat on his lap. He made a proposal to me and I readily consented. Why I did so, I do not know, but that I did is true. He visited me several times after that and each time I was indiscreet. I did not care after the first time. In fact I could not have resisted, and had no desire to resist."

When asked by her husband why she told him she had been outraged, she said: "I had several reasons for telling you. One was the neighbors saw the fellows [sic] here, another was, I was afraid I had contracted a loathsome disease, and still another was that I feared I might give birth to a Negro baby. I hoped to save my reputation by telling you a deliberate lie." Her husband horrified by the confession had Offett, who had already served four years, released and secured a divorce.

There are thousands of such cases throughout the South, with the difference that the Southern white men in insatiate fury wreak their vengeance without intervention of law upon the Afro-Americans who consort with their women. A few instances to substantiate the assertion that some white

192

women love the company of the Afro-American will not be out of place. Most of these cases were reported by the daily papers of the South.

In the winter, of 1885-86 the wife of a practicing physician in Memphis, in good social standing whose name has escaped me, left home, husband and children, and ran away with her black coachman. She was with him a month before her husband found and brought her home. The coachman could not be found. The doctor moved his family away from Memphis, and is living in another city under an assumed name.

In the same city last year a white girl in the dusk of evening screamed at the approach of some parties that a Negro had assaulted her on the street. He was captured, tried by a white judge and jury, that acquitted him of the charge. It is needless to add if there had been a scrap of evidence on which to convict him of so grave a charge he would have been convicted.

Sarah Clark of Memphis loved a black man and lived openly with him. When she was indicted last spring for miscegenation, she swore in court that she was *not* a white woman. This she did to escape the penitentiary and continue her illicit relation undisturbed. That she is of the lower class of whites does not disturb the fact that she is a white woman. "The leading citizens" of Memphis are defending the "honor" of *all* white women, *demi-monde* included.

Since the manager of the "Free Speech" has been run away from Memphis by the guardians of the honor of Southern white women, a young girl living on Poplar St., who was discovered in intimate relations with a handsome mulatto young colored man, Will Morgan by name, stole her father's money to send the young fellow away from that father's wrath. She has since joined him in Chicago.

The Memphis "Ledger" for June 8th has the following; "If Lillie Bailey, a rather pretty white girl seventeen years of age, who is now at the City Hospital, would be somewhat less reserved about her disgrace there would be some very nauseating details in the story of her life. She is the mother of a little coon. The truth might reveal fearful depravity or it might reveal the evidence of a rank outrage. She will not divulge the name of the man who has left such black evidence of her disgrace, and, in fact, says it is a matter in which there can be no interest to the outside world. She came to Memphis nearly three months ago and was taken in at the Woman's Refuge in the southern part of the city. She remained there until a few weeks ago, when the child was born. The ladies in charge of the Refuge were horrified. The girl was at once sent to the City Hospital, where she has been since May 30th. She is a country girl. She came to Memphis from her father's farm, a short distance from Hernando, Miss. Just when she left there she would not say. In fact she says she came to Memphis from Arkansas, and says her home is in that State. She is rather good looking, has blue eyes, a low forehead and dark red hair. The ladies at the Woman's Refuge do not know anything about the girl further than what they learned when she was an inmate of the institution; and she would not tell much. When the child was born an attempt was made to get the girl to reveal the name of the Negro who had disgraced her, she obstinately refused and it was impossible to elicit any information from her on the subject."

Note the wording. "The truth might reveal fearful depravity or rank outrage." If it had been a white child or Lillie Bailey had told a pitiful story of Negro outrage, it would have been a case of woman's weakness or assault and she could have remained at the Woman's Refuge. But a Negro child and to withhold its father's name and thus prevent the killing of another Negro "rapist." A case of "fearful depravity." The very week the "leading citizens" of Memphis were making a spectacle of themselves in defense of all white women of every kind, an Afro-American, M. Stricklin, was found in a white woman's room in that city. Although she made no outcry of rape, he was jailed and would have been lynched, but the woman stated she bought curtains of him (he was a furniture dealer) and his business in her room that night was to put them up. A white woman's word was taken as absolutely in this case as when the cry of rape is made, and he was freed.

What is true of Memphis is true of the entire South. The daily papers last year reported a farmer's wife in Alabama had given birth to a Negro child. When the Negro farm hand who was plowing in the field heard it he took the mule from the plow and fled. The dispatches also told of a woman in South Carolina who gave birth to a Negro child and charged three men with being its father, every *one of whom has since disappeared*. In Tuscumbia, Ala., the colored boy who was lynched there last year for assaulting a white girl told her before his accusers that he had met her there in the woods often before.

Frank Weems of Chattanooga who was not lynched in May only because the prominent citizens became his body guard until the doors of the penitentiary closed on him, had letters in his pocket from the white woman in the case, making the appointment with him. Edward Coy, who was burned alive in Texarkana January 1, 1892, died protesting his innocence. Investigation since as given by the Bystander in the Chicago Inter-Ocean, October 1, proves:

1. The woman who was paraded as a victim of violence was of bad character; her husband was a drunkard and a gambler.
2. She was publicly reported and generally known to have been criminally intimate with Coy for more than a year previous.

3. She was compelled by threats, if not by violence, to make the charge against the victim.

4. When she came to apply the match Coy asked her if she would burn him after they had "been sweethearting" so long.

5. A large majority of the "superior" white men prominent in the affair are the reputed fathers of mulatto children.

These are not pleasant facts, but they are illustrative of the vital phase of the so-called "race question," which should properly be designated an earnest inquiry as to the best methods by which religion, science, law and political power may be employed to excuse injustice, barbarity and crime done to a people because of race and color. There can be no possible belief that these people were inspired by any consuming zeal to vindicate God's law against miscegenationists of the most practical sort. The woman was a willing partner in the victim's guilt, and being of the "superior" race must naturally have been more guilty.

In Natchez, Miss., Mrs. Marshall, one of the *creme de la creme* of the city, created a tremendous sensation several years ago. She has a black coachman who was married and had been in her employ several years. During this time she gave birth to a child whose color was remarked, but traced to some brunette ancestor, and one of the fashionable dames of the city was its godmother. Mrs. Marshall's social position was unquestioned, and wealth showered every dainty on this child which was idolized with its brothers and sisters by its white papa. In course of time another child appeared on the scene, but it was unmistakably dark. All were alarmed, and "rush of blood, strangulation" were the conjectures, but the doctor, when asked the cause, grimly told them it was a Negro child. There was a family conclave, the coachman heard of it and leaving his own family went West, and has never returned. As soon as Mrs. Marshall was able to travel she was sent away in deep disgrace. Her husband died within the year of a broken heart.

Ebenzer Fowler, the wealthiest colored man in Issaquena County, Miss., was shot down on the street in Mayersville, January 30, 1885, just before dark by an armed body of white men who filled his body with bullets. They charged him with writing a note to a white woman of the place, which they intercepted and which proved there was an intimacy existing between them.

Hundreds of such cases might be cited, but enough have been given to prove the assertion that there are white women in the South who love the Afro-American's company even as there are white men notorious for their preference for Afro-American women.

There is hardly a town in the South which has not an instance of the kind which is well-known, and hence the assertion is reiterated that "nobody in the South believes the old thread-bare lie that negro men rape white women." Hence there is a growing demand among Afro-Americans that the guilt or innocence of parties accused of rape be fully established. They know the men of the section of the country who refuse this are not so desirous of punishing rapists as they pretend. The utterances of the leading white men show that with them it is not the crime but the *class*. Bishop Fitzgerald has become apologist for lynchers of the rapists of *white* women only. Governor Tillman, of South Carolina, in the month of June, standing under the tree in Barnwell, S.C., on which eight Afro-Americans were hung last year, declared that he "would lead a mob to lynch a *negro* who raped a *white* woman." So say the pulpits, officials and newspapers of the South. But when the victim is a colored woman it is different.

Last winter in Baltimore, Md., three white ruffians assaulted a Miss Camphor, a young Afro-American girl, while out walking with a young man of her own race. They held her escort and outraged the girl. It was a deed dastardly enough to arouse Southern blood, which gives its horror of rape as excuse for lawlessness, but she was an Afro-American. The case went to the courts, an Afro-American lawyer defended the men and they were acquitted.

In Nashville, Tenn., there is a white man, Pat Hanifan, who outraged a little Afro-American girl, and, from the physical injuries received, she has been ruined for life. He was jailed for six months, discharged, and is now a detective in that city. In the same city, last May, a white man outraged an Afro-American girl in a drug store. He was arrested, and released on bail at the trial. It was rumored that five hundred Afro-Americans had organized to lynch him. Two hundred and fifty white citizens armed themselves with Winchesters and guarded him. A cannon was placed in front of his home, and the Buchanan Rifles (State Militia) ordered to the scene for his protection. The Afro-American mob did not materialize. Only two weeks before Eph. Grizzard, who had only been *charged* with rape upon a white woman, had been taken from the jail, with Governor Buchanan and the police and militia standing by, dragged through the streets in broad daylight, knives plunged into him at every step, and with every fiendish cruelty a frenzied mob could devise, he was at last swung out on the bridge with hands cut to pieces as he tried to climb up the stanchions. A naked bloody example of the blood-thirstiness of the nineteenth-century civilization of the Athens, of the South! No cannon or military was called out in his defense. He dared to visit a white woman.

At the very moment these civilized whites were announcing their determination "to protect their wives and daughters" by murdering Grizzard, a white man was in the same jail for raping eight-year-old Maggie Reese, an Afro-American girl. He was not harmed. The "honor" of grown women who were glad enough to be supported by the Grizzard boys and Ed Coy, as long as the liaison was not known, needed protection; they were white. The outrage upon helpless childhood needed no avenging in this case; she was black.

A white man in Guthrie, Oklahoma Territory, two months ago inflicted such injuries upon another Afro-American child that she died. He was not punished, but an attempt was made in the same town in the month of June to lynch an Afro-American who visited a white woman.

In Memphis, Tenn., in the month of June, Ellerton L. Dorr, who is the husband of Russell Hancock's widow, was arrested for attempted rape on Mattie Cole, a neighbor's cook; he was only prevented from accomplishing his purpose by the appearance of Mattie's employer. Dorr's friends say he was drunk and not responsible for his actions. The grand jury refused to indict him and he was discharged.

CHAPTER III
THE NEW CRY

The appeal of Southern whites to Northern sympathy and sanction, the adroit, insidious plea made by Bishop Fitzgerald for suspension of judgment because those "who condemn lynching express no sympathy for the *white* woman in the case," falls to the ground in the light of the foregoing.

From this exposition of the race issue in lynch law, the whole matter is explained by the well-known opposition growing out of slavery to the progress of the race. This is crystalized in the oft-repeated slogan: "This is a white man's country and the white man must rule." The South resented giving the Afro-American his freedom, the ballot box and the Civil Rights Law. The raids of the Ku-Klux and White Liners to subvert reconstruction government, the Hamburg and Ellerton, S.C., the Copiah County Miss., and the Lafayette Parish, La., massacres were excused as the natural resentment of intelligence against government by ignorance.

Honest white men practically conceded the necessity of intelligence murdering ignorance to correct the mistake of the general government, and the race was left to the tender mercies of the solid South. Thoughtful Afro-Americans with the strong arm of the government withdrawn and with the hope to stop such wholesale massacres urged the race to sacrifice its political rights for sake of peace. They honestly believed the race should fit itself for government, and when that should be done, the objection to race participation in politics would be removed.

But the sacrifice did not remove the trouble, nor move the South to justice. One by one the Southern States have legally (?) disfranchised the Afro-American, and since the repeal of the Civil Rights Bill nearly every Southern State has passed separate car laws with a penalty against their infringement. The race regardless of advancement is penned into filthy, stifling partitions cut off from smoking cars. All this while, although the political cause has been removed, the butcheries of black men at Barnwell, S.C., Carrolton, Miss., Way-cross, Ga., and Memphis, Tenn., have gone on; also the flaying alive of a man in Kentucky, the burning of one in Arkansas, the hanging of a fifteen year old girl in Louisiana, a woman in Jackson, Tenn., and one in Hollendale, Miss., until the dark and bloody record of the South shows 728 Afro-Americans lynched during the past 8 years. Not 50 of these were for political causes; the rest were for all manner of accusations from that of rape of white women to the case of the boy Will Lewis who was hanged at Tullahoma, Tenn., last year for being drunk and "sassy" to white folks.

These statistics compiled by the Chicago "Tribune" were given the first of this year (1892). Since then, not less than one hundred and fifty have been known to have met violent death at the hands of cruel bloodthirsty mobs during the-past nine months.

To palliate this record (which grows worse as the Afro-American becomes intelligent) and excuse some of the most heinous crimes that ever stained the history of a country, the South is shielding itself behind the plausible screen of defending the honor of its women. This, too, in the face of the fact that only *one-third* of the 728 victims to mobs have been *charged* with rape, to say nothing of those of that one-third who were innocent of the charge. A white correspondent of the Baltimore Sun declares that the Afro-American who was lynched in Chestertown, Md., in May for assault on a white girl was innocent; that the deed was done by a white man who had since disappeared. The girl herself maintained that her assailant was a white man. When that poor Afro-American was murdered, the whites excused their refusal of a trial on the ground that they wished to spare the white girl the mortification of having to testify in court.

This cry has had its effect. It has closed the heart, stifled the conscience, warped the judgment and hushed the voice of press and pulpit on the subject of lynch law throughout this "land of liberty." Men who stand high in the esteem of the public for Christian character, for moral and physical courage, for devotion to the principles of equal and exact justice to all, and for great sagacity, stand as cowards who fear to open their mouths before this great outrage. They do not see that by their tacit encouragement, their silent acquiescence, the black shadow of lawlessness in the form of lynch law is spreading its wings over the whole country.

Men who, like Governor Tillman, start the ball of lynch law rolling for a certain crime, are powerless to stop it when drunken or criminal white toughs feel like hanging an Afro-American on any pre-text.

Even to the better class of Afro-Americans the crime of rape is so revolting they have too often taken the white man's word and given lynch law neither the investigation nor condemnation it deserved.

They forget that a concession of the right to lynch a man for a certain crime, not only concedes the right to lynch any person for any crime, but (so frequently is the cry of rape now raised) it is in a fair way to stamp us a race of rapists and desperadoes. They have gone on hoping and believing that general education and financial strength would solve the difficulty, and are devoting their energies to the accumulation of both.

The mob spirit has grown with the increasing intelligence of the Afro-American. It has left the out-of-the-way places where ignorance prevails, has thrown off the mask and with this new cry stalks in broad daylight in large cities, the centres of civilization, and is encouraged by the "leading citizens" and the press.

CHAPTER IV
THE MALICIOUS AND UNTRUTHFUL WHITE PRESS

The "Daily Commercial" and "Evening Scimitar" of Memphis, Tenn., are owned by leading business men of that city, and yet, in spite of the fact that there had been no white woman in Memphis outraged by an Afro-American, and that Memphis possessed a thrifty law-abiding, property owning class of Afro-Americans the "Commercial" of May 17th, under the head of "More Rapes, More Lynchings" gave utterance to the following:

The lynching of three Negro scoundrels reported in our dispatches from Anniston, Ala., for a brutal outrage committed upon a white woman, will be a text for much comment on 'Southern barbarism' by Northern newspapers; but we fancy it will hardly prove effective for campaign purposes among intelligent people. The frequency of these lynchings calls attention to the frequency of the crimes which causes lynching. The 'Southern barbarism' which deserves the serious attention of all people North and South, is the barbarism which preys upon weak and defenseless women. Nothing but the most prompt, speedy and extreme punishment can hold in check the horrible and bestial propensities of the Negro race. There is a strange similarity about a number of cases of this character which have lately occurred.

In each case the crime was deliberately planned and perpetrated by several Negroes. They watched for an opportunity when the women were left without a protector. It was not a sudden yielding to a fit of passion, but the consummation of a devilish purpose which has been seeking and waiting for the opportunity. This feature of the crime not only makes it the most fiendishly brutal, but it adds to the terror of the situation in the thinly settled country communities. No man can leave his family at night without the dread that some roving Negro ruffian is watching and waiting for this opportunity. The swift punishment which invariably follows these horrible crimes doubtless acts as a deterring effect upon the Negroes in that immediate neighborhood for a short time. But the lesson is not widely learned nor long remembered. Then such crimes, equally atrocious, have happened in quick succession, one in Tennessee, one in Arkansas, and one in Alabama. The facts of the crime appear to appeal more to the Negro's lustful imagination than the facts of the punishment do to his fears. He sets aside all fear of death in any form when opportunity is found for the gratification of his bestial desires.

There is small reason to hope for any change for the better. The commission of this crime grows more frequent every year. The generation of Negroes which have grown up since the war have lost in large measure the traditional and wholesome awe of the white race which kept the Negroes in subjection, even when their masters were in the army, and their families left unprotected except by the slaves themselves. There is no longer a restraint upon the brute passion of the Negro.

What is to be done? The crime of rape is always horrible, but [for] the Southern man there is nothing which so fills the soul with horror, loathing and fury as the outraging of a white woman by a Negro. It is the race question in the ugliest, vilest, most dangerous aspect. The Negro as a political factor can be controlled. But neither laws nor lynchings can subdue his lusts. Sooner or later it will force a crisis. We do not know in what form it will come.

In its issue of June 4th, the Memphis "Evening Scimitar" gives the following excuse for lynch law:

Aside from the violation of white women by Negroes, which is the outcropping of a bestial perversion of instinct, the chief cause of trouble between the races in the South is the Negro's lack of manners. In the state of slavery he learned politeness from association with white people, who took pains to teach him. Since the emancipation came and the tie of mutual interest and regard between master and servant was broken, the Negro has drifted away into a state which is neither freedom nor bondage. Lacking the proper inspiration of the one and the restraining force of the other, he has taken up the idea that boorish insolence is independence, and the exercise of a decent degree of breeding toward white people is identical with servile submission. In consequence of the prevalence of this notion there are many Negroes who use every opportunity to make themselves offensive, particularly when they think it can be done with impunity.

We have had too many instances right here in Memphis to doubt this, and our experience is not exceptional. *The white people won't stand this sort of thing, and whether they be insulted as individuals are* [sic] *as a race, the response will be prompt and effectual.* The bloody riot of 1866, in which so many Negroes perished, was brought on principally by the outrageous conduct of the blacks toward the whites on the streets. It is also a remarkable and discouraging fact that the majority of such scoundrels are Negroes who have received educational advantages at the hands of the white taxpayers. They have got just enough of learning to make them realize how hopelessly their race is behind the other in everything that makes a great people, and they attempt to 'get even' by insolence, which is ever the resentment of inferiors. There are well-bred Negroes among us, and it is truly unfortunate that they should have to pay, even in part, the penalty of the offenses committed by the baser sort, but this is the way of the world. The innocent must suffer for the guilty. If the Negroes as a people possessed a hundredth part of the self-respect which is evidenced by the courteous bearing of some that the "Scimitar" could name, the friction between the races would be reduced to a minimum. It will not do to beg the question by pleading that many white men are also stirring up strife. The Caucasian blackguard simply obeys the promptings of a depraved disposition, and he is seldom deliberately rough or offensive toward strangers or unprotected women.

The Negro tough, on the contrary, is given to just that kind of offending, and he almost invariably singles out white people as his victims.

On March 9th, 1892, there were lynched in this same city three of the best specimens of young since-the-war Afro-American manhood. They were peaceful, law-abiding citizens and energetic business men.

They believed the problem was to be solved by eschewing politics and putting money in the purse. They owned a flourishing grocery business in a thickly populated suburb of Memphis, and a white man named Barrett had one on the opposite corner. After a personal difficulty, which Barrett sought by going into the "People's Grocery" drawing a pistol and was thrashed by Calvin McDowell, he (Barrett) threatened to "clean them out." These men were a mile beyond the city limits and police protection; hearing that Barrett's crowd was coming to attack them Saturday night, they mustered forces and prepared to defend themselves against the attack.

When Barrett came he led a *posse* of officers, twelve in number, who afterward claimed to be hunting a man for whom they had a warrant. That twelve men in citizen's clothes should think it necessary to go in the night to hunt one man who had never before been arrested, or made any record as a criminal has never been explained. When they entered the back door the young men thought the threatened attack was on, and fired into them. Three of the officers were wounded, and when the *defending* party found it was officers of the law upon whom they had fired, they ceased and got away.

Thirty-one men were arrested and thrown in jail as "conspirators," they all declared more than once they did not know they were firing on officers. Excitement was at fever heat until the morning papers, two days after, announced that the wounded deputy sheriffs were out of danger. This hindered rather than helped the plans of the whites. There was no law on the statute books which would execute an Afro-American for wounding a white man, but the "unwritten law" did. Three of these men, the president, the manager and clerk of the grocery—"the leaders of the conspiracy"—were secretly taken from jail and lynched in a shockingly brutal manner. "The Negroes are getting too independent," they say, "we must teach them a lesson."

What lesson? The lesson of subordination. "Kill the leaders and it will cow the Negro who dares to shoot a white man, even in self-defense."

Although the race was wild over the outrage, the mockery of law and justice which disarmed men and locked them up in jails where they could be easily and safely reached by the mob—the Afro-American ministers, newspapers and leaders counselled obedience to the law which did not protect them.

Their counsel was heeded and not a hand was uplifted to resent the outrage; following the advice of the "Free Speech," people left the city in great numbers.

The dailies and associated press reports heralded these men to the country as "toughs," and "Negro desperadoes who kept a low dive." This same press service printed that the Negro who was lynched at Indianola, Miss., in May, had outraged the sheriff's eight-year-old daughter. The girl was more than eighteen years old, and was found by her father in this man's room, who was a servant on the place.

Not content with misrepresenting the race, the mob spirit was not to be satisfied until the paper which was doing all it could to counteract this impression was silenced. The colored people were resenting their bad treatment in a way to make itself felt, yet gave the mob no excuse for further murder, until the appearance of the editorial which is construed as a reflection on the "honor" of the Southern white women. It is not half so libelous as that of the "Commercial" which appeared four days before, and which has been given in these pages. They would have lynched the manager of the "Free Speech" for exercising the right of free speech if they had found him as quickly as they would have hung a rapist, and glad of the excuse to do so. The owners were ordered not to return, "The Free Speech" was suspended with as little compunction as the business of the "People's Grocery" broken up and the proprietors murdered.

CHAPTER V
THE SOUTH'S POSITION

Henry W. Grady[18] in his well-remembered speeches in New England and New York pictured the Afro-American as incapable of self-government. Through him and other leading men the cry of the South to the country has been "Hands off! Leave us to solve our problem." To the Afro-American the South says, "the white man must and will rule." There is little difference between the Ante-bellum South and the New South.

Her white citizens are wedded to any method however revolting, any measure however extreme, for the subjugation of the young manhood of the race. They have cheated him out of his ballot, deprived him of civil rights or redress therefor in the civil courts, robbed him of the fruits of his labor, and are still murdering, burning and lynching him.

The result is a growing disregard of human life. Lynch law has spread its insidious influence till men in New York State, Pennsylvania and on the free Western plains feel they can take the law in their own hands with impunity, especially where an Afro-American is concerned. The South is brutalized to a degree not realized by its own inhabitants, and the very foundation of government, law and order are imperilled.

Public sentiment has had a slight "reaction" though not sufficient to stop the crusade of lawlessness and lynching. The spirit of Christianity of the great M.E. Church was aroused to the frequent and revolting crimes against a weak people, enough to pass strong condemnatory resolutions at its General Conference in Omaha last May. The spirit of justice of the grand old party asserted itself sufficiently to secure a denunciation of the wrongs, and a feeble declaration of the belief in human rights in the

Republican platform at Minneapolis, June 7th. Some of the great dailies and weeklies have swung into line declaring that lynch law must go. The President of the United States issued a proclamation that it be not tolerated in the territories over which he has jurisdiction. Governor Northern and Chief Justice Bleckley of Georgia have proclaimed against it. The citizens of Chattanooga, Tenn., have set a worthy example in that they not only condemn lynch law, but her public men demanded a trial for Weems, the accused rapist, and guarded him while the trial was in progress. The trial only lasted ten minutes, and Weems chose to plead guilty and accept twenty-one years sentence, than invite the certain death which awaited him outside that cordon of police if he had told the truth and shown the letters he had from the white woman in the case.

Col. A.S. Colyar, of Nashville, Tenn., is so overcome with the horrible state of affairs that he addressed the following earnest letter to the Nashville "American." "Nothing since I have been a reading man has so impressed me with the decay of manhood among the people of Tennessee as the dastardly submission to the mob reign. We have reached the unprecedented low level; the awful criminal depravity of substituting the mob for the court and jury, of giving up the jail keys to the mob whenever they are demanded. We do it in the largest cities and in the country towns; we do it in midday; we do it after full, not to say formal, notice, and so thoroughly and generally is it acquiesced in that the murderers have discarded the formula of masks. They go into the town where everybody knows them, sometimes under the gaze of the governor, in the presence of the courts, in the presence of the sheriff and his deputies, in the presence of the entire police force, take out the prisoner, take his life, often with fiendish glee, and often with acts of cruelty and barbarism which impress the reader with a degeneracy rapidly approaching savage life. That the State is disgraced but faintly expresses the humiliation which has settled upon the once proud people of Tennessee. The State, in its majesty, through its organized life, for which the people pay liberally, makes but one record, but one note, and that a criminal falsehood, 'was hung by persons to the jury unknown.' The murder at Shelbyville is only a verification of what every intelligent man knew would come, because with a mob a rumor is as good as a proof."

These efforts brought forth apologies and a short halt, but the lynching mania has raged again through the past three months with unabated fury.

The strong arm of the law must be brought to bear upon lynchers in severe punishment, but this cannot and will not be done unless a healthy public sentiment demands and sustains such action.

The men and women in the South who disapprove of lynching and remain silent on the perpetration of such outrages are particeps criminis,[19] accomplices, accessories before and after the fact, equally guilty with actual law-breakers who would not persist if they did not know that neither the law nor militia would be employed against them.

CHAPTER VI
SELF HELP

In the creation of this healthier public sentiment, the Afro-American can do for himself what no one else can do for him. The world looks on with wonder that we have conceded so much and remain law-abiding under such great outrage and provocation.

To Northern capital and Afro-American labor the South owes its rehabilitation. If labor is withdrawn capital will not remain. The Afro-American is thus the backbone of the South. A thorough knowledge and judicious exercise of this power in lynching localities could many times effect a bloodless revolution. The white man's dollar is his god, and to stop this will be to stop outrages in many localities.

The Afro-Americans of Memphis denounced the lynching of three of their best citizens, and urged and waited for the authorities to act in the matter and bring the lynchers to justice. No attempt was made to do so, and the black men left the city by thousands, bringing about great stagnation in every branch of business. Those who remained so injured the business of the street car company by staying off the cars, that the superintendent, manager and treasurer called personally on the editor of the "Free Speech," asked them to urge our people to give them their patronage again. Other business men became alarmed over the situation and the "Free Speech" was run away that the colored people might be more easily controlled. A meeting of white citizens in June, three months after the lynching, passed resolutions for the first time, condemning it. *But they did not punish the lynchers.* Every one of them was known by name, because they had been selected to do the dirty work, by some of the very citizens who passed these resolutions. Memphis is fast losing her black population, who proclaim as they go that there is no protection for the life and property of any Afro-American citizen in Memphis who is not a slave.

The Afro-American citizens of Kentucky, whose intellectual and financial improvement has been phenomenal, have never had a separate car law until now. Delegations and petitions poured into the Legislature against it, yet the bill passed and the Jim Crow Car of Kentucky is a legalized institution. Will the great mass of Negroes continue to patronize the railroad? A special from Covington, Ky., says:

Covington, June 13th. — The railroads of the State are beginning to feel very markedly the effects of the separate coach bill recently passed by the Legislature. No class of people in the State have so many and so largely attended excursions as the blacks. All these have been abandoned, and regular travel is reduced to a minimum. A competent authority says the loss to the various roads will reach $1,000,000 this year.

A call to a State Conference in Lexington, Ky., last June had delegates from every county in the State. Those delegates, the ministers, teachers, heads of secret and other orders, and the head of every family should pass the word around for every member of the race in Kentucky to stay off railroads unless obliged to ride. If they did so, and their advice was followed persistently the convention would not need to petition the Legislature to repeal the law or raise money to file a suit. The railroad corporations would be so effected they would in self-defense lobby to have the separate car law repealed. On the other hand, as long as the railroads can get Afro-American excursions they will always have plenty of money to fight all the suits brought against them. They will be aided in so doing by the same partisan public sentiment which passed the law. White men passed the law, and white judges and juries would pass upon the suits against the law, and render judgment in line with their prejudices and in deference to the greater financial power.

The appeal to the white man's pocket has ever been more effectual than all the appeals ever made to his conscience. Nothing, absolutely nothing, is to be gained by a further sacrifice of manhood and self-respect. By the right exercise of his power as the industrial factor of the South, the Afro-American can demand and secure his rights, the punishment of lynchers, and a fair trial for accused rapists.

Of the many inhuman outrages of this present year, the only case where the proposed lynching did *not* occur, was where the men armed themselves in Jacksonville, Fla., and Paducah, Ky., and prevented it. The only times an Afro-American who was assaulted got away has been when he had a gun and used it in self-defense.

The lesson this teaches and which every Afro-American should ponder well, is that a Winchester rifle should have a place of honor in every black home, and it should be used for that protection which the law refuses to give. When the white man who is always the aggressor knows he runs as great risk of biting the dust every time his Afro-American victim does, he will have greater respect for Afro-American life. The more the Afro-American yields and cringes and begs, the more he has to do so, the more he is insulted, outraged and lynched.

The assertion has been substantiated throughout these pages that the press contains unreliable and doctored reports of lynchings, and one of the most necessary things for the race to do is to get these facts before the public. The people must know, before they can act, and there is no educator to compare with the press.

The Afro-American papers are the only ones which will print the truth, and they lack means to employ agents and detectives to get at the facts. The race must rally a mighty host to the support of their journals, and thus enable them to do much in the way of investigation.

A lynching occurred at Port Jarvis, N.Y., the first week in June. A white and colored man were implicated in the assault upon a white girl. It was charged that the white man paid the colored boy to make the assault, which he did on the public highway in broad day time, and was lynched. This, too was done by "parties unknown." The white man in the case still lives. He was imprisoned and promises to fight the case on trial. At the preliminary examination, it developed that he had been a suitor of the girl's. She had repulsed and refused him, yet had given him money, and he had sent threatening letters demanding more.

The day before this examination she was so wrought up, she left home and wandered miles away. When found she said she did so because she was afraid of the man's testimony. Why should she be afraid of the prisoner? Why should She yield to his demands for money if not to prevent him exposing something he knew? It seems explainable only on the hypothesis that a *liaison* existed between the colored boy and the girl, and the white man knew of it. The press is singularly silent. Has it a motive? We owe it to ourselves to find out.

The story comes from Larned, Kansas, Oct. 1st, that a young white lady held at bay until daylight, without alarming any one in the house, "a burly Negro" who entered her room and bed. The "burly Negro" was promptly lynched without investigation or examination of inconsistant stories.

A house was found burned down near Montgomery, Ala., in Monroe County, Oct. 13th, a few weeks ago; also the burned bodies of the owners and melted piles of gold and silver.

These discoveries led to the conclusion that the awful crime was not prompted by motives of robbery. The suggestion of the whites was that "brutal lust was the incentive, and as there are nearly 200 Negroes living within a radius of five miles of the place the conclusion was inevitable that some of them were the perpetrators."

Upon this "suggestion" probably made by the real criminal, the mob acted upon the "conclusion" and arrested ten Afro-Americans, four of whom, they tell the world, confessed to the deed of murdering Richard L. Johnson and outraging his daughter, Jeanette. These four men, Berrell Jones, Moses Johnson, Jim and John Packer, none of them 25 years of age, upon this conclusion, were taken from jail, hanged, shot, and burned while yet alive the night of Oct. 12th. The same report says Mr. Johnson was on the best of terms with his Negro tenants.

The race thus outraged must find out the facts of this awful hurling of men into eternity on supposition, and give them to the indifferent and apathetic country. We feel this to be a garbled report, but how can we prove it?

Near Vicksburg, Miss., a murder was committed by a gang of burglars. Of course it must have been done by Negroes, and Negroes were arrested for it. It is believed that 2 men, Smith Tooley and John Adams belonged to a gang controlled by white men and, fearing exposure, on the night of July 4th, they were hanged in the Court House yard by those interested in silencing them. Robberies since committed in the same vicinity have been known to be by white men who had their faces blackened. We strongly believe in the innocence of these murdered men, but we have no proof. No other news goes out to the world save that which stamps us as a race of cut-throats, robbers and lustful wild beasts. So great is Southern hate and prejudice, they legally hung poor little thirteen year old Mildrey Brown at Columbia, S.C., Oct. 7th, on the circumstantial evidence that she poisoned a white infant. If her guilt had been proven unmistakably, had she been white, Mildrey Brown would never have been hung.

The country would have been aroused and South Carolina disgraced forever for such a crime. The Afro-American himself did not know as he should have known as his journals should be in a position to have him know and act.

Nothing is more definitely settled than he must act for himself. I have shown how he may employ the boycott, emigration and the press, and I feel that by a combination of all these agencies can be effectually stamped out lynch law, that last relic of barbarism and slavery. "The gods help those who help themselves."

Ida B. Wells [Barnett], "The Negro's Case in Equity." *The Independent*, 26 April 1900: 1010–11

[Ms Barnett was driven out of Tennessee at the time of the destruction by a mob of the colored paper of which she was an editor. She has since carried on a campaign in England and America against lynching, and is chairman of the Anti-lynching Bureau of the Afro-American Council—EDITOR.]

The Independent publishes an earnest appeal to negro editors, preachers and teachers "to tell their people to defend the laws and their own rights even to blood, but never, never to take guilty participation in lynching

Figure 3.1: Ida B. Wells

white man or black." This advice is given by way of comment on the double lynching in Virginia the other day. Theoretically the advice is all right, but viewed in the light of circumstances and conditions it seems like giving a stone when we ask for bread.

For twenty years past the negro has done nothing else but defend the law and appeal to public sentiment for defense *by* the law. He has seen hundreds of men of his race murdered in cold blood by connivance of officers of the law, from the governors of the States down to sheriffs of counties, as in this Virginia case, and that upon the unsupported word of some white man or woman. He has seen his women and children stripped and strung up to trees or riddled with bullets for the gratification of spite, as in the case of Postmaster Baker's family two years ago, and in that in Alabama a few weeks ago, when an entire family was wiped out of existence because a white man had been murdered.

The negro has seen scores of his race, absolutely innocent of any charge whatever, used as scapegoats for some white man's crime, as in the case of

C.J. Miller, lynched in Bardwell, Ky., in 1893, and John Peterson, of Denmark, S.C., the same year. Miller was stripped, hung with a log chain to a telegraph pole, riddled with bullets, then burned, since which proceeding he was found to have suffered for a crime committed by a white man. Peterson had sought protection from Governor (now Senator) Tillman,[20] but was given over to the mob, and altho the girl in the case said he was not the man, yet the lynchers, led by a State Senator, said a crime had been committed and somebody had to hang for it; so Peterson was swung up and five hundred bullets fired into his body. Such also was the case of a negro woman in Jackson, Tenn., who was stripped and hung in the court house yard by a mob led by the woman's employer. Her mistress had died suddenly of arsenical poisoning and the negro cook was accused because a box of rat poison was found in her room. The husband of the woman who was poisoned, and who led the mob, has since been confined in the insane asylum, and his ravings prove him to have been the poisoner of his wife.

All this and more the negro has seen and suffered without taking the law into his hands for, lo, these many years. There have been no Nat Turner insurrections[21] and San Domingan horrors[22] in retaliation for all the wrongs he has suffered. When the negro has appealed to the Christian and moral forces of the country—asking them to create a sentiment against this lawlessness and unspeakable barbarism; demanding justice and the protection of the law for every human being regardless of color—that demand has been met with general indifference or entirely ignored. Where this is not true he has been told that these same forces upon which he confidently depends refuse to make the demand for justice, because they believe the story of the mob that negroes are lynched because they commit unspeakable crimes against white women. For this reason the Christian and moral forces are silent in the presence of the horrible barbarities alleged to be done in the name of woman.

When the negro, confident in the justice of his cause and the sincerity of the aforesaid Christian and moral forces, seeks the opportunity to disprove this slander, he is refused, except in very rare instances. The columns of the powerful dailies, religious periodicals and thoughtful magazines have printed these charges wholesale until the civilized world has accepted them, but few wish to consider the refutation of them or give space for the possible other side. The leading pulpits of the country are open to stories of the negro's degradation and ignorance, but not to his defense from slander.

Again and again, during the present session of Congress, in both the House and Senate, the negro has been attacked and this foul slander against his good name made in several speeches and sent broadcast. Except a brief rejoinder by Congressman George White,[23] there was no attempt at refutation or rebuke in Congress or out by any of the champions of truth and justice.

Notwithstanding all this is true and has been true for twenty years past, while ten thousand men, women and children have been done to death in the same manner as in the late Virginia case; in spite of the fact that the governors of States, commanders of militia, sheriffs and police have taken part in these disgraceful exhibitions; and with absolute proof that the public sentiment of the country was with the mob—who, if not the negro preachers, editors and teachers, are to be credited with the fact that there are few, if any, instances of negroes who have had "guilty participation in lynching white men or black?"

And if all the negro preachers, editors and teachers should charge themselves with the responsibility of this one lapse after years of the greatest human provocation, should not all the white preachers, editors and teachers charge themselves with the thousands of lynchings by white men? Ought not they to tell their people over and over again that ten human beings have been burned alive in this country during the past seven years—three of them during the year 1899? For the seven years the negro has been agitating against lynching he has made this appeal to the leaders of thought and action among the white race. If they will do their duty in this respect the negroes will soon have no bad examples of the lynching kind set, which in their desperation they may be tempted to follow.

As matters now stand, the negroes down in Virginia the other day would have fared badly had they attempted to defend the law in either case. A band of negroes prevented a lynching in Jacksonville, Fla., in the summer of 1893 by guarding the jail, tho not a shot was fired. The man who led the band has been an exile from his home ever since. He was indicted for "conspiracy" and about to be sent to the penitentiary for preventing white men from lynching a negro, when he forfeited his bond by leaving home and sacrificing his property. Only last summer the same thing happened in Darien, Ga. A white woman gave birth to a negro child, and the mob prepared to lynch the father for the "usual crime." The negroes got wind of it, guarded the jail and prevented the lynching. They were all indicted for that "conspiracy" and lodged in jail. John Delegal, who helped guard his father when the mob was after him, lived in the country. The posse went after him as a "conspirator," broke open his house and entered firing. He returned the fire, killing the leader instantly. Those negroes have all been tried since by a jury of the kind of men who tried to lynch Delegal's father, found guilty of "conspiracy," and are now doing time in the penitentiary. John was sent up for life. In the present apathetic condition of public sentiment,

North and South, this is what the negro gets who attempts to "defend the law and his rights." Not until the white editors, preachers and teachers of the country join with him in his fight for justice and protection by law can there be any hope of success.

CHICAGO, ILL.

Mary Church Terrell, "Lynching from a Negro's Point of View." *North American Review* 178 (1904): 853–68

Before 1904 was three months old, thirty-one negroes had been lynched. Of this number, fifteen were murdered within one week in Arkansas, and one was shot to death in Springfield, Ohio, by a mob composed of men who did not take the trouble to wear masks. Hanging, shooting and burning black men, women and children in the United States have become so common that such occurrences create but little sensation and evoke but slight comment now. Those who are jealous of their country's fair name feel keenly the necessity of extirpating this lawlessness, which is so widespread and has taken such deep root. But means of prevention can never be devised, until the cause of lynching is more generally understood.

The reasons why the whole subject is deeply and seriously involved in error are obvious. Those who live in the section where nine-tenths of the lynchings occur do not dare to tell the truth, even if they perceive it. When men know that the death-knell of their aspirations and hopes will be sounded as soon as they express views to which the majority in their immediate vicinage are opposed, they either suppress their views or trim them to fit the popular mind. Only martyrs are brave and bold enough to defy the public will, and the manufacture of martyrs in the negro's behalf is not very brisk just now. Those who do not live in the section where most of the lynchings occur borrow their views from their brothers who do, and so the errors are continually repeated and inevitably perpetuated.

In the discussion of this subject, four mistakes are commonly made.

In the first place, it is a great mistake to suppose that rape is the real cause of lynching in the South. Beginning with the Ku-Klux Klan, the negro has been constantly subjected to some form of organized violence ever since he became free. It is easy to prove that rape is simply the pretext and not the cause of lynching. Statistics show that, out of every hundred negroes who are lynched, from seventy-five to eighty-five are not even accused of this crime, and many who are accused of it are innocent. And, yet, men who admit the accuracy of these figures gravely tell the country that lynching can never be suppressed, until negroes cease to commit a crime with which less than one-fourth of those murdered by mobs are charged.

The prevailing belief that negroes are not tortured by mobs unless they are charged with the "usual" crime, does not tally with the facts. The savagery which attended the lynching of a man and his wife the first week in March of the present year was probably never exceeded in this country or anywhere else in the civilized world. A white planter was murdered at Doddsville, Miss., and a negro was charged with the crime. The negro fled, and his wife, who was known to be innocent, fled with him to escape the fate which she knew awaited her, if she remained. The two negroes were pursued and captured, and the following account of the tragedy by an eye-witness appeared in the "Evening Post," a Democratic daily of Vicksburg, Miss.

"When the two negroes were captured, they were tied to trees, and while the funeral pyres were being prepared they were forced to suffer the most fiendish tortures. The blacks were forced to hold out their hands while one finger at a time was chopped off. The fingers were distributed as souvenirs. The ears of the murderers were cut off. Holbert was beaten severely, his skull was fractured, and one of his eyes, knocked out with a stick, hung by a shred from the socket. Neither the man nor the woman begged for mercy, nor made a groan or plea. When the executioner came forward to lop off fingers, Holbert extended his hand without being asked. The most excruciating form of punishment consisted in the use of a large corkscrew in the hands of some of the mob. This instrument was bored into the flesh of the man and the woman, in the arms, legs and body, and then pulled out, the spirals tearing out big pieces of raw, quivering flesh every time it was withdrawn. Even this devilish torture did not make the poor brutes cry out. When finally they were thrown on the fire and allowed to be burned to death, this came as a relief to the maimed and suffering victims."

The North frequently sympathizes with the Southern mob, because it has been led to believe the negro's diabolical assaults upon white women are the chief cause of lynching. In spite of the facts, distinguished representatives from the South are still insisting, in Congress and elsewhere, that "whenever negroes cease committing the crime of rape, the lynchings and burnings will cease with it." But since three-fourths of the negroes who have met a violent death at the hands of Southern mobs have not been accused of this crime, it is evident that, instead of being the "usual" crime, rape is the most unusual of all the crimes for which negroes are shot, hanged and burned.

Although Southern men of prominence still insist that "this crime is more responsible for mob violence than all other crimes combined," it is gratifying to observe that a few of them, at least, are beginning to feel ashamed to pervert the facts. During the past few years, several Southern gentlemen, of unquestioned ability and integrity, have publicly exposed the falsity of this plea. Two years ago, in a masterful article on the race problem, Professor Andrew Sledd, at that time an instructor in a Southern college, admitted that only a small number of the negroes who are lynched are even accused of assaulting white women.[24] Said he:

"On the contrary, a frank consideration of all the facts, with no other desire than to find the truth, the whole truth and nothing but the truth, however contrary to our wishes and humiliating to our section the truth may be, will show that by far the most of our Southern lynchings are carried through in *sheer, unqualified and increasing brutality*."

But a heavy penalty was paid by this man who dared to make such a frank and fearless statement of facts. He was forced to resign his position as professor, and lost prestige in his section in various ways. In the summer of 1903, Bishop Candler of Georgia[25] made a strong protest against lynching, and called attention to the fact that, out of 128 negroes who had been done to death in 1901, only 16 were even accused of rape.

In the second place, it is a mistake to suppose that the negro's desire for social equality sustains any relation whatsoever to the crime of rape. According to the testimony of eye-witnesses, as well as the reports of Southern newspapers, the negroes who are known to have been guilty of assault have, as a rule, been ignorant, repulsive in appearance and as near the brute creation as it is possible for a human being to be. It is safe to assert that, among the negroes who have been guilty of ravishing white women, not one had been taught that he was the equal of white people or had ever heard of social equality. And if by chance he had heard of it, he had no clearer conception of its meaning than he had of the principle of the binomial theorem. In conversing with a large number of ignorant negroes, the writer has never found one who seemed to have any idea of what social equality means, or who expressed a desire to put this theory into practice when it was explained to him.

Negroes who have been educated in Northern institutions of learning with white men and women, and who for that reason might have learned the meaning of social equality and have acquired a taste for the same, neither assault white women nor commit other crimes, as a rule. A careful review of the facts will show that negroes who have the "convention habit" developed to a high degree, or who are able to earn their living by editing newspapers, do not belong to the criminal class, although such negroes are always held up by Southern gentlemen as objects of ridicule, contempt and scorn. Strange as it may appear, illiterate negroes, who are the only ones

214

contributing largely to the criminal class, are coddled and caressed by the South. To the educated, cultivated members of the race, they are held up as bright and shining examples of what a really good negro should be. The dictionary is searched in vain by Southern gentlemen and gentlewomen for words sufficiently ornate and strong to express their admiration for a dear old "mammy" or a faithful old "uncle," who can neither read nor write, and who assure their white friends they would not, if they could.

On the other hand, no language is sufficiently caustic, bitter and severe, to express the disgust, hatred and scorn which Southern gentlemen feel for what is called the "New Issue," which, being interpreted, means, negroes who aspire to knowledge and culture, and who have acquired a taste for the highest and best things in life. At the door of this "New Issue," the sins and shortcomings of the whole race are laid. This "New Issue" is beyond hope of redemption, we are told, because somebody, nobody knows who, has taught it to believe in social equality, something, nobody knows what. The alleged fear of social equality has always been used by the South to explain its unchristian treatment of the negro and to excuse its many crimes. How many crimes have been committed, and how many falsehoods have been uttered, in the name of social equality by the South! Of all these, the greatest is the determination to lay lynching at its door. In the North, which is the only section that accords the negro the scrap of social equality enjoyed by him in the United States, he is rarely accused of rape. The only form of social equality ever attempted between the two races, and practised to any considerable extent, is that which was originated by the white masters of slave women, and which has been perpetuated by them and their descendants even unto the present day. Of whatever other crime we may accuse the big, black burly brute, who is so familiar a figure in the reports of rape and lynching-bees sent out by the Southern press, surely we cannot truthfully charge him with an attempt to introduce social equality into this republican form of government, or to foist it upon a democratic land. There is no more connection between social equality and lynching to-day than there was between social equality and slavery before the war, or than there is between social equality and the convict-lease system, or any other form of oppression to which the negro has uniformly been subjected in the South.

The third error on the subject of lynching consists of the widely circulated statement that the moral sensibilities of the best negroes in the United States are so stunted and dull, and the standard of morality among even the leaders of the race is so low, that they do not appreciate the enormity and heinousness of rape. Those who claim to know the negro best and to be his best friends declare that he usually sympathizes with the black victim of mob violence rather than with the white victim of the black fiend's lust, even when he does not go so far as to condone the crime of rape. Only those who are densely ignorant of the standards and sentiments of the best negroes, or who wish wilfully to misrepresent and maliciously to slander a race already resting under burdens greater than it can bear, would accuse its thousands of reputable men and women of sympathizing with rapists, either black or white, or of condoning their crime. The negro preachers and teachers who have had the advantage of education and moral training, together with others occupying positions of honor and trust, are continually expressing their horror of this one particular crime, and exhorting all whom they can reach by voice or pen to do everything in their power to wash the ugly stain of rape from the race's good name. And whenever slightest pity for the victim of mob violence is expressed by a negro who represents the intelligence and decency of his race, it is invariably because there is a reasonable doubt of his innocence, rather than because there is condonation of the alleged crime.

Everybody who is well informed on the subject of lynching knows that many a negro who has been accused of assault or murder, or other violation of the law, and has been tortured to death by a mob, has afterward been proved innocent of the crime with which he was charged. So great is the thirst for the negro's blood in the South, that but a single breath of suspicion is sufficient to kindle into an all-consuming flame the embers of hatred ever smouldering in the breasts of the fiends who compose a typical mob. When once such a bloodthirsty company starts on a negro's trail, and the right one cannot be found, the first available specimen is sacrificed to their rage, no matter whether he is guilty or not.

A white man who died near Charleston, South Carolina, in March of the present year, confessed on his death-bed that he had murdered his wife, although three negroes were lynched for this crime at Ravenel, South Carolina, in May, 1902. This murder was one of the most brutal ever committed in the State, and the horrible tortures to which the three innocent negroes were subjected indicated plainly that the mob intended the punishment to fit the crime. In August, 1901, three negroes, a mother, her daughter and her son, were lynched in Carrollton, Miss., because it was rumored that they had heard of a murder before it was committed, and had not reported it. A negro was accused of murdering a woman, and was lynched in Shreveport, Louisiana, in April, 1902, who was afterward proved innocent. The woman who was lynched in Mississippi this year was not even accused of a crime. The charge of murder had not been proved against her husband, and, as the white man who was murdered had engaged in an altercation with him, it is quite likely that, if the negro had been tried in a court of law, it would have been shown to be a case of justifiable homicide. And so other cases might easily be cited to prove that the charge that innocent negroes are sometimes lynched is by no means without foundation. It is not strange, therefore, that even reputable, law-abiding negroes should protest against the tortures and cruelties inflicted by mobs which wreak vengeance upon the guilty and innocent and upon the just and unjust of their race alike. It is to the credit and not to the shame of the negro that he tries to uphold the sacred majesty of the law, which is so often trailed in the dust and trampled under foot by white mobs.

In the fourth place, it is well to remember, in discussing the subject of lynching, that it is not always possible to ascertain the facts from the accounts in the newspapers. The facts are often suppressed, intentionally or unintentionally, or distorted by the press. The case of Sam Hose, to which reference has so often been made, is a good illustration of the unreliability of the press in reporting the lynching of negroes. Sam Hose, a negro, murdered Alfred Cranford, a white man, in a dispute over wages which the white employer refused to pay the colored workman. It was decided to make an example of a negro who dared to kill a white man. A well-known, influential newspaper immediately offered a reward of $500 for the capture of Sam Hose. This same newspaper predicted a lynching, and stated that, though several modes of punishment had been suggested, it was the consensus of opinion that the negro should be burned at the stake and tortured before being burned. A rumor was started, and circulated far and wide by the press, that Sam Hose had assaulted the wife of Alfred Cranford, after the latter had been killed. One of the best detectives in Chicago was sent to Atlanta to investigate the affair.[26] After securing all the information it was possible to obtain from black and white alike, and carefully weighing the evidence, this white detective declared it would have been a physical impossibility for the negro to assault the murdered man's wife, and expressed it as his opinion that the charge of assault was an invention intended to make the burning a certainty.

The Sunday on which Sam Hose was burned was converted into a holiday. Special trains were made up to take the Christian people of Atlanta to the scene of the burning, a short distance from the city. After the first train moved out with every inch of available space inside and out filled to overflowing, a second had to be made up, so as to accommodate those who had just come from church. After Sam Hose had been tortured and burned to death, the great concourse of Christians who had witnessed the tragedy scraped for hours among his ashes in the hope of finding a sufficient number of his bones to take to their friends as souvenirs. The charge has been made that Sam Hose boasted to another negro that he intended to assault Alfred Cranford's wife. It would be difficult for anybody who understands conditions in the South to believe that a sane negro would announce his purpose to violate a white woman there, then deliberately enter her husband's house, while all the family were present, to carry out his threat.

Two years ago a riot occurred in Atlanta, Georgia, in which four white policemen were killed and several wounded by a colored man named Richardson, who was himself finally burned to death. Through the press the public was informed that the negro was a desperado. As a matter of fact, Richardson was a merchant, well to do and law-abiding. The head and front of his offending was that he dared to reprimand an ex-policeman for living in open adultery with a colored woman. When it was learned that this negro had been so impudent to a white man, the sheriff led out a posse, consisting of the city police, to arrest Richardson. Seeing the large number of officers surrounding his house, and knowing what would be his fate, if caught, the negro determined to sell his life dear, and he did. With the exception of the Macon "Telegraph," but few white newspapers ever gave the real cause of the riot, and so Richardson has gone down to history as a black desperado, who shot to death four officers of the law and wounded as many more. Several years ago, near New Orleans, a negro was at work in a corn-field. In working through the corn he made considerable noise, which frightened a young white woman, who happened to be passing by. She ran to the nearest house, and reported that a negro had jumped at her. A large crowd of white men immediately shouldered guns and seized the negro, who had no idea what it meant. When told why he was taken, the negro protested that he had not even seen the girl whom he was accused of frightening, but his protest was of no avail and he was hanged to the nearest tree. The press informed the country that this negro was lynched for attempted rape. Instance after instance might be cited to prove that facts bearing upon lynching, as well as upon other phases of the race problem, are often garbled—without intention, perhaps—by the press.

What, then, is the cause of lynching? At the last analysis, it will be discovered that there are just two causes of lynching. In the first place, it is due to race hatred, the hatred of a stronger people toward a weaker who were once held as slaves. In the second place, it is due to the lawlessness so prevalent in the section where nine-tenths of the lynchings occur. View the question of lynching from any point of view one may, and it is evident that it is just as impossible for the negroes of this country to prevent mob violence by any attitude of mind which they may assume, or any course of conduct which they may pursue, as it is for a straw dam to stop Niagara's flow. Upon the same spirit of intolerance and of hatred the crime of lynching must be fastened as that which called into being the Ku-Klux Klan, and which has prompted more recent exhibitions of hostility toward the negro, such as the disfranchisement acts, the Jim Crow Car Laws, and the new slavery called "peonage," together with other acts of oppression which make the negro's lot so hard.

Lynching is the aftermath of slavery. The white men who shoot negroes to death and flay them alive, and the white women who apply flaming torches to their oil-soaked bodies to-day, are the sons and daughters of women who had but little, if any, compassion on the race when it was enslaved. The men who lynch negroes to-day are, as a rule, the children of women who sat by their firesides happy and proud in the possession and affection of their own children, while they looked with unpitying eye and adamantine heart upon the anguish of slave mothers whose children had been sold away, when not overtaken by a sadder fate. If it be contended, as it often is, that negroes are rarely lynched by the descendants of former slaveholders, it will be difficult to prove the point. According to the reports of lynchings sent out by the Southern press itself, mobs are generally composed of the "best citizens" of a place, who quietly disperse to their homes as soon as they are certain that the negro is good and dead. The newspaper who predicted that Sam Hose would be lynched, which offered a reward for his capture and which suggested burning at the stake, was neither owned nor edited by the poor whites. But if it be conceded that the descendants of slaveholders do not shoot and burn negroes, lynching must still be regarded as the legitimate offspring of slavery. If the children of the poor whites of the South are the chief aggressors in the lynching-bees of that section, it is because their ancestors were brutalized by their slaveholding environment. In discussing the lynching of negroes at the present time, the heredity and the environment, past and present, of the white mobs are not taken sufficiently into account. It is as impossible to comprehend the cause of the ferocity and barbarity which attend the average lynching-bee without taking into account the brutalizing effect of slavery upon the people of the section where most of the lynchings occur, as it is to investigate the essence and nature of fire without considering the gases which cause the flame to ignite. It is too much to expect, perhaps, that the children of women who for generations looked upon the hardships and the degradation of their sisters of a darker hue with few if any protests, should have mercy and compassion upon the children of that oppressed race now. But what a tremendous influence for law and order, and what a mighty foe to mob violence Southern white women might be, if they would arise in the purity and power of their womanhood to implore their fathers, husbands and sons no longer to stain their hands with the black man's blood!

While the men of the South were off fighting to keep the negro in bondage, their mothers, wives and daughters were entrusted to the black man's care. How faithfully and loyally he kept his sacred trust the records of history attest! Not a white woman was violated throughout the entire war. Can the white women of the South forget how black men bore themselves throughout that trying time? Surely it is not too much to ask that the daughters of mothers who were shielded from harm by the black man's constancy and care should requite their former protectors, by at least asking that, when the children of the latter are accused of crime, they should be treated like human beings and not like wild animals to be butchered and shot.

If there were one particularly heinous crime for which an infuriated people took vengeance upon the negro, or if there were a genuine fear that a guilty negro might escape the penalty of the law in the South, then it might be possible to explain the cause of lynching on some other hypothesis than that of race hatred. It has already been shown that the first supposition has no foundation in fact. It is easy to prove that the second is false. Even those who condone lynching do not pretend to fear the delay or the uncertainty of the law, when a guilty negro is concerned. With the courts of law entirely in the hands of the white man, with judge and jury belonging to the superior race, a guilty negro could no more extricate himself from the meshes of the law in the South than he could slide from the devilfish's embrace or slip from the anaconda's coils. Miscarriage of justice in the South is possible only when white men transgress the law.

In addition to lynching, the South is continually furnishing proof of its determination to wreak terrible vengeance upon the negro. The recent shocking revelations of the extent to which the actual enslavement of negroes has been carried under the peonage system of Alabama and Mississippi, and the unspeakable cruelties to which men, women and children are alike subjected, all bear witness to this fact. In January of the present year, a government detective found six negro children ranging in age from six to sixteen years working on a Georgia plantation in bare feet, scantily clad in rags, although the ground was covered with snow. The owner of the plantation is one of the wealthiest men in northeast Georgia, and is said to have made his fortune by holding negroes in slavery. When he was tried it was shown that the white planter had killed the father of the six children a few years before, but was acquitted of the murder, as almost invariably happens, when a white man takes a negro's life. After the death of their father, the children were treated with incredible cruelty. They were often chained in a room without fire and were beaten until the blood streamed from their backs, when they were unable to do their stint of work. The planter was placed under $5,000 bail, but it is doubtful whether he will ever pay the penalty of his crime. Like the children just mentioned hundreds of negroes are to-day groaning under a bondage more crushing and more cruel than that abolished forty years ago.

This same spirit manifests itself in a variety of ways. Efforts are constantly making to curtail the educational opportunities of colored children. Already one State has enacted a law by which colored children in the public schools are prohibited from receiving instruction higher than the sixth grade, and other States will, doubtless, soon follow this lead. It is a well-known fact that a Governor recently elected in one of the Southern States owes his popularity and his votes to his open and avowed opposition to the education of negroes. Instance after instance might be cited to prove that the hostility toward the negro in the South is bitter and pronounced, and that lynching is but a manifestation of this spirit of vengeance and intolerance in its ugliest and most brutal form.

To the widespread lawlessness among the white people of the South lynching is also due. In commenting upon the blood-guiltiness of South Carolina, the Nashville "American" declared some time ago that, if the killings in the other States had been in the same ratio to population as in South Carolina, a larger number of people would have been murdered in the United States during 1902 than fell on the American side in the Spanish and Philippine wars.

Whenever Southern white people discuss lynching, they are prone to slander the whole negro race. Not long ago, a Southern writer of great repute declared without qualification or reservation that "the crime of rape is well-nigh wholly confined to the negro race," and insisted that "negroes furnish most of the ravishers." These assertions are as unjust to the negro as they are unfounded in fact. According to statistics recently published, only one colored male in 100,000 over five years of age was accused of assault upon a white woman in the South in 1902, whereas one male out of every 20,000 over five years of age was charged with rape in Chicago during the same year. If these figures prove anything at all, they show that the men and boys in Chicago are many times more addicted to rape than are the negroes in the South. Already in the present year two white men have been arrested in the national capital for attempted assault upon little children. One was convicted and sentenced to six years in the penitentiary. The crime of which the other was accused was of the most infamous character. A short account of the trial of the convicted man appeared in the Washington dailies, as any other criminal suit would have been reported; but if a colored man had committed the same crime, the newspapers from one end of the United States to the other would have published it broadcast. Editorials upon the total depravity and the hopeless immorality of the negro would have been written, based upon this particular case as a text. With such facts to prove the falsity of the charge that "the crime of rape is well-nigh wholly confined to the negro race," it is amazing that any writer of repute should affix his signature to such a slander.

But even if the negro's morals were as loose and as lax as some claim them to be, and if his belief in the virtue of women were as slight as we are told, the South has nobody to blame but itself. The only object lesson in virtue and morality which the negro received for 250 years came through the medium of slavery, and that peculiar institution was not calculated to set his standards of correct living very high. Men do not gather grapes of thorns nor figs of thistles. Throughout their entire period of bondage colored women were debauched by their masters. From the day they were liberated to the present time, prepossessing young colored girls have been considered the rightful prey of white gentlemen in the South, and they have been protected neither by public sentiment nor by law. In the South, the negro's home is not considered sacred by the superior race. White men are neither punished for invading it, nor lynched for violating colored women and girls. In discussing this phase of the race problem last year, one of the most godly and eloquent ministers in the Methodist Episcopal Church (white) expressed himself as follows: "The negro's teachers have been white. It is from the white man the negro has learned to lie and steal. If you wish to know who taught the negro licentiousness, you have only to look into the faces of thousands of mulatto people and get your answer." When one thinks how the negro was degraded in slavery, which discouraged, when it did not positively forbid, marriage between slaves, and considers the bad example set them by white masters, upon whom the negroes looked as scarcely lower than the angels, the freedman's self-control seems almost like a miracle of modern times. In demanding so much of the negro, the South places itself in the anomalous position of insisting that the conduct of the inferior race shall be better, and its standards higher, than those of the people who claim to be superior.

The recent lynching in Springfield, Ohio, and in other cities of the North, show how rapidly this lawlessness is spreading throughout the United States. If the number of Americans who participate in this wild and diabolical carnival of blood does not diminish, nothing can prevent this country from becoming a byword and a reproach throughout the civilized world. When Secretary Hay appealed to Roumania in behalf of the Jews, there were many sarcastic comments made by the press of that country and of other foreign lands about the inhuman treatment of the negro in the United States. In November, 1903, a manifesto signed by delegates from all over the world was issued at Brussels, Belgium, by the International Socialist

Bureau, protesting against the lynching of negroes in the United States.

It is a source of deep regret and sorrow to many good Christians in this country that the church puts forth so few and such feeble protests against lynching. As the attitude of many ministers on the question of slavery greatly discouraged the abolitionists before the war, so silence in the pulpit concerning the lynching of negroes to-day plunges many of the persecuted race into deep gloom and dark despair. Thousands of dollars are raised by our churches every year to send missionaries to Christianize the heathen in foreign lands, and this is proper and right. But in addition to this foreign missionary work, would it not be well for our churches to inaugurate a crusade against the barbarism at home, which converts hundreds of white women and children into savages every year, while it crushes the spirit, blights the hearth and breaks the heart of hundreds of defenceless blacks? Not only do ministers fail, as a rule, to protest strongly against the hanging and burning of negroes, but some actually condone the crime without incurring the displeasure of their congregations or invoking the censure of the church. Although the church court which tried the preacher in Wilmington, Delaware, accused of inciting his community to riot and lynching by means of an incendiary sermon, found him guilty of "unministerial and unchristian conduct," of advocating mob murder and of thereby breaking down the public respect for the law, yet it simply admonished him to be "more careful in the future" and inflicted no punishment at all. Such indifference to lynching on the part of the church recalls the experience of Abraham Lincoln, who refused to join church in Springfield, Illinois, because only three out of twenty-two ministers in the whole city stood with him in his effort to free the slave. But, however unfortunate may have been the attitude of some of the churches on the question of slavery before the war, from the moment the shackles fell from the black man's limbs to the present day, the American Church has been most kind and generous in its treatment of the backward and struggling race. Nothing but ignorance or malice could prompt one to disparage the efforts put forth by the churches in the negro's behalf. But, in the face of so much lawlessness today, surely there is a role for the Church Militant to play. When one reflects upon the large number of negroes who are yearly hurled into eternity, unshriven by priest and untried by law, one cannot help realizing that as a nation we have fallen upon grave times, indeed. Surely, it is time for the ministers in their pulpits and the Christians in their pews to fall upon their knees and pray for deliverance from this rising tide of barbarism which threatens to deluge the whole land.

How can lynching be extirpated in the United States? There are just two ways in which this can be accomplished. In the first place, lynching can never be suppressed in the South, until the masses of ignorant white people in that section are educated and lifted to a higher moral plane. It is difficult for one who has not seen these people to comprehend the density of their ignorance and the depth of their degradation. A well-known white author who lives in the South describes them as follows:

"Wholly ignorant, absolutely without culture, apparently without even the capacity to appreciate the nicer feelings or higher sense, yet conceited on account of their white skin which they constantly dishonor, they make, when aroused, as wild and brutal a mob as ever disgraced the face of the earth."

In lamenting the mental backwardness of the white people of the South, the Atlanta "Constitution" expressed itself as follows two years ago: "We have as many illiterate white men over the age of twenty-one years in the South to-day as there were fifty-two years ago, when the census of 1850 was taken." Over against these statistics stands the record of the negro, who has reduced his illiteracy 44.5 per cent in forty years. The hostility which has always existed between the poor whites and the negroes of the South has been greatly intensified in these latter days, by the material and intellectual advancement of the negro. The wrath of a Spanish bull, before whose maddened eyes a red flag is flaunted, is but a feeble attempt at temper compared with the seething, boiling rage of the average white man in the South who beholds a well-educated negro dressed in fine or becoming clothes. In the second place, lynching cannot be suppressed in the South until all classes of white people who dwell there, those of high as well as middle and low degree, respect the rights of other human beings, no matter what may be the color of their skin, become merciful and just enough to cease their persecution of a weaker race and learn a holy reverence for the law.

It is not because the American people are cruel, as a whole, or indifferent on general principles to the suffering of the wronged or oppressed, that outrages against the negro are permitted to occur and go unpunished, but because many are ignorant of the extent to which they are carried, while others despair of eradicating them. The South has so industriously, persistently and eloquently preached the inferiority of the negro, that the North has apparently been converted to this view—the thousands of negroes of sterling qualities, moral worth and lofty patriotism to the contrary notwithstanding. The South has insisted so continuously and belligerently that it is the negro's best friend, that it understands him better than other people on the face of the earth and that it will brook interference from nobody in its method of dealing with him, that the North has been persuaded or intimidated into bowing to this decree.

Then, too, there seems to be a decline of the great convictions in which this government was conceived and into which it was born. Until there is a renaissance of popular belief in the principles of liberty and equality upon which this government was founded, lynching, the Convict Lease System, the Disfranchisement Acts, the Jim Crow Car Laws, unjust discriminations in the professions and trades and similar atrocities will continue to dishearten and degrade the negro, and stain the fair name of the United States. For there can be no doubt that the greatest obstacle in the way of extirpating lynching is the general attitude of the public mind toward this unspeakable crime. The whole country seems tired of hearing about the black man's woes. The wrongs of the Irish, of the Armenians, of the Roumanian and Russian Jews, of the exiles of Russia and of every other oppressed people upon the face of the globe, can arouse the sympathy and fire the indignation of the American public, while they seem to be all but indifferent to the murderous assaults upon the negroes in the South.

The Anti-Lynching Crusaders, "The Anti-Lynching Crusaders." *The Crisis* (November 1922): 8

Under the leadership of Mrs. Mary B. Talbert[27] of Buffalo and an executive committee of 15 supported by over 700 state workers, there has been started the "Anti-Lynching Crusade," the object of which is to "unite a million women to stop lynching." These crusaders are planning a short, sharp campaign beginning immediately and ending January 1, 1923. They seek to arouse the conscience of the women of America, both white and black. They are in deadly earnest and they put forward as the first fact in the lynching campaign the horrid truth that 83 American women have been lynched by mobs in the last 30 years in addition to 3,353 men. This, in part, is the prayer which the Anti-Lynching Crusaders have sent out:

"We are slain all the day long in the land of our nativity, which is the land of our loyalty and of our love. The vials of race vengeance are wreaked upon our defenceless heads. The inhuman thirst for human blood takes little heed of innocence or guilt. Any convenient victim identified with our race suffices to slake the accursed thirst. We are beaten with many stripes. Our bodies are bruised, burned and tortured and torn asunder for the ghoulish mirth of the blood-lusty multitude. Whenever such atrocity is perpetrated upon any one of our number, because of his race, it is done unto us all. Vengeance and wrath are not invoked for the fit atonement of committed crime, nor yet for the just punishment of evil doer; but the sinister aim is to cow our spirit, enslave our soul and to give our name an evil repute in the eyes of the world..."

"Lawlessness is weakening the pillars of the temple of liberty. Laxity of law is speeding this people to the abyss of moral anarchy and social ruin. Thou didst set apart this nation in the wilderness of the new world to be an example unto all people of the blessings of liberty and law. May our nation measure up to the fulfillment of this high privilege. The land of lynchers can not long remain in the land of liberty. The nation that fails to destroy lawlessness will be destroyed by it. Save us from this evil fate.

"We pray Thee to enlighten the understanding and nerve the hearts of our lawmakers with the political wisdom and the moral courage to pass the Dyer Bill,[28] now hanging on the balance of doubt and uncertainty.

"Have mercy upon any of our legislators who may be so embittered with the gall of race hatred and fettered by the bonds of political iniquity as to advocate or apologize for lynching, rapine and murder.

"Quicken the conscience of the people with the moral firmness and determination to demand and to uphold the effective enforcement of this measure and of all righteous laws.

"May liberty and law, peace and good will, prevail through the length and breadth of our beloved land, and may equity and justice be meted out with equal and impartial hand, unto the least even as unto the greatest... Amen."

At the meeting of the executive committee of the National Council of Women[29] held at Fort Des Moines Hotel, Des Moines, Iowa, a body representing thirteen million American women, the following resolution was unanimously adopted: "Resolved, That the National Council of Women endorse the Anti-Lynching Crusade recently launched by the colored women of this country."

Persons interested in this crusade should write to Mrs. M.B. Talbert, 521 Michigan Avenue, Buffalo, New York.

Notes

1. Immediately preceding Harper's address, Alice Fletcher had declared that (white) women had a duty to minister to "the negro" and "the Indian" as "dependent races," a duty she could exercise with reform work and her responsible use of the suffrage. Fletcher's remarks focused on "the Red Man" and his ability to "bre[e]d evil among" whites "by turning loose the lightly-leased savage elements of our nature" as evidenced by "the conduct of white men...in the West among the Indians" (Fletcher 1891, 83-84). Fletcher, an anthropologist and reformer, was active in implementing land allotment among the Omaha and Nez Percé. She drafted the *Omaha Severalty Act* of 1882, regarded as the precursor to the national allotment program initiated by the *Dawes Act*.

2. Genesis 39: When Joseph is sold by his brothers into slavery, he becomes a household slave to Potiphar. Potiphar's wife attempts to seduce Joseph, and when he resists she accuses him of attempting to rape her.

3. In 1770 Crispus Attucks, a fugitive, became the first casualty of the American Revolution.

4. In 1888 the Crispus Attucks monument was erected on Boston Common.

5. Harper quotes General Jackson's Address to the "Men Of Color," given on 18 December 1814 at New Orleans.

6. This refers to the ritual of public penance of condemned heretics under the Spanish Inquisition. Harper draws on its popular circulation as burning at the stake.

7. From the "Rock of Ages."

8. Isaiah 65:5.

9. John 12:32.

10. Matthew 18:16.

11. Acts 10:43.

12. James 2:9.

13. Colossians 3:11.

14. Matthew 7:12.

15. "Exiled," New York *Age* 25 June 1892, sold 10,000 copies (Streitmatter 1993, 54).

16. In early March of 1892 Calvin McDowell, Will Stewart, and Thomas Moss were lynched by a white mob of ten men. Prominent black citizens who were members of the People's Grocery Company cooperative, a black-owned store competing with a white-owned grocery in Memphis's racially mixed neighborhood the "Curve," these men were accused of injuring three deputies in an armed stand-off incited by rumors of an impending mob raid on their store. Despite two weeks of hearings, no one was indicted or tried for their murder (McMurry 1998, 135). Wells was close friends with Thomas Moss and his widow, and the *Free Speech* covered the lynchings and hearings extensively. It was not until Wells ran an editorial in the 21 May edition, questioning the well-worn claim that rape motivated lynching, that her own life was threatened by the specter of a white mob and her paper destroyed.

17. Wells's speech to over 200 elite black women of New York, Boston, and Philadelphia at the Lyric Hall in New York on 5 October 1892 solidified her reputation among African Americans as a "heroine" ("A Distinguished Woman" 1892). Organized by Victoria Earle Matthews, Sarah Garnett, and Maritcha Lyons, the event raised over $600, much of which was given to Wells to fund her anti-lynching efforts. Attended by highly visible and respected African American women like Josephine St. Pierre Ruffin and Gertrude Mossell, Wells's address was given the stamp of respectability and caused Wells to be invited to speak on a "frantic tour of eastern cities" (McMurry 1998, 174). The text of her Lyric Hall address closely

followed her New York *Age* article, and Wells promptly published these in this pamphlet *Southern Horrors: Lynch Law in All Its Phases*, in late October 1892.

18. Henry Woodfin Grady (1850-89) was a journalist and orator who, as spokesman for the "New South," helped reintegrate the states of the former Confederacy into the Union after the American Civil War.

19. A partaker in the crime, an accessory.

20. An outspoken advocate of white supremacy, Benjamin R. Tillman (1847-1918) was governor of South Carolina, from 1890 to 1894, and a federal senator from 1895 until his death. During Reconstruction, he fought to overthrow the interracial Republican coalition in the state and disempower the black majority. He was also largely responsible for calling the state constitutional convention in 1895 that disfranchised most of South Carolina's black men and instituted Jim Crow laws.

21. Nat Turner (1800-31), an enslaved preacher, led an insurrection in Southampton County, Virginia on 21 August 1831 that included some 50 free and enslaved African Americans. Quashed by militia, Turner's insurrection killed 57 whites and made white slaveowners fearful for years that similar rebellions would arise.

22. A 1791 slave rebellion instigated the Haitian Revolution, culminating in the independent Republic of Haïti in 1804.

23. George E. White (1848-1935) was a Republican congressman from Illinois from 1895 to 1899.

24. Sledd was a professor of Latin at Emory when he published his denunciation of lynching in the *Atlantic Monthly* in 1902, leading Emory's president, James Dickey, to call for his resignation. See Sledd 1902.

25. Warren Akin Candler (1857-1941) was the tenth president and the first chancellor of Emory University, and a Southern Methodist Episcopal bishop. For three decades Candler wrote a column in the *Atlanta Journal* in addition to writing articles for religious publications and 15 books on biographical and religious topics. Although he wrote of his belief in Anglo-Saxon superiority, Candler spoke out strongly against lynching (Kemp 2002).

26. Following the lynching of Sam Hose, Ida B. Wells-Barnett organized a committee to raise funds to pay a detective to investigate the case (McMurry 1998, 255).

27. Mary Burnett Talbert (1866-1923) was an orator, activist, suffragist, and reformer, who was called "the best known colored woman in the United States." Talbert was a co-founder of the Niagara Movement, the predecessor for the NAACP (National Association for the Advancement of Colored People), was president of the NACW (National Association of Colored Women) from 1916 to 1921, and co-founded the International Council of Women of the Darker Races in 1922.

28. Congressman Leonidas Dyer of Missouri first introduced his anti-lynching

bill—the Dyer Bill—into Congress in 1918. The Dyer Bill was passed by the House of Representatives on the 26 January 1922, but its passage was halted by a filibuster in the Senate.

29. Founded in 1888, during the fortieth year commemoration of the Seneca Falls Convention, the NCW's first president was temperance activist Francis Willard, whose equivocal remarks on lynching and racist characterization of Southern African Americans as the "black-faced mob" that "menaces" the "safety of women, of children, of the home" in 1890 alienated her from many black feminists, reformers, and anti-lynching activists.

4

Defending
Black Womanhood
and the Black Women's
Club Movement

Frances Harper called the 1890s the "woman's era," as it was in that decade that African American women organized nationally through the black women's club movement. Given the wealth of black feminist work earlier in the century, we might consider whether the "woman's era" had actually been underway for some time before the networks of women's clubs in cities like New York, Chicago, Washington, DC, Philadelphia, and Boston gained national attention through federation. The National Association of Colored Women's Clubs (NACWC) was organized in Washington, DC on 21 July 1896, with Mary Church Terrell as president, through the merger of the National Federation of Afro-American Women, the Women's Era Club of Boston, and the Colored Women's League of Washington, DC. Harper, herself, became president of the NACWC in 1897. Nevertheless, there are important connections between the work undertaken by African American women within the club movement and the black feminist work that predates it in areas such as anti-lynching agitation and attention to employment, education, and suffrage. Moreover, the rhetoric of black feminism for which the club movement is known—domestic feminism and maternal feminism[1]—can be found in documents dating from the 1870s, well before the ostensible dawn of the "woman's era."

The club movement, for both black and white women, had its roots in what were commonly known as self-improvement clubs, which filled the need for continued learning for women denied a college education.

Clubwomen developed study plans that emphasized literature, history, or the arts. During the Progressive Era, black women's clubs, like the benevolent and mutual aid societies that preceded them, focused on the betterment of their communities, by advocating safe workplaces, particularly for women; establishing kindergartens, youth clubs, and homes for the elderly; and engaging in fundraising activities to benefit working-class and poor African Americans. They also pursued anti-lynching activism and have been regarded as the prime mobilizer for suffrage politics among African American women at the end of the nineteenth century. Black clubwomen were predominantly middle-class and elite women in their communities, though they came from a variety of class and regional backgrounds.

The national federation of black women's clubs is believed to have been organized by Josephine St. Pierre Ruffin[2] in response to a vicious attack on African American womanhood by the president of the Missouri Press Association, James Jacks. Indignant at the picture Ida B. Wells was painting of the South during her 1894 anti-lynching lecture tour of Britain, Jacks wrote an open letter to British anti-lynching organizations in 1895 denouncing her arguments. This letter, circulated by Josephine St. Pierre Ruffin among black women's clubs, claimed that African Americans were "devoid of morality" and referred to black women as "prostitutes" and all blacks as "natural thieves and liars." Ruffin issued a call to action, citing the Jacks letter as the veritable last straw: the first national meeting of African American women's organizations was held in Boston in late July 1895 with the organization of a national federation following a year later.

This chapter collects writings on the defense of black womanhood, some predating the Jacks letter. This "discourse of defense," persisting for at least a decade after his attack and beginning at least 20 years before it, foregrounds the ways in which African American women, regardless of their class position, continued to find their reputations impugned. Using what Evelyn Brooks Higginbotham (1993) has called a "bicultural voice," African American clubwomen worked to revise negative perceptions of and attitudes towards African American women and promoted a domestic and maternal feminism in their communities that stressed the importance of motherhood, the home, and the welfare of children. With aims such as "moral education" and "mental elevation" and proving that their "aims and interests are identical with those of all good aspiring women," the NACWC aligned itself with the discourse of domesticity (Lerner 1972, 441–42).[3] Consequently, the club movement has been frequently indicted for adopting white bourgeois mores and regarding working-class African Americans as the objects of a reforming philanthropy designed to elevate the middle-class black woman through an appeal to "racial respectability." Despite their goals of "race pride...the defence of the black community and home, and...race advancement" (Lerner 1972, 437), clubwomen's apparent endorsements of bourgeois mores have been interpreted by many contemporary readers as attempts to assimilate by adopting a "white is right" policy. Regarded as constructing a black middle-class or elite woman as its ideal, the club movement has been said to promote the middle-class woman's responsibility to "lift" the working-class woman "as she climbed," "correct[ing] many of the evils which militate so seriously against us" (Terrell 1990, 348). Many critics have thus charged that club leaders perpetuated class divisions in "the" black community and distanced themselves from working-class African Americans.

While this may be true of some clubwomen and is revealed in some of the writings collected here, scholars like Anne Meis Knupfer are quick to point out that while club policies might reflect "selectivity, privilege, and cultural capital," they also "illustrated the richness and complexity of the club movement," which needs to be understood as located "within larger socio-political structures"(1996, 13).[4] This complexity saw some clubwomen advocating the propriety of domesticity while others were vocal about its limitations.[5]

Recently, Francille Rusan Wilson (2002) has argued that scholarship on the black women's club movement has interrogated the "lifting" of that movement's motto—"Lifting as we climb"—while little attention has been paid to the necessary "climbing" of middle-class black women. As Wilson contends, that these women did have to "climb" speaks to the sexism in black communities and the racism in white feminist networks that they encountered.[6] Certainly the defenses of black womanhood included in this chapter are evidence of the "climbing" even elite black women felt they had to undertake.

DEFENSE OF BLACK WOMANHOOD

Fannie Barrier Williams, "The Intellectual Progress of the Colored Women of the United States Since the Emancipation Proclamation." In *The World's Congress of Representative Women*, ed. May Wright Sewall. New York: Rand, McNally, 1894. 696–711

Less than thirty years ago the term progress as applied to colored women of African descent in the United States would have been an anomaly. The recognition of that term to-day as appropriate is a fact full of interesting significance. That the discussion of progressive womanhood in this great assemblage of the representative women of the world is considered incomplete without some account of the colored women's status is a most noteworthy evidence that we have not failed to impress ourselves on the higher side of American life.[7]

Less is known of our women than of any other class of Americans.

No organization of far-reaching influence for their special advancement, no conventions of women to take note of their progress, and no special literature reciting the incidents, the events, and all things interesting and instructive concerning them are to be found among the agencies directing their career. There has been no special interest in their peculiar condition as native-born American women. Their power to affect the social life of America, either for good or for ill, has excited not even a speculative interest.

Though there is much that is sorrowful, much that is wonderfully heroic, and much that is romantic in a peculiar way in their history, none of it has as yet been told as evidence of what is possible for these women. How few of the happy, prosperous, and eager living Americans can appreciate what it all means to be suddenly changed from irresponsible bondage to the responsibility of freedom and citizenship!

The distress of it all can never be told, and the pain of it all can never be felt except by the victims, and by those saintly women of the white race who for thirty years have been consecrated to the uplifting of a whole race of women from a long-enforced degradation.

The American people have always been impatient of ignorance and poverty. They believe with Emerson that "America is another word for opportunity," and for that reason success is a virtue and poverty and ignorance are inexcusable. This may account for the fact that our women have excited no general sympathy in the struggle to emancipate themselves from the demoralization of slavery. This new life of freedom, with its far-reaching responsibilities, had to be learned by these children of darkness mostly without a guide, a teacher, or a friend. In the mean vocabulary of slavery there was no definition of any of the virtues of life. The meaning of such precious terms as marriage, wife, family, and home could not be learned in a school-house. The blue-back speller, the arithmetic, and the copy-book contain no magical cures for inherited inaptitudes for the moralities. Yet it must ever be counted as one of the most wonderful things in human history how promptly and eagerly these suddenly liberated women tried to lay hold upon all that there is in human excellence. There is a touching pathos in the eagerness of these millions of new home-makers to taste the blessedness of intelligent womanhood. The path of progress in the picture

234

is enlarged so as to bring to view these trustful and zealous students of freedom and civilization striving to overtake and keep pace with women whose emancipation has been a slow and painful process for a thousand years. The longing to be something better than they were when freedom found them has been the most notable characteristic in the development of these women. This constant striving for equality has given an upward direction to all the activities of colored women.

Freedom at once widened their vision beyond the mean cabin life of their bondage. Their native gentleness, good cheer, and hopefulness made them susceptible to those teachings that make for intelligence and righteousness. Sullenness of disposition, hatefulness, and revenge against the master class because of two centuries of ill-treatment are not in the nature of our women.

But a better view of what our women are doing and what their present status is may be had by noticing some lines of progress that are easily verifiable.

First it should be noticed that separate facts and figures relative to colored women are not easily obtainable. Among the white women of the country independence, progressive intelligence, and definite interests have done so much that nearly every fact and item illustrative of their progress and status is classified and easily accessible. Our women, on the contrary, have had no advantage of interests peculiar and distinct and separable from those of men that have yet excited public attention and kindly recognition.

In their religious life, however, our women show a progressiveness parallel in every important particular to that of white women in all Christian churches. It has always been a circumstance of the highest satisfaction to the missionary efforts of the Christian church that the colored people are so susceptible to a religion that marks the highest point of blessedness in human history.

Instead of finding witchcraft, sensual fetishes, and the coarse superstitions of savagery possessing our women, Christianity found them with hearts singularly tender, sympathetic, and fit for the reception of its doctrines. Their superstitions were not deeply ingrained, but were of the same sort and nature that characterize the devotees of the Christian faith everywhere.

While there has been but little progress toward the growing rationalism in the Christian creeds, there has been a marked advance toward a greater refinement of conception, good taste, and the proprieties. It is our young women coming out of the schools and academies that have been insisting upon a more godly and cultivated ministry. It is the young women of a new generation and new inspirations that are making tramps of the minister who once dominated the colored church, and whose intelligence and piety were mostly in their lungs. In this new and growing religious life the colored people have laid hold of those sweeter influences of the King's Daughters, of the Christian Endeavor and Helping Hand societies, which are doing much to elevate the tone of worship and to magnify all that there is blessed in religion.

Another evidence of growing intelligence is a sense of religious discrimination among our women. Like the nineteenth-century woman generally, our women find congeniality in all the creeds, from the Catholic creed to the no-creed of Emerson. There is a constant increase of this interesting variety in the religious life of our women.

Closely allied to this religious development is their progress in the work of education in schools and colleges. For thirty years education has been the magic word among the colored people of this country. That their greatest need was education in its broadest sense was understood by these people more strongly than it could be taught to them. It is the unvarying testimony of every teacher in the South that the mental development of the colored women as well as men has been little less than phenomenal. In twenty-five years, and under conditions discouraging in the extreme, thousands of our women have been educated as teachers. They have adapted themselves to the work of mentally lifting a whole race of people so eagerly and readily that they afford an apt illustration of the power of self-help. Not only have these women become good teachers in less than twenty-five years, but many of them are the prize teachers in the mixed schools of nearly every Northern city.

These women have also so fired the hearts of the race for education that colleges, normal schools, industrial schools, and universities have been reared by a generous public to meet the requirements of these eager students of intelligent citizenship. As American women generally are fighting against the nineteenth-century narrowness that still keeps women out of the higher institution of learning, so our women are eagerly demanding the best of education open to their race. They continually verify what President Rankin of Howard University recently said, "Any theory of educating the Afro-American that does not throw open the golden gates of the highest culture will fail on the ethical and spiritual side."

It is thus seen that our women have the same spirit and mettle that characterize the best of American women. Everywhere they are following in the tracks of those women who are swiftest in the race for higher knowledge.

To-day they feel strong enough to ask for but one thing, and that is the same opportunity for the acquisition of all kinds of knowledge that may be accorded to other women. This granted, in the next generation these progressive women will be found successfully occupying every field where the highest intelligence alone is admissible. In less than another generation

American literature, American art, and American music will be enriched by productions having new and peculiar features of interest and excellence.

The exceptional career of our women will yet stamp itself indelibly upon the thought of this country.

American literature needs for its greater variety and its deeper soundings that which will be written into it out of the hearts of these self-emancipating women. The great problems of social reform that are now so engaging the highest intelligence of American women will soon need for their solution the reinforcement of that new intelligence which our women are developing. In short, our women are ambitious to be contributors to all the great moral and intellectual forces that make for the greater weal of our common country.

If this hope seems too extravagant to those of you who know these women only in their humbler capacities, I would remind you that all that we hope for and will certainly achieve in authorship and practical intelligence is more than prophesied by what has already been done, and more that can be done, by hundreds of Afro-American women whose talents are now being expended in the struggle against race resistance.

The power of organized womanhood is one of the most interesting studies of modern sociology. Formerly women knew so little of each other mentally, their common interests were so sentimental and gossipy, and their knowledge of all the larger affairs of human society was so meager that organization among them, in the modern sense, was impossible. Now their liberal intelligence, their contact in all the great interests of education, and their increasing influence for good in all the great reformatory movements of the age has created in them a greater respect for each other, and furnished the elements of organization for large and splendid purposes. The highest ascendancy of woman's development has been reached when they have become mentally strong enough to find bonds of association interwoven with sympathy, loyalty, and mutual trustfulness. Today union is the watchword of woman's onward march.

If it be a fact that this spirit of organization among women generally is the distinguishing mark of the nineteenth-century woman, dare we ask if the colored women of the United States have made any progress in this respect?

For peculiar and painful reasons the great lessons of fraternity and altruism are hard for the colored women to learn. Emancipation found the colored Americans of the South with no sentiments of association. It will be admitted that race misfortune could scarcely go further when the terms fraternity, friendship, and unity had no meaning for its men and women.

If within thirty years they have begun to recognize the blessed significance of these vital terms of human society, confidence in their social development should be strengthened. In this important work of bringing the race together to know itself and to unite in work for a common destiny, the women have taken a leading part.

Benevolence is the essence of most of the colored women's organizations. The humane side of their natures has been cultivated to recognize the duties they owe to the sick, the indigent and ill-fortuned. No church, school, or charitable institution for the special use of colored people has been allowed to languish or fail when the associated efforts of the women could save it.

It is highly significant and interesting to note that these women, whose hearts have been wrung by all kinds of sorrows, are abundantly manifesting those gracious qualities of heart that characterize women of the best type. These kinder sentiments arising from mutual interests that are lifting our women into purer and tenderer relationship to each other, and are making the meager joys and larger griefs of our conditions known to each other, have been a large part of their education.

The hearts of Afro-American women are too warm and too large for race hatred. Long suffering has so chastened them that they are developing a special sense of sympathy for all who suffer and fail of justice. All the associated interests of church, temperance, and social reform in which American women are winning distinction can be wonderfully advanced when our women shall be welcomed as co-workers, and estimated solely by what they are worth to the moral elevation of all the people.

I regret the necessity of speaking to the question of the moral progress of our women, because the morality of our home life has been commented upon so disparagingly and meanly that we are placed in the unfortunate position of being defenders of our name.

It is proper to state, with as much emphasis as possible, that all questions relative to the moral progress of the colored women of America are impertinent and unjustly suggestive when they relate to the thousands of colored women in the North who were free from the vicious influences of slavery. They are also meanly suggestive as regards thousands of our women in the South whose force of character enabled them to escape the slavery taints of immorality. The question of the moral progress of colored women in the United States has force and meaning in that discussion only so far as it tells the story of how the once-enslaved women have been straggling for twenty-five years to emancipate themselves from the demoralization of their enslavement.

While I duly appreciate the offensiveness of all references to American slavery, it is unavoidable to charge to that system every moral imperfection that mars the character of the colored American. The whole life and power of slavery depended upon an enforced degradation of everything human in the slaves. The slave code recognized only animal distinctions between the sexes, and ruthlessly ignored those ordinary separations that belong to the social state.

It is a great wonder that two centuries of such demoralization did not work a complete extinction of all the moral instincts. But the recuperative power of these women to regain their moral instincts and to establish a respectable relationship to American womanhood is among the earlier evidences of their moral ability to rise above their conditions. In spite of a cursed heredity that bound them to the lowest social level, in spite of everything that is unfortunate and unfavorable, these women have continually shown an increasing degree of teachableness as to the meaning of woman's relationship to man.

Out of this social purification and moral uplift have come a chivalric sentiment and regard from the young men of the race that give to the young women a new sense of protection. I do not wish to disturb the serenity of this conference by suggesting why this protection is needed and the kind of men against whom it is needed.

It is sufficient for us to know that the daughters of women who thirty years ago were not allowed to be modest, not allowed to follow the instincts of moral rectitude, who could cry for protection to no living man, have so elevated the moral tone of their social life that standards of personal worth have been created, and new ideals of womanhood, instinct with grace and delicacy, are everywhere recognized and emulated.

This moral regeneration of a whole race of women is no idle sentiment —it is a serious business; and everywhere there is witnessed a feverish anxiety to be free from the mean suspicions that have so long underestimated the character strength of our women.

These women are not satisfied with the unmistakable fact that moral progress has been made, but they are fervently impatient and stirred by a sense of outrage under the vile imputations of a diseased public opinion.

Loves that are free from the dross of coarseness, affections that are unsullied, and a proper sense of all the sanctities of human intercourse felt by thousands of these women all over the land plead for the recognition of their fitness to be judged, not by the standards of slavery, but by the higher standards of freedom and of twenty-five years of education, culture, and moral contact.

The moral aptitudes of our women are just as strong and just as weak as those of any other American women with like advantages of intelligence and environment.

It may now perhaps be fittingly asked. What mean all these evidences of mental, social, and moral progress of a class of American women of whom you know so little? Certainly you can not be indifferent to the growing needs and importance of women who are demonstrating their intelligence and capacity for the highest privileges of freedom.

The most important thing to be noted is the fact that the colored people of America have reached a distinctly new era in their career so quickly that the American mind has scarcely had time to recognize the fact, and adjust itself to the new requirements of the people in all things that pertain to citizenship.

Thirty years ago public opinion recognized no differences in the colored race. To our great misfortune public opinion has changed but slightly. History is full of examples of the great injustice resulting from the perversity of public opinion, and its tardiness in recognizing new conditions.

It seems to daze the understanding of the ordinary citizen that there are thousands of men and women everywhere among us who in twenty-five years have progressed as far away from the non-progressive peasants of the "black belt" of the South as the highest social life in New England is above the lowest levels of American civilization.

This general failure of the American people to know the new generation of colored people, and to recognize this important change in them, is the cause of more injustice to our women than can well be estimated. Further progress is everywhere seriously hindered by this ignoring of their improvement.

Our exclusion from the benefits of the fair play sentiment of the country is little less than a crime against the ambitions and aspirations of a whole race of women. The American people are but repeating the common folly of history in thus attempting to repress the yearnings of progressive humanity.

In the item of employment colored women bear a distressing burden of mean and unreasonable discrimination. A Southern teacher of thirty years' experience in the South writes that "one million possibilities of good through black womanhood all depend upon an opportunity to make a living."

It is almost literally true that, except teaching in colored schools and menial work, colored women can find no employment in this free America. They are the only women in the country for whom real ability, virtue, and special talents count for nothing when they become applicants for respectable employment. Taught everywhere in ethics and social economy that merit always wins, colored women carefully prepare themselves for all kinds of occupation only to meet with stern refusal, rebuff, and disappointment. One of countless instances will show how the best as well as the meanest of American society are responsible for the special injustice to our women.

240

Not long ago I presented the case of a bright young woman to a well-known bank president of Chicago, who was in need of a thoroughly competent stenographer and typewriter. The president was fully satisfied with the young woman as exceptionally qualified for the position, and manifested much pleasure in commending her to the directors for appointment, and at the same time disclaimed that there could be any opposition on account of the slight tinge of African blood that identified her as a colored woman. Yet, when the matter was brought before the directors for action, these mighty men of money and business, these men whose prominence in all the great interests of the city would seem to lift them above all narrowness and foolishness, scented the African taint, and at once bravely came to the rescue of the bank and of society by dashing the hopes of this capable yet helpless young woman. No other question but that of color determined the action of these men, many of whom are probably foremost members of the humane society and heavy contributors to foreign missions and church extension work.

This question of employment for the trained talents of our women is a most serious one. Refusal of such employment because of color belies every maxim of justice and fair play. Such refusal takes the blessed meaning out of all the teachings of our civilization, and sadly confuses our conceptions of what is just, humane, and moral.

Can the people of this country afford to single out the women of a whole race of people as objects of their special contempt? Do these women not belong to a race that has never faltered in its support of the country's flag in every war since Attucks fell in Boston's streets?[8]

Are they not the daughters of men who have always been true as steel against treason to everything fundamental and splendid in the republic? In short, are these women not as thoroughly American in all the circumstances of citizenship as the best citizens of our country? If it be so, are we not justified in a feeling of desperation against that peculiar form of Americanism that shows respect for our women as servants and contempt for them when they become women of culture? We have never been taught to understand why the unwritten law of chivalry, protection, and fair play that are everywhere the conservators of women's welfare must exclude every woman of a dark complexion.

We believe that the world always needs the influence of every good and capable woman, and this rule recognizes no exceptions based on complexion. In their complaint against hindrances to their employment colored women ask for no special favors.

They are even willing to bring to every position fifty per cent more of ability than is required of any other class of women. They plead for opportunities untrammeled by prejudice. They plead for the right of the individual to be judged, not by tradition and race estimate, but by the present evidences of individual worth. We believe this country is large enough and the opportunities for all kinds of success are great enough to afford our women a fair chance to earn a respectable living, and to win every prize within the reach of their capabilities.

Another, and perhaps more serious, hindrance to our women is that nightmare known as "social equality." The term equality is the most inspiring word in the vocabulary of citizenship. It expresses the leveling quality in all the splendid possibilities of American life. It is this idea of equality that has made room in this country for all kinds and conditions of men, and made personal merit the supreme requisite for all kinds of achievement.

When the colored people became citizens, and found it written deep in the organic law of the land that they too had the right to life, liberty, and the pursuit of happiness, they were at once suspected of wishing to interpret this maxim of equality as meaning social equality.

Everywhere the public mind has been filled with constant alarm lest in some way our women shall approach the social sphere of the dominant race in this country. Men and women, wise and perfectly sane in all things else, become instantly unwise and foolish at the remotest suggestion of social contact with colored men and women. At every turn in our lives we meet this fear, and are humiliated by its aggressiveness and meanness. If we seek the sanctities of religion, the enlightenment of the university, the honors of politics, and the natural recreations of our common country, the social equality alarm is instantly given, and our aspirations are insulted. "Beware of social equality with the colored American" is thus written on all places, sacred or profane, in this blessed land of liberty. The most discouraging and demoralizing effect of this false sentiment concerning us is that it utterly ignores individual merit and discredits the sensibilities of intelligent womanhood. The sorrows and heartaches of a whole race of women seem to be matters of no concern to the people who so dread the social possibilities of these colored women.

On the other hand, our women have been wonderfully indifferent and unconcerned about the matter. The dread inspired by the growing intelligence of colored women has interested us almost to the point of amusement. It has given to colored women a new sense of importance to witness how easily their emancipation and steady advancement is disturbing all classes of American people. It may not be a discouraging circumstance that colored women can command some sort of attention, even though they be misunderstood. We believe in the law of reaction, and it is reasonably certain that the forces of intelligence and character being developed in our women will yet change mistrustfulness into confidence and contempt into sympathy and respect. It will soon appear to those who are not hopelessly monomaniacs on the subject that the colored people are in no way responsible for the social equality nonsense. We shall yet be credited with knowing better than our enemies that social equality can neither be enforced by law nor prevented by oppression. Though not philosophers, we long since learned that equality before the law, equality in the best sense of that term under our institutions, is totally different from social equality.

We know, without being exceptional students of history, that the social relationship of the two races will be adjusted equitably in spite of all fear and injustice, and that there is a social gravitation in human affairs that eventually overwhelms and crushes into nothingness all resistance based on prejudice and selfishness.

Our chief concern in this false social sentiment is that it attempts to hinder our further progress toward the higher spheres of womanhood. On account of it, young colored women of ambition and means are compelled in many instances to leave the country for training and education in the salons and studios of Europe. On many of the railroads of this country women of refinement and culture are driven like cattle into human cattle-cars lest the occupying of an individual seat paid for in a first-class car may result in social equality. This social quarantine on all means of travel in certain parts of the country is guarded and enforced more rigidly against us than the quarantine regulations against cholera.

Without further particularizing as to how this social question opposes our advancement, it may be stated that the contentions of colored women are in kind like those of other American women for greater freedom of development. Liberty to be all that we can be, without artificial hindrances, is a thing no less precious to us than to women generally.

We come before this assemblage of women feeling confident that our progress has been along high levels and rooted deeply in the essentials of intelligent humanity. We are so essentially American in speech, in instincts, in sentiments and destiny that the things that interest you equally interest us.

We believe that social evils are dangerously contagious. The fixed policy of persecution and injustice against a class of women who are weak and defenseless will be necessarily hurtful to the cause of all women. Colored women are becoming more and more a part of the social forces that must help to determine the questions that so concern women generally. In this Congress we ask to be known and recognized for what we are worth. If it be the high purpose of these deliberations to lessen the resistance to woman's progress, you can not fail to be interested in our struggles against the many oppositions that harass us.

Women who are tender enough in heart to be active in humane societies, to be foremost in all charitable activities, who are loving enough to unite Christian womanhood everywhere against the sin of intemperance, ought to be instantly concerned in the plea of colored women for justice and humane treatment. Women of the dominant race can not afford to be responsible for the wrongs we suffer, since those who do injustice can not escape a certain penalty. But there is no wish to overstate the obstacles to colored women or to picture their status as hopeless. There is no disposition to take our place in this Congress as faultfinders or suppliants for mercy. As women of a common country, with common interests, and a destiny that will certainly bring us closer to each other, we come to this altar with our contribution of hopefulness as well as with our complaints.

When you learn that womanhood everywhere among us is blossoming out into greater fullness of everything that is sweet, beautiful, and good in woman; when you learn that the bitterness of our experience as citizen-women has not hardened our finer feelings of love and pity for our enemies; when you learn that fierce opposition to the widening spheres of our employment has not abated the aspirations of our women to enter successfully into all the professions and arts open only to intelligence, and that everywhere in the wake of enlightened womanhood our women are seen and felt for the good they diffuse, this Congress will at once see the fullness of our fellowship, and help us to avert the arrows of prejudice that pierce the soul because of the color of our bodies.

If the love of humanity more than the love of races and sex shall pulsate throughout all the grand results that shall issue to the world from this parliament of women, women of African descent in the United States will for the first time begin to feel the sweet release from the blighting thrall of prejudice.

The colored women, as well as all women, will realize that the inalienable right to life, liberty, and the pursuit of happiness is a maxim that will become more blessed in its significance when the hand of woman shall take it from its sepulture in books and make it the gospel of every-day life and the unerring guide in the relations of all men, women, and children.

Josephine St. Pierre Ruffin, "A Charge to be Refuted." *Woman's Era* 2.3 (June 1895): 9

The editors of the WOMAN'S ERA are in receipt of a letter from Miss Florence Belgarnie,[9] Honorable Secretary of the Anti-Lynching Society of England, in which she encloses a letter from Mr. James W. Jacks, president of the Missouri Press Association. The letter of Mr. Jacks to Miss Belgarnie is a denouncement of the morality of the colored women of America, and also a criticism of the peculiar ideas of virtue and morality held by everybody but the people of the south and west. Miss Belgarnie forwards the letter for publication in the ERA,[10] with an expression of sympathy and indignation for the slurs we, as colored women, are subjected to. As the charges in this letter are so sweeping and so base, we have decided not to act hastily upon it, but to be very careful in our method of bringing it before the public. Our line of action has already begun; the letter will be printed and forwarded to leading men and women and heads of educational institutions, particularly in the south, people of reputation and standing, whose words carry weight; and in the next issue it is hoped to print the charge, with these signed replies.

The matter is a solemn one, and one upon which we shall call all our women all over the country to act. In the meantime we wish to move with discretion, and so not defeat the ultimate aim, which is the confusion of Jacks and that host of traducers who are so free in bringing the charge of immorality upon all colored women.

Lucy Craft Laney, "The Burden of the Educated Colored Woman." *Hampton Negro Conference* 3 (July 1899): 37-43

The Woman's Conference[11] opened on Thursday morning with a paper by Miss Lucy Laney, whose simplicity of manner, and evident common sense, won for her many friends. The discussion that followed was earnest and spirited,—one of the very best of the conference.

If the educated colored woman has a burden,—and we believe she has—what is that burden? How can it be lightened, how may it be lifted? What it is can be readily seen perhaps better than told, for it constantly annoys to irritation; it bulges out as did the load of Bunyan's Christian—ignorance—with its inseparable companions, shame and crime and prejudice. That our position may be more readily understood, let us refer to the past; and it will suffice for our purpose to begin with our coming to America in 1620, since prior to that time, we claim only heathenism. During the days of training in our first mission school—slavery—that which is the foundation, of right training and good government, the basic rock of all true culture—the home, with its fire-side training, mother's moulding, woman's care, was not only neglected but utterly disregarded. There was no time in the institution for such teaching. We know that there were, even in the first days of that school, isolated cases of men and women of high moral character and great intellectual worth, as Phillis Wheatley, Sojourner Truth, and John Chavers, whose work and lives should have taught, or at least suggested to their instructors, the capabilities and possibilities of their dusky slave pupils. The progress and the struggles of these for noble things should have led their instructors to see how the souls and minds of this people then yearned for light—the real life. But alas! these dull teachers, like many modern pedagogues and school-keepers, failed to know their pupils—to find out their real needs, and hence had no cause to study methods of better and best development of the boys and girls under their care. What other result could come from such training or want of training than a conditioned race such as we now have?

For two hundred and fifty years they married, or were given in marriage. Oft times marriage ceremonies were performed for them by the learned minister of the master's church; more often there was simply a consorting by the master's consent, but it was always understood that these unions for cause, or without cause, might be more easily broken, than a divorce can be obtained in Indiana or Dakota. Without going so long a distance as from New York to Connecticut, the separated could take other companions for life, for a long or short time; for during those two hundred and fifty years there was not a single marriage legalized in a single southern state, where dwelt the mass of this people. There was something of the philosopher in the plantation preacher, who, at the close of the marriage ceremony, had the dusky couple join their right hands, and then called upon the assembled congregation to sing as he lined it out, "Plunged in a gulf of dark despair," for well he knew the sequel of many such unions. If it so happened that a husband and wife were parted by those who owned them, such owners often consoled those thus parted with the fact that he could get another wife; she, another husband. Such was the sanctity of the marriage vow that was taught and held for over two hundred and fifty years.

Habit is indeed second nature. This is the race inheritance. I thank God not of all, for we know, each of us, of instances, of holding most sacred the plighted love and keeping faithfully and sacredly the marriage vows. We know of pure homes and of growing old together. Blessed heritage! If we only had the gold there might be many "Golden Weddings." Despair not; the crushing burden of immorality which has its root in the disregard of the marriage vow, can be lightened. It must be, and the educated colored woman can and will do her part in lifting this burden.

In the old institution there was no attention given to homes and to home-making. Homes were only places in which to sleep, father had neither responsibility nor authority; mother, neither cares nor duties. She wielded no gentle

246

sway nor influence. The character of their children was a matter of no concern to them; surroundings were not considered. It is true, house cleaning was sometimes enforced as a protection to property, but this was done at stated times and when ordered. There is no greater enemy of the race than these untidy and filthy homes; they bring not only physical disease and death, but they are very incubators of sin; they bring intellectual and moral death. The burden of giving knowledge and bringing about the practice of the laws of hygiene among a people ignorant of the laws of nature and common decency is not a slight one. But this, too, the intelligent women can and must help to carry.

The large number of young men in the state prison is by no means the least of the heavy burdens. It is true that many of these are unjustly sentenced; that longer terms of imprisonment are given Negroes than white persons for the same offences; it is true that white criminals by the help of attorneys, money, and influence, oftener escape the prison, thus keeping small the number of prisoners recorded, for figures never lie. It is true that many are tried and imprisoned for trivial causes, such as the following, clipped from the *Tribune,* of Elberyon, Ga.: "Seven or eight Negroes were arrested and tried for stealing two fish-hooks last week. When the time of our courts is wasted in such a manner as this, it is high time to stop and consider whither we are driving. Such picaunyish[12] cases reflect on the intelligence of a community. It is fair to say the courts are not to blame in this matter." Commenting on this *The South Daily* says: "We are glad to note that the sentiment of the paper is against the injustice. Nevertheless these statistics will form the basis of some lecturer's discourse." This fact remains, that many of our youth are in prison, that large numbers of our young men are serving out long terms of imprisonment, and this is a very sore burden. Five years ago while attending a Teacher's Institute at Thomasville, Ga., I saw working on the streets in the chain gang, with rude men and ruder women, with ignorant, wicked, almost naked men, criminals guilty of all the sins named in the decalogue, a large number of boys from ten to fifteen years of age, and two young girls between the ages of twelve and sixteen. It is not necessary that prison statistics be quoted, for we know too well the story, and we feel most sensibly this burden, the weight of which will sink us unless it is at once made lighter and finally lifted.

Last, but not least, is the burden of prejudice, heavier in that it is imposed by the strong, those from whom help, not hindrance, should come. They are making the already heavy burden of their victims heavier to bear, and yet they are commanded by One who is even the Master of all: "Bear ye one another's burdens, and thus fulfil the law."[13] This is met with, and must be borne everywhere. In the South, in public conveyances, and at all points of race contact; in the North, in hotels, at the baptismal pool, in cemeteries; everywhere, in some shape or form, it is to be borne. No one suffers under the weight of this burden as the educated Negro woman does; and she must help to lift it.

Ignorance and immorality, if they are not the prime causes, have certainly intensified prejudice. The forces to lighten and finally to lift this and all of these burdens are true culture and character, linked with that most substantial coupler, cash. We said in the beginning that the past can serve no further purpose than to give us our present bearings. It is a condition that confronts us. With this we must deal, it is this we must change. The physician of today inquires into the history of his patient, but he has to do especially with diagnosis and cure. We know the history; we think a correct diagnosis has often been made—let us attempt a cure. We would prescribe: homes—better homes, clean homes, pure homes; schools—better schools; more culture; more thrift; and work in large doses; put the patient at once on this treatment and continue through life. Can woman do this work? She can; and she must do her part, and her part is by no means small.

Nothing in the present century is more noticeable than the tendency of women to enter every hopeful field of wage-earning and philanthropy, and attempt to reach a place in every intellectual arena. Women are by nature fitted for teaching very young children; their maternal instinct makes them patient and sympathetic with their charges. Negro women of culture, as kindergartners and primary teachers have a rare opportunity to lend a hand to the lifting of these burdens, for here they may instill lessons of cleanliness, truthfulness, loving kindness, love for nature, and love for Nature's God. Here they may daily start aright hundreds of our children; here, too, they may save years of time in the education of the child; and may save many lives from shame and crime by applying the law of prevention. In the kindergarten and primary school is the salvation of the race.

For children of both sexes from six to fifteen years of age, women are more successful as teachers than men. This fact is proven by their employment. Two-thirds of the teachers in the public schools of the United States are women. It is the glory of the United States that good order and peace are maintained not by a large, standing army of well trained soldiers, but by the sentiment of her citizens, sentiments implanted and nourished by her well trained army of four hundred thousand school teachers, two-thirds of whom are women.

The educated Negro woman, the woman of character and culture is needed in the schoolroom not only in the kindergarten, and in the primary and the secondary school; but she is needed in high school, the academy, and the college. Only those of character and culture can do successful lift-

248

ing, for she who would mould character must herself possess it. Not alone in the schoolroom can the intelligent woman lend a lifting hand, but as a public lecturer she may give advice, helpful suggestions, and important knowledge, that will change a whole community and start its people on the upward way. To be convinced of the good that can be done for humanity by this means one need only recall the names of Lucy Stone, Mary Livermore, Frances Harper, Frances Willard and Julia Ward Howe. The refined and noble Negro woman may lift much with this lever. Women may also be most helpful as teachers of sewing schools and cooking classes, not simply in the public schools and private institutions, but in classes formed in neighborhoods that sorely need this knowledge. Through these classes girls who are not in school may be reached; and through them something may be done to better their homes, and inculcate habits of neatness and thrift. To bring the influence of the schools to bear upon these homes is the most needful thing of the hour. Often teachers who have labored most arduously, conscientiously, and intelligently have become discouraged on seeing that society had not been benefited, but sometimes positively injured by the conduct of their pupils.

The work of the schoolroom has been completely neutralized by the training of the home. Then we must have better homes, and better homes mean better mothers, better fathers, better born children. Emerson says, "To the well-born child all the virtues are natural, not painfully acquired."

But "The temporal life which is not allowed to open into the eternal life becomes corrupt and feeble even in its temporalness." As a teacher in the Sabbath school, as a leader in young people's meetings and missionary societies, in women's societies and Bible classes our cultured women are needed to do a great and blessed work. Here they may cause many budding lives to open into eternal life. Froebel urged teachers and parents to see to the blending of the temporal and divine life when he said, "God created man in his own image; therefore man should create and bring forth like God."[14] The young people are ready and anxiously await intelligent leadership in Christian work. The less fortunate women already assembled in churches are ready for work. Work they do and work they will; that it may be effective work, they need the help and leadership of their more favored sisters.

A few weeks ago this country was startled by the following telegram of southern women of culture sent to Ex-Governor Northen of Georgia, just before he made his Boston speech: "You are authorized to say in your address tonight that the women of Georgia, realizing the great importance to both races of early moral training of the Negro race, stand ready to undertake this work when means are supplied." But more startled was the world the next day, after cultured Boston had supplied a part of the means,

$20,000, to read the glaring head lines of the southern press, "Who Will Teach the Black Babies?" because some of the cultured women who had signed the telegram had declared when interviewed, that Negro women fitted for the work could not be found, and no self-respecting southern white woman would teach a colored kindergarten. Yet already in Atlanta, Georgia, and in Athens, Georgia, southern women are at work among Negroes. There is plenty of work for all who have the proper conception of the teacher's office, who know that all men are brothers, God being their common father. But the educated Negro women *must* teach the "Black Babies"; she must come forward and inspire our men and boys to make a successful onslaught upon sin, shame, and crime.

The burden of the educated colored woman is not diminished by the terrible crimes and outrages that we daily hear of, but by these very outrages and lawlessness her burdens are greatly increased.

Somewhere I read a story, that in one of those western cities built in a day, the half-dozen men of the town labored to pull a heavy piece of timber to the top of a building. They pushed and pulled hard to no purpose, when one of the men on the top shouted to those below: "Call the women." They called the women; the women came; they pushed; soon the timber was seen to move, and ere long it was in the desired place. Today not only the men on top call, but a needy race — the whole world, calls loudly to the cultured Negro women to come to the rescue. Do they hear? Are they coming? Will they push?

The discussion following Miss Laney's paper brought to light the fact that educated colored women are aware of their responsibilities, and that they have already accomplished much toward making lighter the burdens that weigh down the race. There was no lack of frankness in the relation of incidents showing the great need of help for the ignorant and degraded classes; nor was there any lack of willingness to undertake whatever the conference might decide upon as the best thing to be done. The session was especially marked by harmony and unanimity of feeling, no disposition being shown by anyone to shirk responsibility or to belittle the work of her neighbors.

Addie Hunton, "Negro Womanhood Defended." *Our Woman's Number. The Voice of the Negro* 1.7 (July 1904): 280–82

Out of that ever vexing and mysterious hydra headed evil we name the "race problem," there seems to have grown of late a sentiment, if you will, whose particular function it is to magnify the moral weakness of Negro womanhood. While her character had been assailed from without many times, it remained for a Judas Iscariot, in an awful and sinful malediction, to make the assertion that "not only are ninety per cent of the Negro women of America unchaste, but the social degradation of our freedwomen is without parallel in all modern civilization."[15] This assertion, which the author himself unconsciously repudiates before he closes his foul tirade, seems to have given this phase of the "problem" a sudden boom, and to have made a delightfully new and inviting theme for our many enemies and harping critics. Unwarned, unasked, with no sense of delicacy for her feelings, the Negro woman has been made the subject of an increasing and unmerciful criticism. To her, at this time, is being charged every weakness of the race, even though this weakness may have been common to humanity since the days of Adam. Everywhere, her moral defects are being portrayed by her enemies; sometimes, veiled in hypocritical pity, and again, in language bitter and unrelenting.

In taking up the gauntlet of defense, we desire to have it understood that we are in no sense an apologist. We are neither unconscious or unmindful of our shortcomings; we are simply asking now that, in the clear light of truth and justice, her case be given a hearing by all who are interested in moral and social problems, and who value the principles of justice, freedom and fraternity, or even by those who regard all humanity as something above the common clod. This hearing the Negro woman claims as her right, upon the basis that whatever is a benefit or injury to one, that he has a right to concern himself about.

Whence come these base aspersions to blight and dwarf the spirit of the Negro woman? Who in all this land can be so forgetful of her service and servitude as to seek to crush her already wounded and bleeding soul? Wounded by the violence and shame forced upon her in times when she had no voice to speak her woe; bleeding because of the constant irritation of these wounds by those who, while spending their best energies to vilify her to the world, are at the same time ever secretly seeking to make these vilifications true; she asks, Whence comes all this talk about the immorality of the Negro woman?

It is a fact to be noted that most of the articles that bear upon this subject are written not by those who have made a systematic and careful study of the question from every point of view, but rather by those whose conclusions are born of their own limited experiences with and observations of one class or kind of Negro women. The statement has been made often of late that there are different classes of Negro women as there are different classes of other women, but it seems so difficult for some to grasp this idea that it will bear further repetition. It is also a fact that there is a wide gulf—which seemingly grows wider—between the white people of the

South and the better class of colored people. They are as Jew and Samaritan, so that those who write most about the moral degradation of the Negro woman know little or nothing of that best element of our women who are quietly and unobtrusively working out the salvation of the race. Because the Negro women with whom they come in contact exhibit none of those higher qualities that are based upon virtue, it is assumed that these women are typical of all Negro women, and, upon this assumption, an attempt is made to prove to the shame of all, a wholesale immorality.

But what of the Negro woman herself? Of her condition and environments? Any argument that does not take more than passing note of the heritage of shame with which she found herself burdened when emerging from slavery, or that does not take more than a mere glance at her very peculiar environment, is at best but erroneous.

For two centuries the Negro woman was forced by cruelty too diverse and appalling to mention to submit her body to those who bartered for it. She was voiceless and there was no arm lifted in her defense. And yet there is hardly a daughter of a slave mother who has not heard of the sublime and heroic soul of some maternal ancestor that went home to the God that gave it rather than live a life of enforced infamy. There is an unwritten and an almost unmentionable history of the burdens of those soul-trying times when, to bring profit to the slave trade and to satisfy the base desires of a stronger hand, the Negro woman was the subject of compulsory immorality. Not only did she emerge from that dark period crushed by an experience more bitter than death, but her teachers had given her a false conception of the marriage vow and its sanctity. That slavery might be made as profitable as possible, masters reserved the right to join or separate their slaves at will. Prostitution was not only encouraged but fostered.

Stepping suddenly out of the darkness of slavery, the Negro woman was bewildered by the temptations and trials awaiting her. In many instances, they were no less intense than those to which she had been subjected in the past. It is not strange that those whose prey she had been for so long should have followed her into her new environments, and, as they had used cruel force when it was their right, now that this was no longer possible, should seek to subvert her with glittering baubles. With a blighted past, no fireside training nor home life, driven to and fro at will in a world of poverty and ignorance, it would have been strange and unusual had she not, in many cases, fallen by the wayside.

The wages paid the Negro laboring woman are so paltry as to scarcely provide for her the necessities of life. One writer has said "the severest poverty is unfavorable to moralty." Then, where, as in this case, the tempter stands on every side, it calls for no ordinary strength to resist his allurements.

That versatile and soulful writer of the race in "The Souls of Black Folk"[16] has given a chapter entitled "Of the Coining of John." Therein is a picture of the temptation which forces itself upon the average comely Negro servant girl, and therein, too, is portrayed the tragedy that comes when the Negro man dares raise his hand in the defense of his own. And yet in the face of all this ignominy—all this immorality and cruel oppression—she has staggered up through the ages ladened with the double burden of excessive maternal care and physical toil, and she has, while climbing, thrown off much of the dross and become more chastened and purified, conforming herself as fast as possible to the demand for upright Christian living. To all who are fair-minded and unprejudiced, it must be certain that nothing can stay the tide of her progress in its onward flow.

It is quite likely that too much attention has hitherto been given to theorizing on this grave question, while real study, friendly fairness and appreciation of her progress have found no place in the arguments. This fact alone might be sufficient to discourage her and blight her hopes did she not inherit that rare faith of her ancestors who trusted so implicitly in God. Let those who desire to write of her from a moral standpoint hereafter realize the justice and wisdom of studying her in her best as well as her worst condition.

Immorality and thrift do not mate very well, and in spite of all accusations, the Negro woman has been the motive power in whatever has been accomplished by the race. She early realized that the moral and conservative qualities of a race reside in its womanhood, and with this realization came a longing and a reaching after a virtuous home-life: hence, we have thousands of homes dotting this Southland, some mere cottages, others more pretentious residences, but all are citadels of purity and virtue, presided over by women of intelligence and housewifely care. The beneficent influence of these homes is felt in every community, and it will be appreciated more largely by coming generations than it is now possible to realize. The Negro woman is rightly making her first effort for parity and truth at her own fireside. By her thrift she has helped to accumulate property, real and personal, to the value of more than $700,000,000. She has helped to raise nearly $14,000,000 for the education of her children. She has educated more than 25,000 teachers of her own race, and all of this, in her hampered condition, in less than a half century. With her deeper interest in her people, her larger knowledge of their needs, with the culture and character that education give, she is constantly at work for the uplift of her race.

Finally, we are confronting new conditions which make stern demands upon the wisdom and conscience of both races. Let it not be forgotten that the high virtue of the South has its basis on the souls and bodies of Negro

women; therefore, it is now time that Southern chivalry, which ever pro-
claims its right to "keep pure and undefiled the spirit that worships at the
family shrine," should extend itself to the protection of the Negro man who
seeks to establish the same principle for his home. In the light of Christianity
all women must be protected if for no other reason than that they are akin
to the Christ-mother. Until this is done, it would, at least, be charitable to
leave the discussion of the morality of the Negro woman to those who are
earnestly laboring for her uplift.

CLUB MOVEMENT

Mary Church Terrell, "The Duty of the National Association of Colored Women to the Race." *AME Church Review* 16.3 (January 1900): 340–54

The National Association of Colored Women[17] had at its second convention every reason to rejoice and be exceeding glad. From its birth in July,
1896, till the present moment its growth has been steady and its march ever
onward and upward to the goal of its ambition.

An infant of but three years is this organization, over which I have had
the honor to preside, ever since it first saw the light of day in the Capital
of the Nation, and yet in those short years it has accomplished a vast
amount of good. So tenderly has this child of the organized womanhood
of the race been nurtured, and so wisely ministered unto by all who have
watched prayerfully and waited patiently for its development, that it comes
before you, to-day a child hale, hearty and strong, of which its fond mothers have every reason to be proud. As individuals, colored women have
always been ambitious for their race. From the day when shackles first fell
from their fettered limbs till now, they have often, single-handed and alone,
struggled against the most desperate and discouraging odds, in order to
secure for their loved ones and themselves that culture of the head and
heart for which they hungered and thirsted so long in vain. But it dawned
upon them finally, that individuals working alone, or scattered here and
there in small companies, might be ever so honest in purpose, so indefatigable in labor, so conscientious about methods, and so wise in projecting
plans, yet they would accomplish little, compared with the possible
achievement of many individuals, all banded together throughout the
entire land, with heads and hearts fixed on the same high purpose and

hands joined in united strength. As a result of a general realization of this fact, the National Association of Colored Women was born.

Though we are young in years, and have been unable to put into execution some plans on which we had built high hopes, the fruits of organized effort are already apparent to all. If in the short space of three years the National Association had done nothing but give an impressive object lesson in the necessity for, and the efficacy of, organization, it would have proved its reason for existence and its right to live; but, seriously handicapped though we have been, both because of the lack of experience and lack of funds, our efforts have for the most part been crowned with success.

In the kindergartens established by some of our organizations, children have been cultivated and trained. A sanatorium with a training school for nurses has been set on such a firm foundation in a Southern city, and has given such abundant proof of its utility and necessity, that the municipal government has voted it an annual appropriation of several hundred dollars. To our poor benighted sisters in the black belt of Alabama we have gone, and have been both a help and a comfort to these women, through the darkness of whose ignorance of everything that makes life sweet or worth the living, no ray of light would have penetrated but for us. We have taught them the A, B, C, of living, by showing them how to make their huts more habitable and decent with the small means at their command, and how to care for themselves and their families more in accordance with the laws of health. Plans for aiding the indigent, orphaned and aged have been projected and in some instances have been carried to a successful execution. Mother's meetings have been generally held and sewing classes formed. Abuses like lynching, the convict lease system and the Jim Crow car laws have been discussed with a view of doing something to remedy these evils. In Chicago, magnificent work has been done by the Illinois Federation of Colored Women's Clubs through whose instrumentality schools have been visited, truant children looked after, parents and teachers urged to co-operate with each other, public institutions investigated, rescue and reform work engaged in to reclaim unfortunate women and tempted girls, garments cut, made and distributed to the needy poor. In short, what our hands have found to do, that we have cheerfully done. It is not, therefore, because I feel that the National Association of Colored Women has been derelict, or has failed, that I shall discuss its duty to our race, but because I wish to emphasize some special lines of work in which it is already engaging, but to which I would pledge its more hearty support.

The more closely I study the relation of this Association to the race, the more clearly defined becomes its duty to the children.

Believing in the saving grace of the kindergarten for our little ones, at *education for young kindergartens*

our first convention, as some may remember, I urged with all the earnestness that I could command, that the Association should consider the establishment of kindergartens as the special mission it is called upon to fulfill. The importance of engaging extensively in this effort to uplift the children, particularly those to whom the opportunity of learning by contact what is true and good and beautiful could come through no other source, grows on me more and more every day. Through the kindergarten alone, which teaches its lessons in the most impressionable years of childhood, shall we be able to save countless thousands of our little ones who are going to destruction before our very eyes. To some the task of establishing kindergartens may seem too herculean for the Association to undertake, because of the great expense involved. Be that as it may, we shall never accomplish the good it is in our power to do, nor shall we discharge our obligation to the race, until we engage in this work in those sections at least where it is most needed.

In many cities and towns the kindergarten has already been incorporated in the public school system. Here it may not be necessary for the Association to work. But wherever the conditions are such that our children are deprived of the training which they can receive from the kindergarten alone, deprived of that training which from the very nature of the case, they so sorely need, there the Association should establish these schools, from which so much benefit to our little ones will accrue.

Side by side in importance with the kindergarten stands the day nursery, a charity of which there is an imperative need among us. Thousands of our wage-earning mothers with large families dependent upon them for support are obliged to leave their infants all day to be cared for either by young brothers and sisters, who know nothing about it, or by some good-natured neighbor, who promises much, but who does little. Some of these infants are locked alone in a room from the time the mother leaves in the morning until she returns at night. Their suffering is, of course, unspeakable. Not long ago, I read in a southern newspaper that an infant thus locked alone in a room all day, while its mother went out to wash, had cried itself to death. Recently I have had under direct observation a day nursery, established for infants of working women, and I have been shocked at some of the miserable little specimens of humanity brought in by mothers, who had been obliged to board them out with either careless or heartless people. In one instance the hands and legs of a poor little mite of only fourteen months had been terribly drawn and twisted with rheumatism contracted by sleeping in a cold room with no fire during the severe winter, while the family with whom it boarded enjoyed comfortable quarters overhead. And so I might go on enumerating cases, showing how terrible is the suffering of infants of working women, who have no one with whom to leave them, while they earn their daily bread. Establishing day nurseries is clearly a practical charity, of the need of which there is abundant proof in every community where our women may be found.

What a vast amount of good would be accomplished, if by every branch of the Association, a home were provided for the infants of working women, who no matter how tender may be their affection for their little ones, are forced by stern necessity to neglect them all day themselves, and at best, can only entrust them to others, from whom, in the majority of cases, they do not receive the proper care. It would not only save the life, and preserve the health of many a poor little one, but it would speak eloquently of our interest in our sisters, whose lot is harder than our own, but to whom we should give unmistakable proof of our regard, our sympathy, and our willingness to render any assistance in our power. When one thinks of the slaughter of the innocents which is occurring with pitiless persistency every day, and reflects upon how many are maimed for life through neglect, how many there are whose intellects are clouded because of the treatment received during their helpless infancy, establishing day nurseries can seem neither unnecessary nor far-fetched; but must appeal directly to us all. No great amount is required to establish a day nursery, and part of the money necessary for its maintenance might be secured by charging each of the mothers who take advantage of it a small sum. In no other way could the investment of the same amount of money bring such large and blessed returns.

To each and every branch of the Association, then, I recommend the establishment of a day nursery, as a means through which it can render one of the greatest services possible to humanity and the race.

For the sake of argument, let us suppose that absolute lack of means prevents an organization from establishing either a kindergarten or a day nursery. Even under such circumstances a part of its obligation to the children may be discharged.

For no organization is so poor both in mental resources and in money that it cannot form a children's club, through which we can do a vast amount of good. Lessons may be taught and rules of conduct impressed, while the children of a neighborhood are gathered together for amusement and play, as in no other way. Both by telling and reading stories, teaching kindness to animals, politeness to elders, pity for the unfortunate and weak, seeds may be sown in youthful minds, which in after years will spring up and bear fruit, some an hundred fold. What a revolution we should work, for instance, by the time the next generation stands at the helm, if the children of to-day were taught that they are responsible for their thoughts that they can learn to control them, that an impure life is the result of impure

257

thoughts, that crime is conceived in thought before it is executed in deed. No organization of the Association should feel entirely satisfied with its work, unless some of its energy, or some of its brain, or some of its money is used in the name, and for the sake of the children, either by establishing a day nursery, a kindergarten, informing a children's club, which last is possible to all.

Let us remember that we are banded together to do good, to work most vigorously and conscientiously upon that which will redound most to the welfare and progress of the race. If that be true, I recommend to you, I plead to you, for the children, for those who will soon represent us, for those by whom as a race we shall soon stand or fall in the estimation of the world, for those upon whom the hope of every people must necessarily be built. As an Association, let us devote ourselves enthusiastically, conscientiously, to the children, with their warm little hearts, their susceptible little minds, their malleable, pliable characters. Through the children of to-day, we must build the foundation of the next generation upon such a rock of integrity, morality, and strength, both of body and mind, that the floods of proscription, prejudice, and persecution may descend upon it in torrents, and yet it will not be moved. We hear a great deal about the race problem, and how to solve it. This theory, that and the other, may be advanced, but the real solution of the race problem, both so far as we, who are oppressed and those who oppress us are concerned, lies in the children.

Let no one suppose that I would have a large organization like ours a body of one idea, with no thought, plan or purpose except that which centers about the children. I am an optimist, because I see how we are broadening and deepening out into the various channels of generosity and beneficence, which indicates what a high state of civilization we have already reached. Homes for the orphaned and aged must be established; sanatoriums, hospitals, and training schools for nurses founded; unfortunate women and tempted girls encircled by the loving arms of those who would woo them back to the path of rectitude and virtue; classes formed for cultivating the mind; schools of domestic science opened in every city and village in which our women and girls may be found. All this is our duty, all this is an obligation, which we should discharge as soon as our means will permit. But in connection with such work let us not neglect, let us not forget, the children, remembering that when we love and protect the little ones, we follow in the footsteps of Him, who when He wished to paint the most beautiful picture of Beulah land it is possible for the human mind to conceive, pointed to the children and said—"Of such is the kingdom of heaven."[18]

It is frequently charged against the more favored among us who have been blessed with advantages of education and moral training superior to those enjoyed by the majority, that they hold themselves too much aloof from the less fortunate of their people. Without discussing the reasons for such a condition of things, it must be patent to the most careless observer that the more intelligent and influential among us do not exert themselves as much as they should to uplift those beneath them, as it is plainly their duty to do.

It has been suggested, and very appropriately, I think, that this Association should take as its motto — *Lifting as we climb*. In no way could we live up to such a sentiment better than by coming into closer touch with the masses of our women, by whom, whether we will or not, the world will always judge the womanhood of the race. Even though we wish to shun them, and hold ourselves entirely aloof from them, we cannot escape the consequences of their acts. So, that, if the call of duty were disregarded altogether, policy and self-preservation would demand that we go down among the lowly, the illiterate, and even the vicious to whom we are bound by the ties of race and sex, and put forth every possible effort to uplift and reclaim them.

It is useless to talk about elevating the race if we do not come into closer touch with the masses of our women, through whom we may correct many of the evils which militate so seriously against us, and inaugurate the reforms without which, as a race, we cannot hope to succeed. It is often difficult, I know, to persuade people who need help most to avail themselves of the assistance offered by those who wish to lift them to a higher plane. If it were possible for us to send out a national organizer, whose duty it would be to form clubs throughout the length and breadth of the land, it would be no easy matter, I am sure, to persuade some of our women to join them, even though they knew that by so doing they would receive just that kind of instruction and counsel which they so greatly need. This fault is not peculiar to our women alone, but is common to the whole human race. Difficult though it be for us to uplift some of our women, many of whose practices in their own homes and in the service of their employers rise like a great barrier to our progress, we should nevertheless work unceasingly to this end until we win their confidence so that they will accept our aid.

Through such clubs as I have just mentioned, the attention of our women might be called to the alarming rapidity with which they are losing ground in the world of labor — a fact patent to all who observe and read the signs of the times. So many families are supported entirely by our women, that if this movement to withold employment from them continues to grow, we shall soon be confronted by a condition of things serious and disastrous indeed. It is clearly the duty of this, the only organized body of colored women in the country, to study the labor question, not only as it affects the women, but also as it affects the men. When those who formerly employed colored women as domestics, but who refuse to do so now, are asked why they have established what is equivalent to a boycott against us, they invariably tell us that colored women are now neither skilled in the trades nor reliable as working women. While we know that in the majority of cases colored women are not employed because of the cruel, unreasonable prejudice which rages so violently against them, there is just enough truth in the charge of poor workmanship and unreliability to make us wince when it is preferred.

To stem this tide of popular disfavor against us should be the desire and determination of every colored woman in the country who has the interest of her race at heart. It is we, the National Association, who must point out to our women how fatal it will be to their highest, best interests, and to the highest, best interests of their children, if they do not build up a reputation for reliability and proficiency, by establishing schools of domestic science as soon as our means will permit; and it is the duty of this Association to raise funds to start a few of these schools immediately—we should probably do more to solve the labor question, so far as it affects the women than by using any other means we could possibly employ. Let us explain the situation as we may, the fact remains that trades and avocations, which formerly by common consent belonged almost exclusively to our men and women are gradually slipping from their grasp.

Whom does such a condition of things affect more directly and disastrously than the women of the race? As parents, teachers and guardians, we teach our children to be honest and industrious, to cultivate their minds, to become skilled workmen, to be energetic and then to be hopeful. It is easy enough to impress upon them the necessity of cultivating their minds, and of becoming skilled workmen, of being energetic, honest and industrious, but how difficult it is for colored women to inspire their children with hope, or offer them an incentive for their best endeavor under the existing condition of things in this country.

As a mother of the dominant race looks into the sweet innocent face of her babe, her heart thrills not only with happiness in the present, but also with joyful anticipations of the future. For well she knows that honor, wealth, fame and greatness in any vocation he may choose, are all his, if he but possess the ability and determination to secure them. She knows that if it is in him to be great, all the exterior circumstances, which can help him to the goal of his ambition, such as the laws of his country, the public opinion of his countrymen and manifold opportunities, are all his, without the asking. From his birth he is king in his own right, and is no suppliant for justice.

But how bitter is the contrast between the feelings of joy and hope which thrill the heart of the white mother and those which stir the soul of her colored sister. As a mother of the weaker race clasps to her bosom the babe which she loves with an affection as tender and deep as that the white mother bears her child, she cannot thrill with joyful anticipation of the future. For before her babe she sees the thorny path of prejudice and proscription his little feet must tread. She knows that no matter how great his ability, or how lofty his ambition, there are comparatively few trades and avocations in which any one of his race may hope to succeed. She knows that no matter how skillful his hand, how honest his heart, or how great his need, trades unions will close their doors in his face and make his struggle for existence desperate indeed. So rough does the way of her infant appear to many a poor colored mother, as she thinks of the hardships and humiliations to which he will be subjected, when he tries to earn his daily bread, that instead of thrilling with joy and hope, she trembles with apprehension and despair.

This picture, though forbidding to look upon, is not overdrawn, as those who have studied the labor question in its relation to our race can testify. What, then, shall we do? Shall we sit supinely by, with folded hands, drooping heads, and weeping eyes, or shall we be up and doing, determined to smooth out the rough roads of labor over which tiny feet that now patter in play, will soon stumble and fall? To our own youth, to our own tradesmen, we must preach efficiency, reliability, thorough preparation for any work in which they choose to engage. Let us also appeal directly to the large-hearted, broad-minded women of the dominant race, and lay our case clearly before them. In conversing with many of them privately I have discovered that our side of the labor question has never been made a living, breathing, terrible reality to them. In a vague way they know that difficulties do confront colored men and women in their effort to secure employment, but they do not know how almost insurmountable are the obstacles which lie in the path of the rank and file who want to earn an honest living. Let us ask these women both to follow, themselves, and teach their children, the lofty principles of humanity, charity and justice which they profess to observe. Let us ask that they train their children to be just and broad enough to judge men and women by their intrinsic merit, rather than by the adventitious circumstances of race or color or creed. Let the Association of colored women ask the white mothers of this country to teach their children that when they grow to be men and women, if they deliberately prevent their fellow creatures from earning their daily bread by closing the doors of trade against them the Father of all men will hold them responsible for the crimes which are the result of their injustice, and for the human wrecks which the ruthless crushing of hope and ambition always makes. In the name of our children, let us ask, also, that they do all in their power to secure for our youth opportunities of earning a living and

261

...ing unto the full stature of manhood and womanhood, which they
...for their own. In the name of justice and humanity, in the name of
the innocence and helplessness of childhood, black childhood, as well as
white childhood, let us appeal to the white mothers of this country to do
all in their power to make the future of our boys and girls as bright and
promising as should be that of every child, born on this free American soil.
It is the women of the country who mould public opinion, and when they
say that trades and avocations shall not be closed against men and women
on account of race or color, then the day of proscription and prejudice will
darken to dawn no more.

As individuals, we have presented our case again and again. Let us now
try the efficacy of organized effort; on this, I build great hope. Organization
is one of the most potent forces in the world to-day, and the good it is possible for the National Association to accomplish has not yet been approximated by those most sanguine of its success.

And now, I must briefly call your attention to a subject fraught with
interest to us all. The health of our race is becoming a matter of deep concern to many who are alarmed by statistics showing how great is the death
rate among us as compared with that of the Whites.

There are many reasons why this proportion is so great among us—chief
of which are poverty and ignorance of the laws of health. Our children are
sent illy clad through inclement weather to school, for instance. Girls just
budding into womanhood are allowed to sit all day in wet boots and damp
skirts, in both the high and graded schools which they attend. Thus it happens that some of our most promising and gifted young women succumb
to diseases, which are the result of carelessness on the part both of parents
and teachers. We must call the attention of our mothers to this fact, and
urge the school officials to protect the health of our children as far as possible by wise legislation, and thus stop the awful ravages made by diseases
which a little care and precaution might prevent.

I must not neglect to mention another duty which the Association owes
the race, and which it must not fail to discharge. Creating a healthful, wholesome public opinion in every community in which we are represented, is
one of the greatest services we can render. The duty of setting a high moral
standard and living up to it devolves upon us as colored women in a peculiar way. Slanders are circulated against us every day, both in the press and
by the direct descendants of those who in years past were responsible for
the moral degradation of their female slaves. While these calumnies are not
founded in fact, they can nevertheless do us a great deal of harm, if those
who represent the intelligence and virtue among us do not, both in our
public and private life, avoid even the appearance of evil. In spite of the

fateful inheritance left us by slavery, in spite of the manifold temptations and pitfalls to which our young girls are subjected all over the country, and though the safeguards usually thrown around maidenly youth and innocence are in some sections entirely withheld from colored girls, statistics compiled by men not inclined to falsify in favor of my race show that immorality among colored women is not so great as among women in countries like Austria, Italy, Germany, Sweden and France.

If I were called upon to state in a word where I thought the Association should do its most effective work, I should say unhesitatingly, "in the home." The purification of the home must be our first consideration and care. It is in the home where woman is really queen, that she wields her influence with the most telling effect. It is through the home, therefore, that the principles which we wish to promulgate can be most widely circulated and most deeply impressed. In the mind and heart of every good and conscientious woman, the first place is occupied by home. We must always remember in connection with this fact, however, that observation has shown and experience has proved that it is not the narrow-minded, selfish woman who think of naught save their families and themselves, who have no time to work for neglected children, the helpless sick and the needy poor—it is not such women, I say, who exert in their homes the most powerful influence for good.

And now, finally, let us be up and doing wherever a word may be spoken for principle, or a hand lifted to aid. We must study carefully and conscientiously the questions which affect us most deeply and directly. Against lynching, the convict lease system, the Jim Crow car laws, and all other barbarities and abuses which degrade and dishearten us, we must agitate with such force of logic and intensity of soul that the oppressor will either be converted to principles of justice or be ashamed to openly violate them. Let loyalty to race, as displayed by employing and patronizing our own, in refusing to hold up our own to public ridicule and scorn, let allegiance to those whose ability, character and general fitness qualify them to lead, be two of the cardinal principles by which each and every member of this Association is guided. If we are to judge the future by the past, as dark as that past has sometimes been since our emancipation, there is no reason why we should view it with despair. Over almost insurmountable obstacles as a race we have forged ahead until today there is hardly a trade, a profession, or an art in which we have not at least one worthy representative. I challenge any other race to show such wonderful progress along all lines in so short a time, under circumstances so discouraging as that made by the ex-slaves of the United States of America. And though today some of us are cast down by the awful barbarities constantly inflicted upon some of our unfortunate race in the South who have been shot and burned to death by mobs which took no pains to establish the guilt of their victims, some of whom were doubtless innocent, we must remember that the darkest hour is just before the dawn.

As an Association, by discharging our duty to the children, by studying the labor question in its relation to our race, by coming into closer touch with the masses of our women, by urging parents and teachers to protect the health of our boys and girls, by creating a wholesome, healthful public sentiment in every community in which we are represented, by setting a high moral standard and living up to it, and purifying the home, we shall render the race a service, whose magnitude and importance it is not in my power to express.

Let us love and cherish our Association, with such loyalty and zeal, that it will wax strong and great, that it may soon become that bulwark of strength and source of inspiration to our women that it is destined to be.

In spite of rock and tempest's roar,
In spite of false lights on the shore,
Sail on, nor fear to breast the sea!
Our hearts, our hopes are all with Thee,
Our hearts, our hopes, our prayers, our tears,
Our faith, triumphant o'er our fears,
Are all with Thee, are all with Thee.[19]

Margaret Murray Washington, "The Gain in the Life of Negro Women." *The Outlook* 76.5 (30 January 1904): 271-74

In the many-tongued discussion of negro problems there is no fallacy so common or so insidious as that by which a proposition found true of a particular group of negroes is, in virtue of that fact, proclaimed true of all or of the great mass. To maintain that since from the negroes in a certain town no superior class has emerged, the negroes of America have no superior class—to maintain that is to feel with the Africans that, because the white slave-catchers were merciless, all white men are merciless. The specific problem which is the subject of this paper—Gain in the Life of Negro Women—is often similarly befuddled. There are 8,840,789 negroes in this country, of whom 4,447,568 are women. These women live in States from Massachusetts to Mississippi; some live on plantations, some in towns, some in cities; some are ignorant, some intelligent; some are rich, some poor; some good, some bad. To make propositions that will hold true of these many and essentially different groups of negro women is a task which I do not essay—a task to which Edmund Burke referred when he said that no man can indict a whole race of people.[20]

Moreover, you can no more find the "average" negro woman than you can multiply eggs by treaties. Just as eggs are different from treaties, so good negro women are different from bad negro women, and no average can be struck. The best we can do is to estimate the size of the various groups of negro women, but even this is not enough; the influence, efficiency, significance of one superior woman's life may be indefinitely more than that of ten dull drudges. And so the statistical method could not do justice to this essentially human problem; statistics negate individuality.

I propose to speak of the superior class of negro women, and roughly to indicate something of the import of their organized endeavor.

Every census teems with information that testifies to the material and spiritual gain of the negro population and notably of negro women. To cite a few illustrations from school enrollment, I may say that in the census year 1,096,774 negroes attended school, of whom 510,007 were males and 586,767 were females; 27,858 females as against 28,268 males attended school from two to three months; 160,231 females as against 136,028 males attended school from four to five months; and 227,546 females as against 187,173 males attended school six months and more. These figures indicate the well-known fact that girls attend school more continuously than boys; the boys must go to work while the girls are in school.

In the one hundred public high schools for negroes, 3,659 girls as against 2,974 boys were enrolled in elementary grades, and in secondary grades 3,933 girls and 1,634 boys. In these schools 154 girls were enrolled in the business course; 792 in the classical course; 1,098 girls in the scientific course. In the normal course of the high schools there were 221 girls and 65 boys. In the industrial training courses, there were 709 girls and 550 boys. 501 girls and 177 boys graduated in 1900-1 from the high-school course.

In the secondary and higher schools of the colored race there were 13,306 females and 9,587 males in elementary grades; 7,383 females and 6,164 males in the secondary grades; 740 females and 2,339 males in the collegiate course. In secondary and higher schools there were 17,138 colored students receiving the industrial training, of whom 11,012 were females.

These young negro women have not come through the schools on "flowery beds of ease." While their mothers and fathers of the generation of yesterday have not been able to give them that home training essential to the best development, they have by the sweat of their brows aided their boys and girls to get the education for which they themselves had yearned in vain. The average young negro woman has either helped her parents on the cotton patch or her mother with her laundry work, during vacation, and in that way has helped to defray her expenses through school. The large majority have worked their way through school in spite of the heavy odds against them. Better home training might have aided them the better to meet the problems confronting them in their lives and service.

At any rate, the schools are each year appreciably increasing the number of educated women of negro blood. The educational provision is of course dangerously inadequate; thus, I know of a great Southern State where there has not for years been a nearly sufficient number of candidates for positions as teachers who could meet the minimum requirements. However, the proportion of educated negro women to-day is very much greater than in 1860. The crucial question is always whether, in the environment in which the negro school or college girl eventually finds herself, she will be able to maintain in her life the ideals of school and college. A superior class of negro women, realizing this situation, have organized a system of clubs to meet the difficulty in some measure. The educated negro girl, these women say, must not go back to the blanket! The woman's club organizes the social life of educated negro women on rational principles, and urges those women to intelligent social service. From this point of view, and from many others, the club movement is interesting.

The club movement among negro women, with social betterment as the aim, began fifteen years ago. So educative was the force that a National Association was organized in 1895. To-day West Virginia, Ohio, Iowa, Pennsylvania, Illinois, Missouri, Mississippi, and Alabama have State federations. The Northeastern Federation of forty-five clubs confines its work to the Northeast. The Southern Federation of two hundred and twenty-five clubs is devoted to work in the Southern States, but its clubs are affiliated with the National organization.

The work of the individual club is varied. The largest of these have departments directed by women interested in certain phases of uplift—free kindergartens, day nurseries, temperance, prison work, social purity, Mothers' Unions, and the like. The intellectual development has an outlet by discussions of live topics. Here is a typical evening's programme of one of these clubs:

Music, Vocal.
Russia, Past and Present.
Quartet.
The Representative People of Russia.
Life of the Russian Peasant Women as Compared with that of Negro Women.
Instrumental Music.

Our women are wide awake to the necessity of social culture, and no more pleasing feature is there than to receive their friends in their best attire in tastefully furnished reception-rooms. This is a diversion on the club pro-gramme perhaps once a year. But the earnest, faithful work of these women in their chosen fields of labor is the aim of their existence. By their efforts free kindergartens, day nurseries, sewing and cooking schools, are supported. Hundreds of untaught mothers living with their children in their cabin homes or in the crowded tenements of the cities are taught how to live. In some of the large towns weekly meetings are held with an aver-age attendance of one hundred and fifty women. Helpful talks are given on such subjects as:

How to Keep Close to the Children.
How to Keep the Confidence of Children.
Mother's Authority in Selecting Company for the Children.
How a Mother can Help her Daughter to Avoid Mistakes as Regards
   the Young Man she Loves.
White Cross Leagues for Boys.
Relation of Brother and Sister.
Teaching a Boy to Protect Women.

In the conferences that follow, many a revolution is promised that tells that the hints have struck home. House-to-house visits show that progress is made. Where crowded conditions have not seemed to promote a healthy moral atmosphere, attempts have been made to gain privacy by a simple screen device, and in many instances this has been a spur to save money and buy homes. These Mothers' Unions or Conferences are training-schools for social betterment, and the cities, towns, and settlements of the plantations all over the South are giving evidences of these helpful influences brought to bear on the lives of our women belonging to the generation of yesterday.

For the past five years the Southern Federation of Colored Women's Clubs has met in the cities of Montgomery, Alabama; Atlanta, Georgia; Vicksburg, Mississippi; New Orleans, Louisiana; and recently in Jacksonville, Florida. After each yearly meeting the impetus gained in the work has been won-derful. Club life has a strong hold in all the cities and States of the South. Each year the new accessions come better prepared to lend a hand in the service. Mothers, business women, school-teachers, are equally active in their efforts to reach out after those who should be awakened to the neces-sity of proper home making and training for their children.

In the story of the evolution of a club woman in one of our periodicals the trend of the club idea of the white woman seems to take her away from home duties. But our negro women are American daughters of aliens whose home life has not generations of culture behind it, and our work must be practical.

Yet a large percentage of our negro women preside in homes of their own in all these cities where the Southern Federation of Negro Women's Clubs has been privileged to meet. The majority of these club women have helped their husbands to purchase homes by their thrift and economy. Many of these residences are situated on prominent streets. They are well-designed, painted cottages of six and eight rooms, with bath and hot and cold water contrivances, well ventilated, and constructed with an eye to sanitary arrangements. These homes are tastefully furnished.

The hostesses who have entertained the delegations of the Federation as the years have passed, not only know how to keep house, but how to cook and serve well-prepared meals properly in well-appointed dining-rooms. The same women have attended the daily sessions of the conventions, and are those who give the addresses of welcome, direct the federated clubs of the city, and conduct those Mothers' Conferences that are proving vital helps. These women are the leaders in the side trips, trolley rides, and local receptions given as recreations to the visiting workers. They are women following their chosen pursuits — dressmaking, millinery, manicuring. They are clerks, stenographers, trained nurses, teachers, workers in every field of labor that helps them to make a living and buy homes. In many of our largest cities a goodly percentage of the bank depositors are negro women. This means a nest-egg for the purchase and ownership of homes. The negro women are unmodern in that they assume a share in working to pay for homes for their families. In many instances young married couples unite their savings in buying homes — in this order of helpmate may lie some of the reason for gain in the sacredness of the marriage tie.

From all these club centers of the South there radiates over each State an influence that has caused marked improvement in the home life of women gaining instruction in domestic affairs from the club conferences to which they belong.

I have emphasized the educative force of the club, because it has been by this means, certainly, that the passing generation of negro women has been able to meet the demands of family responsibilities.

Young negro women of to-day are developing under fairer conditions. The home training combined with the school training of head, hand, and heart develops that steadiness of purpose that underlies strong, sturdy character.

Our young woman is already taking her place in various spheres of life, regardless of precedent. Her training fits her for home life and the larger social service of the schoolroom. She does with her might what her hands find to do. A college girl directs a steam laundry or makes soap in a large laundering establishment. She has spent four years at Greek and Latin, but has charge of a broom factory where girls are manufacturing brooms of all sorts and sizes. She has gained all the training possible in the schools of her native heath, and by arduous sacrifice has worked her way through the best New England schools of domestic science that she might be thoroughly prepared to teach. She has a laboratory for her theory classes in cooking. She teaches practical cooking daily to large classes of white-capped, white-aproned girls, with individual towels and holders, and at the end of each week in one school alone four hundred and fifty negro girls have learned to cook by doing. No more helpful encouragement has come for this work than the testimonials from white women of the South interested in the improvement of some of these girls.

Young negro women are teaching hundreds of their sisters the same principles of dressmaking and millinery that they were taught in the train-ing-schools of Pratt and Teachers' College. And these young women are not misfits. They are not despondent in their calling. They are putting in brain with the would-be drudgery, and are making marked success of industries where women with fewer advantages might have failed to show their pupils the true dignity of labor.

The present indications of advance in the life of negro women are most hopeful for the future of the race. With the home training that is becom-ing possible, with the training that our schools afford, with the inheritance of true worth that made the parents do their utmost to bequeath to their children honest, upright lives, the young negro women will possess that wealth of character that will be the means eventually of dispelling the great-est barriers that may confront the race.

Whether or not we attribute this gain to school, club, or religious influ-ence, we do know that much is due to the club, and we know that the future of the race is dependent upon the women and their standards of liv-ing. Whatever force is at work that is developing that strength of character which is the bulwark of an individual or race, we hope it will obtain a per-manent hold in the life of negro women.

It remains with the greater mass of our women to make the weal or woe come quickly or linger. But the signs of the times are bright. The educa-tive forces are at work. The greater mass is being leavened, and we thank God that there will be no retrograde. There has been none and there will be none!

Tuskegee, Alabama.

Josephine Silone-Yates, "The National Association of Colored Women." *Our Woman's Number. The Voice of the Negro* 1.7 (July 1904): 283-87

We have but faith, we cannot know.
For knowledge is of things we see.
And yet we trust it comes from thee.
A beam in darkness, let it grow.[21]

The history of this organization, the National Association of Colored Women, and of its formation, is somewhat unique, and has for its members, possibly, also for the sociologist, and the casual observer, a special interest, because of the manner of this formation; the causes surrounding, or leading, to the same; and the additional fact that, outside of secret orders this organization represents the largest, possibly the only national, non-sectarian body of educated Negro women organized for the definite and avowed purpose of "race elevation."

It is not the purpose of this article to go into the details of the causes or chain of events that led to its formation, but rather to tell of the work it is accomplishing: however, as a bit of history, it is interesting to note that it literally was a child born of "prayers and tears," and was organized in the City of Washington in 1896, by the consolidation of two National bodies of Negro women, known, the one, as the "National League" and the other as the "National Federation."[22] The name of the new organization thus formed was, out of deference to the parent bodies, a compromise, in which the word "Association" was substituted for the words "League" or "Federation."

The prime object of the organization, as stated in article II of its constitution is, "To secure harmony of action and cooperation among all women in raising to the highest plane, home, moral, and civil life," and under the very beautiful motto, soon adopted by its leaders, "Lifting as we climb," in many ways highly suggestive of its aims. Many things have been accomplished during the seven years of its existence.

The first convention of the National Association was held in the city of Nashville in 1897; the second in Chicago in 1899; the third in Buffalo in 1901; the fourth will be held in the city of St. Louis, July 11-16, 1904.

Each convention thus far held has been an inspiration to those attending and a wonderful revelation to the interested on-looker as to the work and development of Afro-American women, not only with reference to papers read and discussions of the same, but also because of more tangible proofs through exhibits of painting, of literature, of music, and of other forms of art that prove the growth and development of a race in its efforts to struggle upward "through all the spires of form."[23]

From its initial period, all clubs of women that have some well defined aim for the elevation of the race have been eligible to membership; and while much stress is placed upon the Mother's Club, the establishment of kindergartens and day nurseries, for the reason that these organizations strike, as it were, at the root of the whole matter, at the same time the Association urges the formation of musical clubs, for the study of high class music, believing that music in the Negro is a heaven born gift that should be cultivated to its highest extent, and that should never be allowed to degenerate into a low and unseemly amusement, calculated to degrade rather than to elevate the race.

It urges the formation of temperance clubs, knowing that intemperance is one of the greatest foes to the progress and development of the Negro as well as to other races.

It urges the formation of domestic science clubs, cooking classes, and similar forms, because unsanitary methods of living, of cooking, etc. prevent the masses of our people from doing their best work from economic and from other standpoints.

It urges the formation of benevolent and charitable institutions, since above all else, the race as a unit should be taught to be self-sustaining, independent, self-reliant; should learn to think logically, and act accordingly.

It encourages the formation of Women's Exchanges and other varieties of business clubs, or organizations, in order that our women and girls may learn the value of a "penny," how to make and how to invest a dollar, as well as how to spend one; for, Mrs. Thompson,[24] and others to the contrary, with reference to woman as an "Industrial failure," the Negro woman has been, and for some time must continue to be, at least "an assistant" breadwinner if the finances of the race are to be improved; and fortunately for her, she has, generally speaking, managed in such manner that few of the conditions mentioned in Mrs. Thompson's article in a recent number of the North American Review, have attained with our women, possibly because, with but comparatively few exceptions, the Negro women instinctively knows the art of "managing"; but this is another story, and returning to the original discussion, it may be added that the National Association of Colored Women encourages the foundation of all forms of clubs that have as an object the general improvement of society.

It now represents a membership of at least fifteen thousand educated, cultured, refined Negro women, with the local branches that compose it, scattered abroad in twenty-six States, Indian and Oklahoma Territories. In more than half of these States, as in Michigan, Minnesota, Missouri, Iowa, Illinois, Indiana, Ohio, Kentucky, Mississippi, Pennsylvania, New York, Rhode Island, Louisiana, West Virginia, Kansas, etc, a flourishing federation exists, and in several of the larger cities, as in St. Louis, Cleveland, and elsewhere, a city federation.

Each of these States holds annually a highly successful State meeting, in which a line of work for the year is mapped out, officers elected, and papers on questions of the day are read, discussed, and the usual business of a State Federation carefully conducted.

The value of such training to our women along the line of parliamentary and of business organizations, the inspiration they receive from contact, the unity they acquire, which is so much to be desired, so necessary in race development, and that can only come from thus working together for a common cause, are all points that cannot be overestimated from a sociological point of view.

Among Afro-American people the church is the leading organization; and the endorsement of the church affords a highway to the hearts of the people.

The church, irrespective of creed or denomination, has endorsed the work of the National Association of Colored Women, and looking upon it as one of its strongest allies, has pledged and given it hearty support in innumerable ways.

The teaching fraternity, next to the church, perhaps, sways the multitude, and in every section of this broad land teachers have enlisted to carry forward the good work.

The Department of Professional Women's Clubs, which consists very largely of teachers, united with other professional women, promises to become one of the most valuable departments in the organization, and from it great things are expected.

The Association supports a national organ, known at "Notes," edited by Mrs. Margaret Washington, and an able corps of associates. Ten numbers per year are furnished for the small annual subscription price of twenty-five cents. It is thus within reach of every one; keeps members in touch, furnishes helpful suggestions, and is a general means of communication.

Undoubtedly the conservative tone adopted by this paper, and the determination of the National Organization from its incipiency, diligently "to saw wood," and thus find no time for controversy, has had much to do in dignifying its aims and in increasing its scope and influence.

In addition to "Notes," several State papers are published at the expense of respective States, as "Queen's Gardens," of Ohio, Mrs. Carrie Clifford, editor; "The Outlook," of Missouri, Miss Victoria Wallace, editor.

The press of the country at large has been very kind to the National

Association of Colored Women, freely placing the columns at the disposal of the organization, and for some time a "Woman's World Department" was conducted in the "Colored American," thus giving in addition to "Notes," a general survey of the work for the outer reading public; while special articles, as called for relative to the work of the organization, have from time to time appeared in such leading papers as the Boston "Transcript," Boston "Herald," Los Angeles "Herald," "The Evangelist," "The Voice of Missions," "Church Reviews," etc.

The National Council of Women, an organization founded in 1888, composed of twenty large national bodies, and as many local councils, and itself one of the affiliated branches of the International Council of Women, recently in quinquennial session in Berlin, deserves the hearty and sincere gratitude of a race for the breadth of thought evidenced and the advanced ground taken by its leaders in inviting to membership in its organization the National Association of Colored Women; and its act of affiliating this organization with the Council, as it did in the year 1900, was such a gracious recognition of the worth and merit of Negro womanhood that it goes far toward the mitigation of the contumely that is from time to time and from various sources, unjustly heaped upon it.

The leaders of the Council have at all times remained firm and steadfast to their self-imposed obligations and this at a sacrifice best known only within the organization.

Similarly, the National Association has had membership and representation in the "National Congress of Mothers," which embodies another great altruistic movement of the age; and as an affiliated member of the National Council has membership and representation in the International Council, composed of national organizations from eighteen civilized countries, working in unison under the motto, "Do unto others as ye would that others should do unto you"; with the motto of the Council, "Lead Kindly Light," and that of the National Association, "Lifting as we climb," it is readily seen that we have a chain of beautiful sentiments, which if exemplified in the acts of members, show this club movement among women to be one of the world's great unifying forces, destined to establish beyond disputation, "The brotherhood of man, the Fatherhood of God."

With reference to work accomplished by the national body it may be stated that while not in any sense condoning crime, not in any sense unduly sympathizing with the criminal, at each convention resolutions have been passed denouncing lynching as a barbarous mode of punishment, and condemning the convict lease system. Three notable addresses upon this latter subject have been read before the convention. The first, prepared by Mrs. Butler of Atlanta, Ga., and read at the Nashville meeting, was published in 1897, at the expense of the National Organization, and placed on sale in order that the ideas contained therein might reach the public eye, and if possible effect some change in the system.[25]

The second equally good the product of one of our brainiest young women, Miss Josephine Holmes, also of Atlanta, was read at the Chicago meeting 1899.

The third was the famous lecture on this subject, "The Convict Lease System" prepared by Mrs. Frederic Douglass, since deceased, widow of our deceased race leader, and was given before the Buffalo Convention 1901.[26]

Said the Buffalo "Express" in referring to this address[:] Mrs Douglass' statement threw new light on the origin as well as the working of a system by which some of the States have re-established slavery under the guise of penal law.

At the Chicago meeting in 1899, and again in Buffalo in 1901, the Association assumed the cost of publishing pamphlets written by Mrs. M.C. Terrell, then president of the organization[;] the proceeds of the sales of these publications Mrs. Terrell very generously contributed to the National Ways and Means Committee as a gift to start a fund to be used in establishing kindergartens and day nurseries. Various additions have been made to this fund and from it money has been sent as ordered to assist the Maggie Murray Kindergarten of Atlanta, Ga., the Alice D. Karey Kindergarten of Charleston, S.C., and the Butler Mission Kindergarten of Chicago.

Every effective organized body has had its period of development and growth, as well as of actual accomplishment.

The National Association of Colored Women, so dear to the hearts of its earnest workers, long since passed the experimental stage, and entered upon an aggressive campaign of growth, with "push organization" as its battle cry, meanwhile accomplishing as much in the line of work as reasonably can be expected, when one reflects that few Negro women are women of leisure, or, of large means; and that the time and money they give to public work is usually at a sacrifice practically unknown to the women of other races engaged in similar work.

It should also be considered that it has been for various reasons a difficult task to enlist in the movement more than a comparatively small number of colored women well adapted by means and influence to carry forward this work, but this condition is gradually changing, and the recognition that the National Association of Colored Women has received at the hands of the National Council of America, the International Congress, and from the Commissioners of the World's Fair in St. Louis, in which instance this body of women was the first Negro organization outside of Fisk University (and this is hardly a parallel case), to receive a World's

Fair Day, will tend greatly to increase the respect in which the organization will be held on all sides.

As to the national work, in this its period of organization, when most of its force must be spent upon organizing individual clubs, State Federations, Department work, and in the thorough systematization of this work, it cannot with truth be said that it has at any time remained at a standstill, or that it has swerved from its original purpose of "Raising to a higher plane, home, moral and civil life," as set forth in its Constitution.

It has at all times hewn directly to the line in carrying forward this purpose, and, leaving each State and each community free to take up the line of work most needed therein, according to the best judgment of the leading minds of the State or community, has favored as national work the kindergarten and day nursery idea, as before stated, mainly as a method of getting at the root of the problem of race elevation—"the children."

In this idea it has not wavered, as may be seen from the fact that aid has been extended to several kindergartens from money donated to the Ways and Means Committee from the sale of pamphlets published at the cost of the national body; and from the additional fact that the resolution introduced by the present president of the Association at the last Triennial Council of Women of the United States, and unanimously passed by that august body, pledged the members of that organization to assist the National Association of Colored Women in every possible way in their very laudable efforts to establish kindergartens and day nurseries.

The National has been urged at each biennial meeting to set aside a fund, however small, for this same purpose, and with the art of incorporation will be in a position to receive bequests, legacies and endowments, to carry forward this and many other forms of national work that will help to make the National Association of Colored Women one of the great forces of the century in the solution of the race problem, a problem that can be solved only by race elevation.

Notes

1. The domestic feminism that the club movement championed through a "discourse on raising the standards of home, family life, and motherhood…insist[ed] that the future of the race was moored to African American mothers' moral guardianship" (Knupfer 1996, 12).

2. The National Federation of Afro-American Women was founded in 1895 with Margaret Murray Washington as president, and the Colored Women's League of Washington was founded in 1893 with Helen Cook as president. Ruffin founded and led the Women's Era Club in 1894 with the help and support of her daugh-

ter Florida Ruffin Ridley, who was also an anti-lynching activist and who support-ed Ida B. Wells's work in her writing in Boston's *Woman's Era*. Ruffin founded this periodical, the first magazine in the United States published by and for black women. The earliest extant copy is dated March 1894.

3. It is important to note that the NACWC's charter also echoes ideals of racial uplift promoted by African American men since antebellum times.

4. Class differences within "the" African American community were, in fact, cen-tral to black political culture generally at this time, which is frequently represented as divided between bourgeois Du Boisian and working-class Washingtonian politics.

5. For example, Mary Church Terrell believed that women should be political-ly involved and a strong moral influence in the home. She was also an advocate for working mothers even as she characterized the working class and the poor as the "lowly" and "vicious" in need of uplift. See Mary Church Terrell, "The Duty of the National Association of Colored Women" in this chapter.

6. See Wilson 2002 and Wilson 2008.

7. The World's Congress of Representative Women opened on 15 May 1893 at the World's Columbian Exposition in Chicago and attracted 500 delegates rep-resenting 27 countries and 126 organizations. Many of the delegates were suffra-gists, including African American women and feminists. In addition to Williams's address, were speeches by Anna Julia Cooper, Fannie Jackson Coppin, Sarah J. Early, and Hallie Quinn Brown.

8. See Chapter 3, note 3.

9. When Florence Balgarnie (a supporter of Ida B. Wells and secretary of the British Anti-Lynching Committee founded in 1894 largely due to Wells's anti-lynching lecture tour of Britain) wrote American journalists to recruit them in anti-lynching efforts, John Jacks replied with a bitter attack on black women's morality. Histories of the black women's club movement cite this letter as crystal-lizing "the determination of black women to speak for themselves" against such attacks (McMurry 1998, 246). The call for the 1895 National Conference of Colored Women held in Boston issued by Josephine St. Pierre Ruffin included a copy of Jacks's letter.

10. *Woman's Era* was founded by Josephine St. Pierre Ruffin, who served as editor and publisher from 1890 to 1897. It was the first newspaper published by and for African American women; it highlighted their achievements and champi-oned their rights.

11. The first Hampton Negro Conference was held in 1897 at the Hampton Institute, founded near Hampton, Virginia by the American Missionary Society in 1868 and directed by General Samuel Armstrong. It offered freedmen moral train-ing and an industrial education that focused on domestic and agricultural practices. One of its most famous graduates was Booker T. Washington, who headed Tuskegee Institute, which shared Hampton's focus on training black men and

women to become teachers or self-sufficient craftspeople and industrial workers. Hampton was a boarding school that also offered instruction to Native American students, who first attended in 1878. Hampton was also committed to women's education, endorsing the position that "women's influence was a key factor in the progress of Afro-Americans" (Neverdon-Morton 1989, 23).

12. Trivial.

13. Galatians 6:2.

14. Friedrich Froebel (1782-1852) laid the foundation for modern education based on the recognition that children have unique needs and capabilities.

15. See Thomas 1901. As a result of his assertions in this book, Thomas came to be known as the black Judas.

16. W.E.B. DuBois, 1903.

17. As we saw at the beginning of this chapter, the National Association of Colored Women Clubs (NACWC) was established in Washington, DC by the merger in 1896 of the National Federation of Afro-American Women, the Women's Era Club of Boston, and the National League of Colored Women of Washington, DC, as well as smaller organizations that had arisen from the black women's club movement. Founders of the NACWC included Harriet Tubman, Frances Harper, Ida B. Wells-Barnett, and Mary Church Terrell. By 1915, the NACWC consisted of over 1,000 clubs with 50,000 members (Giddings 1984, 95). By 1927 the NACWC represented over 250,000 black women (Salem 1993, 842-45).

18. Matthew 19:14.

19. Henry Wadsworth Longfellow, "The Building of the Ship" (1849).

20. Edmund Burke (1729-97) was an Anglo-Irish statesman, author, orator, political theorist, and philosopher, who served in the British House of Commons as a member of the Whig Party and who supported the American colonies in the dispute with King George III that led to the American Revolution.

21. Alfred Lord Tennyson, *In Memoriam* (1850).

22. The earliest formal association of black women's clubs was the Colored Women's League of Washington, DC formed in 1829. In 1885 both the Women's Loyal Union and the National Federation of Colored Women's Clubs were founded. The Colored Women's League and the National Federation of Colored Women's Club were in a position of rivalry until they merged to become the NACWC with Mary Church Terrell as its first president (McMurry 1998, 248).

23. Ralph Waldo Emerson, *Nature* (1836).

24. Quite likely Mrs. Joseph Thompson of Georgia, head of the Women's Board of the Atlanta Exposition of 1895. She spoke immediately before Booker T. Washington delivered his famous "Atlanta Compromise" address.

25. Selena S. Butler, "The Chain-Gang System," Nashville, 16 September 1897. Selena Butler was a delegate to the founding convention of the National Association

of Colored Women's Clubs, the first president of the Georgia Federation of Colored Women's Clubs, and a member of the Georgia Commission on Interracial Cooperation.

26. Helen Pitts Douglass (1838-1903), second wife of Frederick Douglass. Following her husband's death in 1895 up until the last year of her own life, Helen Pitts Douglass lectured throughout the northeast. "A form letter advertising her talks bore the heading, 'Mrs. Frederick Douglass—Popular Lectures: Convict Lease System of the Southern States; Lost Opportunities, the Hittites with stereopticon illustrations; Modern Egypt with stereopticon illustrations.' The letter's text advised, 'I would be willing to lecture before your people for $25 per night and expenses, the latter not to exceed $15 and in many cases less than that sum.'" She used the money she raised to establish the Frederick Douglass Memorial and Historical Association ("Stories in Stone" 2008).

5

Woman's Rights, Suffrage, Temperance

African American women's work within and frequent critiques of the woman's rights, suffrage, and temperance movements further attest to the ways in which their work with white feminists was frequently fraught. Since these feminist reform movements were interracial in character, and relations between black and white feminists were complicated by racism and class, this chapter also incorporates black feminist calls for interracial cooperation as well as writings that convey the divisiveness of questions over black male suffrage and woman suffrage. These writings and speeches return to questions opened in Chapter 1 about the nature of black feminist access to and participation in reform networks that pursued a (sometimes unstated) focus on white women's rights, the reliability of representations of black feminists within archives documenting these movements, and the schisms that developed when black feminists refused to choose between "race or gender."

Events such as the American Equal Rights Association (AERA) meetings in New York City in the spring of 1867 when Susan B. Anthony went on record opposing black male suffrage before (white) female suffrage, and scandals such as Frances Willard's denunciation of Ida B. Wells's anti-lynching work while Willard was an internationally recognized leader of the Women's Christian Temperance Union (WCTU) are represented here, as are the selective approbation of particular black feminists within reform movements, such as Sojourner Truth within woman's rights and Frances Harper within temperance. Moreover, a focus on events like the AERA meetings in 1867 and the resulting 1869 split within the suffrage movement that created the American Woman Suffrage Association (AWSA) and the National Woman Suffrage Association (NWSA) reveal black feminism as varied in its political responses, with some feminists choosing to affiliate with the AWSA despite its opposition to the Fifteenth Amendment and others affiliating with the NWSA, which argued for universal suffrage.[1] When these rival suffrage associations joined to become the National American Woman Suffrage Association (NAWSA) in 1890, African American feminists had now to contend with "conservative strategies," including "ignor[ing] the priorities of Black women" in order "to bring…white southern women" into the suffrage movement. Despite the alienation they experienced, some black feminists continued to attend NAWSA meetings while others focused their efforts on black women's political agendas (Terborg-Penn 1998, 55).

Still others founded suffrage organizations for African American women, such as Mary Ann Shadd Cary's Colored Women's Professional Franchise Association founded in 1890. Black women's suffrage clubs, like the Alpha Suffrage Club founded in 1913 by Ida B. Wells, were fueled by the larger mobilization of black women's clubs for suffrage begun in earnest at the turn of the century. These clubs included not only those affiliated with the NACWC, but "independent clubs formed in churches and in neighbor-hoods to aid the community" (Terborg-Penn 1998, 97). The Alpha Suffrage Club published the *Alpha Suffrage Record* to educate its members and the wider community about election issues and candidates, signaling an aware-ness of the continued "pedagogy of the press" begun with Maria Stewart's pieces in the *Liberator* and Wells's earlier anti-lynching journalism and arguably continued in publications like Ruffin's *Woman's Era* as well as the larger phenomenon of black feminist journalism in the late 1880s and 1890s. At this time black women journalists were also pursuing feminist and suffrage arguments in the papers for which they regularly wrote or which they edited, including Mary E. Britton (Meb), Gertrude Mossell, and Josephine St. Pierre Ruffin. Pre-eminent black periodicals, such as *The Crisis* (August 1915) and *Voice of the Negro* (July 1904) ran special suffrage and woman's numbers in which feminists wrote defenses of black woman-hood and arguments for suffrage, signaling their importance not only to black women but to black communities at large.

Temperance organizations and the WCTU also became venues to mobilize support for suffrage, since both black and white reformers work-ing in temperance recognized that the suffrage would mean greater input on legislation controlling public drinking. Frances Harper's organizing is indicative of the link black feminists quickly saw between suffrage and temperance reforms. In 1885, two years before she became Superintendent of Work among the Colored People of the North in the WCTU, she was director of the Woman's Congress, "a group organized by white feminist

Pauline Davis to discuss the moral and humanitarian activities of woman suffragists" (Terborg-Penn 1998, 85). Other black feminists, such as Mamie Dillard, credited the WCTU with gaining school suffrage for women and encouraged black women to join the temperance movement once Frances Harper became superintendent and segregated black unions were possible within the national organization. Women like Mary Church Terrell also spoke of the importance of the suffrage to the battle against intemperance (Terborg-Penn 1998, 86). As this chapter indicates, temperance activism could take the form of speeches, writings, and symposia in the Afro-Protestant press, as well as the publication of fiction.

WOMAN'S RIGHTS

Sojourner Truth, "Woman's Rights Convention." *The Anti-Slavery Bugle*, 21 June 1851

One of the most unique and interesting speeches of the Convention was made by Sojourner Truth, an emancipated slave. It is impossible to transfer it to paper, or convey any adequate idea of the effect it produced upon the audience. Those only can appreciate it who saw her powerful form, her whole-souled earnest gestures, and listened to her strong and truthful tones. She came forward to the platform and addressing the President said with great simplicity:

May I say a few words? Receiving an affirmative answer, she proceeded; I want to say a few words about this matter. I am a woman's rights. I have as much muscle as any man, and can do as much work as any man. I have plowed and reaped and husked and chopped and mowed, and can any man do more than that? I have heard much about the sexes being equal; I can carry as much as any man, and can eat as much too, if I can get it. I am as strong as any man that is now. As for intellect, all I can say is, if woman have a pint and man a quart—why cant she have her little pint-full? You need not be afraid to give us our rights for fear we will take too much— for we cant take more than our pint'll hold. The poor men seem to be all in confusion, and dont know what to do. Why children, if you have woman's rights give it to her and you will feel better. You will have your own rights, and they wont be so much trouble. I cant read, but I can hear. I have heard the bible and have learned that Eve caused man to sin. Well if woman upset the world, do give her a chance to set it right side up again. The Lady has spoken about Jesus, how he never spurned woman from him, and she was right. When Lazarus died, Mary and Martha came to him with faith and love and besought him to raise their brother. And Jesus wept—and Lazarus came forth. And how came Jesus into the world? Through God who created him and woman who bore him. Man, where is your part? But the women are coming up blessed be God and a few of the men are coming up with them. But man is in a tight place, the poor slave is on him, woman is coming on him, and he is surely between a hawk and a buzzard.[2]

Sojourner Truth, "Woman's Rights Convention. Meeting at the Broadway Tabernacle." *New York Daily Times*, 8 September 1853

Excitement at Yesterday's Session
SECOND DAY

Long after 9 o'clock yesterday, the Tabernacle presented a desolate appearance not very encouraging to the Woman's Rights Reformers. Scarcely a dozen people had assembled, who, spread through the large building, rather added to the loneliness. At the regular hour for meeting, about two hundred had assembled [...]

Sojourner Truth, a negro woman asked permission to speak in the afternoon, which was granted by the Chair. [Yells and hooting from the gallery.]

The meeting was declared adjourned to 3 o'clock.

Cries of "We'll be here to hear SOJOURNER—Hurrah."

AFTERNOON SESSION
[...]
The President ascended the platform, and with commendable composure took her seat. She was soon followed by Miss Lucy[3] in pants, and Miss or Mrs. Sojourner Truth, a colored lady of some sixty winters. In a woman's blue gown and black pinafore. A white cotton 'kerchief was bound around her sable brows, and in the immensity of its folds her phrenological developments were concealed, and her hair retained in proper position [...]

The President then announced to the audience that Miss or Mrs. Sojourner Truth was about to make a few remarks. Miss or Mrs. Sojourner Truth arose, and so did a perfect storm of applause, hisses, groans and undignified ejaculations. One young lad, with red hair, whose education had evidently been previously neglected, insinuated that the colored lady was not then acting in her accustomed sphere, by calling for "an oyster stew with plenty of crackers." Another young rascal, with a dirty shirt and face, said he would take a "half dozen on half shell." Another scape-grace called vociferously for a "sixpenny plate of clam soup."

Notwithstanding these unmannerly, unhandsome, and ill-timed calls for bivalves, Sojourner Truth came forward to the desk, rolled up her eye-balls in scorn, frowned indignantly, and raised her hand and voice in wrath. She spoke. Ye who have not heard the roar of the cataract can form but a meager idea of the volume of sound that rushed forth upon the devoted audience. Imagine Trinity Church organ, forgetful for a time of its sacred duties with its low bass and trumpet-stops pulled out, all the keys down, and two men and a boy working for dear life at the bellows, and you have a gentle specimen of the angry voice of Sojourner Truth.

She said: It is good for me to come forth for to see what kind of spirit you are made of. I see some of you have got the spirit of a goose, and a good many of you have got the spirits of snakes.[4] [Great applause and cries of "Go on" — "That's the style" — "Show your pluck" — "Give it to them"; during which that young scape-grace in the gallery called for a "small fry."] I feel at home here. [A venerable old gentleman occupying a front seat, said, "So you ought."] I was born in this State, I've been a slave in this State, and now I'm a good citizen of this State. [Vociferous demonstrations of applause.] I was born here, and I can tell you I feel to home here. [Queer man under the gallery: That's right. Make yourself at home, you're welcome; take a chair.] I've been looking round and watching things, and I know a little might 'bout Woman's Rights, too. [Applause, and cries of "got it lively; you'll have a fair show."] I know it feels funny, kinder funny and tickling to see a colored woman get up and tell you about things and woman's rights, when we've all been trampled down and nobody thought we'd ever git up agin. But we have come up, and I'm here. There was a king in old times in the Scripters that said he'd give away half of his kingdom, and hang some body as Haman.[5] Now, he was more liberaler than the present King of the United States, 'cause he wouldn't do that for the women. [Roars of laughter, on the conclusion of which a middle-aged gentleman, with a florid countenance, short hair and old-fashioned shirt collar, ventured to correct the lady as to the title of our present Chief Magistrate, but the lady would not change the name, and continued.] But we don't want him to kill the men, nor we don't want half of his kingdom; we only want half of our rights, and we don't get them neither. But we'll have them see 'f we don't, and you can't stop us, neither; see 'f you can! [Applause, and some hissing.] Oh, you may hiss as much as you please, like any other lot of geese, but you can't stop it; its bound to come. [That young rascal with the dirty shirt and face — "Hurry up that stew; its bilin."] You see the women don't get half as much rights as they ought to get. We want more, and will have it. [Loud laughter.] Then you see the Bible says, sons and daughters ought to behave themselves before their mothers; but they don't; I'm wa'ching, and I can see them a spickering, and pinting and laughing at their mothers up here on the stage. [That young scape-grace again—"My mother ain't up there, an' I don't believe anybody's mother is." Applause.] They ought to be ashame! They ought to know better, an' if they'd been brought up proper they would. [Queer man under the gallery—"They ought to be spanked." Roars of laughter.] Woman's sphere ought to rise— rise as high as hanged Haman, and spread out all over. [Great applause, and that queer man under the gallery insinuated that that might be done by the least possible extension of their bustles.] I'm round watching things, and I wanted to come up and say these few things to you, and I'm much obliged for your listening. I wanted to tell you a little might about Woman's Rights, and so I come out and said so. I'll be around agin sometime. I'm watching things, and I'll git up agin, an' tell you what time o'night it is. [Great applause.] And, with another request from the young rascals to "hurry up them stews and things," the lady took a seat on the steps, which lead to the platform.

Harriet Beecher Stowe, "Sojourner Truth, The Libyan Sibyl." *The Atlantic Monthly* 11 (April 1863): 473–81

Many years ago, the few readers of radical Abolitionist papers must often have seen the singular name of Sojourner Truth, announced as a frequent speaker at Anti-Slavery meetings, and as travelling on a sort of self-appointed agency through the country. I had myself often remarked the name, but never met the individual. On one occasion, when our house was filled with company, several eminent clergymen being our guests, notice was brought up to me that Sojourner Truth was below, and requested an interview. Knowing nothing of her but her singular name, I went down, prepared to make the interview short, as the pressure of many other engagements demanded.

When I went into the room, a tall, spare form arose to meet me. She was evidently a full-blooded African, and though now aged and worn with many hardships, still gave the impression of a physical development which in early youth must have been as fine a specimen of the torrid zone as Cumberworth's celebrated statuette of the Negro Woman at the Fountain.[6] Indeed, she so strongly reminded me of that figure, that, when I recall the events of her life, as she narrated them to me, I imagine her as a living, breathing impersonation of that work of art.

I do not recollect ever to have been conversant with any one who had more of that silent and subtle power which we call personal presence than this woman. In the modern Spiritualistic phraseology, she would be described as having a strong sphere. Her tall form, as she rose up before me, is still vivid to my mind. She was dressed in some stout, grayish stuff, neat and clean, though dusty from travel. On her head, she wore a bright Madras handkerchief, arranged as a turban, after the manner of her race. She seemed perfectly self-possessed and at her ease, — in fact, there was almost an unconscious superiority, not unmixed with a solemn twinkle of humor, in the odd, composed manner in which she looked down on me. Her whole air had at times a gloomy sort of drollery which impressed one strangely.

"So this is *you*," she said.

"Yes," I answered.

"Well, honey, de Lord bless ye! I jes' thought I'd like to come an' have a look at ye. You's heerd o' me, I reckon?" she added.

"Yes, I think I have. You go about lecturing, do you not?"

"Yes, honey, that's what I do. The Lord has made me a sign unto this nation, an' I go round a'testifyin', an' showin' on 'em their sins agin my people."

So saying, she took a seat, and, stooping over and crossing her arms on her knees, she looked down on the floor, and appeared to fall into a sort of reverie. Her great gloomy eyes and her dark face seemed to work with some undercurrent of feeling; she sighed deeply, and occasionally broke out, —

"O Lord! O Lord! Oh, the tears, an' the groans, an' the moans! O Lord!"

I should have said that she was accompanied by a little grandson of ten years, — the fattest, jolliest woolly-headed little specimen of Africa that one can imagine. He was grinning and showing his glistening white teeth in a state of perpetual merriment, and at this moment broke out into an audible giggle, which disturbed the reverie into which his relative was falling.

She looked at him with an indulgent sadness, and then at me.

"Laws, Ma'am, *he* don't know nothin' about it—*he* don't. Why, I've seen them poor critters, beat an' 'bused an' hunted, brought in all torn, — ears hangin' all in rags, where the dogs been a'bitin' of 'em!"

This set off our little African Puck into another giggle, in which he seemed perfectly convulsed.

She surveyed him soberly, without the slightest irritation.

"Well, you may bless the Lord you *can* laugh; but I tell you, 't wa'n't no laughin' matter."

By this time I thought her manner so original that it might be worth while to call down my friends; and she seemed perfectly well pleased with the idea. An audience was what she wanted, — it mattered not whether high or low, learned or ignorant. She had things to say, and was ready to say them at all times, and to any one.

I called down Dr. Beecher,[7] Professor Allen,[8] and two or three other clergymen, who, together with my husband and family, made a roomful. No princess could have received a drawing-room with more composed dignity than Sojourner her audience. She stood among them, calm and erect, as one of her own native palm-trees waving alone in the desert. I presented one after another to her, and at last said, —

"Sojourner, this is Dr. Beecher. He is a very celebrated preacher."

"*Is* he?" she said, offering her hand in a condescending manner, and looking down on his white head. "Ye dear lamb, I'm glad to see ye! De Lord bless ye! I loves preachers. I'm a kind o' preacher myself."

"You are?" said Dr. Beecher. "Do you preach from the Bible?"

"No, honey, can't preach from de Bible, — can't read a letter."

"Why, Sojourner, what do you preach from, then?"

Her answer was given with a solemn power of voice, peculiar to herself, that hushed every one in the room.

"When I preaches, I has jest one text to preach from, an' I always preaches from this one. *My* text is, 'WHEN I FOUND JESUS.'"

"Well, you couldn't have a better one," said one of the ministers.

She paid no attention to him, but stood and seemed swelling with her own thoughts, and then began this narration: —

"Well, now, I'll jest have to go back, an' tell ye all about it. Ye see, we was all brought over from Africa, father an' mother an' I, an' a lot more of us; an' we was sold up an' down, an' hither an' yon; an' I can 'member, when I was a little thing, not bigger than this 'ere," pointing to her grandson, "how my ole mammy would sit out o' doors in the evenin', an' look up at the stars an' groan. She'd groan an' groan, an' says I to her, —

"'Mammy, what makes you groan so?'

"an' she'd say, —

"'Matter enough, chile! I'm groanin' to think o' my poor children: they don't know where I be, an' I don't know where they be; they looks up at the stars, an' I looks up at the stars, but I can't tell where they be.

"'Now,' she said, 'chile, when you're grown up, you may be sold away from your mother an' all your ole friends, an' have great troubles come on ye; an' when you has these troubles come on ye, ye jes' go to God, an' He'll help ye.'

"An' says I to her, —

"'Who is God, anyhow, mammy?'

"An' says she, —

"'Why, chile, you jes' look up *dar*! It's Him that made all *dem*!'

"Well, I didn't mind much 'bout God in them days. I grew up pretty lively an' strong, an' could row a boat, or ride a horse, or work round, an' do 'most anything.

"At last I got sold away to a real hard massa an' missis. Oh, I tell you, they *was* hard! 'Peared like I couldn't please 'em, nohow. An' then I thought o' what my old mammy told me about God; an' I thought I'd got into trouble, sure enough, an' I wanted to find God, an' I heerd some one tell a story about a man that met God on a threshin'-floor, an' I thought, 'Well an' good, I'll have a threshin'-floor, too.' So I went down in the lot, an' I threshed down a place real hard, an' I used to go down there every day, an' pray an' cry with all my might, a-prayin' to the Lord to make my massa an' missis better, but it didn't seem to do no good; an' so says I, one day, —

"'O God, I been a-askin' ye, an' askin' ye, an' askin' ye, for all this long time, to make my massa an' missis better, an' you don't do it, an' what *can* be the reason? Why, maybe you *can't*. Well, I shouldn't wonder ef you couldn't. Well, now, I tell you, I'll make a bargain with you. Ef you'll help me to git away from my massa an' missis, I'll agree to be good; but ef you don't help me, I really don't think I can be. Now,' says I, 'I want to git away; but the trouble's jest here: ef I try to git away in the night, I can't see; an' ef I try to git away in the daytime, they'll see me, an' be after me.'

"Then the Lord said to me, 'Git up two or three hours afore daylight, an' start off.'

"An' says I, 'Thank 'ee, Lord! that's a good thought.'

"So up I got, about three o'clock in the mornin', an' I started an' travelled pretty fast, till, when the sun rose, I was clear away from our place an' our folks, an' out o' sight. An' then I begun to think I didn't know nothin' where to go. So I kneeled down, and says I, —

"'Well, Lord, you've started me out, an' now please to show me where to go.'

"Then the Lord made a house appear to me, an' He said to me that I was to walk on till I saw that house, an' then go in an' ask the people to take me. An' I travelled all day, an' didn't come to the house till late at night; but when I saw it, sure enough, I went in, an' I told the folks that the Lord sent me; an' they was Quakers, an' real kind they was to me. They jes' took me in, an' did for me as kind as ef I'd been one of 'em; an' after they'd giv me supper, they took me into a room where there was a great, tall, white bed; an' they told me to sleep there. Well, honey, I was kind o' skeered when they left me alone with that great white bed; 'cause I never had been in a bed in my life. It never came into my mind they could mean me to sleep in it. An' so I jes' camped down under it, on the floor, an' then I slep' pretty well. In the mornin', when they came in, they asked me ef I hadn't been asleep; an' I said, 'Yes, I never slep' better.' An' they said, 'Why, you haven't been in the bed!' An' says I, 'Laws, you didn't think o' such a thing as my sleepin' in dat 'ar' *bed*, did you? I never heerd o' such a thing in my life.'

"Well, ye see, honey, I stayed an' lived with 'em. An' now jes' look here: instead o' keepin' my promise an' bein' good, as I told the Lord I would, jest as soon as everything got a'goin' easy, *I forgot all about God.*

"Pretty well don't need no help; an' I gin up prayin. I lived there two or three years, an' then the slaves in New York were all set free, an' ole massa came to our home to make a visit, an' he asked me ef I didn't want to go back an' see the folks on the ole place. An' I told him I did. So he said, ef I'd jes' git into the wagon with him, he'd carry me over. Well, jest as I was goin' out to git into the wagon, *I met God!* an' says I, 'O God, I didn't know as you was so great!' An' I turned right round an' come into the house, an' set down in my room; for 't was God all around me. I could feel it burnin', burnin', burnin' all around me, an' goin' through me; an' I saw I was so wicked, it seemed as ef it would burn me up. An' I said, 'O somebody, somebody, stand between God an' me! for it burns me!' Then, honey, when I said so, I felt as it were somethin' like an *amberill* [umbrella] that came between me an' the light, an' I felt it was *somebody*, — somebody that stood between me an' God; an' it felt cool, like a shade; an' says I, 'Who's this that stands between me an' God? Is it old Cato?' He was a pious old preacher; but then I seemed to see Cato in the light, an' he was all polluted an' vile, like me; an' I said, 'Is it old Sally?' an' then I saw her, an' she seemed jes' so. An' then says I, '*Who* is this?' An' then, honey, for a while it was like the sun shinin' in a pail o' water, when it moves up an' down; for I begun to feel 't was somebody that loved me; an' I tried to know him. An' I said, 'I know you! I know you! I know you!' — an' then I said, 'I don't know you! I don't know you! I don't know you!' An' when I said, 'I know you, I know you,' the light came; an' when I said, 'I don't know you, I don't know you,' it went, jes' like the sun in a pail o' water. An' finally somethin' spoke out in me an' said, '*This is Jesus!*' An' I spoke out with all my might, an' says I, '*This ·is Jesus!* Glory be to God!' An' then the whole world grew bright, an' the trees they waved an' waved in glory, an' every little bit o' stone on the ground shone like glass; an' I shouted an' said, 'Praise, praise, praise to the Lord!' An' I begun to feel such a love in my soul as I never felt before, — love to all creatures. An' then, all of a sudden, it stopped, an' I said, 'Dar's de white folks, that have abused you an' beat you an' abused your people, — think o' them!' But then there came another rush of love through my soul, an' I cried out loud, — 'Lord, Lord, I can love *even de white folks!*'

"Honey, I jes' walked round an' round in a dream. Jesus loved me! I knowed it, — I felt it. Jesus was my Jesus. Jesus would love me always. I didn't dare tell nobody; 't was a great secret. Everything had been got away from me that I ever had; an' I thought that ef I let white folks know about this, maybe they'd get *Him* away,—so I said, 'I'll keep this close. I won't let any one know.'"

"But, Sojourner, had you never been told about Jesus Christ?"

"No, honey. I hadn't heerd no preachin',—been to no meetin'. Nobody hadn't told me. I'd kind o' heerd of Jesus, but thought he was like Gineral Lafayette, or some o' them. But one night there was a Methodist meetin' somewhere in our parts, an' I went; an' they got up an' begun for to tell der 'speriences; an' de fust one begun to speak. I started, 'cause he told about Jesus. 'Why,' says I to myself, 'dat man's found him, too!' An' another got up an' spoke, an I said, 'He's found him, too!' An' finally I said, 'Why, they all know him!' I was so happy! An' then they sung this hymn": (Here Sojourner sang, in a strange, cracked voice, but evidently with all her soul and might, mispronouncing the English, but seeming to derive as much elevation and comfort from bad English as from good):—

"There is a holy city,
A world of light above,
Above the stairs and regions,[9]
Built by the God of Love.

"An Everlasting temple,
And saints arrayed in white
There serve their great Redeemer
And dwell with him in light.

"The meanest child of glory
Outshines the radiant sun;
But who can speak the splendor
Of Jesus on his throne?

"Is this the man of sorrows
Who stood at Pilate's bar,
Condemned by haughty Herod
And by his men of war?

"He seems a mighty conqueror,
Who spoiled the powers below,
And ransomed many captives
From everlasting woe.

"The hosts of saints around him
Proclaim his work of grace,
The patriarchs and prophets,
And all the godly race,

"Who speak of fiery trials
And tortures on their way;
They came from tribulation
To everlasting day.

"And what shall be my journey,
How long I'll stay below,
Or what shall be my trials,
Are not for me to know.

"In every day of trouble
I'll raise my thoughts on high,
I'll think of that bright temple
And crowns above the sky."

I put in this whole hymn, because Sojourner, carried away with her own feeling, sang it from beginning to end with a triumphant energy that held the whole circle around her intently listening. She sang with the strong barbaric accent of the native African, and with those indescribable upward turns and those deep gutturals which give such a wild, peculiar power to the negro singing,—but above all, with such an overwhelming energy of personal appropriation that the hymn seemed to be fused in the furnace of her feelings and come out recrystallized as a production of her own.

It is said that Rachel was wont to chant the "Marseillaise" in a manner that made her seem, for the time, the very spirit and impersonation of the gaunt, wild, hungry, avenging mob which rose against aristocratic oppression; and in like manner, Sojourner, singing this hymn, seemed to impersonate the fervor of Ethiopia, wild, savage, hunted of all nations, but burning after God in her tropic heart, and stretching her scarred hands towards the glory to be revealed.

"Well, den ye see, after a while, I thought I'd go back an' see de folks on de ole place. Well, you know, de law had passed dat de culled folks was all free; an' my old missis, she had a daughter married about dis time who went to live in Alabama,—an' what did she do but give her my son, a boy about de age of dis yer, for her to take down to Alabama?[10] When I got back to de ole place, they told me about it, an' I went right up to see ole missis, an' says I, —

"'Missis, have you been an' sent my son away down to Alabama?'

"'Yes, I have,' says she; 'he's gone to live with your young missis.'

"'Oh, Missis,' says I, 'how could you do it?'

"'Poh!' says she, 'what a fuss you make about a little nigger! Got more of 'em now than you know what to do with.'

"I tell you, I stretched up. I felt as tall as the world!

"'Missis,' says I, '*I'll have my son back agin!*'

"She laughed.

"'*You* will, you nigger? How you goin' to do it? You ha'n't got no money.'

"'No, Missis, — but *God* has, — an' you'll see He'll help me!' — an' I turned round an' went out.

"Oh, but I *was* angry to have her speak to me so haughty an' so scornful, as ef my chile wasn't worth anything. I said to God, 'O Lord, render unto her double!' It was a dreadful prayer, an' I didn't know how true it would come.

"Well, I didn't rightly know which way to turn; but I went to the Lord, an' I said to Him, 'O Lord, ef I was as rich as you be, an' you was as poor as I be, I'd help you, — you *know* I would; and, oh, do help me!' An' I felt sure then that He would.

"Well, I talked with people, an' they said I must git the case before a grand jury. So I went into the town when they was holdin' a court, to see ef I could find any grand jury. An' I stood round the court-house, an' when they was a-comin' out, I walked right up to the grandest-lookin' one I could see, an' says I to him, —

"'Sir, be you a grand jury?'

"An' then he wanted to know why I asked, an' I told him all about it; an' he asked me all sorts of questions, an' finally he says to me, —

"'I think, ef you pay me ten dollars, that I'd agree to git your son for you.' An' says he, pointin' to a house over the way, 'You go 'long an' tell your story to the folks in that house, an' I guess they'll give you the money.'

"Well, I went, an' I told them, an' they gave me twenty dollars; an' then I thought to myself, 'Ef ten dollars will git him, twenty dollars will git him *sartin*.' So I carried it to the man all out, an' said, —

"'Take it all, — only be sure an' git him.'

"Well, finally they got the boy brought back; an' then they tried to frighten him, an' to make him say that I wasn't his mammy, an' that he didn't know me; but they couldn't make it out. They gave him to me, an' I took him an' carried him home; an' when I came to take off his clothes, there was his poor little back all covered with scars an' hard lumps, where they'd flogged him.

"Well, you see, honey, I told you how I prayed the Lord to render unto her double. Well, it came true; for I was up at ole missis' house not long after, an' I heerd 'em readin' a letter to her how her daughter's husband had murdered her,—how he'd thrown her down an' stamped the life out of her, when he was in liquor; an' my ole missis, she giv a screech, an' fell flat on the floor. Then says I, 'O Lord, I didn't mean all that! You took me up too quick.'

"Well, I went in an' tended that poor critter all night. She was out of her mind,—a-cryin', an' callin' for her daughter; an' I held her poor ole head on my arm, an' watched for her as ef she'd been my babby. An' I watched by her, an' took care on her all through her sickness after that, an' she died in my arms, poor thing!"

"Well, Sojourner, did you always go by this name?"

"No, 'deed! My name was Isabella; but when I left the house of bondage, I left everything behind. I wa'n't goin' to keep nothin' of Egypt on me, an' so I went to the Lord an' asked Him to give me a new name. And the Lord gave me Sojourner, because I was to travel up an' down the land, showin' the people their sins, an' bein' a sign unto them. Afterwards I told the Lord I wanted another name, 'cause everybody else had two names; and the Lord gave me Truth, because I was to declare the truth to the people.

"Ye see some ladies likely have given me a white satin banner," she said, pulling out of her pocket and unfolding a white banner, printed with many texts, such as, "Proclaim liberty throughout all the land unto all the inhabitants thereof," and others of like nature. "Well," she said, "I journeys round to camp-meetins, an' wherever folks is, an' I sets up my banner, an' then I sings, an' then folks always comes up round me, an' then I preaches to 'em. I tells 'em about Jesus, an' I tells 'em about the sins of this people. A great many always comes to hear me; an' they're right good to me, too, an' say they want to hear me agin."

We all thought it; and as the company left her, they shook hands with her, and thanked her for her very original sermon; and one of the ministers was overheard to say to another, "There's more of the gospel in that story than in most sermons."

Sojourner stayed several days with us, a welcome guest. Her conversation was so strong, simple, shrewd, and with such a droll flavoring of humor, that the Professor was wont to say of an evening, "Come, I am dull, can't you get Sojourner up here to talk a little?" She would come up into the parlor, and sit among pictures and ornaments, in her simple stuff gown, with her heavy travelling-shoes, the central object of attention both to parents and children, always ready to talk or to sing, and putting into the common flow of conversation the keen edge of some shrewd remark.

"Sojourner, what do you think of Women's Rights?"

"Well, honey, I's ben to der meetins, an' harked a good deal. Dey wanted me for to speak. So I got up. Says I, — 'Sisters, I a'n't clear what you'd be after. Ef women want any rights more 'n dey's got, why don't dey jes' *take 'em*, an' not be talkin' about it?' Some on 'em came round me, an' asked why I didn't wear Bloomers. An' I told 'em I had Bloomers enough when I was in bondage. You see," she said, "dey used to weave what dey called nigger-cloth, an' each one of us got jes' sech a strip, an' had to wear it widthwise. Them that was short got along pretty well, but as for me" — She gave an indescribably droll glance at her long limbs and then at us, and added, — "Tell *you*, I had enough of Bloomers in them days."

Sojourner then proceeded to give her views of the relative capacity of the sexes, in her own way.

"S'pose a man's mind holds a quart, an' a woman's don't hold but a pint; ef her pint is *full*, it's as good as his quart."

Sojourner was fond of singing an extraordinary lyric, commencing, —

"I'm on my way to Canada,
That cold, but happy land;
The dire effects of Slavery
I can no longer stand.
O righteous Father,
Do look down on me,
And help me on to Canada,
Where colored folks are free!"

The lyric ran on to state, that, when the fugitive crosses the Canada line,

"The Queen comes down unto the shore,
With arms extended wide,
To welcome the poor fugitive
Safe onto Freedom's side."

In the truth thus set forth she seemed to have the most simple faith. But her chief delight was to talk of "glory," and to sing hymns whose burden was,

"O glory, glory, glory,
Won't you come along with me?"

and when left to herself, she would often hum these with great delight, nodding her head.

On one occasion, I remember her sitting at a window singing and fervently keeping time with her head, the little black Puck of a grandson meanwhile amusing himself with ornamenting her red-and-yellow turban with green dandelion-curls, which shook and trembled with her emotions, causing him perfect convulsions of delight.

"Sojourner," said the Professor to her, one day, when he heard her singing, "you seem to be very sure about heaven."

"Well, I be," she answered, triumphantly.

"What makes you so sure there is any heaven?"

"Well, 'cause I got such a hankerin' arter it in here," she said, — giving a thump on her breast with her usual energy.

There was at the time an invalid in the house, and Sojourner, on learning it, felt a mission to go and comfort her. It was curious to see the tall, gaunt, dusky figure stalk up to the bed with such an air of conscious authority, and take on herself the office of consoler with such a mixture of authority and tenderness. She talked as from above, — and at the same time, if a pillow needed changing or any office to be rendered, she did it with a strength and handiness that inspired trust. One felt as if the dark, strange woman were quite able to take up the invalid in her bosom, and bear her as a lamb, both physically and spiritually. There was both power and sweetness in that great warm soul and that vigorous frame.

At length, Sojourner, true to her name, departed. She had her mission elsewhere. Where now she is I know not; but she left deep memories behind her. To these recollections of my own I will add one more anecdote, related by Wendell Phillips.[11]

Speaking of the power of Rachel to move and bear down a whole audience by a few simple words, he said he never knew but one other human being that had that power, and that other was Sojourner Truth. He related a scene of which he was witness. It was at a crowded public meeting in Faneuil Hall,[12] where Frederick Douglas was one of the chief speakers. Douglas had been describing the wrongs of the black race, and as he proceeded, he grew more and more excited, and finally ended by saying that they had no hope of justice from the whites, no possible hope except in their own right arms. It must come to blood; they must fight for themselves, and redeem themselves, or it would never be done.

Sojourner was sitting, tall and dark, on the very front seat, facing the platform; and in the hush of deep feeling, after Douglas sat down, she spoke out in her deep, peculiar voice, heard all over the house, —

"Frederick, *is God dead?*"

The effect was perfectly electrical, and thrilled through the whole house, changing as by a flash the whole feeling of the audience. Not another word she said or needed to say; it was enough.

It is with a sad feeling that one contemplates noble minds and bodies, nobly and grandly formed human beings, that have come to us cramped, scarred, maimed, out of the prison-house of bondage. One longs to know what such beings might have become, if suffered to unfold and expand under the kindly developing influences of education.

It is the theory of some writers, that to the African is reserved, in the later and palmier days of the earth, the full and harmonious development of the religious element in man. The African seems to seize on the tropical fervor and luxuriance of Scripture imagery as something native; he appears to feel himself to be of the same blood with those old burning, simple souls, the patriarchs, prophets, and seers, whose impassioned words seem only grafted as foreign plants on the cooler stock of the Occidental mind.

I cannot but think that Sojourner with the same culture might have spoken words as eloquent and undying as those of the African Saint Augustine or Tertullian. How grand and queenly a woman she might have been, with her wonderful physical vigor, her great heaving sea of emotion, her power of spiritual conception, her quick penetration, and her boundless energy! We might conceive an African type of woman so largely made and moulded, so much fuller in all the elements of life, physical and spiritual, that the dark hue of the skin should seem only to add an appropriate charm,—as Milton says of his Penseroso, whom he imagines

"Black, but such as in esteem
Prince Memnon's sister might beseem,
Or that starred Ethiop queen that strove
To set her beauty's praise above
The sea-nymph's."[13]

But though Sojourner Truth has passed away from among us as a wave of the sea, her memory still lives in one of the loftiest and most original works of modern art, the Libyan Sibyl, by Mr. Story, which attracted so much attention in the late World's Exhibition.[14] Some years ago, when visiting Rome, I related Sojourner's history to Mr. Story at a breakfast at his house. Already had his mind begun to turn to Egypt in search of a type of art which should represent a larger and more vigorous development of nature than the cold elegance of Greek lines. His glorious Cleopatra was then in process of evolution, and his mind was working out the problem of her broadly developed nature, of all that slumbering weight and fulness [sic] of passion with which this statue seems charged, as a heavy thunder-cloud is charged with electricity.

The history of Sojourner Truth worked in his mind and led him into the deeper recesses of the African nature,—those unexplored depths of being and feeling, mighty and dark as the gigantic depths of tropical forests, mysterious as the hidden rivers and mines of that burning continent whose life-history is yet to be. A few days after, he told me that he had conceived the idea of a statue which he should call the Libyan Sibyl. Two years subsequently, I revisited Rome, and found the gorgeous Cleopatra finished, a thing to marvel at, as the creation of a new style of beauty, a new manner of art. Mr. Story requested me to come and repeat to him the history of Sojourner Truth, saying that the conception had never left him. I did so; and a day or two after, he showed me the clay model of the Libyan Sibyl. I have never seen the marble statue; but am told by those who have, that it was by far the most impressive work of art at the Exhibition.

A notice of the two statues from the London "Athenaeum" must supply a description which I cannot give.

"The Cleopatra and the Sibyl are seated, partly draped, with the characteristic Egyptian gown, that gathers about the *torso* and falls freely around the limbs; the first is covered to the bosom, the second bare to the hips. Queenly Cleopatra rests back against her chair in meditative ease, leaning her cheek against one hand, whose elbow the rail of the seat sustains; the other is outstretched upon her knee, nipping its forefinger upon the thumb thoughtfully, as though some firm, wilful [sic] purpose filled her brain, as it seems to set those luxurious features to a smile as if the whole woman 'would.' Upon her head is the coif, bearing in front the mystic *uraeus*, or twining basilisk of sovereignty, while from its sides depend the wide Egyptian lappels, [sic] or wings, that fall upon her shoulders. The *Sibilla Libica* has crossed her knees,—an action universally held amongst the ancients as indicative of reticence or secrecy, and of power to bind. A secret-keeping looking dame she is, in the full-bloom proportions of ripe womanhood, wherein choosing to place his figure the sculptor has deftly gone between the disputed point whether these women were blooming and wise in youth, or deeply furrowed with age and burdened with the knowledge of centuries, as Virgil, Livy, and Gellius say. Good artistic example might be quoted on both sides. Her forward elbow is propped upon one knee; and to keep her secrets close, for this Libyan woman is the closest of all the Sibyls, she rests her shut mouth upon one closed palm, as if holding the African mystery deep in the brooding brain that looks out through mournful, warning eyes, seen under the wide shade of the strange horned (ammonite) crest, that bears the mystery of the Tetragrammaton upon its upturned front. Over her full bosom, mother of myriads as she was, hangs the same symbol. Her face has a Nubian cast, her hair wavy and plaited, as is meet."

We hope to see the day when copies both of the Cleopatra and the Libyan Sibyl shall adorn the Capitol at Washington.

Frances D. Gage, "Sojourner Truth." *National Anti-Slavery Standard*, 2 May 1863

The story of "Sojourner Truth," by Mrs. H.B. Stowe, in the April number of *The Atlantic*,[15] will be read by thousands in the East and West with intense interest; and as those who knew this remarkable woman will lay down this periodical, there will be heard in home-circles throughout Ohio, Michigan, Wisconsin, and Illinois many an anecdote of the weird, wonderful creature, who was at once a marvel and a mystery.

Mrs. Stowe's remarks on Sojourner's opinion of Woman's Rights bring vividly to my mind a scene in Ohio, never to be forgotten by those who witnessed it. In the spring of 1851, a Woman's Rights Convention was called in Akron, Ohio, by the friends of that then wondrously unpopular cause. I attended that Convention. No one at this day can conceive of the state of feeling of the multitude that came together on that occasion.

The Convention in the spring of 1850, in Salem, Ohio, reported at length in *The New York Tribune* by that stanch friend of human rights, Oliver Johnson,[16] followed in October of the same year by another convention at Worcester, Mass., well reported and well abused, with divers minor conventions, each amply vilified and caricatured, had set the world all agog, and the people, finding the women *in earnest*, turned out in large numbers to see and hear.

The leaders of the movement, staggering under the weight of disapprobation already laid upon them, and tremblingly alive to every appearance of evil that might spring up in their midst, were many of them almost thrown into panics on the first day of the meeting, by seeing a tall, gaunt black woman in a gray dress and white turban, surmounted by an uncouth sun-bonnet, march deliberately into the church, walk with the air of a queen up the aisle, and take her seat upon the pulpit steps. A buzz of disapprobation was heard all over the house, and such words as these fell upon listening ears:

"An abolition affair!" "Women's Rights and niggers!" "We told you so. Go it, old darkey!"

I chanced upon that occasion to wear my first laurels in public life, as president of the meeting. At my request, order was restored, and the business of the hour went on. The morning session closed; the afternoon session was held; the evening exercises came and went; old Sojourner, quiet and reticent as the "Libyan Statue,"[17] sat crouched against the wall on a corner of the pulpit stairs, her sun-bonnet shading her eyes, her elbow on her knee, and her chin resting on her broad, hard palm.

At intermissions she was busy selling the "Life of Sojourner Truth," a narrative of her own strange and adventurous life.

Again and again timorous and trembling ones came to me and said with earnestness, "Don't let her speak, Mrs. G. It will ruin us. Every newspaper in the land will have our cause mixed with abolition and niggers, and we shall be utterly denounced." My only answer was, "We shall see when the time comes."

The second day the work waxed warm. Methodist, Baptist, Episcopal, Presbyterian, and Universalist ministers came in to hear and discuss the resolutions brought forth. One claimed superior rights and privileges for man because of superior intellect; another because of the manhood of Christ. If God had desired the equality of woman, he would have given some token of his will through the birth, life, and death of the Savior. Another gave us a theological view of the awful sin of our first mother. There were few women in those days that dared to "speak in meeting," and the august teachers of the people, with long-winded bombast, were seeming to get the better of us, while the boys in the galleries and sneerers among the pews were enjoying hugely the discomfiture, as they supposed, of the strong-minded. Some of the tender-skinned friends were growing indignant and on the point of losing dignity, and the atmosphere of the convention betokened a storm.

Slowly from her seat in the corner rose Sojourner Truth, who, till now, had hardly lifted her head. "Don't let her speak" gasped a half-dozen in my ear. She moved slowly and solemnly to the front; laid her old bonnet at her feet, and turned her great speaking eyes to me.

There was a hissing sound of disapprobation above and below. I rose and announced "Sojourner Truth," and begged the audience to keep silence for a few moments. The tumult subsided at once, and every eye was fixed on this almost Amazon form, which stood nearly six feet high, head erect, and eye piercing the upper air like one in a dream. At her first word there was a profound hush. She spoke in deep tones, which, though not loud, reached every ear in the house, and away through the throng at the doors and windows.

"Well, chillen, whar dar's so much racket dar must be som'ting out o' kilter. I tink dat, 'twixt de niggers of de South and de women at de Norf, all a-talking 'bout rights, de white man will be in a fix pretty soon. But what's all this here talking bout? Dat man ober dar say dat woman needs to be helped into carriages, and lifted over ditches, and to have de best place ebery whar. Nobody eber helps me into carriages, or ober mud-puddles, or gives me any best place"; and, raising herself to her full height, and her voice to a pitch like rolling thunder, she asked. "and ar'n't I a woman? Look at me. Look at my arm," and she bared her right arm to the shoulder, show-ing its tremendous muscular power. "I have plowed and planted and gath-ered into barns, and no man could head me—and ar'n't I a woman? I could work as much and eat as much as a man, (when I could get it,) and bear de lash as well—and ar'n't I a woman? I have borne thirteen chillen, and seen 'em mos' all sold off into slavery, and when I cried out with a mother's grief, none but Jesus heard—and ar'n't I a woman? Den dey talks 'bout dis ting in de head. What dis dey call it?" "Intellect," whispered some one near. "Dat's it, honey. What's dat got to do with woman's rights or niggers' rights? If my cup won't hold but a pint and yourn holds a quart, wouldn't ye be mean not to let me have my little half-measure full?" and she point-ed her significant finger and sent a keen glance at the minister who had made the argument. The cheering was long and loud. "Den dat little man in black dar, he say woman can't have as much right as man 'cause Christ wasn't a woman. *Whar did your Christ come from?*"

Rolling thunder could not have stilled that crowd as did those deep wonderful tones, as she stood there with outstretched arms and eye of fire. Raising her voice still louder, she repeated,

"Whar did your Christ come from? From God and a woman. Man had nothing to do with him." Oh! what a rebuke she gave the little man. Turning again to another objector, she took up the defence of Mother Eve. I cannot follow her through it all. It was pointed and witty and solemn, eliciting at almost every sentence deafening applause; and she ended by asserting "that if de fust woman God ever made was strong enough to turn de world upside down all her one lone, all dese togeder," and she glanced her eye over us, "ought to be able to turn it back and git it right side up again, and now dey is asking to, de men better let 'em." (Long continued cheering.) "'Bleeged to ye for hearin' on me, and now ole Sojourner ha'n't got nothin' more to say."

Amid roars of applause she turned to her corner, leaving more than one of us with streaming eyes and hearts beating with gratitude. She had taken us up in her great strong arms and carried us safely over the slough of dif-ficulty, turning the whole tide in our favor.

I have given but a faint sketch of her speech. I have never in my life seen anything like the magical influence that subdued the mobbish spirit of the day, and turned the jibes and sneers of an excited crowd into notes of respect and admiration. Hundreds rushed up to shake hands and congratulate the glorious old mother, and bid her "God-speed" on her mission of "testifying agin concernin' the wickedness of this here people."

Once upon a Sabbath in Michigan an abolition meeting was held. Parker Pillsbury[18] was speaker, and expressed himself freely upon the conduct of the churches regarding slavery. While he spoke, there came up a fearful thunder-storm. A young Methodist arose and, interrupting him, said he felt alarmed; he felt as if God's judgment was about to fall upon him for daring to sit and hear such blasphemy; that it made his hair almost rise with terror. Here a voice sounding above the rain that beat upon the roof, the sweeping surge of the winds, the crashing of the limbs of trees; swaying of branches, and the rolling of thunder, spoke out: "Chile, don't be skeered; you're not goin' to be harmed. I don't speck God's ever heern tell on ye!"

It was all she said, but it was enough. I might multiply anecdotes (and some of the best cannot be told) till your pages would not contain them, and yet the fund not be exhausted. Therefore, I will close, only saying to those who think public opinion does not change, that they have only to look at the progress of ideas from the stand-point of old Sojourner Truth twelve years ago.

The despised and mobbed African, now the heroine of an article in the most popular periodical in the United States. Then Sojourner could say, "If woman wants rights, let her take 'em." Now, women do take them, and public opinion sustains them.

Sojourner Truth is not dead; but, old and feeble, she rests from her labors near Battle Creek, Michigan.

**Frances Ellen Watkins Harper, "We Are All Bound Up Together."
Proceedings of the Eleventh National Woman's Rights
Convention, Held at the Church of the Puritans, New York, May
10, 1866. New York: Robert J. Johnston, 1866. 45–48**

Mrs. Harper,[19] of Ohio, said:

I feel I am something of a novice upon this platform. Born of a race whose inheritance has been outrage and wrong, most of my life had been spent in battling against those wrongs. But I did not feel as keenly as others, that I had these rights, in common with other women, which are now demanded. About two years ago, I stood within the shadows of my home. A great sorrow had fallen upon my life. My husband had died suddenly, leaving me a widow, with four children, one my own, and the others step-children. I tried to keep my children together. But my husband died in debt; and before he had been in his grave three months, the administrator had swept the very milk-crocks and wash tubs from my hands. I was a farmer's wife and made butter for the Columbus market; but what could I do, when they had swept all away? They left me one thing—and that was a looking-glass! Had I died instead of my husband, how different would have been the result! By this time he would have had another wife, it is likely; and no administrator would have gone into his house, broken up his home, and sold his bed, and taken away his means of support.

I took my children in my arms, and went out to seek my living. While I was gone, a neighbor to whom I had once lent five dollars, went before a magistrate and swore that he believed I was a nonresident, and laid an attachment on my very bed. And I went back to Ohio with my orphan children in my arms, without a single feather bed in this wide world, that was not in the custody of the law. I say, then, that justice is not fulfilled so long as woman is unequal before the law.

We are all bound up together in one great bundle of humanity, and society cannot trample on the weakest and feeblest of its members without receiving the curse in its own soul. You tried that in the case of the negro. You pressed him down for two centuries; and in so doing you crippled the moral strength and paralyzed the spiritual energies of the white men of the country. When the hands of the black were fettered, white men were deprived of the liberty of speech and the freedom of the press. Society cannot afford to neglect the enlightenment of any class of its members. At the South, the legislation of the country was in behalf of the rich slaveholders, while the poor white man was neglected. What is the consequence to-day? From that very class of neglected poor white men comes the man who stands to-day with his hand upon the helm of the nation. He fails to catch the watchword of the hour, and throws himself, the incarnation of meanness, across the pathway of the nation. My objection to Andrew Johnson[20] is not that he has been a poor white man; my objection is that he keeps "poor whites" all the way through. (Applause.) That is the trouble with him.

This grand and glorious revolution which has commenced, will fail to reach its climax of success, until throughout the length and breath of the American Republic, the nation shall be so color-blind, as to know no man by the color of his skin or the curl of his hair. It will then have no privileged class, trampling upon and outraging the unprivileged classes, but will be then one great privileged nation, whose privilege will be to produce the loftiest manhood and womanhood that humanity can attain.

I do not believe that giving the woman the ballot is immediately going to cure all the ills of life. I do not believe that white women are dewdrops just exhaled from the skies. I think that like men they may be divided into three classes, the good, the bad, and the indifferent. The good would vote according to their convictions and principles; the bad, as dictated by prejudice or malice; and the indifferent will vote on the strongest side of the question, with the winning party.

You white women speak here of rights. I speak of wrongs. I, as a colored woman, have had in this country an education which has made me feel as if I were in the situation of Ishmael, my hand against every man, and every man's hand against me. Let me go tomorrow morning and take my seat in one of your street cars—I do not know that they will do it in New York, but they will in Philadelphia—and the conductor will put up his hand and stop the car rather than let me ride.

A Lady—They will not do that here.

Mrs. Harper—They do in Philadelphia. Going from Washington to Baltimore this Spring, they put me in the smoking car. (Loud Voices—"Shame.") Aye, in the capital of the nation, where the black man consecrated himself to the nation's defence, faithful when the white man was faithless they put me in the smoking car! They did it once; but the next time they tried it, they failed; for I would not go in. I felt the fight in me; but I don't want to have to fight all the time. To-day I am puzzled where to make my home. I would like to make it in Philadelphia, near my own friends and relations. But if I want to ride in the streets of Philadelphia, they send me to ride on the platform with the driver. (Cries of "Shame.") Have women nothing to do with this? Not long since, a colored woman took her seat in an Eleventh street car in Philadelphia, and the conductor stopped the car, and told the rest of the passengers to get out, and left the car with her in it alone, when they took it back to the station. One day I took my seat in a car, and the conductor came to me and told me to take another seat. I just screamed "murder." The man said if I was black I ought to behave myself. I knew that if he was white he was not behaving himself. Are there not wrongs to be righted?

In advocating the cause of the colored man, since the Dred Scott decision,[21] I have sometimes said I thought the nation had touched bottom. But let me tell you there is a depth of infamy lower than that. It is when the nation, standing upon the threshold of a great peril, reached out its hands to a feebler race, and asked that race to help it, and when the peril was over, said, You are good enough for soldiers, but not good enough for citizens. When Judge Tansy said that the men of my race had no rights which the white man was bound to respect, he had not seen the bones of the black man bleaching outside of Richmond. He had not seen the thinned ranks and the thickened graves of the Louisiana Second,[22] a regiment which went into battle nine hundred strong, and came out with three hundred. He had not stood at Olustee and seen defeat and disaster crashing down the pride of our banner, until word was brought to Col. Hallowell, "The day is lost; go in and save it"; and black men stood in the gap, beat back the enemy, and saved your army.[23] (Applause.)

We have a woman in our country who has received the name of "Moses," not by lying about it, but by acting it out (applause)—a woman who has gone down into the Egypt of slavery and brought out hundreds of our people into liberty.[24] The last time I saw that woman, her hands were swollen. That woman who had led one of Montgomery's most successful expeditions, who was brave enough and secretive enough to act as a scout for the American army, had her hands all swollen from a conflict with a brutal conductor, who undertook to eject her from her place. That woman, whose courage and bravery won a recognition from our army and from every black man in the land, is excluded from every thoroughfare of travel. Talk of giving women the ballot-box? Go on. It is a normal school, and the white women of this country need it. While there exists this brutal element in society which tramples upon the feeble and treads down the weak, I tell you that if there is any class of people who need to be lifted out of their airy nothings and selfishness, it is the white women of America. (Applause.)

Mrs. Martha Wright,[25] of Auburn, stated that the outrage upon Harriet Tubman, just referred to, was perpetrated upon the Camden and Amboy Railroad.

Susan B. Anthony[26] presented the following resolution, and moved its adoption:

Whereas, by the act of Emancipation and the Civil Rights bill, the negro and woman now hold the same civil and political *status*, alike needing only the ballot; and whereas the same arguments apply equally to both classes, proving all partial legislation fatal to republican institutions, therefore

Resolved, That the time has come for an organization that shall demand Universal Suffrage, and that hereafter we shall be known as the "American Equal Rights Association."[27]

SUFFRAGE

Sojourner Truth, "Female Suffrage." *New York World*, **10 May 1867**

FEMALE SUFFRAGE
Speeches, Songs, and Resolutions of Sojourner Truth, Elizabeth
Cady Stanton, Parker Pillsbury, Lucretia Mott, Charles Barfey, Ernestine
L. Rose, Rev. Mr. May, Susan B. Anthony, Maj. Haggerty,
Frances D. Gage, and Others.
Woman Demands Equality with the Negro.
REPUBLICAN HYPOCRISY DENOUNCED,
&c, &c, &c.

The first anniversary of the American Equal Rights Association took place
at the Church of the Puritans yesterday. The morning session was to have
opened at 10 o'clock, but at that hour the attendance was so slim that the
opening was delayed. The audience comprised the customary assortment of
both sexes and all colors, including a fair sprinkling of the latest styles of
fashion, as well as the most antiquated costumes…

A CHARACTER

Miss Sojourner Truth was announced as the next speaker, and her appearance
was the signal for general good humor. Sojourner has been a slave forty years
and free forty years, and is not at all afraid of speaking before white folks or
speaking out in meeting. She dresses much as she used to do on the plantation, and wears a white 'kerchief around her head, *a la* maums all over the
South. She spoke in a clear, loud tone, with a strong African accent, as follows:

SPEECH OF SOJOURNER TRUTH

My friends, I am rejoiced. I come for another appeal. I appealed to the
public many years on behalf of the poor slave, and now he has got his liberty there is more in de land dat ain't got done at all. I believe that women
should have their rights. We have had so much good luck to have slavery
partially destroyed, not entirely. I want root and branch destroyed. We will
then feel that we are free indeed; that we can fill every place that is open
to all that have got their rights. I feel that if I've got to answer for the sins
done in my body just as much as a man has, I have a right to have just as
much as a man. (Laughter and applause.)

WIFE SLAVERY

Well, children, I am old enough to be the mother of all here. (Laughter.) You see, the colored man has got his rights; but has the colored woman? (Laughter.) The colored man has got his rights, but nobody makes [...] about de colored women's rights. (Applause.) Why, de colored man will be massa ober de woman, an' it will be jus as bad as before. (Laughter.) Now, while this stir is going on, I want to keep it stirrin' till it goes right— (Laughter.)—because if you stop, it will be terrible hard work to start de engine agin. (Laughter.) So I appeal on that of de women. The white woman knows a good deal; the colored woman don't know it—that is, those that are lately 'mancipated. The colored men will learn like the rest of the men, that they are a kind of masters. They will try to be masters over their colored wives. (Laughter.)

WASHING AND IRONING

I want the colored woman to understand that if she earns anything it is her own. But if a colored wife goes out to do a little washing—that is about as high as black folks get—(laughter), when she comes back with a little money the husband comes in.

"Where have you been?" "To work." "Well, you got paid?" "Yes." "Then let me have it."

"But I want to buy so and so for the children."

"Well, I don't want words about it. So hand it over." (Laughter.) So he takes it and walks away, nobody knows where. Then he comes in at night.

"Got anything to eat?" "No." "What's the reason?" "No money." "Well, you might ha' got it." That's the way it is; a woman can't claim anything that she can call her own. Why? She stands on the same footing that he does. She can't put her money in her pocket; he can get it. He can spend his'n, and he can hold her'n. She can't get what she wants for her and her children. The man claims her money, body, and everything for himself. (Laughter and applause.)

NOW'S THE TIME

It's not right. Now's the time to make a strong appeal for woman's rights. How beautiful it will be when you can see women sitting like the lawyers and judges. You see a poor woman coming up to be tried by men. If you are going to be tried by men, why can't you have a part in the matter and try him too? When the poor woman stands before the bar perhaps the man who looks down on her has a nose red like a cigar. (Laughter.) No woman dares speak in her behalf. They ask her certain questions for their amusement and no women are to speak. Men haven't all the majesty. I want women in their places. (Laughter.) They would know what to ask and what to say, which the men don't know, for I have been standing and listening, and have seen the poor women go off and the men go "he, he, he." (Giggling.)

JURY WOMEN WANTED

Now I want women there to sit and hear—not these pettifoggers. I mean these lawyers, judges, and jurymen. If it ain't decent for women to be there it ain't decent for men to be there, (laughter), you ought'nt to be anywhere if it ain't decent enough for women to be there. (Applause). This is the trouble with some of the men. They are so mean they don't want the women to know it. Let nobody be ashamed to go to the bar and give testimony. Nobody will be daunted. You know it is a sister sits in judgment, she will not ask you any question if it is unworthy. (Applause.)

HER AGE

I have been here eighty years—that is long enough for anybody. There is a great deal of work to be done, so I will have to tarry. I was forty years a slave and forty years free, and I would wish to live forty years longer if I could have equal rights for those that live. I suppose that the reason I stayed —to fight this battle for the right; that every human being shall have that God-given right. As I said a good many years ago, there is some men who believe that if women got their rights men would have no rights left. They seem to be half scared. (Laughter.) They were so frightened that some of them turned to crying. (Laughter.)

HER LOGIC ABOUT WORK AND PAY

Did God ever have men to have women's rights? "No, No!" Men have all the rights says I. Are you afeard that women will take your rights? They don't want 'em. I have done as much work as the biggest part of men. If I do as much work as a man, why can't I be paid so? (Applause.) If I write and make accounts as well as a man, why can't I have as much money? They don't do more than I, why should they get more pay? There is the German women, they do as much work as a man, but he gets a dollar and she gets a half. Because she is a woman. She eats as much as a man if she can get it. (Applause and laughter.) Nobody must sit in judgment how much she must eat, or how much sense—you can't help that. (Laughter.) I have seen some women that had better sense than the men had. (Laughter.) I have talked with them. Give them a chance. That is what the men fear—they fear that women will degrade them. They ought to out-grow men for a while to bring them to their place. (Great laughter and applause.)

A PREDICTION AND COMPLAINT

This cause must move. Yes, it must. They used to say to me: "Sojourner, it's no use. You will never see de freedom ob de slave." "Well," says I, "let me be in de body or out ob de body, I shall see it." When the dark days were here I thought I should not live to see it. Did me and you know that it would come to pass, men would be better, and women would be better. But men fear to give women their rights. Even the children are brought up to say to the women; "Oh you are only a woman; you don't know." They talk so to their mothers. (Laughter.) Like Adam when God asked what he had been doing, he laid it all to God and the woman. (Laughter.) Just so when children grow up they lay all the blame to women.

SUPPLIES WANTED FROM THE ENEMY

We want woman's rights, but we look to you for the money. When woman's rights come we will have it in our own pockets. (Laughter.) We won't run to men for money; we will have it ourselves. (Applause.) The men will have to ask us for some money. (Laughter.) We want them to give us a little now, until we get our rights, then we won't be troubled any more about asking for money. Then you will have peace; you will be joyful; you and your wife and daughter will stand beside you. You will feel like standing without being propped up. (Applause.) Let's keep the work moving while it is moving, then you won't be asked for money. Women will have money as well as men.

MISS ANTHONY'S INEVITABLE COLLECTION

Susan B. Anthony at this appropriate point announced that the finance committee would take up a collection and receive subscriptions. They didn't want all small stamps either, but would not refuse them.

SOJOURNER CONTINUES

Truth continued with some reiteration of her preceding remarks. She said the men had held the women in slavery so long that they thought they owned them, just as the slaveholders had held the slaves until they thought they owned them. She had been in Washington three years.[28] She felt that the colored women in Washington had a right to vote as well as the colored men. She wanted the whole people to speak out for equal rights. In conclusion, she said: "Now, I will sing a little. There ought to be singing here. I ain't heard no singing since I've been here. I can't sing a great deal. Can't sing as well as I used to."

SOJOURNER'S CHANT

Sojourner then commenced a weird, wailing song, with a very queer time, an odd though clear pronunciation of words, and her old head swaying to and fro in harmony. As best the reporter could catch the words the song was as follows:

> We are goin' home—we had visions bright
> Of that holy land, that world of light,
> Where the cold and dark night of time is passed,
> And the morning of eternity is come at last;
> Where the weary saints no more shall roam,
> But dwell in their peaceful and sunny home;
> Where the light celestial gems our crown,
> And the waves of bliss are dashin' roun'—
>   Oh-h-h-h!
>   Oh, that beautiful home;
>   Oh-h, that beautiful world.

> We are goin' home; we soon shall be
> Where the sky is clear and the soil is free;
> Where the victor's song floats from the plains,
> And the anthems of Seraphs and glorious strains;
> Where the sun rolls down his brilliant flood,
> And beams on a world that's fair and good;
> And the stars that shine on nature's dome,
> Will sparkle and dance from their spirit's home.
>   Oh-h-h-h!
>   Oh, that beautiful home;
>   Oh-h, that beautiful world.

> There tears and sighs, which here are given,
> Will change for the glad songs of heaven;

308

There beauteous forms will sing and shine,
If guarded well by the hand Divine;
Pure love and friendship will be joined
Waiting before that princely band;
And the glory of God, like a molten sea,
Will bathe that immortal company.
  Oh-h-h-h!
  Oh, that beautiful home;
  Oh-h, that beautiful world.

The ransomed throng they see and bless
The holy city of gorgeousness;
The verdant earth and angel's choir,
The flowers that never winter wear:
The conqueror's song it sounds afar
As wafted on the ambrosial air;
Through endless years we then shall prove
The depths of a saviour's matchless love.
  Oh-h-h-h!
  Oh, that beautiful home;
  Oh-h, that beautiful world.[29]

SOJOURNER CONCLUDES

There, chil'ren we'll res' from all our labors; there we shall res' in that bu'-ful world, where we shall go out no moah. Now let's do as we can do; now let's all work for that bu'ful place for I'm boun', my chil'ren, for that, and I'm determin', by the grace o'God, to stop no shorter than that bu'ful place.

Sojourner then bowed to the audience, showing the hideous white handkerchief bound round the top of her head, exactly the shape of a chignon, and where the chignon ought to be, and possibly containing as many gregarines[30] as the *bona fide* article.

Naomi Talbert, "A Colored Woman's Voice [delivered at 1869 NWSA convention in Chicago]." *The Revolution* 3 (4 March 1869): 139[31]

The colored women, of all other American women, should be devoted to the cause of Suffrage. One appeared in the recent Chicago Convention to the following effect:[32]

I present myself to you as a composition of humanity, for there flows through my veins a combination of the blood of four distinct nations, of which the greater part is Dutch, part Indian, part African, and the lesser part Irish. (Applause and laughter.) I am an American, because here I was born. I am true, because I love the dear old flag. I am on the right side of the question, because I believe woman was made a helpmate for man; that he is but half a man without woman (applause), and you need her help as well in political affairs as you do in private or domestic affairs. And, gentlemen, I warn you no longer to stand out in refusing the right for which we contend; in trying to withhold from these noble ladies here and their darker sisters the franchise they now demand. Miss Anthony and Mrs. Stanton, with their high moral and intellectual power, have shaken the states of New England, and the shock is felt here to-day. The echo comes back from St. Louis and all through the west; a sensation is aroused in England; and soon the whole world will be awakened to a sense of the value and importance of our cause. Woman has a power within herself, and the God that reigns above, who commanded Moses to lead the children of Israel from out the land of Egypt, from out the house of bondage, who walled the waters of the Red Sea, who endowed Samson with power to slay his enemies with the jaw-bone of an ass, who furnished Abraham Lincoln with knowledge to write the emancipation proclamation, whereby four millions of blacks were set free—that God, our God, is with and for us, and will hear the call of woman, and her rights will be granted, and she shall be permitted to vote.

Mary Ann Shadd Cary, "Speech to Judiciary Committee Re: The Right of Women to Vote." 1874. Mary Ann Shadd Cary Papers, Moorland-Spingarn Research Center, Howard University[33]

Mr. Chairman, and gentlemen of the Judiciary Committee:—
In respectfully appearing before you, to solicit in concert with *these* ladies, your good offices, in securing to the women of the United States, and *particularly*, to the women of the District of Columbia, the right to *vote*—a right exerc[ized] by a portion of American women, at one period, in the hi[story] of this country,—I am not vain enough to suppose, for [a] moment, that words of mine could add one iota of weight to the arguments from these learned and earnest women, nor that I could bring out material facts not heretofore used by them in one stage or another of this advocacy. But, as a colored woman, a resident of this District, a tax-payer of the same;—as one of a *class* equal in point of *numbers* to the male colored voters herein; claiming affilliation with two and a half millions of the same

sex, in the country at-large, — included in the provisions of recent constitutional amendments, — and not least, by virtue of a decision of the Supreme Court of this District a *citizen*, — my presence, at this time, and on an errand so important, may not I trust be without slight significance.

The crowning glory of American citizenship is that it may be shared equally by people of every nationality, complexion and sex, should they of foreign birth so *desire*; and in the inscrutable rulings of an All-wise providence, millions of citizens of every complexion, and embracing *both sexes*, are born upon the soil and claim the honor. I would be particularly clear upon this point. By the provisions of the 14th & 15th amendments to the Constitution of the United States, — a logical sequence of which is the representation by colored men of time-honored commonwealths in both houses of Congress, — millions of colored *women*, to-day, share with colored men the responsibilities of freedom from chattel slavery. From the introduction of African slavery to its extinction, a period of more than two hundred years, they *equally* with fathers, brothers, [were] denied the right to vote. This fact of their investiture with the privileges of free women of the same time and by the same amendments which disenthralled their kinsmen and conferred upon the latter the right of franchise, without so endowing themselves is one of the anomalies of a measure of legislation otherwise grand in conception and consequences beyond comparison. The colored women of this country though heretofore silent, in great measure upon this question of the right to vote by the women of the [sic], so long and ardently the cry of the noblest of the land, have neither been indifferent to their own just claims under the amendments, in common with colored men, nor to the demand for political recognition so justly made every where throughout the land.

Women everywhere throughout the land. The strength and glory of a free nation, is *not so much* in the size and equipments of its armies, as in the *loyal hearts* and willing hands of its *men* and *women*. And this fact has been illustrated in an eminent degree by well-known events in the history of the United States. To the women of the nation conjointly with the men, is it indebted for arduous and dangerous personal service, and generous expenditure of time, wealth and counsel, so indispensable to success in its hour of danger. The colored *women* though humble in sphere, and unendowed with worldly goods, yet, led as by inspiration, — not only fed, and sheltered, and guided in *safety* the prisoner soldiers of the Union when escaping from the enemy, or the soldier who was compelled to risk life *itself* in the struggle to break the back-bone of rebellion, but gave their *sons* and brothers to the armies of the nation and their prayers to high Heaven for the success of the Right.

The surges of fratricidal war have passed we hope never to return; the premonitions of the future are peace and good will; these blessings, so greatly to be desired, can only be made permanent, in responsible governments,—based as you affirm upon the consent of the governed,—by giving to both sexes practically the equal powers conferred in the provisions of the Constitution as amended. In the District of Columbia the women in common with the women of the states and territories, feel keenly the discrimination against them in the retention of the word *male* in the organic act for the same, and as by reason of its retention, all the evils incident to partial legislation are endured by them, they sincerely hope that the word *male* may be stricken out by Congress on your recommendation without delay. Taxed, and governed in other respects, without their consent, they respectfully demand, that the principles of the *founders* of the government may *not* be disregarded in their case; but, as there are *laws* by which they are tried, with penalties attached thereto, that they may be invested with the right to vote as do men, that thus as in all Republics *indeed*, they may in future be governed by their own consent.

Mary E. ("Meb") Britton, "Woman's Suffrage. A Potent Agency in Public Reforms." *American Catholic Tribune*, 22 July 1887

It affords me great pleasure to present to you this evening, my views on this important question. The atmosphere in which I live is not a very healthy one in favor of woman suffrage; and for that reason I had seen only one side of the question, but now that I am able to see both sides, I am convicted of my error, and fastly, am converted to truth and justice. Humanity is composed of peculiarites of character and talents.

In woman as much so as in man. One person takes to letters, another to mechanics, one to philanthropy, another to money, because impelled thereto by strong innate proclivities.

Poets are born not educated. Blind Tom is a musical prodigy though a born fool.[34] From my early youth I was a strong advocate of human rights; as I grew older and more decided steps were taken in this direction, I was talked of as a strong minded woman[;] not knowing the import I argued against the term, always saying however, that I favored human rights, not woman's rights. Now to the noble women, who read my article on "Higher Education of Woman" published in the *Louisville Courant* last fall, I wish to retract, so much as was said to deprive them of the liberty to follow freely their own natural gifts, and the reluctant recognition of the right to do whatever they can do well. Wherever there is a gift, there is a propecy [sic] pointing to its use, and a silent command of God to use it. The possession of a gift is a charter conveying to the possessor permission to use it. It was both unjust and inconsistent to tell women to prepare themselves, to rear talented children and then to close up the way by which the girls could use natural gifts. Women inherit all the natural gifts that men do. Each has something of the other's gifts, and each has a superiority of its own over the other. The fundamental principle of woman suffrage is, "That every human being has a right to mark out his or her own destiny, subject only to those restraints of society which are applied to all alike." I now throw away the old ignorant prejudices, which I am ashamed to have ever held, and stand here this evening, fearlessly defending woman suffrage, as a potent agency in public reforms. In all history, the ruling classes are cruel to the subordinate classes. Woman was of the subordinate class. She was relegated to the realm of ignorance and servitude. Given in marriage, bartered, or sold as thing of merchandise.

Under the old Roman law, the husband controlled her property and earnings. He had the power of life and death over her, and she could invoke no law against him. She had no power over her children, and was in general thought to have no soul. Many of to-day defend the old Roman custom. They never think a woman too weak to do all the drudgery, and even to do extreme heavy work, but when it comes to giving her protection of the law, over her children and her property, there is a strong fight against it. God's thought of woman changed matters, and the great change has been going on ever since.

He appointed Huldah[35] to be a prophet and Deborah to be a warrior, judge and prophet,[36] just as he appointed men at other times. This equality was a feature of the Messiah's reign of truth and justice. At Nazareth Jesus said: "The spirit of the Lord is upon me, because He hath annointed me to preach good tidings to the poor. He hath sent me to proclaim release to the captives, and recovery of sight to the blind; to set at liberty those that are bruised."[37]

The advocates of the subjection of women have studiously avoided Christ and made much of Paul. Jesus speaks of women as fellow workers in Christ, and gives as much praise to them.

There is no intimation that a woman ever spoke a word against him.

Men were in power and took for themselves the license of lust, and applied the law of purity to women, the acknowledged weaker vessel.

Jesus made chastity equally binding on both. (Matt.v. 28.) When a band of men with the arrogance of those who have the law in their own hands, brought a physically helpless woman to Jesus, saying that she had been guilty of sin, (but they had never been) He put them to flight by applying the law of justice, said He: "He that is without sin among you, let him first cast a stone at her."[38] Apply that law to-day, and there will not be such a cry to save women from falling. This strong rebuke was new to the world, and bad men immediately turned against Jesus, because He hated their lusts, and evil deeds. Christ inaugurated the refom [sic] and its progress has been the long continued efforts in Europe and America to rid the statute books of laws made in the sole interests of men, and denying to wives and mothers their just rights.

There must be men of honor among you here this evening; who are ashamed that women bear equally with men the support of their families; in many instances working harder, better, and of longer duration, and yet receive smaller compensation for their labor, only because they are women.

Christ gave the golden rule — "All things whatsoever ye would that men should do to you, do ye even so to them."[39] Would you like to be treated that way? Then you opposers of this needed reform, come down from your high perches of superiority and give to woman what is justly hers. Follow that golden rule, and you will vitalize every humane movement while the world stands.

The humane question is stirring women's hearts, and breaking down their prejudices. Man alone is not the true fruit of the human race and man only a blossom, good to give him a start, then perishing, to let him swell to full proportion.

It is power made skillful by exercise that makes both men and women richer in domestic life. Whatever makes woman a better thinker, a larger minded actor, a deep thoughted observer, a more potent writer or teacher makes her just so much a better wife or mother. No one is better for being ignorant, no one is a better companion for being weak and helpless.

Our homes demand great heads. Man thinks from the physical and passional [sic] stand-point, this gives him power and outward victory. Woman thinks from the standpoint of affection and moral sentiment, and this gives her purity and rectitude. The union of the two will make the perfect one.

Public sentiment gives much praise to Mesdames Jno. A. Logan, Horace Mann, Wendel Phillips,[40] and other great women, for the success of their husbands in public life.

They were not men who closeted their wives, thereby losing the benefit of their rich minds to combine with what may have been deficient in their own. I would not rob woman of her nature. Her sphere is that of woman, not of man.

Experience has shown that as woman is made to be worth more to society at large, and in public interests, she becomes richer at home and is capable of building it better. She is richer in all household excellences.

In the engagement of her sphere she has forsaken no duty of home, and lost no grace of tenderness and love.

We see the divine fact that civilization as it becomes Christianized will make increasing demands upon creation's gentle half. Woman has steadily risen in the growth of civilization, her sphere is enlarged and she has grown better by just that enlargement it was predicted would unsex her. She has not only learned the alphabet, but has also learned the verbs, conjugations, and declensions of all the languages, ancient and modern. She has taken the first prize in mathematics, science and philosophy. She has taken degrees in law, medicine and theology. She is employed in the mills and manufactories. She is a stenographer, type writer, cashier, clerk, telegraph and telephone operator. She is in the trades and professions, indeed she can go almost anywhere she choses [sic] to go. She suffers all the wrong and impositions of the working man, and the addition of a still greater injustice, that a woman shall receive less wages than a man for the same amount and quality of work, simply because she is a woman.

Woman of the nineteenth century is not keeping silence in the church, home or society. The great foreign missionary work is chiefly upheld by woman. She is the first to teach the gospel of the resurrection of Christ, to the heathen. She was the first to see our risen Savior.

With woman's vote, the saloons all over the land that tempt boys to ruin can be closed. The experiment has been tried in Kansas and was crowned with success. *Women's morality*

"Taxation without representation is tyranny." It is because woman is not like man, that she refuses to be represented by him in making laws to spend her tax money, and to judge her in court. If woman is the same as man then she has the same rights, if she is distinct from man then she has a right to the ballot to help make laws for her government. The only practical method of promoting temperance legislation is to unite in securing municipal suffrage to woman all over the land. The voting of woman will be the safety of men throughout the nation. If men are selected for office whose election depend as much upon the votes of woman as upon those of men, not one bad man will be put up, where there are fifty now. The only thing that will help the world is that men shall do right. When woman begins to tell the bad men this, they say: "Mind your own business, as you are out of your sphere." Well, she is minding her own business in her sphere. When woman becomes a voter, law makers will stop spending the *moral power of* public money for cigars and fine drinks. They will no longer vote upon questions of public interest in an insensible state of mind.

Drink destroys both body and soul. Bad men will receive their quieteus[41] the day woman is enfranchised. She is said to have tempted, man, *from* good, and it is her mission to restore him to his former state. In 1860, Henry Ward Beecher said "The moment you bring into our public affairs woman's influence, her stronger moral sentiment, her moral courage, and faith in all that is good, then will you have God's foundation for moral and public peace. Then principles will not only be discussed but applied, and legislation will grow heroic." Fred. Douglas said the noble work of woman in the slavery movement caused him to believe her deprived of rights justly hers.

Wendell Phillips declared woman suffrage to be the most magnificent reform ever launched upon the world.

Chas. Sumner said "In the progress of human civilization, woman suffrage is sure to come, Justice and common sense must conquer in the long run." The light is dawning and the time is fast approaching.

Among the unusual departures of woman, one young woman in the West is following the profession of civil engineer. A Cincinnati girl has been licensed as stationery engineer, two women are steamboat captains and one has lately secured her license as pilot. A woman is mayor of Argona Kan. Woman as school superintendents, notary publics, and deputy county officers has ceased to be a novelty. If she did not successfully fill these positions, charity would not retain her. One result of the equal rights agitation has been that woman is now employed in 222 of the 265 different occupations enumerated in the census of 1808. Previous to the reform movement, the number of occupations was less than twenty. A humorous incident is told of the work of woman on the New York School Board. A janitor complained to one of the principals, saying that he had been employed there nineteen years, and no one had ever asked him to see the basement until meddlesome old Mrs. — came one day and said she wanted to make an examination, he added plaintively "And that basement wasn't in a fit condition for any one to see."

Every material interest of human life demands that man and woman shall be united.

Whatever strength masculine element may have, it is deficient in moral refinement. Judge Fox said in a political speech at Lexington not long since, that the Republican and Democratic conventions were never known to observe such good order, as had been observed at the last ones, and they had been forced to it by the [...] party and woman's influence in politics. Woman is appointed for the refinement of the race. The need of moral influence in the administration of political affairs is universally conceded.

Since the world began to refine, society has been woman's function. She has carried refinement to the households, to the church, to social life, to literature, to art, to everything, and lastly to government.

Hear from woman in Kansas.[42] The ladies held a caucus, as none of the tickets in the field exactly suited them. They made up a ticket composed of the best men on the three tickets in the fields. Their ticket was elected and the leading paper of the place says: "This election establishes the fact that we have a new factor in politics that will determine every election in which there is a moral or religious issue."

Garden city paper says: "The rum power made a great fight, but the ladies worked hard, the most influential ladies of the town giving their time to the work. The entire temperance ticket was elected."

Topeka Commonwealth says: "A goodly number of ladies have gone to the polls and voted."

We hear of no homes disrupted, of no insults being offered, of no unlady-like performance, of no verification of the hundred ills predicted by the croakers. The babies have been properly cared for, the meals have been furnished regularly, every household duty has been performed satisfactorily and the ceaseless sound of domestic cares goes on in its accustomed channel.

Langston Leader—The ladies voted in fine shape and showed their appreciation of their privelege,[sic].

Winchester Argus—Municipal suffrage for females in Kansas has resulted in much good at this election. The experiment has proved a success.

Independence Tribune—After all we dont see, but that the women vote just as easily as the men, and moreso. With their ballots all ready to cast, they walk up to the voting places, announce their names, deposit their ballots and quietly walk away, leaving all unnecessary discussions on election day to the men.

Thus you see the right of suffrage was used by the best and most refined women. It is no more than going to the post office and dropping in a letter. Some argue that the polls are not decent places. As soon as woman suffrage is general they will be made decent for gentlemen as well as for ladies. So soon as the School Suffrages for women became the law in Mass.,[43] the Legislature passed without opposition a statute to prohibit smoking and drinking at the polls. If politics are naturally corrupting, advise good men as well as good women not to vote.

No movement of any great importance has ever taken place in the world, in which woman has not taken a prominent part as a worker—then most assuredly is Woman Suffrage a Potent Agency in Public Reforms.

Anna Julia Cooper, "Woman versus the Indian." *A Voice from the South*. Xenia, OH: Aldine, 1892. 80–126

In the National Woman's Council convened at Washington in February 1891,[44] among a number of thoughtful and suggestive papers read by eminent women, was one by the Rev. Anna Shaw,[45] bearing the above title.

That Miss Shaw is broad and just and liberal in principle is proved beyond contradiction. Her noble generosity and womanly firmness are unimpeachable. The unwavering stand taken by herself and Miss Anthony in the subsequent color ripple in Wimodaughsis[46] ought to be sufficient to allay forever any doubts as to the pure gold of these two women.

Of Wimodaughsis (which, being interpreted for the uninitiated, is a woman's culture club whose name is made up of the first few letters of the four words wives, mothers, daughters, and sisters) Miss Shaw is president, and a lady from the Blue Grass State *was* secretary.

Pandora's box is opened in the ideal harmony of this modern Eden without an Adam when a colored lady, a teacher in one of our schools, applies for admission to its privileges and opportunities.

The Kentucky secretary, a lady zealous in good works and one who, I can't help imagining, belongs to that estimable class who daily thank the Lord that He made the earth that they may have the job of superintending its rotations, and who really would like to help "elevate" the colored people (in her own way of course and so long as they understand their places) is filled with grief and horror that any persons of Negro extraction should aspire to learn type-writing or languages or to enjoy any other advantages offered in the sacred halls of Wimodaughsis. Indeed, she had not calculated that there were any wives, mothers, daughters, and sisters, except white ones; and she is really convinced that *Whimodaughsis* would sound just as well, and then it need mean just *white mothers, daughters and sisters.* In fact, so far as there is anything in a name, nothing would be lost by omitting for the sake of euphony, from this unique mosaic, the letters that represent wives. *Whiwimodaughsis* might be a little startling, and on the whole wives would better yield to white; since clearly all women are not wives, while surely all wives are daughters. The daughters therefore could represent the wives and this immaculate assembly for propagating liberal and progressive ideas, and disseminating a broad and humanizing culture might be spared the painful possibility of the sight of a black man coming in the future to escort from an evening class this solitary cream-colored applicant. Accordingly the Kentucky secretary took the cream-colored applicant aside, and, with emotions befitting such an epoch-making crisis, told her, "as kindly as she could," that Colored people were not admitted to the classes, at the same time refunding the money which said cream-colored applicant had paid for lessons in type-writing.

When this little incident came to the knowledge of Miss Shaw, she said firmly and emphatically, NO. As a minister of the gospel and as a Christian woman, she could not lend her influence to such unreasonable and uncharitable discrimination; and she must resign the honor of president of Wimodaughsis if persons were to be proscribed solely on account of their color.

To the honor of the board of managers, be it said, they sustained Miss Shaw; and the Kentucky secretary, and those whom she succeeded in inoculating with her prejudices, resigned.

'Twas only a ripple,—some bewailing of lost opportunity on the part of those who could not or would not seize God's opportunity for broadening and enlarging their own souls—and then the work flowed on as before.

Susan B. Anthony and Anna Shaw are evidently too noble to be held in thrall by the provincialisms of women who seem never to have breathed the atmosphere beyond the confines of their grandfathers' plantations. It is only from the broad plateau of light and love that one can see petty prejudice and narrow priggishness in their true perspective; and it is on this high ground, as I sincerely believe, these two grand women stand.

As leaders in the woman's movement of today, they have need of clearness of vision as well as firmness of soul in adjusting recalcitrant forces, and wheeling into line the thousand and one none-such, never-to-be-modified, won't-be-dictated-to banners of their somewhat mottled array.

The black woman and the southern woman, I imagine, often get them into the predicament of the befuddled man who had to take singly across a stream a bag of corn, a fox and a goose. There was no one to help, and to leave the goose with the fox was death—with the corn, destruction. To re-christen the animals, the lion could not be induced to lie down with the lamb unless the lamb would take the inside berth.

The black woman appreciates the situation and can even sympathize with the actors in the serio-comic dilemma.

But, may it not be that, as women, the very lessons which seem hardest to master now are possibly the ones most essential for our promotion to a higher grade of work?

We assume to be leaders of thought and guardians of society. Our country's manners and morals are under our tutoring. Our standards are law in our several little worlds. However tenaciously men may guard some prerogatives, they are our willing slaves in that sphere which they have always conceded to be woman's. Here, no one dares demur when her fiat has gone forth. The man would be mad who presumed, however inexplicable and past finding out any reason for her action might be, to attempt to open a door in her kingdom officially closed and regally sealed by her.

The American woman of to-day not only gives tone directly to her immediate world, but her tiniest pulsation ripples out and out, down and down, till the outermost circles and the deepest layers of society feel the vibrations. It is pre-eminently an age of organizations. The "leading woman," the preacher, the reformer, the organizer "enthuses" her lieutenants and captains, the literary women, the thinking women, the strong, earnest, irresistible women; these in turn touch their myriads of church clubs, social clubs, culture clubs, pleasure clubs and charitable clubs, till the same lecture has been duly administered to every married man in the land (not to speak of sons and brothers) from the President in the White House to the stone-splitter of the ditches. And so woman's lightest whisper is heard as in Dionysius' ear, by quick relays and endless reproductions, through every recess and cavern as well as on every hilltop and mountain in her vast domain. And her mandates are obeyed. When she says "thumbs up," woe to the luckless thumb that falters in its rising. They may be little things, the amenities of life, the little nothings which cost nothing and come to nothing, and yet can make a sentient being so comfortable or so miserable in this life, the oil of social machinery, which we call the courtesies of life, all are under the magic key of woman's permit.

The American woman then is responsible for American manners. Not merely the right ascension and declination of the satellites of her own drawing room; but the rising and the setting of the pestilential or life-giving orbs which seem to wander afar in space, all are governed almost wholly through her magnetic polarity. The atmosphere of street cars and parks and boulevards, of cafes and hotels and steamboats is charged and surcharged with her sentiments and restrictions. Shop girls and serving maids, cashiers and accountant clerks, scribblers and drummers, whether wage earner, salaried toiler, or proprietress, whether laboring to instruct minds, to save souls, to delight fancies, or to win bread—the working women of America in whatever station or sailing they may be found, are subjects, officers, or rulers of a strong centralized government, and bound together by a system of codes and countersigns, which, though unwritten, forms a network of perfect subordination and unquestioning obedience as marvelous as that of the Jesuits. At the head and center in this regime stands the Leading Woman in the principality. The one talismanic word that plays along the wires from palace to cook-shop, from imperial Congress to the distant plain, is *Caste*. With all her vaunted independence, the American woman of to-day is as fearful of losing caste as a Brahmin in India. That is the law under which she lives, the precepts which she binds as frontlets between her eyes and writes on the door-posts of her homes, the lesson which she instils into her children with their first baby breakfasts, the injunction she lays upon husband and lover with direst penalties attached.

The queen of the drawing room is absolute ruler under this law. Her pose gives the cue. The microscopic angle at which her pencilled brows are elevated signifies who may be recognized and who are beyond the pale.

The delicate intimation is, quick as electricity, telegraphed down. Like the wonderful transformation in the House that Jack Built (or regions thereabouts) when the rat began to gnaw the rope, the rope to hang the butcher, the butcher to kill the ox, the ox to drink the water, the water to quench the fire, the fire to burn the stick, the stick to beat the dog, and the dog to worry the cat, and on, and on, and on—when miladi causes the inner arch over her matchless orbs to ascend the merest trifle, *presto!* the Miss at the notions counter grows curt and pert, the dress goods clerk becomes indifferent and taciturn, hotel waiters and ticket dispensers look the other way, the Irish street laborer snarls and scowls, conductors, policemen and park superintendents jostle and push and threaten, and society suddenly seems transformed into a band of organized adders, snapping, and striking and hissing just because they like it on general principles. The tune set by the head singer, sung through all keys and registers, with all qualities of tone—the smooth, flowing, and gentle, the creaking, whizzing, grating, screeching, growling—according to ability, taste, and temperament of the singers. Another application of like master, like man. In this case, like mistress, like nation.

It was the good fortune of the Black Wo[man] of the South to spend some weeks, not long since, in a land over which floated the Union Jack.[47] The Stars and Stripes were not the only familiar experiences missed. A uniform, matter-of-fact courtesy, a genial kindliness, quick perception of opportunities for rendering any little manly assistance, a readiness to give information to strangers—a hospitable, thawing-out atmosphere everywhere—in shops and waiting rooms, on cars and in the streets, actually seemed to her chilled little soul to transform the commonest boor in the service of the public into one of nature's noblemen, and when the old whipped-cur feeling was taken up and analyzed she could hardly tell whether it consisted mostly of self pity for her own wounded sensibilities, or of shame for her country and mortification that her countrymen offered such an unfavorable contrast.

Some American girls, I noticed recently, in search of novelty and adventure, were taking an extended trip through our country unattended by gentleman friends; their wish was to write up for a periodical or lecture the ease and facility, the comfort and safety of American travel, even for the weak and unprotected, under our well-nigh perfect railroad systems and our gentlemanly and efficient corps of officials and public servants. I have some material I could furnish these young ladies, though possibly it might not be just on the side they wish to have illuminated. The Black Woman of the South has to do considerable travelling in this country, often unattended. She thinks she is quiet and unobtrusive in her manner, simple and inconspicuous in her dress, and can see no reason why in any chance assemblage of *ladies*, or even a promiscuous gathering of ordinarily well-bred and dignified individuals, she should be signaled out for any marked consideration. And yet she has seen these same "gentlemanly and efficient" railroad conductors, when their cars had stopped at stations having no raised platforms, making it necessary for passengers to take the long and trying leap from the car step to the ground or step on the narrow little stool placed under by the conductor, after standing at their posts and handing woman after woman from the steps to the stool, thence to the ground, or else relieving her of satchels and bags and enabling her to make the descent easily, deliberately fold their arms and turn round when the Black Woman's turn came to alight—bearing her satchel, and bearing besides another unnamable burden inside the heaving bosom and tightly compressed lips. The feeling of slighted womanhood is unlike every other emotion of the soul. Happily for the human family, it is unknown to many and indescribable to all. Its poignancy, compared with which even Juno's *spretae injuria formae*[48] is earthly and vulgar, is holier than that of jealousy, deeper than indignation, tenderer than rage. Its first impulse of wrathful protest and proud self vindication is checked and shamed by the consciousness that self assertion would outrage still further the same delicate instinct. Were there a brutal attitude of hate or of ferocious attack, the feminine response of fear or repulsion is simple and spontaneous. But when the keen sting comes through the finer sensibilities, from a hand which, by all known traditions and ideals of propriety, should have been trained to reverence and respect them, the condemnation of man's inhumanity to woman is increased and embittered by the knowledge of personal identity with a race of beings so fallen.

I purposely forbear to mention instances of personal violence to colored women travelling in less civilized sections of our country, where women have been forcibly ejected from cars, thrown out of seats, their garments rudely torn, their person wantonly and cruelly injured. America is large and must for some time yet endure its out-of-the-way jungles of barbarism as Africa its uncultivated tracts of marsh and malaria. There are murderers and thieves and villains in both London and Paris. Humanity from the first has had its vultures and sharks, fine representatives of the fraternity who prey upon mankind may be expected no less in America than elsewhere. That this virulence breaks out most readily and commonly against colored persons in this country is due of course to the fact that they are, generally speaking, weak and can be imposed upon with impunity. Bullies are always cowards at heart and may be credited with a pretty safe instinct in scenting their prey. Besides, society, where it has not exactly said to its dogs "s-s-sik him!" has at least engaged to be looking in another direction or studying the rivers on Mars. It is not of the dogs and their doings, but of society holding the leash that I shall speak. It is those subtile [sic] exhalations of atmospheric odors for which woman is accountable, the indefinable, unplaceable aroma which seems to exude from the very pores in her finger tips like the delicate sachet so dexterously hidden and concealed in her linens; the essence of her teaching, guessed rather than read, so adroitly is the lettering and wording manipulated; it is the undertones of the picture laid finely on by woman's own practiced hand, the reflection of the lights and shadows on her own brow; it is, in a word, the reputation of our nation for general politeness and good manners and of our fellow citizens to be somewhat more than cads or snobs that shall engage our present study. There can be no true test of national courtesy without travel. Impressions and conclusions based on provincial traits and characteristics can thus be modified and generalized. Moreover, the weaker and less influential the experimenter, the more exact and scientific the deductions. Courtesy "for revenue only" is not politeness, but diplomacy. Any rough can assume civilty [sic] toward those of "his set," and does not hesitate to carry it even to servility toward those in whom he recognizes a possible patron or his master in power, wealth, rank, or influence. But, as the chemist prefers distilled H_2O in testing solutions to avoid complications and unwarranted reactions, so the Black Woman holds that her femineity [sic] linked with the impossibility of popular affinity or unexpected attraction through position and influence in her case makes her a touchstone of American courtesy exceptionally pure and singularly free from extraneous modifiers. The man who is courteous to her is so, not because of anything he hopes or fears or sees, but because *he is a gentleman.*

I would eliminate also from the discussion all uncharitable reflections upon the orderly execution of laws existing in certain states of this Union, requiring persons known to be colored to ride in one car, and persons supposed to be white in another. A good citizen may use his influence to have existing laws and statutes changed or modified, but a public servant must not be blamed for obeying orders. A railroad conductor is not asked to dictate measures, nor to make and pass laws. His bread and butter are conditioned on his managing his part of the machinery as he is told to do. If, therefore, I found myself in that compartment of a train designated by the sovereign law of the state for presumable Caucasians, and for colored persons only when travelling in the capacity of nurses and maids, should a conductor inform me, as a gentleman might, that I had made a mistake, and offer to show me the proper car for black ladies, I might wonder at the expensive arrangements of the company and of the state in providing special and separate accommodations for the transportation of the various hues of humanity, but I certainly could not take it as a want of courtesy on the conductor's part that he gave the information. It is true, public sentiment precedes and begets all laws, good or bad; and on the ground I have taken, our women are to be credited largely as teachers and moulders of public sentiment. But when a law has passed and received the sanction of the land, there is nothing for our officials to do but enforce it till repealed; and I for one, as a loyal American citizen, will give those officials cheerful support and ready sympathy in the discharge of their duty. But when a great burly six feet of masculinity with sloping shoulders and unkempt beard swaggers in, and, throwing a roll of tobacco into one corner of his jaw, growls out at me over the paper I am reading, "Here gurl," (I am past thirty) "you better git out 'n dis kyar 'f yer don't, I'll put yer out," —my mental annotation is *Here's an American citizen who has been badly trained. He is sadly lacking in both "sweetness" and "light"*; and when in the same section of our enlightened and progressive country, I see from the car window, working on private estates, convicts from the state penitentiary, among them squads of boys from fourteen to eighteen years of age in a chain-gang, their feet chained together and heavy-blocks attached—not in 1850, but in 1890, '91 and '92, I make a note on the flyleaf of my memorandum, *The women in this section should organize a Society for the Prevention of Cruelty to Human Beings, and disseminate civilizing tracts, and send throughout the region apostles of anti-barbarism for the propagation of humane and enlightened ideas.* And when farther on in the same section our train stops at a dilapidated station, rendered yet more unsightly by dozens of loafers with their hands in their pockets while a productive soil and inviting climate beckon in vain to industry; and when, looking a little more closely, I see two dingy little rooms with "FOR LADIES" swinging over one and "FOR COLORED PEOPLE" over the other; while wondering under which head I come, I notice a little way off the only hotel proprietor of the place whittling a pine stick as he sits with one leg thrown across an empty goods box; and as my eye falls on a sample room next door which seems to be driving the only wide-awake and popular business of the commonwealth, I cannot help ejaculating under my breath, "What a field for the missionary woman." I know that if by any fatality I should be obliged to lie over at that station, and, driven by hunger, should be compelled to seek refreshments or the bare necessaries of life at the only public accommodation in the town, that same stick-whittler would coolly inform me, without looking up from his pine splinter, "We doan uccommodate no niggers hyur." And yet we are so scandalized at Russia's barbarity and cruelty to the Jews! We pay a man a thousand dollars a night just to make us weep, by a recital of such heathenish inhumanity as is practiced on Sclavonic [sic] soil.

A recent writer on Eastern nations[49] says: "If we take through the earth's temperate zone, a belt of country whose northern and southern edges are determined by certain limiting isotherms, not more than half the width of the zone apart, we shall find that we have included in a relatively small extent of surface almost all the nations of note in the world, past or present. Now, if we examine this belt and compare the different parts of it with one another, we shall be struck by a remarkable fact. *The peoples inhabiting it grow steadily more personal as we go west.* So unmistakable is this gradation, that one is almost tempted to ascribe it to cosmical rather than to human causes. It is as marked as the change in color of the human complexion observable along any meridian, which ranges from black at the equator to blonde toward the pole. In like manner the sense of self grows more intense as we follow in the wake of the setting sun, and fades steadily as we advance into the dawn. America, Europe, the Levant, India, Japan, each is less personal than the one before.... *That politeness should be one of the most marked results of impersonality* may appear surprising, yet a slight examination will show it to be a fact. Considered *a priori*, the connection is not far to seek. Impersonality by lessening the interest in one's self, induces one to take an interest in others. Looked at *a posteriori*, we find that where the one trait exists the other is most developed, while an absence of the second seems to prevent the full growth of the first. This is true both in general and in detail. *Courtesy increases as we travel eastward round the world, coincidently with a decrease in the sense of self.* Asia is more courteous than Europe, Europe than America. Particular races show the same concomitance of characteristics. France, the most impersonal nation of Europe, is at the same time the most polite." And by inference, Americans, the most personal, are the least courteous nation on the globe.

The Black Woman had reached this same conclusion by an entirely different route; but it is gratifying to vanity, nevertheless, to find one's self sustained by both science and philosophy in a conviction, wrought in by hard experience, and yet too apparently audacious to be entertained even as a stealthy surmise. In fact the Black Woman was emboldened some time since by a well put and timely article from an Editor's Drawer on the "Mannerless Sex,"[50] to give the world the benefit of some of her experience with the "*Mannerless Race*"; but since Mr. Lowell shows so conclusively that the entire Land of the West is a *mannerless continent*, I have determined to plead with our women, the mannerless sex on this mannerless continent, to institute a reform by placing immediately in our national curricula a department for teaching good manners.

Now, am I right in holding the American Woman responsible? Is it true that the exponents of woman's advancement, the leaders in woman's thought, the preachers and teachers of all woman's reforms, can teach this nation to be courteous, to be pitiful, having compassion one of another, not rendering evil for inoffensiveness, and railing in proportion to the improbability of being struck back; but contrariwise, being *all* of one mind, to love as brethren?

I think so.

It may require some heroic measures, and like all revolutions will call for a determined front and a courageous, unwavering, stalwart heart on the part of the leaders of the reform.

The "*all*" will inevitably stick in the throat of the Southern woman. She must be allowed, please, to except the "darkey" from the "all"; it is too bitter a pill with black people in it. You must get the Revised Version to put it, "*love all white people* as brethren." She really could not enter any society on earth, or in heaven above, or in the waters under the earth, on such unpalatable conditions.

The Black Woman has tried to understand the Southern woman's difficulties; to put herself in her place, and to be as fair, as charitable, and as free from prejudice in judging her antipathies, as she would have others in regard to her own. She has honestly weighed the apparently sincere excuse, "But you must remember that these people were once our slaves"; and that other, "But civility towards the Negroes will bring us on *social equality* with them."

These are the two bugbears; or rather, the two humbugbears: for, though each is founded on a most glaring fallacy, one would think they were words to conjure with, so potent and irresistible is their spell as an argument at the North as well as in the South.

One of the most singular facts about the unwritten history of this country is the consummate ability with which Southern influence, Southern ideas and Southern ideals have from the very beginning even up to the present day, dictated to and domineered over the brain and sinew of this nation. Without wealth, without education, without inventions, arts, sciences, or industries, without well-nigh every one of the progressive ideas and impulses which have made this country great, prosperous and happy, personally indolent and practically stupid, poor in everything but bluster and self-esteem, the Southerner has nevertheless with Italian finesse and exquisite skill, uniformly and invariably so manipulated Northern sentiment as to succeed sooner or later in carrying his point and shaping the policy of this government to suit his purposes. Indeed, the Southerner is a magnificent manager of men, a born educator. For two hundred and fifty years he trained to his hand a people whom he made absolutely his own, in body, mind, and sensibility. He so insinuated differences and distinctions among them, that their personal attachment for him was stronger than for their own brethren and fellow sufferers. He made it a crime for two or three of them to be gathered together in Christ's name without a white man's supervision, and a felony for one to teach them to read even the Word of Life; and yet they would defend his interest with their life blood; his smile was their happiness, a pat on the shoulder from him their reward. The slightest difference among themselves in condition, circumstances, opportunities, became barriers of jealousy and disunion. He sowed his blood broadcast among them, then pitted mulatto against black, bond against free, house slave against plantation slave, even the slave of one clan against like slave of another clan; till, wholly oblivious of their ability for mutual succor and defense, all became centers of myriad systems of repellent forces, having but one sentiment in common, and that their entire subjection to that master hand.

And he not only managed the black man, he also hoodwinked the white man, the tourist and investigator who visited his lordly estates. The slaves were doing well, in fact couldn't be happier—plenty to eat, plenty to drink, comfortably housed and clothed—they wouldn't be free if they could; in short, in his broad brimmed plantation hat and easy aristocratic smoking gown, he made you think him a veritable patriarch in the midst of a lazy, well fed, good natured, over-indulged tenantry.

Then, too, the South represented blood—not red blood, but blue blood. The difference is in the length of the stream and your distance from its source. If your own father was a pirate, a robber, a murderer, his hands are dyed in red blood, and you don't say very much about it. But if your great great great grandfather's grandfather stole and pillaged and slew, and you can prove it, your blood has become blue and you are at great pains to establish the relationship. So the South had neither silver nor gold, but she had blood; and she paraded it with so much gusto that the substantial little Puritan maidens of the North, who had been making bread and canning currants and not thinking of blood the least bit, began to hunt up the records of the Mayflower to see if some of the passengers thereon could not claim the honor of having been one of William the Conqueror's brigands, when he killed the last of the Saxon kings and, red-handed, stole his crown and his lands. Thus the ideal from out the Southland brooded over the nation and we sing less lustily than of yore

"Kind hearts are more than coronets
And simple faith than Norman blood."[51]

In politics, the two great forces, commerce and empire, which would otherwise have shaped the destiny of the country, have been made to pander and cater to Southern notions. "Cotton is King" meant the South must be allowed to dictate or there would be no fun. Every statesman from 1830 to 1860 exhausted his genius in persuasion and compromises to smooth out her ruffled temper and gratify her petulant demands. But like a sullen younger sister, the South has pouted and sulked and cried: "I won't play with you now; so there!" and the big brother at the North has coaxed and compromised and given in, and—ended by letting her have her way. Until 1860 she had as her pet an institution which it was death by the law to say anything about, except that it was divinely instituted, inaugurated by Noah, sanctioned by Abraham, approved by Paul, and just ideally perfect in every way. And when, to preserve the autonomy of the family arrangements, in '61, '62 and '63, it became necessary for the big brother to administer a little wholesome correction and set the obstreperous Miss vigorously down in her seat again, she assumed such an air of injured innocence, and melted away so lugubriously, the big brother has done nothing since but try to sweeten and pacify and laugh her back into a companionable frame of mind.

Father Lincoln did all he could to get her to repent of her petulance and behave herself. He even promised she might keep her pet, so disagreeable to all the neighbors and hurtful even to herself, and might manage it at home to suit herself, if she would only listen to reason and be just tolerably nice. But, no—she was going to leave and set up for herself; she didn't propose to be meddled with; and so, of course, she had to be spanked. Just a little at first—didn't mean to hurt, merely to teach her who was who. But she grew so ugly, and kicked and fought and scratched so outrageously, and seemed so determined to smash up the whole business, the head of the family got red in the face, and said: "Well, now, he couldn't have any more of that foolishness. Arabella must just behave herself or take the consequences." And after the spanking, Arabella sniffed and whimpered and pouted, and the big brother bit his lip, looked half ashamed, and said: "Well, I didn't want to hurt you. You needn't feel so awfully bad about it, I only did it for your good. You know I wouldn't do anything to displease you if I could help it; but you would insist on making the row, and so I just had to. Now, there—there—let's be friends!" and he put his great strong arms about her and just dared anybody to refer to that little unpleasantness—he'd show them a thing or two. Still Arabella sulked—till the rest of the family decided she might just keep her pets, and manage her own affairs and nobody should interfere.

So now, if one intimates that some clauses of the Constitution are a dead letter at the South and that only the name and support of that pet institution are changed while the fact and essence, minus the expense and responsibility, remain, he is quickly told to mind his own business and informed that he is waving the bloody shirt.

Even twenty-five years after the fourteenth and fifteenth amendments to our Constitution, a man who has been most unequivocal in his outspoken condemnation of the wrongs regularly and systematically heaped on the oppressed race in this country, and on all even most remotely connected with them—a man whom we had thought our staunchest friend and most noble champion and defender—after a two weeks' trip in Georgia and Florida immediately gives signs of the fatal inception of the virus. Not even the chance traveller from England or Scotland escapes. The arch-manipulator takes him under his special watch-care and training, uses up his stock arguments and gives object lessons with his choicest specimens of Negro depravity and worthlessness; takes him through what, in New York, would be called "the slums," and would predicate there nothing but the duty of enlightened Christians to send out their light and emulate their Master's aggressive labors of love; but in Georgia is denominated "our terrible problem, which people of the North so little understand, yet vouchsafe so much gratuitous advice about." With an injured air he shows the stupendous and atrocious mistake of reasoning about these people as if they were just ordinary human beings, and amenable to the tenets of the Gospel; and not long after the inoculation begins to work, you hear this old-time friend of the oppressed delivering himself something after this fashion:"Ah, well, the South must be left to manage the Negro. She is most directly concerned and must understand her problem better than outsiders. We must not meddle. We must be very careful not to widen the breaches. The Negro is not worth a feud between brothers and sisters."

Lately a great national and international movement characteristic of this age and country, a movement based on the inherent right of every soul to its own highest development, I mean the movement making for Woman's full, free, and complete emancipation, has, after much courting, obtained the gracious smile of the Southern woman—I beg her pardon—the Southern *lady*.

She represents blood, and of course could not be expected to leave that out; and firstly and foremostly she must not, in any organization she may deign to grace with her presence, be asked to associate with "these people who were once her slaves."

Now the Southern woman (I may be pardoned, being one myself) was never renowned for her reasoning powers, and it is not surprising that just a little picking will make her logic fall to pieces even here.

In the first place she imagines that because her grandfather had slaves who were black, all the blacks in the world of every shade and tint were once in the position of her slaves. This is as bad as the Irishman who was about to kill a peaceable Jew in the streets of Cork, having just learned that Jews slew his Redeemer. The black race constitutes one-seventh the known population of the globe; and there are representatives of it here as elsewhere who were never in bondage at any time to any man—whose blood is as blue and lineage as noble as any, even that of the white lady of the South. That her slaves were black and she despises her slaves, should no more argue antipathy to all dark people and peoples, than that Guiteau,[52] an assassin, was white, and I hate assassins, should make me hate all persons more or less white. The objection shows a want of clear discrimination.

The second fallacy in the objection grows out of the use of an ambiguous middle, as the logicians would call it, or assigning a double signification to the term "*Social equality.*"

Civility to the Negro implies social equality. I am opposed to *associating* with dark persons on terms of social equality. Therefore, I abrogate civility to the Negro. This is like

Light is opposed to darkness.
Feathers are light.
Ergo, Feathers are opposed to darkness.

The "social equality" implied by civility to the Negro is a very different thing from forced association with him socially. Indeed it seems to me that the mere application of a little cold common sense would show that uncongenial social environments could by no means be forced on any one. I do not, and cannot be made to associate with all dark persons, simply on the ground that I am dark; and I presume the Southern lady can imagine some whose faces are white, with whom she would no sooner think of chatting unreservedly than, were it possible, with a veritable "darkey." Such things must and will always be left to individual election. No law, human or divine, can legislate for or against them. Like seeks like; and I am sure with the Southern lady's antipathies at their present temperature, she might enter ten thousand organizations besprinkled with colored women without being any more deflected by them than by the proximity of a stone. The social equality scare then is all humbug, conscious or unconscious, I know not which. And were it not too bitter a thought to utter here, I might add that the overtures for forced association in the past history of these two races were not made by the manacled black man, nor by *the silent and suffering black woman!*

When I seek food in a public cafe or apply for first-class accommodations on a railway train, I do so because my physical necessities are identi-

cal with those of other human beings of like constitution and temperament, and crave satisfaction. I go because I want food, or I want comfort—
not because I want association with those who frequent these places; and I
can see no more "social equality" in buying lunch at the same restaurant,
or riding in a common car, than there is in paying for dry goods at the
same counter or walking on the same street.

The social equality which means forced or unbidden association would
be as much deprecated and as strenuously opposed by the circle in which
I move as by the most hide-bound Southerner in the land. Indeed I have
been more than once annoyed by the inquisitive white interviewer, who,
with spectacles on nose and pencil and note-book in hand, comes to get
some "points" about "*your people*." My "people" are just like other people—
indeed, too like for their own good. They hate, they love, they attract and
repel, they climb or they grovel, struggle or drift, aspire or despair, endure
in hope or curse in vexation, exactly like all the rest of unregenerate humanity. Their likes and dislikes are as strong; their antipathies—and prejudices too I fear, are as pronounced as you will find anywhere; and the
entrance to the inner sanctuary of their homes and hearts is as jealously
guarded against profane intrusion.

What the dark man wants then is merely to live his own life, in his own
world, with his own chosen companions, in whatever of comfort, luxury,
or emoluments his talent or his money can in an impartial market secure.
Has he wealth, he does not want to be forced into inconvenient or unsanitary sections of cities to buy a home and rear his family. Has he art, he does
not want to be cabined and cribbed into emulation with the few who
merely happen to have his complexion. His talent aspires to study without
proscription the masters of all ages and to rub against the broadest and
fullest movements of his own day.

Has he religion, he does not want to be made to feel that there is a white
Christ and a black Christ, a white Heaven and a black Heaven, a white
Gospel and a black Gospel—but the one ideal of perfect manhood and
womanhood, the one universal longing for development and growth, the
one desire for being, and being better, the one great yearning, aspiring, out-
reaching, in all the heart throbs of humanity in whatever race or clime.

A recent episode in the Corcoran art gallery at the American capital is
to the point. A colored woman who had shown marked ability in drawing
and coloring was advised by her teacher, himself an artist of no mean rank,
to apply for admission to the Corcoran school in order to study the mod-
els and to secure other advantages connected with the organization. She
accordingly sent a written application accompanied by specimens of her
drawings, the usual *modus operandi* in securing admission.

The drawings were examined by the best critics and pronounced excellent, and a ticket of admission was immediately issued together with a highly complimentary reference to her work.

The next day my friend, congratulating her country and herself that at least in the republic of art no caste existed, presented her ticket of admission *in propria persona*. There was a little preliminary side play in Delsarte pantomine[53]—aghast—incredulity—wonder; then the superintendent told her in plain unartistic English that of course he had not dreamed a colored person could do such work, and had he suspected the truth he would never have issued the ticket of admission; that, to be right frank, the ticket would have to he cancelled—she could under no condition be admitted to the studio.

Can it be possible that even art in America is to be tainted by this shrivelling caste spirit? If so, what are we coming to? Can any one conceive a Shakespeare, a Michael Angelo, or a Beethoven putting away any fact of simple merit because the thought, or the suggestion, or the creation emanated from a soul with an unpleasing exterior?

What is it that makes the great English bard pre-eminent as the photographer of the human soul? Where did he learn the universal language, so that Parthians, Medes and Elamites, and the dwellers in Mesopotamia, in Egypt and Libya, in Crete and Arabia do hear every one in our own tongue the wonderful revelations of this myriad mind? How did he learn our language? Is it not that his own soul was infinitely receptive to Nature, the dear old nurse, in all her protean forms? Did he not catch and reveal her own secret by his sympathetic listening as she "would constantly sing a more wonderful song or tell a more marvellous tale" in the souls he met around him?

"Stand off! I am better than thou!" has never yet painted a true picture, nor written a thrilling song, nor given a pulsing, a soul-burning sermon. 'Tis only sympathy, another name for love—that one poor word which, as George Eliot says, "expresses so much of human insight"—that can interpret either man or matter.

It was Shakespeare's own all-embracing sympathy, that infinite receptivity of his, and native, all-comprehending appreciation, which proved a key to unlock and open every soul that came within his radius. And *he received as much as he gave*. His own stores were infinitely enriched thereby. For it is decreed

Man like the vine supported lives,
The strength he gains is from th' embrace he gives.

It is only through clearing the eyes from bias and prejudice, and becoming one with the great all pervading soul of the universe that either art or science can

332

"Read what is still unread
In the manuscripts of God."[54]

No true artist can allow himself to be narrowed and provincialized by deliberately shutting out any class of facts or subjects through prejudice against externals. And American art, American science, American literature can never be founded in truth, the universal beauty; can never learn to speak a language intelligible in all climes and for all ages, till this paralyzing grip of caste prejudice is loosened from its vitals, and the healthy sympathetic eye is taught to look out on the great universe as holding no favorites and no black beasts, but bearing in each plainest or loveliest feature the handwriting of its God.

And this is why, as it appears to me, woman in her lately acquired vantage ground for speaking an earnest helpful word, can do this country no deeper and truer and more lasting good than by bending all her energies to thus broadening, humanizing, and civilizing her native land.

"Except ye become as little children"[55] is not a pious precept, but an inexorable law of the universe. God's kingdoms are all sealed to the seedy, moss-grown mind of self-satisfied maturity. Only the little child in spirit, the simple, receptive, educable mind can enter. Preconceived notions, blinding prejudices, and shrivelling antipathies must be wiped out, and the cultivable soul made a *tabula rasa* for whatever lesson great Nature has to teach.

This, too, is why I conceive the subject to have been unfortunately worded which was chosen by Miss Shaw at the Woman's Council and which stands at the head of this chapter.

Miss Shaw is one of the most powerful of our leaders, and we feel her voice should give no uncertain note. Woman should not, even by inference, or for the sake of argument, seem to disparage what is weak. For woman's cause is the cause of the weak; and when all the weak shall have received their due consideration, then woman will have her "rights," and the Indian will have his rights, and the Negro will have his rights, and all the strong will have learned at last to deal justly, to love mercy, and to walk humbly; and our fair land will have been taught the secret of universal courtesy which is after all nothing but the art, the science, and the religion of regarding one's neighbor as one's self, and to do for him as we would, were conditions swapped, that he do for us.

It cannot seem less than a blunder, whenever the exponents of a great reform or the harbingers of a noble advance in thought and effort allow themselves to seem distorted by a narrow view of their own aims and principles. All prejudices, whether of race, sect or sex, class pride and caste distinctions are the belittling inheritance and badge of snobs and prigs.

The philosophic mind sees that its own "rights" are the rights of humanity. That in the universe of God nothing trivial is or mean; and the recognition it seeks is not through the robber and wild beast adjustment of the survival of the bullies but through the universal application ultimately of the Golden Rule.

Not unfrequently has it happened that the impetus of a mighty thought wave has done the execution meant by its Creator in spite of the weak and distorted perception of its human embodiment. It is not strange if reformers, who, after all, but think God's thoughts after him, have often "builded more wisely than they knew"; and while fighting consciously for only a narrow gateway for themselves, have been driven forward by that irresistible "Power not ourselves which makes for righteousness" to open a high road for humanity. It was so with our sixteenth-century reformers. The fathers of the Reformation had no idea that they were inciting an insurrection of the human mind against all domination. None would have been more shocked than they at our nineteenth-century deductions from their sixteenth-century premises. Emancipation of mind and freedom of thought would have been as appalling to them as it was distasteful to the pope. They were right, they argued, to rebel against Romish absolutism — because Romish preaching and Romish practicing were wrong. They denounced popes for hacking heretics and forthwith began themselves to roast witches. The Spanish Inquisition in the hands of Philip and Alva was an institution of the devil; wielded by the faithful, it would become quite another thing. The only "rights" they were broad enough consciously to fight for was the right to substitute the absolutism of their conceptions, their party, their *"ism"* for an authority whose teaching they conceived to be corrupt and vicious. Persecution for a belief was wrong only when the persecutors were wrong and the persecuted right. The sacred prerogative of the individual to decide on matters of belief they did not dream of maintaining. Universal tolerance and its twin, universal charity, were not conceived yet. The broad foundation stone of all human rights, the great democratic principle "A man's a man, *and his own sovereign* for a' that" they did not dare enunciate. They were incapable of drawing up a Declaration of Independence for humanity. The Reformation to the Reformers meant one bundle of authoritative opinions vs. another bundle of authoritative opinions. Justification by faith vs. justification by ritual. Submission to Calvin vs. submission to the Pope. English and Germans vs. the Italians.

To our eye, viewed through a vista of three centuries, it was the death wrestle of the principle of thought enslavement in the throttling grasp of personal freedom; it was the great Emancipation Day of human belief, man's intellectual Independence Day, prefiguring and finally compelling the world-wide enfranchisement of his body and all its activities. Not Protestant vs. Catholic, then; not Luther vs. Leo, not Dominicans vs. Augustinians, nor Geneva vs. Rome—but humanity rationally free, vs. the clamps of tradition and superstition which had manacled and muzzled it.

The cause of freedom is not the cause of a race or a sect, a party or a class—it is the cause of human kind, the very birthright of humanity. Now unless we are greatly mistaken the Reform of our day, known as the Woman's Movement, is essentially such an embodiment, if its pioneers could only realize it, of the universal good. And specially important is it that there be no confusion of ideas among its leaders as to its scope and universality. All mists must be cleared from the eyes of woman if she is to be a teacher of morals and manners: the former strikes its roots in the individual and its training and pruning may be accomplished by classes; but the latter is to lubricate the joints and minimize the friction of society, and it is important and fundamental that there be no chromatic or other aberration when the teacher is settling the point, "Who is my neighbor?"

It is not the intelligent woman vs. the ignorant woman; nor the white woman vs. the black, the brown, and the red—it is not even the cause of woman vs. man. Nay, 'tis woman's strongest vindication for speaking that *the world needs to hear her voice.* It would be subversive of every human interest that the cry of one-half the human family be stifled. Woman in stepping from the pedestal of statue-like inactivity in the domestic shrine, and daring to think and move and speak—to undertake to help shape, mold, and, direct the thought of her age, is merely completing the circle of the world's vision. Hers is every interest that has lacked an interpreter and a defender. Her cause is linked with that of every agony that has been dumb—every wrong that needs a voice.

It is no fault of man's that he has not been able to see truth from her standpoint. It does credit both to his head and heart that no greater mistakes have been committed or even wrongs perpetrated while she sat making tatting and snipping paper flowers. Man's own innate chivalry and the mutual interdependence of their interests have insured his treating her cause, in the main at least, as his own. And he is pardonably surprised and even a little chagrined, perhaps, to find his legislation not considered "perfectly lovely" in every respect. But in any case his work is only impoverished by her remaining dumb. The world has had to limp along with the wobbling gait and one-sided hesitancy of a man with one eye. Suddenly the bandage is removed from the other eye and the whole body is filled with light. It sees a circle where before it saw a segment. The darkened eye restored, every member rejoices with it.

What a travesty of its case for this eye to become plaintiff in a suit, *Eye vs. Foot.* "There is that dull clod, the foot, allowed to roam at will, free and untrammelled; while I, the source and medium of light, brilliant and beautiful, am fettered in darkness and doomed to desuetude." The great burly black man, ignorant and gross and depraved, is allowed to vote; while the franchise is withheld from the intelligent and refined, the pure-minded and lofty souled white woman. Even the untamed and untamable Indian of the prairie, who can answer nothing but "ugh" to great economic and civic questions is thought by some worthy to wield the ballot which is still denied the Puritan maid and the first lady of Virginia.

Is not this hitching our wagon to something much lower than a star? Is not woman's cause broader, and deeper, and grander, than a blue stocking debate or an aristocratic pink tea? Why should woman become plaintiff in a suit versus the Indian, or the Negro or any other race or class who have been crushed under the iron heel of Anglo-Saxon power and selfishness? If the Indian has [been] wronged and cheated by the puissance of this American government, it is woman's mission to plead with her country to cease to do evil and to pay its honest debts. If the Negro has been deceit-fully cajoled or inhumanly cuffed according to selfish expediency or capricious antipathy, let it be woman's mission to plead that he be met as a man and honestly given half the road. If woman's own happiness has been ignored or misunderstood in our country's legislating for bread winners, for rum sellers, for property holders, for the family relations, for any or all the interests that touch her vitally, let her rest her plea, not on Indian inferiority, nor on Negro depravity, but on the obligation of legislators to do for her as they would have others do for them were relations reversed. Let her try to teach her country that every interest in this world is entitled at least to a respectful hearing, that every sentiency is worthy of its own gratification, that a helpless cause should not be trampled down, nor a bruised reed broken; and when the right of the individual is made sacred, when the image of God in human form, whether in marble or in clay, whether in alabaster or in ebony, is consecrated and inviolable, when men have been taught to look beneath the rags and grime, the pomp and pageantry of mere circumstance and have regard unto the celestial kernel uncontaminated at the core—when race, color, sex, condition, are realized to be the accidents, not the substance of life, and consequently as not obscuring or modifying the inalienable title to life, liberty, and pursuit of happiness—then is mastered the science of politeness, the art of courteous contact, which is naught but the practical application of the principle of benevolence, the back bone and marrow of all religion; then woman's lesson is taught and woman's cause is won—not the white woman nor the black woman nor the red woman, but the cause of every man or woman who has writhed silently under a mighty wrong. The pleading of the American woman for the right and the opportunity to employ the American method of influencing the disposal to be made of herself, her property, her children in civil, economic, or domestic relations is thus seen to be based on a principle as broad as the human race and as old as human society. Her wrongs are thus indissolubly linked with all undefended woe, all helpless suffering, and the plenitude of her "rights" will mean the final triumph of all right over might, the supremacy of the moral forces of reason and justice and love in the government of the nation.

God hasten the day.

Frances Ellen Watkins Harper, "Woman's Political Future." In *The World's Congress of Representative Women*, ed. May Wright Sewall. Chicago: Rand, McNally and Co., 1894. 433-38

If before sin had cast its deepest shadows or sorrow had distilled its bitterest tears, it was true that it was not good for man to be alone, it is no less true, since the shadows have deepened and life's sorrows have increased, that the world has need of all the spiritual aid that woman can give for the social advancement and moral development of the human race. The tendency of the present age, with its restlessness, religious upheavals, failures, blunders, and crimes, is toward broader freedom, an increase of knowledge, the emancipation of thought, and a recognition of the brotherhood of man; in this movement woman, as the companion of man, must be a sharer. So close is the bond between man and woman that you can not raise one without lifting the other. The world can not move without woman's sharing in the movement, and to help give a right impetus to that movement is woman's highest privilege.

If the fifteenth century discovered America to the Old World, the nineteenth is discovering woman to herself. Little did Columbus imagine, when the New World broke upon his vision like a lovely gem in the coronet of the universe, the glorious possibilities of a land where the sun should be our engraver, the winged lightning our messenger, and steam our beast of burden. But as mind is more than matter, and the highest ideal always the true real, so to woman comes the opportunity to strive for richer and grander discoveries than ever gladdened the eye of the Genoese mariner.

Not the opportunity of discovering new worlds, but that of filling this old world with fairer and higher aims than the greed of gold and the lust of power, is hers. Through weary, wasting years men have destroyed, dashed in pieces, and overthrown, but to-day we stand on the threshold of woman's era, and woman's work is grandly constructive. In her hand are possibilities whose use or abuse must tell upon the political life of the nation, and send their influence for good or evil across the track of unborn ages.

As the saffron tints and crimson flushes of morn herald the coming day, so the social and political advancement which woman has already gained bears the promise of the rising of the full-orbed sun of emancipation. The result will be not to make home less happy, but society more holy; yet I do not think the mere extension of the ballot a panacea for all the ills of our national life. What we need today is not simply more voters, but better voters. To-day there are red-handed men in our republic, who walk unwhipped of justice, who richly deserve to exchange the ballot of the freeman for the wristlets of the felon; brutal and cowardly men, who torture, burn, and lynch their fellow-men, men whose defenselessness should be their best defense and their weakness an ensign of protection. More than the changing of institutions we need the development of a national conscience, and the upbuilding of national character. Men may boast of the aristocracy of blood, may glory in the aristocracy of talent, and be proud of the aristocracy of wealth, but there is one aristocracy which must ever outrank them all, and that is the aristocracy of character; and it is the women of a country who help to mold its character, and to influence if not determine its destiny; and in the political future of our nation woman will not have done what she could if she does not endeavor to have our republic stand foremost among the nations of the earth, wearing sobriety as a crown and righteousness as a garment and a girdle. In coming into her political estate woman will find a mass of illiteracy to be dispelled. If knowledge is power, ignorance is also power. The power that educates wickedness may manipulate and dash against the pillars of any state when they are undermined and honeycombed by injustice.

I envy neither the heart nor the head of any legislator who has been born to an inheritance of privileges, who has behind him ages of education, dominion, civilization, and Christianity, if he stands opposed to the passage of a national education bill, whose purpose is to secure education to the children of those who were born under the shadow of institutions which made it a crime to read.

To-day women hold in their hands influence and opportunity, and with these they have already opened doors which have been closed to others. By opening doors of labor woman has become a rival claimant for at least some of the wealth monopolized by her stronger brother. In the home she is the priestess, in society the queen, in literature she is a power, in legislative halls law-makers have responded to her appeals, and for her sake have humanized and liberalized their laws. The press has felt the impress of her hand. In the pews of the church she constitutes the majority; the pulpit has welcomed her, and in the school she has the blessed privilege of teaching children and youth. To her is apparently coming the added responsibility of political power; and what she now possesses should only be the means of preparing her to use the coming power for the glory of God and the good of mankind; for power without righteousness is one of the most dangerous forces in the world.

Political life in our country has plowed in muddy channels, and needs the infusion of clearer and cleaner waters, I am not sure that women are naturally so much better than men that they will clear the stream by the virtue of their womanhood; it is not through sex but through character that the best influence of women upon the life of the nation must be exerted.

I do not believe in unrestricted and universal suffrage for either men or women. I believe in moral and educational tests. I do not believe that the most ignorant and brutal man is better prepared to add value to the strength and durability of the government than the most cultured, upright, and intelligent woman. I do not think that willful ignorance should swamp earnest intelligence at the ballot-box, nor that educated wickedness, violence, and fraud should cancel the votes of honest men. The unsteady hands of a drunkard can not cast the ballot of a freeman. The hands of lynchers are too red with blood to determine the political character of the government for even four short years. The ballot in the hands of woman means power added to influence. How well she will use that power I can not foretell. Great evils stare us in the face that need to be throttled by the combined power of an upright manhood and an enlightened womanhood; and I know that no nation can gain its full measure of enlightenment and happiness if one-half of it is free and the other half is fettered. China compressed the feet of her women and thereby retarded the steps of her men. The elements of a nation's weakness must ever be found at the hearthstone.

More than the increase of wealth, the power of armies, and the strength of fleets is the need of good homes, of good fathers, and good mothers.

The life of a Roman citizen was in danger in ancient Palestine, and men had bound themselves with a vow that they would eat nothing until they had killed the Apostle Paul. Pagan Rome threw around that imperiled life a bulwark of living clay consisting of four hundred and seventy human hearts, and Paul was saved. Surely the life of the humblest American citizen should be as well protected in America as that of a Roman citizen was in heathen Rome. A wrong done to the weak should be an insult to the strong. Woman coming into her kingdom will find enthroned three great evils, for whose overthrow she should be as strong in a love of justice and humanity as the warrior is in his might. She will find intemperance sending its flood of shame, and death, and sorrow to the homes of men, a fretting lep-rosy in our politics, and a blighting curse in our social life; the social evil sending to our streets women whose laughter is sadder than their tears, who slide from the paths of sin and shame to the friendly shelter of the grave; and lawlessness enacting in our republic deeds over which angels might weep, if heaven knows sympathy.

How can any woman send petitions to Russia against the horrors of Siberian prisons if, ages after the Inquisition has ceased to devise its tor-tures, she has not done all she could by influence, tongue, and pen to keep men from making bonfires of the bodies of real or supposed criminals?

O women of America! into your hands God has pressed one of the sub-limest opportunities that ever came into the hands of the women of any race or people. It is yours to create a healthy public sentiment; to demand justice, simple justice, as the right of every race; to brand with everlasting infamy the lawless and brutal cowardice that lynches, burns, and tortures your own countrymen.

To grapple with the evils which threaten to undermine the strength of the nation and to lay magazines of powder under the cribs of future gen-erations is no child's play.

Let the hearts of the women of the world respond to the song of the her-ald angels of peace on earth and good will to men. Let them throb as one heart unified by the grand and holy purpose of uplifting the human race, and humanity will breathe freer, and the world grow brighter. With such a purpose Eden would spring up in our path, and Paradise be around our way.

Adella Hunt Logan, "Woman Suffrage." *The Colored American Magazine* (September 1905): 487–89

After more than thirty years of trial some statesmen, real and pseudo, have concluded that the Fourteenth Amendment to the National Constitution was a mistake. It is not the purpose of this brief paper to discuss that opin-ion nor to pass judgment on the validity or wisdom of any of the new state constitutions which have in their own ways restricted manhood suffrage. It is the purpose of this article to direct thought to the justice and desirabil-ity of placing the ballot in the hands of the other half of the American peo-ple, their women citizens. Government of the people, for the people and by the people is but partially realized so long as woman has no vote.

"All persons born or naturalized in the United States and subject to the jurisdiction thereof, are citizens of the United States and of the states in which they reside." In the ordinary affairs of life women are regarded as persons. Why not treat them as such in questions of government? No, they are classed with minors, idiots and paupers.

It is a good plan to read the Declaration of Independence and the National Constitution at least once a year. It is helpful to one's political thought and strengthening to one's patriotism. In the Declaration of Independence we read "All governments derive their just powers from the consent of the governed. Taxation without representation is tyranny." Men generally still accept these teachings as fundamental principles of republican government. Do they in practice live out such theories? Not all of them. Let a woman violate the law, her sex in no measure annuls the law's grip on her or stays the sentence of punishment for her crime. She is punished by man-made laws. She is governed by laws to which her consent has not been asked, much less given. The doctrine is not wrong; the classification is correct. Woman is a governed being. It must be there is abuse of the doctrine, "All governments derive their just powers from the consent of the governed." The power that coerces, that controls without consent, is unjust. Such is the status of most American women. "Taxation without representation is tyranny," is a principle sufficiently strong to have called into being one of the most powerful nations on the globe. In the cool light of justice, as they then viewed it, the oppression of taxation without representation justified the Revolutionary War and its outcome was welcomed by liberty-loving men the world over. Strange to say, it seems exceedingly difficult for this liberty-loving people to apply their love of fair play to women.

Women are assessed and required by male officers to appear and pay their taxes, but when any question of appropriation of tax monies comes to a vote, they are told in most places by these same officers and other good men, that it is immodest for women to be seen in public places and bent on helping to run the government. Every man who thinks knows that every woman who thinks just a little sees through this screen to her modesty.

In Colorado, Wyoming, Idaho and Utah women have for years had full suffrage, and none of the evils that the hysterical anti-suffragists predict have come upon those vigorous Western commonwealths. On the contrary, their schools are better, their prisons less full, and civic affairs generally are in a more satisfactory condition than in many of those states where the women have no vote.

Judge Beu Lindsey of the Denver Juvenile Court says that Colorado has the best laws for the protection of women, children and the home, of any state in the Union; and that in his opinion this is due to woman suffrage.

In many other states women have exercised partial suffrage for years, and there are few or no such states or municipalities in which there have been any backward steps taken. The school vote and the saloon vote have been immensely bettered by reason of enfranchising women on these two issues.

It is claimed by some that women do not want to vote. Many do not. A great many do. The elective franchise has not been made compulsory for men, neither should it be for women. Now, because some men do not want to vote—and some do not—should all men be deprived of the right? It is further charged that women do not know civics and are not interested in politics. The charge is measurably true, and small wonder. Create a demand for this kind of knowledge and woman will speedily qualify. The book-sellers of Denver say they sold more books on government in six months after woman suffrage was introduced than in ten years before.

The fear is expressed by the sympathetic opponents that should woman go forth to vote the baby would be neglected. It would be taken care of by the same one who cares for it while she goes out to earn a dollar or to visit a friend, or to rescue a drunkard's neglected child, or to mail a letter, or even sallies forth in a public office or to pay her taxes.

They tell us, too, that the Australian system of voting is complicated. A few women once mastered as difficult problems! Again, it is claimed that women do not need the ballot, as they are represented by their husbands. How about those women who have no husbands? What of those whose views and lives are so different from their husbands'?

In some states the law allows a man to spend as he pleases the money his wife brings to him as a bride, the money he earns—if he earns any—the money she earns, if any. Should he choose to spend all on wine and women —and they sometimes choose to spend all—the wife has no redress before the law. This same husband may go to the polling booth and vote for open saloons and the licensed brothel. And thus he represents his wife! She meanwhile stays at home to cry, to swear or to suicide—as she chooses— or more probably to earn more money for her liege lord who represents her. The native born Chinaman can vote in California but the late Mrs. Stanford could not. She might direct the great university and her heathen servant might direct the government behind the great founder of the university. Oh, the accident of sex! One humiliating feature of the case[:] the right of suffrage is withheld from women largely by ignorant and vicious men. A large proportion of educated men are ardently in favor of the reform, albeit not all find it expedient to express their sentiments.

England and her provinces have gained greatly by the limited or full suffrage for women that obtains almost everywhere in His Majesty's dominions. The United States has liberalized greatly in these matters, and the time is probably not distant when Charles Sumner's[56] prediction will come to pass. More than a quarter of a century ago Sumner said, "In the progress of civilization woman suffrage is sure to come." And come it has in part, and it will doubtless come more fully with the evolution of the higher civic life on which the United States is now well entered.

If white American women, with all their natural and acquired advantages, need the ballot, that right protective of all other rights; if Anglo Saxons have been helped by it—and they have—how much more do black Americans, male and female, need the strong defense of a vote to help secure their right to life, liberty and the pursuit of happiness? And neither do the colored citizens of the Republic lag behind in the fundamental duties of tax-paying and using the elective franchise. The price of their freedom, as far as that freedom has progressed, was too dear a price to be treated lightly. Every morsel of political right and duty should be cherished; and in the opinions of many wise and eminent men, as well as women, these privileges and duties should be extended even to women. Susan B. Anthony stands to-day easily among the foremost ranks of the world's greatest women and men. Her message to civilization has been a beautiful plea for political justice to the weaker members of the human family, whether the black man or all women.

Many objections growing out of prejudice are given to woman's enfranchisement, but reasons against it are few. It is in process of evolution, and when worked out to its logical conclusion the world will wonder why it came so tardily.

Lord Blackstone said: "The elements of sovereignty are three—wisdom, goodness, power."[57] In the United States of America the greatest power is exercised at the polls. Does the reader know any woman, any colored woman, who measures up to Blackstone's test for sovereignty? The writer knows women, some colored women, who claim and crave the sovereignty of full citizenship.

Mary Church Terrell, "Woman Suffrage and the 15th Amendment." *Votes for Women Issue. The Crisis* 10.4 (August 1915): 191

Even if I believed that women should be denied the right of suffrage, wild horses could not drag such an admission from my pen or my lips, for this reason: precisely the same arguments used to prove that the ballot be withheld from women are advanced to prove that colored men should not be allowed to vote. The reasons for repealing the Fifteenth Amendment differ but little from the arguments advanced by those who oppose the enfranchisement of women. Consequently, nothing could be more inconsistent than that colored people should use their influence against granting the ballot to women, if they believe that colored men should enjoy this right which citizenship confers.

What could be more absurd and ridiculous than that one group of individuals who are trying to throw off the yoke of oppression themselves, so as to get relief from conditions which handicap and injure them, should favor laws and customs which impede the progress of another unfortunate group and hinder them in every conceivable way. For the sake of consistency, therefore, if my sense of justice were not developed at all, and I could not reason intelligently, as a colored woman I should not tell my dearest friend that I opposed woman suffrage.

But how can any one who is able to use reason, and who believes in dealing out justice to all God's creatures, think it is right to withhold from one-half the human race rights and privileges freely accorded to the other half, which is neither more deserving nor more capable of exercising them?

For two thousand years mankind has been breaking down the various barriers which interposed themselves between human beings and their perfect freedom to exercise all the faculties with which they were divinely endowed. Even in monarchies old fetters which formerly restricted freedom, dwarfed the intellect and doomed certain individuals to narrow circumscribed spheres, because of the mere accident of birth, are being loosed and broken one by one. In view of such wisdom and experience the political subjection of women in the United States can be likened only to a relic of barbarism, or to a spot upon the sun, or to an octopus holding this republic in its hideous grasp, so that further progress to the best form of government is impossible and that precious ideal its founders promised it would be it seems nothing more tangible than a mirage.

TEMPERANCE

Frances Ellen Watkins Harper, "The Woman's Christian Temperance Union and the Colored Woman." *AME Church Review* 12 (1888): 313–16

A woman sat beneath the shadow of her home, while the dark waves of intemperance dashed against human hearts and hearthstones, but there came an hour when she found that she could *do* something else besides wring her hands and weep over the ravages of the liquor traffic, which had darkened so many lives and desolated so many homes. Where the enemy spreads his snares for the feet of the unwary, inexperienced and tempted, she, too, could go and strive to stay the tide of ruin which was sending its floods of sorrow, shame and death to the habitations of men, and 1873 witnessed the strange and wondrous sight of the Woman's Crusade, when the mother-heart was roused up in defense of the home and all that the home held dearest.[58] A Divine impulse seemed to fan into sudden flame and touch with living fire earnest hearts, which rose up to meet the great occasion. Lips that had been silent in the prayer meeting were loosened to take part in the wonderful uprising. Saloons were visited, hardships encountered, insults, violence and even imprisonment endured, by women, brave to suffer and strong to endure. Thousands of saloon visits were made, many were closed. Grand enthusiasms were aroused, moral earnestness awakened, and a fire kindled whose beacon lights still stream o'er the gloomy track of our monster evil. Victor Hugo has spoken of the nineteenth century as being woman's era, and among the most noticeable epochs in this era is the uprising of women against the twin evils of slavery and intemperance, which had foisted themselves like leeches upon the civilization of the present age. In the great anti-slavery conflict women had borne a part, but after the storm cloud of battle had rolled away, it was found that an enemy, old and strong and deceptive, was warring against the best interests of society; not simply an enemy to one race, but an enemy to all races—an enemy that had entrenched itself in the strongholds of appetite and avarice, and was upheld by fashion, custom and legislation. To dislodge this enemy, to put prohibition not simply on the statute book, but in the heart and conscience of a nation, embracing within itself such heterogeneous masses, is no child's play, nor the work of a few short moons. Men who were subjects in their own country and legislated for by others, became citizens here, with the power to help legislate for native born Americans. Hundreds of thousands of new citizens have been translated from the old oligarchy of slavery into the new commonwealth of freedom, and are numerically strong enough to hold the balance of power in a number of the States, and sway its legislators for good or evil. With all these conditions, something more is needed than grand enthusiasms lighting up a few consecrated lives with hallowed brightness. We need patient, persevering, Christly endeavor, a consecration of the moral earnestness, spiritual power and numerical strength of the nation to grapple with this evil and accomplish its overthrow.

After the knowledge and experience gained by the crusade, women, instead of letting all their pure enthusiasms become dissipated by expending in feeling what they should utilize in action, came together and formed the Woman's Christian Temperance Union. From Miss Willard[59] we learn that women who had been crusading all winter called conventions for consultation in respective States, and that several organizations, called Temperance Leagues, were formed. Another step was the confederation of the States into the National Christian Temperance Union. A circular, aided by an extensive circulation through the press, was sent out to women in different parts of the country, and a convention was called, which met in Cleveland in November, 1874, to which sixteen States responded. A plan of work was adopted, financial arrangements made, and the publishing of an organ resolved upon. Mrs. Whittemyer, of Philadelphia, was elected President, and Miss Willard, of Illinois, Corresponding Secretary. This Union has increased in numbers and territory until at its last convention it embraced thirty-seven States and Territories. For years I knew very little of its proceedings, and was not sure that colored comradeship was very desirable, but having attended a local Union in Philadelphia, I was asked to join and acceded to the request, and was made city and afterwards State Superintendent of work among colored people. Since then, for several years I have held the position of National Superintendent of work among the colored people of the North.[60] When I became National Superintendent there were no colored women on the Executive Committee or Board of Superintendents. Now there are two colored women on the Executive Committee and two on the Board of Superintendents. As a matter of course the colored question has come into this work as it has into the Sons of Temperance, Good Templars and elsewhere. Some of the members of different Unions have met the question in a liberal and Christian manner; others have not seemed to have so fully outgrown the old shards and shells of the past as to make the distinction between Christian affiliation and social equality, but still the leaven of more liberal sentiments has been at work in the Union and produced some hopeful results.[61]

One of the pleasantest remembrances of my connection with the Woman's Christian Temperance Union was the kind and hospitable reception I met in the Missouri State Convention, and the memorable words of their President, Mrs. Hoffman, who declared that the color-line was eliminated. A Superintendent was chosen at that meeting for colored work in the State, at whose home in St. Louis the National Superintendent was for some time a guest. The State Superintendent said in one of the meetings to the colored sisters, "You can come with us, or you can go by yourselves." There was self-reliance and ability enough among them to form a Union of their own, which was named after the National Superintendent. Our work is divided into about forty departments, and among them they chose several lines of work, and had departments for parlor meetings, juvenile and evangelistic work, all of which have been in working order. The Union held meetings in Methodist and Baptist churches, and opened in the African Methodist Episcopal Church an industrial school for children, which increased in size until from about a dozen children at the beginning, it closed with about one hundred and fifty, as I understand. Some of the Unions, in their outlook upon society, found that there was no orphan asylum for colored children, except among the Catholics, and took the initiative for founding an asylum for colored children, and in a short time were successful in raising several hundred dollars for that purpose. This Union has, I have been informed, gathered into its association seventeen school teachers, and I think comprises some of the best brain and heart of the race in the city. From West Virginia a lady informs the National Superintendent that her Union has invited the colored sisters to join with them, and adds, "Praise God, from whom all blessings flow." In a number of places where there are local Unions in the North the doors have been opened to colored women, but in the farther South separate State Unions have been formed. Southern white women, it may be, fail to make in their minds the discrimination between social equality and Christian affiliation. Social equality, if I rightly understand the term, is the outgrowth of social affinities and social conditions, and may be based on talent, ability or wealth, on either or all of these conditions. Christian affiliation is the union of Christians to do Christly work, and to help build up the kingdom of Christ amid the sin and misery of the world, under the spiritual leadership of the Lord Jesus Christ. At our last National Convention two States were represented by colored representatives. The colored President of an Alabama Union represented a Union composed of white and colored people, and is called No. 2, instead of Colored Union, as it was not composed entirely of colored people, and in making its advent into the National Union brought, as I was informed, more than twice the amount of State dues which was paid by the white Alabama Union, No. 1. The question of admission into the White Ribbon Army was brought before the National President, through a card sent from Atlanta. Twenty-three women had formed a Union, and had written to the National Superintendent of colored work in the North asking in reference to their admission, and if black sheep must climb up some other way to tell them how. I showed the card to Miss Willard, who gave it as her opinion "That the National could not make laws for a State. If the colored women of Georgia will meet and form a Woman's Christian Temperance Union for the State, it is my opinion that their officers and delegates will have the same representation in the National." The President of the Second Alabama was received and recognized in the National as a member of the Executive Committee, and had a place, as I was informed, on the Committee of Resolutions. Believing, as I do, in human solidarity,

I hold that the Woman's Christian Temperance Union has in its hands one of the grandest opportunities that God ever pressed into the hands of the womanhood of any country. Its conflict is not the contest of a social club, but a moral warfare for an imperiled civilization. Whether or not the members of the farther South will subordinate the spirit of caste to the spirit of Christ, time will show. Once between them and the Negro were vast disparities, which have been melting and disappearing. The war obliterated the disparity between freedom and slavery. The civil law blotted out the difference between disfranchisement and manhood suffrage. Schools have sprung up like wells in the desert dust, bringing the races nearer together on the intellectual plane, while as a participant in the wealth of society the colored man has, I believe, in some instances, left his former master behind in the race for wealth. With these old landmarks going and gone, one relic remains from the dead past, "Our social customs." In clinging to them let them remember that the most ignorant, vicious and degraded voter outranks, politically, the purest, best and most cultured woman in the South, and learn to look at the question of Christian affiliation on this subject, not in the shadow of the fashion of this world that fadeth away, but in the light of the face of Jesus Christ. And can any one despise the least of Christ's brethren without despising Him? Is there any path that the slave once trod that Jesus did not tread before him, and leave luminous with the light of His steps? Was the Negro bought and sold? Christ was sold for thirty pieces of silver. Has he been poor? "The birds had nests, the foxes had holes, but the Son of man had not where to lay His head."[62] Were they beaten in the house of bondage? They took Jesus and scourged Him. Have they occupied a low social position? "He made himself of no reputation, and was numbered with the transgressors."[63] Despised and trodden under foot? He was despised and rejected of men; spit upon by the rabble, crucified between thieves, and died as did Rome's meanest criminal slave. Oh, my brothers and sisters, if God chastens every son whom He receiveth, let your past history be a stimulus for the future. Join with the great army who are on the side of our God and His Christ. Let your homes be the best places where you may plant your batteries against the rum traffic. Teach your children to hate intoxicating drinks with a deadly hatred. Though scorn may curl her haughty lip, and fashion gather up her dainty robes from social contact, if your lives are in harmony with God and Christly sympathy with man, you belong to the highest nobility in God's universe. Learn to fight the battle for God and man as athletes armed for a glorious strife, encompassed about with a cloud of witnesses who are in sympathy with the highest and holiest endeavors.

Ida B. Wells, "All things considered..." *AME Church Review* (April 1891): 379-81

All things considered, our race is probably not more intemperate than other races. By reason, though, of poverty, ignorance, and consequent degradation *as a mass*, we are behind in general advancement. We can, therefore, less afford to equal other races in that which still further debases, degrades and impoverishes, when we lack so much of being their equals in noble manhood and womanhood (intellectual, moral, and physical), in houses, lands, gold and most things whatsoever which tend to elevate and ennoble a people. Hence the present treatment of the temperance question will be from a race and economic standpoint.

Races, as individuals, make name and place for themselves by emulating the virtues of those who have made themselves great and powerful. The history of such nations teaches us that temperance is one of the cardinal virtues necessary to success. What headway are we making in cultivating this virtue?

Miss Frances E. Willard, president of the National Women's Christian Temperance Union, lately told the world that the center of power of the race is the saloon; that white men for this reason are afraid to leave their homes; that the Negro, in the late Prohibition campaign, sold his vote for twenty-five cents, etc.[64]

Miss Willard's statements possess the small pro rata of truth of all such sweeping statements. It is well known that the Negro's greatest injury is done to himself.

In his wildest moments he seldom molests others than his own, and this article is a protest against such wholesale self-injury.

Our color stands as a synonym for weakness, poverty and ignorance. It says to other nationalities: "This man belongs to a race possessing little of the power or influence which comes through riches, intellect, or even organization. We may proscribe, insult, ignore and oppress him as we please; he cannot help himself."

The Anglo-Saxon in every avenue of life puts in practice this line of reasoning; and as intemperance is one of the strongest foes to intellectual, material, and moral advancement, it is like playing with fire to take that in the mouth which steals away the brains, and thus gives judges and juries the excuse for filling the convict camps of Georgia alone with fifteen hundred Negroes, out of the sixteen hundred convicts in them, most of whom are young men—the flower of the race, physically speaking.

At the close of the year, when farmers receive pay for the year's work, thousands of dollars, which might flow into honorable channels of trade and build up race enterprises, are spent for liquor to inflame the blood and incite to evil deeds. That which is not directly spent for liquor is lost or wasted; and thus, year in and out, one of the most useful factors in race progress—the farmer—is kept at a dead level, without money, without ambition, and consequently at the mercy of the landholder.

The belief is widespread that our people will patronize the saloon as they do no other enterprise. Desiring to secure some of the enormous profits flowing into Anglo-Saxon coffers, many of our young men are entering the nefarious traffic for the money it brings, and thus every year sacrificing to the Moloch of intemperance hundreds of our young men. Intemperance is general and organized. In the cities it beguiles from every street corner and is found in many homes.

What shall be done to neutralize this power which tempts our young manhood and robs us of their time, talents, labor and money? Throughout the length and breadth of our land there exists little organized effort among ourselves against it. What can we do?

The convention of Educators of Colored Youth[65] in Atlanta, Ga., last December, in discussing the relative mortality of the race, took the ground that intemperance was chiefly the cause of our alarming mortality. The presidents of the schools and colleges in that convention assembled represented thousands of students who are to be the teachers of the race. The subject of temperance and her twin sister, frugality, should not be left for them to touch upon as an abstract matter, or in an incidental or spasmodic manner. An earnest, constant, systematic course of instruction from an economic standpoint in these schools, on this subject, which the students are in turn to impart to the people, is of vital importance, would be far-reaching and beneficial in its results; that association can wield a great power for the spread of temperance.

The National Press Association (representing over one hundred newspapers) which met in Cincinnati last month, speaking weekly to a constituency of perhaps a million readers, as an organized body can revolutionize public sentiment by showing how intemperance is sapping our physical and financial resources. The writer knows one secular journal which has lost many dollars by refusing to advertise saloons. That is the action of one sheet. There is needed, however, harmonious and consistent combination of agitation and effort from the entire body.

Nor must the ministers of the gospel, the most potent agents, who directly reach the masses, cease to preach temperance in their lives and pulpits, line upon line, and precept upon precept.

The Negro's greatest lack is his seeming incapacity for organization for his own protection and elevation. Yet every reader of these lines, who loves his race and feels the force of these statements, can make himself a committee of one to influence some one else. One person does not make a race, but the nation is made up of a multiplicity of units. Not one grain of sand, but countless millions of them, *side by side*, make the ocean bed. A single stream does not form the "Father of Waters," but the conjunctive force of a hundred streams in the bottom of the Mississippi Basin, swells into the broad artery of commerce, which courses the length of this continent, and sweeps with resistless current to the sea. So, too, an organized combination of all these agencies for humanity's good will sweep the country with a wave of public sentiment which shall make the liquor traffic unprofitable and dishonorable, and remove one of the principal stumbling blocks to race progress.

Carrie W. Clifford, "Love's Way (A Christmas Story)." *Alexander's Magazine* 1.8 (December 1905): 55-58

"Where is now the merry party—
I remember long ago,
Laughing round the chimney-fire,
Brightened by its ruddy glow;
Or, in summer's balmy evening
In the field upon the hay?
They have all dispensed and wandered
Far away, far away."[66]

Oh, the pathos in the tones, the world of sorrow, regret, despair in the thin, quavering voice of Miss Milly as she sang! Christmas eve had come again, and with it the sad memories of another Christmas eve, 30 years before when she had been so young, so pretty, so gay and happy. And she had sung this same song; only then, it had been sung for the pure joy of singing. For surrounded as she was with her merry party of Christmas guests (boys and girls who were her girlhood friends) and better than all else, her heart's idol among them—he to whom she had plighted her troth—what power could have foreseen this lonely desolate ending to all her dreams of bliss!

Then she had been Millicent Clarke, the belle of the village, and her voice was full, sweet and clear as a lark's, and when Tom Wentworth joined her in singing, with his deep, rich bass, one was constrained to stop and listen to the ravishing melody.

Thirty long, lonely weary years had passed since that happy Christmas eve, and she had now long been known as "Miss Milly," the village old maid.

For she, and her lover had quarreled, as lovers will; she had been firm and unyielding; he, proud and stubborn.

On Christmas, the day after the memorable party, Tom Wentworth had called alone upon his beautiful sweetheart. Her face, beaming with love and joy, she ran to meet him; and with all the eagerness of a young lover he stretched out his arms to draw her to his breast. Tenderly he bent and kissed her; but quick as a flash, she wrenched herself free, and with horror in face and eyes asked whether he had not been drinking.

"Certainly," he said; he had had a glass or two with the boys, but surely this was no great sin, and on Christmas day, too, when every one was making merry.

But this little maiden had serious objections to "making merry" after this fashion, at any time or season, and said so plainly. Further, she exacted a pledge that he would abstain thenceforth from all intoxicating liquors.

He could see no reason in such a demand; he was no drunkard; he seldom tasted wine; it was only on occasions like this that he drank with his fellows simply to be sociable. He would take no such pledge; she would accept nothing less; neither would yield, and so they parted in anger.

After Tom had stamped through the hall and closed the door with some vehemence behind him, Millicent's heart began to misgive her. Had she not been a little too hasty? And yet, would he not have promised her anything, if he had truly loved her? So she cried herself sick, and went to bed firmly believing that he would see things in a different light by morning, and be anxious to be restored to her favor.

As he strode down the street, his heart was hot within him. Surely she did not love him, or she would not be so unreasonable! What had he done to merit such treatment at her hands? A single glass with his comrade, who had toasted "the prettiest girl in N—, Millicent Clarke."

He was very, very angry with Millicent; and to show how little he cared that she had cast him off, he went back to the club where he drank again and again in a spirit of pure bravado.

The next morning when Millicent was anxiously awaiting a penitent letter or perhaps a call, the gentleman in question was nursing a very bad head, and feeling like a low-down, contemptible fellow. By nature very impetuous, and being angry with Millicent and angrier with himself, he determined to throw over all his bright prospects and enlist in the navy. He got up and out into the street. Once there, he felt a mighty yearning to go to his darling and heal the breach. But with that thought, came the remembrance of how he had acted upon leaving her. Were not the effects of his night's debauch still plain upon him? How could he see her thus?

In sheer desperation, he turned and hurried in the opposite direction toward the wharf.

★ ★ ★ ★

Like wild fire spread the news that Tom and Millicent had quarreled and Tom had gone to sea! The effect of this news upon Millicent was terrible. When she learned that he had gone without one line, one word, and that he could not if he would return for five long years, she uttered one heart-breaking moan and fell like a broken lily.

A long and serious illness followed; then she began to return slowly to health, but the old Millicent was gone forever. This wan, sad-eyed, serious woman was not the round, rosy, hoydenish creature whose high spirits and wild pranks had been the pride of N—.

Thirty years had passed since then, and Miss Milly, as she was now called, was left alone in the great house in the park. Old friends had passed away; those near of kin were sleeping in the dust. For many years now, Miss Milly had been the good angel of the village. Her hand was ever ready to help, her purse ready to succor the poor, the miserable, the destitute.

The children whose fathers were the victims of the drink-habit, were her especial wards. For these despairing ones, there was in her heart a bottomless well of sympathy.

On this Christmas eve of which we write, she had again invited a little party to her home; but, oh, how different from that first one!

The other party had been composed of bright, joyous young men and women, rich in wealth, in happiness, and worldly store; this was a company of that most pathetic thing in life — careworn, burdened children, old in want, in misery and woe.

When Miss Milly finished her singing, her mind traveled away back into the past. In the first years of her sorrow, she had waited and watched for some word from her erring lover; she thought he must return, at the end of those five, cruel, silent years. But five, ten, and 20 passed, and still no word, no sign!

But Miss Milly's faithfulness to the absent one never wavered. She took all the blame upon herself.

She had been hasty, stubborn, unjust, she had earned her punishment, so she told herself.

Thirty years went by, and tonight as she sat alone she thought of the stream of years that had rolled into eternity since that night when she had been so deliciously happy.

During all this time, Miss Milly had never missed sitting alone in the *why doesn't Milly find someone else?*

parlor on Christmas eve, singing that never-to-be-forgotten song, and calling up visions of the past.

Long since she had ceased to expect the return of the wanderer; her cry now was ever, "If I could but know his fate. I would be satisfied!"

A ring at the door bell recalled Miss Milly with a start! She hurried into the hall, and with a face glowing with love and good fellowship, admitted her quaint little guests.

The first thing Miss Milly did was to sit them down to such a feast as never was before. "All the delicacies of the season" failed to express the abundance of the good things to eat. And how the children enjoyed it! Miss Milly had never before seen victuals vanish, as did turkey, oysters, sweet potatoes, cranberry sauce, pickles, mince pies, pumpkin pies, custard pies and plum pudding on this occasion.

When they could eat no more, games of all kinds were indulged in, ending in a big romp of blind man's buff and hide and seek. After this came the nuts and fruit, and then each was given a well-filled basket to ferry home. At last the wraps were all on, the baskets distributed, and the thoroughly tired youngsters starting for home.

As Miss Milly stood in the hall door with the light streaming upon her angelic face, she called after the retreating forms. "A Merry Christmas to you, children, and God bless you every one!" And the happy children shouted back, "The same to you, Miss Milly."

With a patient little sigh, and her hand pressed over her heart, which was never quite free from the old aching pain, she stood for a moment in the doorway. Suddenly she became aware of the figure of a man approaching. Laboriously he mounted the steps and with a muttered "At last," fell senseless at her feet.

Oh, the unspeakable chord of love! Old, changed, broken as he was, one glance was all-sufficient to assure Millicent Clarke that this was her old lover—Tom Wentworth.

"Thank God," was all she said. She rang for the butler, and together they lifted him into the sitting room, and laid him upon the couch. Everything that could be done was resorted to, until the doctor, who had been telephoned for, should arrive.

The years had given him back—changed, but a shadow of his former self, almost dead; yet Miss Milly was as happy as a queen. How she hovered over him, kissing his brow, chafing his hands, bathing his forehead, moaning in those plaintive dovelike accents.

God had heard her prayer. He had ended the suspense. He had granted that she should know his fate whatever it was to be, and she dared ask no more!

When Tom Wentworth returned to consciousness, he was lying in a massive bed in an elegant chamber, and Millicent Clarke was bending over him. As though the intervening years had been a dream, he whispered "Millicent," and drawing her head down upon his bosom he kissed her.

When he was strong enough he related a tale of a wasted life, of wanderings, of carousings, of a stubborn pride, then of longing and regret and shame.

For many years pride had kept him from returning; then shame had stepped in to torture and harass him. But at last he swore that nothing should keep him from her longer. Like the prodigal, he would return.

With all his sin, his heart had ever remained true to her. Even in wildest excesses he had ever borne good will to his fellow man. Whatever else he was, he was no coward, and many were the lives he had saved at risk of his own. Many letters testifying to his bravery and many medals for gallant seamanship were his.

"But the tempter in the wine cup has ever been my undoing," he confessed at last when all was told. "Each returning Christmas night has seen a wilder debauch. At first only on Christmas did the fiend have power over me; but as the years rolled by, the outbreak grew more frequent, so that each succeeding year rendered it more impossible for me to return to you. But I have come at last. You will not cast me off, oh, say you will not cast me off!"

"If you knew, if you could but realize the desperate battle I've fought with the fiend to reach your side untainted! But, thank God. I've won! Old, scarred, dying, yet blessed to come into your presence without the taint of liquor. Will you receive me again? Milly, can you forgive me?"

More than once during the recital she had vainly striven to check him. Now, all her loving, tender woman's heart was overflowing. She baptized him with her tears, she covered him with kisses, she called him by every endearing name under heavens.

Forgive him! Why she had done so 30 years ago. In fact, the fault had all been hers; her hasty temper, her imperiousness had been the cause of all.

And so mutually forgiving and forgetting the past, under the influence of her caressing hand he fell asleep.

The full light of the glad Christmas day was shining into the room, when he again opened his eyes. He was very weak, he knew the sands of life were running low. "Milly," he called softly. Instantly she was beside him.

"Did you call, dearest one?" A pause, then he answered, "I have a strange fancy—the fancy of a dying man. Can you—will you marry me, Milly? It will not be for long and I can die happier."

"I have been betrothed to you for 30 years," was her low fervid reply.

"Then send for the minister; there is no time to be lost."

The intervening hour was spent in that blessed communion, known only to lovers. It was a bit of Paradise here below.

When the minister came, the woman knelt by the bedside, and took upon herself the vows, "for richer, for poorer, for better, for worse, in sickness, in health until death us do part"; and so they were married.

To one unacquainted with their story, the wedding would have seemed a sad one; but to them it was one of unspeakable joy, for it was so much more than they had believed it possible to be granted to them!

The day was dying in the west when Tom, his head pillowed on Millicent's arm and a smile of infinite sweetness on his lips, entered into rest.

And Milly, though with streaming eyes, was looking longingly into the future; satisfied that she would follow soon, and that the glimpse of Paradise vouchsafed them here, would be continued there, into infinity.

The value of true friendship cannot be estimated.

Notes

1. Terborg-Penn notes that black feminists such as Charlotte Forten, Frances Harper, Lottie Rollin, Josephine St. Pierre Ruffin and Sojourner Truth affiliated with the AWSA, while Naomi Talbert, Mary Ann Shadd Cary, Harriet and Hattie Purvis, and Charlotte Ray chose the NWSA (1998, 42).

2. Carla Peterson has pointed out that Truth is using an African Americanism here: "'[H]awk' and 'buzzard' are…figures from an African American folktale in which the two vultures are as oppositional and come into conflict in a struggle for survival, the buzzard, a descendant of the powerful African 'King Buzzard,' always gaining the ascendancy" (1995, 54).

3. Lucy Stone (1818-93) was a prominent suffragist, best known for being the first American woman to keep her surname upon marriage and the first Massachusetts woman to earn a college degree from Oberlin in 1847. A leader of the suffrage movement, she was also a lecturer for the Massachusetts Anti-Slavery Society and helped found the Woman's National Loyal League and later the AERA. When Elizabeth Cady Stanton and Susan B. Anthony left the AERA in 1869 in opposition to the passage of the Fifteenth Amendment and formed the National Woman Suffrage Association, Stone, her husband, and Julia Ward Howe founded the American Woman Suffrage Association (AWSA), which was committed to woman suffrage and African American civil rights.

4. See Peterson on the significance of Truth's reference to the spirit of a goose and snake in this speech (1995, 54-55).

5. See the Book of Esther. On the invocation of "Queen Esther" by American woman's rightists, see Yellin 1989, 30, 40-41.

6. Charles Cumberworth (1811-52) was a French sculptor, admitted to the Beaux-Arts in 1829. His work—portrait-busts of women and children, and allegorical statues of classical figures—was exhibited from 1833 to 1848 in the Salon de Paris.

7. Henry Ward Beecher (1813-87) was a prominent clergyman, social reformer, abolitionist, and brother of Harriet Beecher Stowe.

8. Frederic de Forest Allen (1844-97) graduated from Oberlin College in 1863 and was a professor of foreign languages before becoming chair of classical philology at Harvard 1880-97.

9. Starry regions.

10. Truth's son Peter (born c.1820) was sold by John Dumont to Dr. Gedney (an in-law) in 1826. Gedney then sold Peter to his brother Solomon, who resold him to his brother-in-law Fowler, an Alabama planter, who was married to Gedney's sister Eliza (Painter 1996, 32-33; Mabee 1993, 16-20). Because Peter had been illegally sold out of state, the judge hearing Truth's case declared him entirely free.

11. Wendell Philips (1811-84), abolitionist, orator, and advocate of Native American rights.

12. Faneuil Hall, the central marketplace and meeting hall in Boston, was erected in 1742 with an open ground floor and assembly room above, for the purposes of meetings, speeches, and community activity.

13. Milton's "Il Penseroso" is a pastoral poem written in 1631 in praise of contemplation, philosophy, and meditative study. Stowe quotes lines 17-21.

14. William Wetmore Story (1819-95) was an American sculptor, critic, poet, and editor, who moved to Rome in 1856 to pursue his artistic endeavors. The "Libyan Sibyl" (1861) was sculpted in marble, and, as Painter argues, Story "never connected Truth or Stowe with what he considered his best work" (1996, 158).

15. Harriet Beecher Stowe, "Sojourner Truth, The Libyan Sibyl," *The Atlantic Monthly* 11 (April 1863): 473-81.

16. Oliver Johnson (1809-99) assisted William Lloyd Garrison with establishing the *Liberator*, lectured for the Western Anti-Slavery Society, and helped organize the New England Anti-Slavery Society. Johnson edited the *Anti-Slavery Bugle* for two years before becoming managing editor of the *Independent* in 1865 and editor of the *New York Tribune* in 1870 (Galbreath 1921, 392).

17. See note 14.

18. Parker Pillsbury (1809-98) was a minister and a lecturing agent for the New Hampshire, Massachusetts, and American anti-slavery societies for over two decades. He edited the *Herald of Freedom* (1840, 1845-46) and the *National Anti-Slavery Standard* (1866), and was the American Anti-Slavery Society emissary to Britain in 1854. Pillsbury helped to draft the constitution of the American Equal Rights Association (AERA) in 1865, served as vice-president of the New Hampshire Woman Suffrage Association, and co-edited the women's rights newsletter *The Revolution*, founded in 1868, with Elizabeth Cady Stanton.

19. Frances Smith Foster notes that "this speech marked the beginning of Harper's prominence in national feminist organizations" (1990, 216). This national woman's rights convention was the first held since the Civil War and was the meeting at which the American Equal Rights Association (AERA) was formed.

20. Andrew Johnson (1808-75) became the seventeenth president of the United States (1865-69) upon the assassination of Abraham Lincoln. He adopted conciliatory policies towards the South, including rushing to reincorporate the former Confederates back into the union and vetoing civil rights bills.

21. See Chapter 1, note 81.

22. African American regiments from Louisiana who fought at Port Hudson for the Union were the first black units in the Civil War engaged in large-scale combat against white soldiers. The First Louisiana was largely comprised of free men of color, while the Second and Third Louisiana were composed of both free blacks and former slaves.

23. The Battle of Olustee or Battle of Ocean Pond was fought near Lake City, Florida on 20 February 1864. It was the largest battle fought in Florida during the Civil War. The 54th Massachusetts Volunteer Infantry and the First North Carolina who Harper notes "saved your army" were comprised of African American soldiers.

24. Harriet Tubman (c.1820-1913) was an abolitionist, Union spy during the Civil War, and activist for woman suffrage. She helped numerous enslaved African Americans escape North and to Canada on 13 covert missions and recruited men for John Brown's raid on Harpers Ferry (1859). Tubman was the keynote speaker at the inaugural meeting of the National Federation of Afro-American Women (1896). See Clinton 2004 and Larson 2004.

25. Martha Coffin Wright (1806-75) was an abolitionist, woman's rights activist, and a signatory of the Declaration of Sentiments at the Seneca Falls Convention (1848). Her home was a station on the Underground Railroad, and she was a friend and supporter of Harriet Tubman.

26. Susan Brownell Anthony (1820-1906) played a pivotal role in the women's rights movement to secure women's suffrage in the United States. In 1869, she and Elizabeth Cady Stanton founded the National Women's Suffrage Association (NWSA) when the American Equal Rights Association (AERA) split over the Fifteenth Amendment and woman suffrage. In 1890, Anthony orchestrated the merger of the NWSA with the American Woman Suffrage Association (AWSA), creating the National American Woman Suffrage Association (NAWSA).

27. The America Equal Rights Association (AERA) founded in 1866 by Susan B. Anthony, Frederick Douglass, and Elizabeth Cady Stanton to pursue racial and sexual equality split in 1869 over conflicted views of the Fifteenth Amendment enfranchising black men before women were granted the suffrage.

28. From 1864 through 1867, Truth worked in Washington counseling, teaching, and resettling freedpeople. See Mabee 1993, Ch. 11 and Painter 1996, Ch. 22.

29. Carleton Mabee (1993, 225-26) documents this song as one of Truth's favorites, which she sang twice at this convention and may have sung for the first time in public at New Lisbon, Ohio in 1852. For a slightly different version of this song, see Fitch and Mandziuk 1997, 215-16.

30. Gregarines are intestinal parasites.

31. Rosalyn Terborg-Penn importantly notes that Talbert's speech, given at an NWSA convention, positioned her as identified with Susan B. Anthony and Elizabeth Cady Stanton, "at a time when they severely criticized Blacks and the pending Fifteenth Amendment, offend[ing] many of the African Americans of Chicago.... [S]he was severely censured as a result....Talbert seemed caught in her attempts to deal with the problems of racism and sexism at the same time" (1998, 49).

32. Following the first National Woman Suffrage Convention, held in Washington, DC on 19-20 January 1869, Elizabeth Cady Stanton and Susan B. Anthony embarked on a tour of Missouri, Illinois, Wisconsin, and Ohio. They spoke at several state suffrage conventions, including the convention held in Chicago in February 1869. See Cady Stanton *et al.* 1969[1882], II: 345-78.

33. As Jane Rhodes documents, Shadd Cary delivered this speech before the Judiciary Committee of the House of Representatives on 21 January 1874 as part of a group of women petitioning the House on behalf of 600 women in the District of Columbia seeking the vote. In 1871 Shadd Cary, on the basis of being a resident in the Second district of DC, attempted to register to vote as did 62 other women in the District that year (Rhodes 1998, 194-95).

34. Thomas "Blind Tom" Wiggins (1849-1908) was an African American autistic savant and musical prodigy on the piano. He achieved significant fame and played before President Buchanan at the White House in 1860.

35. 2 Kings 22; Books of Chronicles 2:34.

36. Judges 4 and 5.

37. Luke 4:18.

38. John 8:7.

39. Matthew 7:12.

40. Mary Simmerson Cunningham Logan (1785-1805), wife of John A. Logan, Union general and Illinois senator, held anti-slavery views much of her life; Mary Tyler Peabody Mann (1806-87) was Horace Mann's second wife and an educator active in the kindergarten movement with her sister, Elizabeth Peabody; Ann Terry Greene Phillips (1813-86) was active in the Boston Female Anti-slavery Society and is regarded as having influenced Wendel Phillips to become more involved with the anti-slavery movement.

41. Medieval Latin; discharge from obligation, but also a final stroke that effectually ends or settles a point or issue.

42. While unsuccessful in their first attempt petitioning for a bill granting municipal suffrage in 1885, Kansas women won that right in 1887.

43. In 1866 and 1867 the Massachusetts legislature was petitioned to allow women to be elected to school boards. In 1874, Boston elected four women to serve on its school committee, and in 1879 the state allowed women to vote for school committee members. By 1892, when the state abolished its poll tax, more women could vote to elect school committee members, even though they were required to be textually literate to do so.

44. The National Council of Women's first triennial meeting was held in Washington, DC, 22-25 February 1891.

45. Touted as the most renowned American woman speaker of all time and "queen" of the suffrage platform, Anna Howard Shaw (1847-1919) attended Boston University Theological School and was licensed as a Methodist preacher in the early 1870s. By the 1880s she was an established temperance lecturer and in 1885 became a full-time lecturer for suffrage, temperance, and social purity. In 1890, Shaw was appointed national lecturer by NAWSA and in 1892 became the organization's vice-president.

46. Wimodaughsis was a suffrage-oriented national woman's club, founded in 1890 by Emma Gillett and headquartered in Washington, DC. Branches of Wimodaughsis continue to be active today. Its name was, as Julia Cooper notes, an amalgam of wife, mother, daughter, and sister; the organization purported to disregard members' race, religion, or class. Incorporated as an educational society to help working women further their education, the Washington, DC headquarters provided courses for women in areas such as French and journalism.

47. Cooper was one of the few women invited to speak at the 1890 Pan-African Conference held in London.

48. "Affront to spurned beauty": Juno's resentment that Paris gave Venus the golden apple as the prize for beauty.

49. Charles Lemert and Esme Bhan, in their edited collection of Cooper's essays, papers, and letters, note this is "presumably Percival Lowell (1855-1916), author of *Soul of the Far East*" (1998, 95, n.3).

50. In 1892 Oscar Fay Adams published *The Presumption of Sex and Other Papers* with Lee and Shepard Publishers of Boston. The book reprinted his essays first published in the *North American Review*, including "The Mannerless Sex."

51. Alfred Lord Tennyson's *Lady Clara Vere de Vere*, part of *The Lady of Shalott, and Other Poems* (1842).

52. On 2 July 1881, Charles Julius Guiteau (1841-82), an American lawyer, assassinated President James A. Garfield.

53. François Alexandre Nicolas Chéri Delsarte (1811-71) was a French musician who developed an acting style that sought to express an actor's emotions through systematized gestures and movements. The "Delsarte" method was taught throughout the world and was particularly popular in America.

54. Henry Wadsworth Longfellow, "The Fiftieth Birthday of Agassiz" 1857.

55. Matthew 18:2-6.

56. Charles Sumner (1811-74) was a lawyer and powerful orator, who led anti-slavery forces in Massachusetts as well as the Radical Republicans in the United States Senate during the Civil War and Reconstruction. As a politician he fought for freedmen's civil and voting rights.

57. See Ch. 1, note 90.

58. The Women's Christian Temperance Union (WCTU) was formed in 1873. It was silent on woman suffrage until Frances Willard endorsed the vote for women as a "weapon of 'home protection' at its Philadelphia Convention in October 1876" (Peterson 2000, 49).

59. Frances Elizabeth Caroline Willard (1839-98) was an educator, temperance reformer, and suffragist. She was elected president of the WCTU in the United States in 1879 and held that position for life. She created the Formed Worldwide WCTU in 1883 and was elected its president in 1888. She also founded the WCTU's magazine, *The Union Signal*, which she edited from 1892 through 1898. Willard was a controversial figure, publicly criticized for refusing to condemn lynching by Ida B. Wells-Barnett during the latter's anti-lynching lecture tour of Britain in 1894. At an address to the WCTU in Cleveland in November 1894, Willard's rebuttal of Wells-Barnett revealed her view that the myth of the black male rapist was a reality and that Southerners were justified in acting to "protect" themselves (Carby 1987, 114).

60. Harper was committed to temperance as early as the 1850s, and she was visible in the WCTU at state, national, and international levels by the late nineteenth century (Peterson 2000, 120). Margaret Hope Bacon notes that Harper was first made part of the WCTU governing body as vice-president of the Women's International Temperance Conference in Philadelphia in 1876 because it was noted there were no non-white delegates. Harper went on to be the only African American delegate to the 1881 WCTU convention, and in 1886 she was named Pennsylvania State Superintendent of Work among the Colored People. By 1888 Harper was the first Superintendent of the Negro Section at the national level and was a national officer until 1893 (Bacon 1989, 42).

61. There were six black unions in the WCTU in 1886, when Harper was appointed Pennsylvania State Superintendent of Work among the Colored People, but the number of so-called colored unions "did not grow substantially until after Lucy Thurman became head of the Colored Division of the national WCTU in 1895. Texas 'Number 2' or 'Thurman' Union formed in Dallas in December 1897, after Mrs. Thurman spent several months in the state organizing fifteen black locals" (McArthur 2008). Terborg-Penn notes that "by the turn of the century, there were several WCTU unions among Black women throughout the nation" in places such as Washington, DC, South Carolina, Tennessee, Washington State, and Rhode Island. Women such as Mamie Dillard and Emma J. Ray were active in organizing these "colored" unions (Terborg-Penn 1998, 86).

62. Luke 9:58.

63. Philippians 2:7 and Isaiah 53:12.

64. Wells–Barnett is referring to an interview Willard gave and published in the October 1890 issue of the *New York Voice*, in which she sympathized with southerners and said, "The colored race multiplies like the locusts of Egypt. The grog-shop is its center of power…. 'Better whisky and more of it' has been the rallying cry of great dark-faced mobs in the Southern localities." Willard was understood as condoning lynching in this interview when she said: "The safety of women, of children, of the home is menaced in a thousand localities at this moment, so men dare not go beyond the sight of their own roof-tree" (quoted in McMurry 1998, 210).

65. The American Association of Educators of Colored Youth held their first meeting in 1889. The Association's members and officers included Booker T. Washington, Frances Harper, Fanny Jackson Coppin, and W.E.B. DuBois (Lee 1913, 132).

66. *The Poetry from Summer Songs of Country Life* (Francis Brooks and Co., 1890).

References and
Further Readings

Acornley, John H. 1987[1892]. *The Colored Lady Evangelist, Being the Life, Labors and Experiences, of Mrs Harriet A. Baker*. New York: Garland.

"A Distinguished Woman Honored." 1892. *American Citizen* 21 October.

Allen, Grant. 1889. "Plain Words on the Woman Question." *Fortnightly Review* 52.46 (October): 448-58.

Almonte, Richard. 1998[1852]. *A plea for emigration, or, Notes of Canada West by Mary Ann Shadd Cary*. Toronto: Mercury P.

AMEC Book of Worship. 1984. Nashville: AMEC Sunday School Union.

Ampadu, Lena. 2007. "Maria W. Stewart and the Rhetoric of Black Preaching." In *Black Women's Intellectual Traditions: Speaking Their Minds*, ed. Kristin Waters and Carol B. Conaway. Burlington: U of Vermont P. 38-54.

Andrews, William L. (Ed.). 1986. "Introduction." *Sisters of the Spirit: Three Black Women's Autobiographies of the Nineteenth Century*. Bloomington: Indiana UP. 1-22.

Angell, Stephen Ward. 1996. "The Controversy Over Women's Ministry in the African Methodist Episcopal Church During the 1880s: The Case of Sarah Ann Hughes." In *This Far By Faith: Readings in African-American Women's Religious Biography*, ed. Judith Weisenfeld and Richard Newman. New York: Routledge. 94-109.

Arnesen, Eric (Ed.). 2003. *Black Protest and the Great Migration*. Boston: Bedford/St. Martin's.

Bacon, Jacqueline. 2002. *The Humblest May Stand Forth: Rhetoric, Empowerment, and Abolition*. Columbia: U of South Carolina P.

Bacon, Margaret Hope. 1989. "'One Great Bundle of Humanity': Frances Ellen Watkins Harper (1825-1911)." *The Pennsylvania Magazine of History and Biography* 113.1: 21-29.

Barkley Brown, Elsa. 1994. "Negotiating and Transforming the Public Sphere: African American Political Life in the Transition from Slavery to Freedom." *Public Culture* 7: 107-46.

Barnes, Reverend A. 1838. *A Manual of Prayer Designed to Assist Young Christians in Learning the Modes and Subjects of Devotion*. Boston: Perkins and Marvin.

Bassard, Katherine Clay. 1999. *Spiritual Interrogations: Culture, Gender, and Community in Early African American Women's Writing*. Princeton: Princeton UP.

Beardin, Jim, and Linda Jean Butler. 1977. *The Life and Times of Mary Shadd Cary*. Toronto: NC Press.

Bell, Michael Davitt. 2000. *Culture, Genre, and Literary Vocation*. Chicago: Chicago UP.

Blackett, R.J.M. 1983. *Building an Antislavery Wall: Black Americans in the Atlantic Abolitionist Movement, 1830-1860*. Baton Rouge and London: Louisiana State UP.

———. 1986. *Beating Against the Barriers: Biographical Essays in Nineteenth-Century Afro-American History*. Baton Rouge and London: Louisiana State UP.

Bordin, Ruth Birgitta Anderson. 1990. *Woman and Temperance: The Quest for Power and Liberty, 1873-1900*. New Brunswick: Rutgers P.

Boyd, Melba Joyce. 1994. *Discarded Legacy: Politics and Poetics in the Life of Frances E.W. Harper 1825-1911*. Detroit: Wayne State UP.

Broughton, Virginia. 1988[1907]. "Twenty Year's Experience of a Missionary." In *Spiritual Narratives*, ed. Susan Houchins. *The Schomburg Library of Nineteenth-Century Black Women Writers*. New York: Oxford UP.

Brown, Annie E. 1909. *Religious Work and Travels*. Chester, PA: Olin T. Pancoast.

Brown, Hallie Quinn. 1988[1926]. *Homespun Heroines and Other Women of Distinction*. New York: Oxford UP.

Bruce, Dickson D., Jr. 1974. *And They All Sang Hallelujah: Plain-Folk Camp-Meeting Religion, 1800-1845*. Knoxville: U of Tennessee P.

Burns, Jacqueline S., and Tracy A. Jefferson. 1997. "African American Community Life In Columbus, Ohio, 1847-1997." http://mediamanager.osu.edu/index.cfm?fuseaction=collections.seeItemInCollection&CollectionID=c27e34ca-989d-4a95-bf1e-8f3fe1be76d3&ItemID=29dd5f7e-f8dd-4d6a-8791-cc8e749a66e8.

Cady Stanton, Elizabeth, Susan B. Anthony, and Matilda Joslyn Gage (Eds.). 1969[1882]. *History of Woman Suffrage*. 10 vols. New York: Arno Press.

Carby, Hazel V. 1987. *Reconstructing Womanhood: The Emergence of the Afro-American Woman Novelist*. New York: Oxford UP.

Carby, Hazel. 1992. "Policing the Black Woman's Body in an Urban Context." *Critical Inquiry* 18: 738-55.

Carter, Linda M. 1996. "Naomi Bowman Talbert Anderson." In *Notable Black American Women*, Vol. II, ed. Jessie Carney Smith. Detroit: Gale Research. 11-12.

Cash, Floris Barnett. 1993. "Associations for the Protection of Negro Women." In *Black Women in America: An Historical Encyclopedia*, ed. Darlene Clark Hine, *et al.* New York: Carlson. 51-52.

———. 1993. "White Rose Mission, New York City." In *Black Women in America: An Historical Encyclopedia*, ed. Darlene Clark Hine, *et al.* New York: Carlson. 1258-59.

Clinton, Catherine. 2004. *Harriet Tubman: The Road to Freedom*. New York: Little, Brown and Company.

Connor, Kimberly Rae. 1994. *Conversions and Visions in the Writings of African-American Women.* Knoxville: U of Tennessee P.

Cooper, Kenneth J. 2007. "A History of African American Newspapers in New England." <http://news.newamericamedia.org/news/view_article.html?article_id=72e2a1771d7c4080744902534e1bd6c9>.

Coppin, Levi Jenkins. 1888. *In Memoriam: Catherine S. Campbell Beckett.* AME Book Concern.

Curtis White, Katherine J. 2005. "Women in the Great Migration: Economic Activity of Black and White Southern-Born Female Migrants in 1920, 1940, and 1970." *Social Science History* 29.3: 413-55.

Davis, Angela Y. 1983. *Women, Race and Class.* New York: Vintage.

———. 1998. *Blues Legacies and Black Feminism: Gertrude "Ma" Rainey, Bessie Smith, and Billie Holiday.* New York: Vintage.

Davis, Elizabeth Lindsay. 1996[1993]. *Lifting as They Climb.* New York: G.K. Hall.

Deegan, Mary Jo (Ed.). 2002. "Fannie Barrier Williams and Her Life as New Woman of Color in Chicago, 1893-1918." In *The New Woman of Color: The Collected Writings of Fannie Barrier Williams, 1893-1918.* DeKalb: Northern Illinois UP. xiii-lx.

Dieter, Melvin Easterday. 1980. *The Holiness Revival of the Nineteenth Century.* Metuchen, NJ: The Scarecrow Press.

Dodson, Jualynne. 1981. "Nineteenth-Century A.M.E. Preaching Women." In *Women in New Worlds*, ed. Hilah F. Thomas and Rosemary Skinner Keller. Nashville: Abingdon. 276-89.

———. 1993. "African Methodist Episcopal Preaching Women of the Nineteenth Century." In *Black Women In America: An Historical Encyclopaedia*, ed. Darlene Clark Hine, *et al.* New York: Carlson. 12-14.

———. 1988a "Introduction." *An Autobiography: The Story of the Lord's Dealings with Mrs. Amanda Smith the Colored Evangelist* (1893). New York: Oxford UP. xxvii-xlii.

———. 1988b. "Power and Surrogate Leadership: Black Women and Organized Religion." *Sage* 5.2: 37-42.

Douglass-Chinn, Richard J. 2001. *Preacher Woman Sings the Blues: The Autobiographies of Nineteenth-Century African American Evangelists.* Columbia: U of Missouri P.

Duster, Alfreda M. (Ed.). 1970. *Crusade for Justice: The Autobiography of Ida B. Wells.* Chicago: U of Chicago P.

Edwards, Wendy J., and Carolyn De Swarte Gifford (Eds.). 2003. *Gender and the Social Gospel.* Urbana: U of Illinois P.

Elizabeth. 1988[1863]. "Memoir of Old Elizabeth, A Coloured Woman." In *Six Women's Slave Narratives*, ed. William L. Andrews. *The Schomburg Library of Nineteenth-Century Black Women Writers.* New York: Oxford UP.

"Elizabeth Jennings." 2008. *Victoria's Past. Com.* http://www.victoriaspast.com/Famous_Black_Americans/elizabeth_jennings.htm.

Fisch, Audrey. 2000. *American Slaves in Victorian England: Abolitionist Politics in Popular Literature and Culture.* Cambridge: Cambridge UP.

Fitch, Suzanne Pullon, and Roseann M. Mandziuk. 1997. *Sojourner Truth as Orator: Wit, Story, and Song.* Westport: Greenwood P.

Fletcher, Alice C. 1891. "Our Duty to Dependent Races." *Transactions of the National Council of Women of the United States, Assembled in Washington, D.C. February 22 to 25, 1891,* ed. Rachel Foster Avery. Philadelphia: J.B. Lippincott. 83–84.

Fletcher, Holly. 2007. *Gender and the American Temperance Movement of the Nineteenth Century.* New York: Routledge.

Foster, Frances Smith (Ed.). 1988. *Iola Leroy, or Shadows Uplifted* (1892). Oxford and New York: Oxford UP.

———. (Ed.). 1990. *A Brighter Coming Day: A Frances Ellen Watkins Harper Reader.* New York: Feminist Press.

———. 1993. *Written By Herself: Literary Production by African American Women, 1746-1892.* Bloomington: Indiana UP.

Frazier, E. Franklin, and C. Eric Lincoln. 1974. *The Negro Church in America.* New York: Schocken.

Fuchs, Sabrina. 2001. "Victoria Earle Smith." *Encyclopedia of African-American Culture and History.* 5 vols. Farmington Hills, MI: Gale Group. <http://galenet.galegroup.com/servlet/HistRC/>.

Fuller, Edward. 1971. *Prudence Crandall: An Incident of Racism in Nineteenth-Century Connecticut.* Middletown: Wesleyan UP.

Fultz, Michael. 1995. "'The Morning Cometh': African-American Periodicals, Education, and the Black Middle Class, 1900-1930." *Journal of Negro History* 80.3: 97-112.

Galbreath, C.B. 1921. "Anti-Slavery Movement in Columbiana County." *Ohio History: The Scholarly Journal of the Ohio Historical Society* 30.4: 355-96.

George, Carol V.R. 1973. *Segregated Sabbaths: Richard Allen and the Emergence of Independent Black Churches, 1740-1840.* New York: Oxford UP.

———. 1996. "Widening the Circle: The Black Church and the Abolitionist Crusade, 1830-1860." In *African American Religion: Interpretive Essays in History and Culture,* ed. Timothy E. Fulop and Albert J. Raboteau. New York: Routledge. 155-73.

Giddings, Paula. 1984. *When and Where I Enter: The Impact of Black Women on Race and Sex in America.* New York: Morrow.

———. 2008. *Ida: A Sword Among Lions: Ida B. Wells And The Campaign Against Lynching.* New York: Amistad P.

Gilbert, Olive, and Frances Titus. 1991[1878]. *Narrative of Sojourner Truth; a Bondswoman of Olden Time, with a History of her Labors and Correspondence Drawn from her "Book of Life,"* ed. Henry Louis Gates, Jr. *The Schomburg Library of Nineteenth-Century Black Women Writers.* New York and Oxford: Oxford UP.

Gilkes, Cheryl Townsend. 1994. "The Politics of 'Silence': Dual-Sex Political

Systems and Women's Traditions of Conflict in African-American Religion." In *African American Christianity: Essays in History*, ed. Paul E. Johnson. Berkeley: U of California P. 80-110.

Glaude, Eddie S., Jr. 2000. *Exodus! Religion, Race, and Nation in Early Nineteenth-Century Black America*. Chicago: U of Chicago P.

Goldsby, Jacqueline. 2006. *A Spectacular Secret: Lynching in American Life and Literature*. Chicago: U of Chicago P.

Gordon, Ann D., and Bettye Collier-Thomas (Eds.). 1997. *African American Women and the Vote: 1837-1965*. Amherst: U of Massachusetts P.

Grammer, Elizabeth. 2002. *Some Wild Visions: Autobiographies by Female Itinerant Evangelists in Nineteenth-Century America*. New York: Oxford UP.

Gredier, Katharine. 2005. "The Schoolteacher on the Streetcar." *New York Times* 13 November. <http://www.nytimes.com/2005/11/13/nyregion/thecity/13jenn. html?pagewanted=all> .

Grossman, Jonathan. 2008. "Black Studies in the Department of Labor, 1897-1907." US Department of Labor, 1 April. <http://www.dol.gov/oasam/ programs/history/blackstudiestext.htm>.

Gunning, Sandra. 1996. *Race, Rape, and Lynching: The Red Record of American Literature, 1890-1912*. Oxford and New York: Oxford UP.

Gusfield, Joseph R. 1986. *Symbolic Crusade: Status Politics and the American Temperance Movement*. Urbana: U of Illinois P.

Guy-Sheftall, Beverly. 1990. *Daughters of Sorrow: Attitudes Towards Black Women, 1880-1920*. New York: Carlson.

Hall, Jacquelyn Dowd. 1979. "'A Truly Subversive Affair': Women Against Lynching in the Twentieth Century South." In *Women of America: A History*, ed. Carol Ruth Berking and Mary Beth Norton. Boston: Houghton Mifflin. 360-83.

———. 1993. "Antilynching Movement." In *Black Women in America: An Historical Encyclopedia*, ed. Darlene Clark Hine. New York: Carlson. Vol 1: 38-41.

Harley, Sharon. 1991. "When your Work is Not Who You Are: The Development of a Working-Class Consciousness among Afro-American Women." In *Gender, Class, Race, and Reform in the Progressive Era*, ed. Noralee Frankel and Nancy S. Dye. Lexington: UP of Kentucky. 42-55.

———, and the Black Women and Work Collective (Eds.). 2002. *Sister Circle: Black Women and Work*. New Brunswick: Rutgers UP.

Haywood, Chanta M. 2003. *Prophesying Daughters: Black Women Preachers and the Word, 1823-1913*. Columbia: U of Missouri P.

"Helen Pitts Douglass—1838-1903." *Stories in Stone: Famous Women in Mount Hope Cemetery*. 2004. Friends of Mount Hope Cemetery. <http://www.fomh.org/ Stories/HDouglass.htm>.

Hersch, Blanche Glassman. 1978. *The Slavery of Sex: Feminist-Abolitionists in America*. Urbana: U of Illinois P.

Higginbotham, Evelyn Brooks. 1993. *Righteous Discontent: The Women's Movement in the Black Baptist Church, 1890-1920*. Cambridge, MA: Harvard UP.

Hine, Darlene Clark. 1994. *Hine Sight: Black Women and the Re-Construction of American History*. Bloomington: Indiana UP.

——, et al. (Eds.). 1990. *Black Women in United States History*. 16 vols. Brooklyn: Carlson, 1990.

——, et al. (Eds.). 1995. *"We Specialize in the Wholly Impossible": A Reader in Black Women's History*. New York: Carlson.

——, and David Barry Gaspar. 1996. *More than Chattel: Black Women and Slavery in the Americas*. Bloomington: Indiana UP.

——, and Kathleen Thompson. 1998. *A Shining Thread of Hope: The History of Black Women in America*. New York: Broadway Books.

Hopkins, Pauline E. 1902. "Famous Women of the Negro Race. IV. Some Literary Workers." *The Colored American Magazine* 4 (March): 276-80.

Horton, James Oliver, and Lois E. Horton. 1997. *In Hope Of Liberty: Culture, Community and Protest Among Northern Free Blacks, 1700-1860*. New York: Oxford UP.

Humez, Jean. 1981. "Introduction." *Gifts of Power: The Writings of Rebecca Jackson, Black Visionary, Shaker Eldress*. Amherst: University of Massachusetts P.

Hunter, Tera W. 1997. *To "Joy My Freedom": Southern Black Women's Lives and Labors After the Civil War*. Cambridge: Harvard UP.

Jackson, Rebecca Cox. 1981[1830-64]. *Gifts of Power: The Writings of Rebecca Jackson, Black Visionary, Shaker Eldress*, ed. Jean McMahon Humez. Amherst: U of Massachusetts P. 1-64.

Jackson-Coppin, Fannie. 1913. *Reminiscences of School Life, and Hints on Teaching*. Philadelphia: AME Book Concern.

James, Edward T., and Janet Wilson James (Eds.). 1971. *Notable American Women, 1607-1950: A Biographical Dictionary*. Cambridge: Harvard UP.

James, Jennifer Lee. 1997. "Jehiel C. Beman: A Leader of the Northern Free Black Community." *The Journal of Negro History* 82.1: 133-57.

Jones, Beverly Washington (Ed.). 1990. *Quest for Equality: The Life and Writings of Mary Eliza Church Terrell: 1863-1954*. New York: Carlson.

Jones, Martha S. 2007. *"All Bound Up Together": The Woman Question in African American Public Culture, 1830-1900*. Chapel Hill: U of North Carolina P.

Kellor, Frances A. 1905. "Southern Girls in the North: The Problem of Their Protection." *Charities* 13.25 (March 18): 584-85.

Kemp, Kathryn W. 2002. "Warren Akin Candler (1857-1941)." *The New Georgia Encyclopedia*, 20 November. <http://www.georgiaencyclopedia.net/nge/Article.jsp?path=/Religion/HistoricalFigures&id=h-754>.

King, Wilma. 2006. *The Essence of Liberty: Free Black Women During the Slave Era*. Columbia: U of Missouri P.

Knupfer Anne Meis. 1996. *Toward a Tenderer Humanity and a Nobler Womanhood:*

African American Women's Clubs in Turn-of-the-Century Chicago. New York: New York UP.

————. 2008. *The Educational Work Of Women's Organizations, 1890-1960.* New York: Palgrave Macmillan.

Larson, Kate Clifford. 2004. *Bound For the Promised Land: Harriet Tubman, Portrait of an American Hero.* New York: Ballantine.

Lasser, Carolyn. 1987. "Century of Struggle, Decades of Revision: A Retrospective on Eleanor Flexner's Suffrage History." *American History* (June): 344-54.

Lee, B.F., Jr. 1913. "Negro Organizations." *Annals of the American Academy of Political and Social Science* 49: 129-37.

Lee, Jarena. 1986[1836]. "The Life and Religious Experience of Jarena Lee." In *Sisters of the Spirit: Three Black Women's Autobiographies of the Nineteenth Century,* ed. William L. Andrews. Bloomington: Indiana UP. 25-48.

————. 1988[1849]. "Religious Experience and Journal of Mrs Jarena Lee, Giving an Account of Her Call to Preach the Gospel." In *Spiritual Narratives,* ed. Susan Houchins. *The Schomburg Library of Nineteenth-Century Black Women Writers.* New York: Oxford UP.

Lemert, Charles, and Esme Bhan. 1998. "The Colored Woman's Office." In *The Voice of Anna Julia Cooper, Including A Voice from the South and Other Important Essays, Papers, and Letters.* Boston: Rowman and Littlefield.

Lerner, Gerda (Ed.). 1992 [1972]. *Black Women in White America: A Documentary History.* New York: Vintage.

Leslie, Kent Anderson. 2008. "Lucy Craft Laney." *The New Georgia Encyclopaedia.* <http://www.newgeorgiaencyclopedia.org/nge/Article.jsp?id=h-820>.

Leslie, William R. 1952. "The Pennsylvania Fugitive Slave Act of 1826." *The Journal of Southern History* 18.4: 429-45.

Lincoln, Eric C., and Lawrence H. Mamiya. 1990. *The Black Church in the African American Experience.* Durham: Duke UP.

Lockwood, Lewis C. (Ed.). 1969. *Two Black Teachers During the Civil War: Mary S. Peake, the Colored Teacher at Fortress Monroe, and Charlotte Forten, Life on the Sea Islands.* New York: Arno P.

Logan, Shirley Wilson. 1999. *"We Are Coming": The Persuasive Discourse of Nineteenth-Century Black Women.* Carbondale: Southern Illinois UP.

Lowenberg, James, and Ruth Bogin (Eds.). 1976. *Black Women in Nineteenth-Century American Life: Their Words, Their Thoughts, Their Feelings.* University Park: Penn State UP.

Mabee, Carleton, with Susan Mabee Newhouse. 1993. *Sojourner Truth: Slave, Prophet, Legend.* New York: New York UP.

Maloney, Thomas N. 2002. "African American Migration to the North: New Evidence for the 1910s." *Economic Inquiry* 40.1 (January): 1-11.

Mayer, Henry. 1998. *All on Fire: William Lloyd Garrison and the Abolition of Slavery.* New York: St. Martin's P.

McArthur, Judith N. 2008. "Woman's Christian Temperance Union." *Handbook of Texas Online*. 11 January. <http://www.tshaonline.org/handbook/online/articles/WW/vaw1.html>.

McCluskey, Audrey Thomas, and Elaine M. Smith (Eds.). 1999. *Mary McLeod Bethune: Building a Better World*. Bloomington: Indiana UP.

McHenry, Elizabeth. 2002. *Forgotten Readers: Recovering the Lost History of African American Literary Societies*. Durham: Duke UP.

McMurry, Linda O. 1998. *To Keep the Waters Troubled: The Life of Ida B. Wells*. Oxford: Oxford UP.

Midgley, Clare. 1992. *Women Against Slavery: The British Campaigns 1780-1870*. London and New York: Routledge.

Ministry of the AME Church; Ministerial Paths and Titles. 2000. <http://www.ame-today.com/abcsofame/ministry.shtml>.

Minutes and Proceedings of the Second Annual Convention, for the Improvement of the Free People of Color in these United States. 1832. Philadelphia: Martin and Boden.

Moody, Joycelyn. 2001. *Sentimental Confessions: Spiritual Narratives of Nineteenth-Century African American Women*. Athens: U of Georgia P.

Moses, Wilson J. 1982. *Black Messiahs and Uncle Toms: Social and Literary Manipulations of a Religious Myth*. University Park: Penn State UP.

Mossell, Mrs. N.F. [Gertrude]. 1885. "Our Woman's Department. Woman Suffrage." *New York Freeman* (26 December): 2.

Neverdon-Morton, Cynthia. 1989. *Afro-American Women of the South and the Advancement of the Race, 1895-1925*. Knoxville: U of Tennessee P.

Painter, Nell Irvin. 1996. *Sojourner Truth: A Life, A Symbol*. New York: W.W. Norton.

Paludan, Phillip Shaw. 2004. "Lincoln and Colonization: Policy or Propaganda?" *Journal of the Abraham Lincoln Association* 25.1: 23-37.

Peterson, Carla L. 1995. *"Doers of the Word": African-American Women Speakers and Writers in the North (1830-1880)*. Oxford: Oxford UP.

———. 2000. "Frances Harper, Charlotte Forten, and African American Literary Reconstruction." In *Challenging Boundaries: Gender and Periodization*, ed. Joyce W. Warren and Margaret Dickie. Athens: U of Georgia P. 39-61.

Pride, Armistead S., and Clint C. Wilson, II. 1997. *A History of the Black Press*. Washington, DC: Howard UP.

Quarles, Benjamin. 1969. *Black Abolitionists*. Oxford and New York: Oxford UP.

Raboteau, Albert J. 1978. *Slave Religion: The "Invisible Institution" in the Antebellum South*. Oxford: Oxford UP.

Reed, Harry. 1994. *Platform for Change: The Foundations of the Northern Free Black Community, 1775-1865*. East Lansing: Michigan State UP.

Rhodes, Jane. 1998. *Mary Ann Shadd Cary: The Black Press and Protest in the Nineteenth Century*. Bloomington: Indiana UP.

Richardson, Marilyn (Ed.). 1987. *Maria W. Stewart, America's First Black Woman Political Writer*. Bloomington: Indiana UP.

———. 1993. "'What If I Am a Woman?' Maria W. Stewart's Defense of Black Women's Political Activism." In *Courage and Conscience: Black and White Abolitionists in Boston*, ed. Donald M. Jacobs. Bloomington: Indiana UP. 191-206.

Ripley, C. Peter, *et al.* (Eds.). 1991. *The Black Abolitionist Papers: The United States, 1830-1846*. Volume I of V. Chapel Hill: U of North Carolina P.

Rouse, Jacqueline, Anne. 1989. *Lugenia Burns Hope: Black Southern Reformer*. Athens: U of Georgia P.

Royster, Jacqueline Jones. 2000. *Traces of a Stream: Literacy and Social Change Among African American Women*. Pittsburgh: U of Pittsburgh P.

Ruiz, Vicki, and Ellen Carol Dubois (Eds.). 2008. *Unequal Sisters: An Inclusive Reader in US Women's History*. 4th ed. New York: Routledge.

Salem, Dorothy. 1990. *To Better Our World: Black Women in Organized Reform, 1890-1920*. New York: Carlson.

———. 1993. "National Association of Colored Women." In *Black Women in America: An Historical Encyclopedia*, ed. Darlene Clark Hine. New York: Carlson.

Santamarina, Xiomara. 2005. *Belabored Professions: Narratives of African American Working Womanhood*. Chapel Hill: U of North Carolina P.

Sasson, Diane. 1993. *The Shaker Spiritual Narrative*. Knoxville: U of Tennessee P.

Schechter, Patricia A. 2001. *Ida B. Wells-Barnett and American Reform, 1880-1930*. Chapel Hill: U of North Carolina P.

Shaw, Stephanie J. 1995. "Black Club Women and the Creation of the National Association of Colored Women." In *"We Specialize in the Wholly Impossible": A Reader in Black Women's History*, ed. Darlene Clark Hine, *et al.* New York: Carlson. 433-47.

Shaw, Stephanie. 1996. *What a Woman Ought to Be and Do: Black Professional Women Workers during the Jim Crow Era*. Chicago: U of Chicago P.

Sinha, Manisha, and Penny Von Eschen (Eds.). 2007. *Contested Democracy: Freedom, Race, And Power In American History*. New York: Columbia UP.

Sledd, Andrew. 1902. "The Negro: Another View." *The Atlantic Monthly* (June): 70-71.

Smith, Amanda Berry. 1988[1893]. *An Autobiography: The Story of the Lord's Dealings with Mrs. Amanda Smith the Colored Evangelist*, ed. Jualynne E. Dodson. *The Schomburg Library of Nineteenth-Century Black Women Writers*. New York: Oxford UP.

Sobel, Mechal. 1988. *Trabelin' On: The Slave Journey to an Afro-Baptist Faith*. Princeton: Princeton UP.

Spruill Wheeler, Marjorie (Ed.). 1995. *One Woman, One Vote: Rediscovering the Woman Suffrage Movement*. Troutdale: NewSage P.

Sterling, Dorothy (Ed.). 1984. *We Are Your Sisters: Black Women in the Nineteenth Century*. New York: Norton.

Stevenson, Brenda (Ed.). 1988. *The Journals of Charlotte Forten Grimké*. New York: Oxford UP.

Streitmatter, Rodger. 1993. "Maria W. Stewart: The First Female African-American Journalist." *Historical Journal of Massachusetts* 21.2: 44-59.

———. 1994. *Raising her Voice: African-American Women Journalists Who Changed History*. Lexington: UP of Kentucky.

Tate, Gayle T. 2003. *Unknown Tongues: Black Women's Political Activism in the Antebellum Era, 1830-1860*. East Lansing: Michigan State UP.

Terborg-Penn, Rosalyn (Ed.). 1978. *The Afro-American Woman: Struggles and Images*. Port Washington: Kennikat P.

———, Rosalyn. 1998. *African American Women in the Struggle for the Vote, 1850-1920*. Bloomington: Indiana UP.

Thomas, William Hannibal. 1901. *The American Negro: What He Was, What He Is, and What He May Become: A Critical and Practical Discussion*. New York: Macmillan.

Thompson, Mildred I. 1990. *Ida B. Wells-Barnett: An Exploratory Study of an American Black Woman, 1893-1930*. New York: Carlson.

Tolnay, Stewart E. 2003. "The African American 'Great Migration' and Beyond." *Annual Review of Sociology* 29: 209-32.

Vandiver, Margaret. 2006. *Lethal Punishment: Lynchings And Legal Executions In The South*. New Brunswick: Rutgers UP.

Waldrep, Christopher. 2006. *Lynching in America: A History in Documents*. New York: NYU Press.

Washington Jones, Beverly (Ed.). 1990. *Quest for Equality: The Life and Writings of Mary Eliza Church Terrell: 1863-1954*. New York: Carlson.

Weisenburger, Steven. 1998. *Modern Medea: A Family Story of Slavery and Child-Murder from the Old South*. New York: Hill and Wang.

Weisenfeld, Judith, and Richard Newman (Eds.). 1996. *This Far By Faith: Readings in African-American Women's Religious Biography*. New York: Routledge.

Wells, Ida B. 1991[1892]. *Southern Horrors: Lynch Law in All its Phases*. Rpt. in *Selected Works of Ida B. Wells-Barnett*, ed. Trudier Harris. New York and London: Oxford UP. 14-45.

———. 1893. "Lynch Law in All Its Phases." *Our Day* 11.65 (May): 333-47.

———. 1991[1895]. *A Red Record: Tabulated Statistics and Alleged Causes of Lynching in the United States, 1892-1893-1894*. Rpt. in *Selected Works of Ida B. Wells-Barnett*, ed. Trudier Harris. New York: Oxford UP. 55-151.

———. 1899. *Lynch Law in Georgia. By Ida B. Wells-Barnett; A Six Weeks' Record in the Center of Southern Civilization, As Faithfully Chronicled by the "Atlanta Journal" and the "Atlanta Constitution." Also The Full Report Of Louis P. Le Vin, The Chicago Detective Sent to Investigate the Burning of Samuel Hose, the Torture and Hanging of Elijah Strickland, the Colored Preacher, and the Lynching of Nine Men for Alleged Arson*. Chicago: Ida B. Wells-Barnett.

————. 1900. "The Negro's Case in Equity." *The Independent* (26 April): 1010-11.

————. 1990[1909]. "Lynching: Our National Crime." Rpt. in *Ida B. Wells-Barnett: An Exploratory Study of an American Black Woman, 1893-1930*, ed. Mildred I. Thompson. New York: Carlson. 261-65.

Welter, Barbara. 1976. "The Cult of True Womanhood 1820-1860." *Dimity Convictions: The American Woman in the Nineteenth Century*. Athens: Ohio UP. 21-41.

White, Deborah Gray. 1999a [1985]. *Aren't I a Woman? Female Slaves in the Plantation South*. New York: W.W. Norton.

————. 1999b. *Too Heavy a Load; Black Women in Defense of Themselves, 1894-1994*. New York: W.W. Norton.

Wiegman, Robyn. 1995. *American Anatomies: Theorizing Race and Gender*. Durham: Duke UP.

Wilson, Francille Rusan. 2002. "All of the Glory…Faded Quickly: Sadie T.M. Alexander and Black Professional Women, 1920-1950." In *Sister Circle: Black Women and Work*, ed. Sharon Harley and the Black Women and Work Collective. New York: Rutgers.

————. 2008. "Becoming 'Woman of the Year': Sadie T.M. Alexander's Construction of a Public Persona as a Black Professional Woman, 1920-1950." *Black Women, Gender, and Families*. 2.2: 1-30.

Winks, Robin W. 1997. *The Blacks in Canada: A History, Second Edition*. McGill-Queen's UP.

Wolcott, Victoria W. 2001. *Remaking Respectability: African American Women in Interwar Detroit*. Chapel Hill: U of North Carolina P.

Wood, Marcus. 2000. *Blind Memory: Visual Representations of Slavery in England and America, 1780-1865*. Manchester: Manchester UP.

Yee, Shirley J. 1992. *Black Women Abolitionists: A Study in Activism, 1828-1860*. Knoxville: U of Tennessee P.

Yellin, Jean Fagan. 1989. *Women and Sisters: The Antislavery Feminists in American Culture*. New Haven and London: Yale UP.

————, and John C. Van Horne (Eds.). 1994. *The Abolitionist Sisterhood: Women's Political Culture in Antebellum America*. Ithaca: Cornell UP.

Zackodnik, Teresa (Ed.). 2007. African American Feminisms, 1828-1923. *6 vol. History of Feminisms Series*. London: Routledge.

Index of Names

Ada. *See* Douglass, Sarah Mapps
Adams, John, 208
Adams, Oscar Fay, 360n50
Allen, Frederic de Forest, 286, 357n8
Allen, Grant, 109–11, 176n48
Allen, Richard, 10, 15–16, 72n7, 74n40, 175n31
Altgeld, John Peter, 178n67
Andrews, William L., 73n18–19
Anthony, Susan B., 279, 303–4, 307, 310, 318–19, 343, 356n3, 358n26–358n27, 359n31–359n32
Armstrong, Samuel, 110, 276n11
Arnold, Matthew, 108
Ashton, Mrs., 69
Atkins, S.G., 176n39
Attucks, Crispus, 227n3

Bacon, Margaret Hope, 361n60
Bailey, Lillie, 193
Baker (Postmaster), 208
Banneker, Benjamin, 116, 177n54
Barfey, Charles, 304
Barry, Charles, 81n95
Beard, Dr., 69
Beecher, Harriet. *See* Stowe, Harriet Beecher
Beecher, Henry Ward, 286, 316, 357n7
Belgarnie, Florence, 244–45, 276n9
Bellamy, Edward, 105, 176n44
Beman, Jehiel, 33–35, 74n41

Bhan, Esme, 360n49
Bickly, George, 79n85
Bishop, F., 69
Blackett, R.J.M., 81n96
Blackstone, William, 67, 80n93, 343
Bleckley, Logan Edwin, 204
Blyden, Edward Wilmot, 116, 177n54
Bonfield, Mr., 134
Bracken, Mrs., 97
Bradenburg, Albert of, 107
Britton, Mary E., 280, 312–17
Brougham, Henry Peter, 71, 81n97
Brown, Annie E., 1
Brown, Elsa Barkley, xv
Brown, Hallie Quinn, 276n7
Brown, John, 173n17
Brown, Mildrey, 208
Bruce, Blanche K., 177n54, 177n57, 178n58
Bruce, Josephine B., 123–28
Bruce, Roscoe Conkling, 116, 177n54
Buchanan, Isaac, 173n18, 196, 359n34
Buchanan, James, 80n86
Burke, Edmund, 265, 277n20
Burns, Anthony, 78n76
Burroughs, Nannie Helen, 114–17, 136–40, 177n52
Butler, Serena, 273, 277n25
Byron, George Gordon Byron, Baron, 109